"This fascinating book reaches striking and the dynamics of African rebel groups, with a Horn, but with much broader applications.'
  Christopher Clapham, Centre of African Stu

"*Insurgent Fragmentation in the Horn of Africa: Rebellion and Its Discontents* combines a pathbreaking theoretical analysis of the fragmentation of rebel movements with a deep and detailed historical study of cases from the Horn of Africa to provide a fascinating account of a much-neglected topic. This is an essential contribution to the literature on the dynamics of civil wars."
  Alex de Waal, Tufts University

"Michael Woldemariam's book offers a new and important explanation of rebel cohesion and fragmentation. By focusing on the impact of battlefield dynamics on rebel unity, Woldemariam helps us understand why insurgent cohesion is so challenging and prone to breakdown. His careful, deeply researched comparative evidence from Ethiopia and Somalia valuably brings these fascinating cases into dialogue with the broader literature on political violence. This book deserves wide attention and engagement."
  Paul Staniland, University of Chicago

"Why do rebel organizations fragment and why does it matter? Drawing on a new database of fragmentation in 171 rebel organizations in sub-Saharan Africa (1946–2006), Woldemariam argues that fortunes on the battlefield hold the key to understanding these dynamics. When rebels lose territory, commitment problems push them apart. But even when they win, the reduced threat encourages fragmentation by weakening their incentives for continued cooperation. Ironically, therefore, rebel organizations are more likely to cohere during stalemates on the battlefield."
  Paul D. Williams, George Washington University

"Theoretically sound and empirically robust, this book is a definitive work on rebel fragmentation in the Horn of Africa. In a region where scholarship has long been tainted by partisan politics, Dr. Woldemariam presents a rare dispassionate analysis of the internal dynamics of insurgent groups in one of the most conflict-ridden regions of the world."
  Assefaw Bariagaber, Seton Hall University

Insurgent Fragmentation in the Horn of Africa

When insurgent organizations factionalize and fragment, it can profoundly shape a civil war: its intensity, outcome, and duration. In an extended treatment of this complex and important phenomenon, Michael Woldemariam examines why rebel organizations fragment through a unique historical analysis of the Horn of Africa's civil wars. Central to his view is that rebel factionalism is conditioned by battlefield developments. While fragmentation is caused by territorial gains and losses, counterintuitively, territorial stalemate tends to promote rebel cohesion and is a critical basis for cooperation in war.

As a rare effort to examine these issues in the context of the Horn of Africa region, based on an extensive fieldwork, this book will interest both scholarly and nonscholarly audiences interested in insurgent groups and conflict dynamics.

MICHAEL WOLDEMARIAM is an assistant professor of international relations at Boston University's Pardee School of Global Studies. His research focuses on the dynamics of armed conflict, the behavior of rebel organizations, and postconflict institution building. He has special expertise on the Horn of Africa region, where he has traveled extensively. His research has been published in *Terrorism and Political Violence*, the *Journal of Strategic Studies*, and *Nationalism and Ethnic Politics*, and is forthcoming in a number of edited volumes. He has been a fellow at the Woodrow Wilson International Center for Scholars, the Bradley Foundation, the Truman National Security Project, and a research specialist with the Innovations for Successful Societies program at Princeton University.

Insurgent Fragmentation in the Horn of Africa

Rebellion and Its Discontents

Michael Woldemariam
Boston University

CAMBRIDGE
UNIVERSITY PRESS

CAMBRIDGE
UNIVERSITY PRESS

University Printing House, Cambridge CB2 8BS, United Kingdom

One Liberty Plaza, 20th Floor, New York, NY 10006, USA

477 Williamstown Road, Port Melbourne, VIC 3207, Australia

314-321, 3rd Floor, Plot 3, Splendor Forum, Jasola District Centre, New Delhi - 110025, India

79 Anson Road, #06-04/06, Singapore 079906

Cambridge University Press is part of the University of Cambridge.

It furthers the University's mission by disseminating knowledge in the pursuit of education, learning and research at the highest international levels of excellence.

www.cambridge.org
Information on this title: www.cambridge.org/9781108435994
DOI: 10.1017/9781108525657

© Michael Woldemariam 2018

This publication is in copyright. Subject to statutory exception and to the provisions of relevant collective licensing agreements, no reproduction of any part may take place without the written permission of Cambridge University Press.

First published 2018
First paperback edition 2020

A catalogue record for this publication is available from the British Library

Library of Congress Cataloging in Publication data
Names: Woldemariam, Michael, 1982– author.
Title: Insurgent fragmentation in the Horn of Africa : rebellion and its discontents / Michael Woldemariam.
Description: New York, NY : Cambridge University Press, 2018. | Revised version of the author's thesis (doctoral) – Princeton University, 2011. | Includes bibliographical references and index.
Identifiers: LCCN 2017061796 | ISBN 9781108423250 (alk. paper)
Subjects: LCSH: Civil war – Horn of Africa. | Insurgency – Horn of Africa. | Horn of Africa – Politics and government. | Eritrea – History – Revolution, 1962–1993. | Ethiopia – History – 1974– | Somalia – History – 1960–1991. | Unit cohesion (Military science)
Classification: LCC DT367.75.W65 2018 | DDC 963.06 – dc23
LC record available at https://lccn.loc.gov/2017061796

ISBN 978-1-108-42325-0 Hardback
ISBN 978-1-108-43599-4 Paperback

Cambridge University Press has no responsibility for the persistence or accuracy of URLs for external or third-party internet websites referred to in this publication, and does not guarantee that any content on such websites is, or will remain, accurate or appropriate.

Contents

List of Figures	*page* viii
List of Tables	ix
Acknowledgments	x
List of Acronyms	xiv

Part I Theory and Concepts

1	Organized Rebellion and Its Intractable Problem	3
2	A Theory of Rebel Fragmentation	23

Part II Rebellion in Ethiopia and Eritrea

3	The Eritrean Liberation Front: *Jebha* in Action, 1960–1982	71
4	The Eritrean People's Liberation Front: *Shaebia* in Action, 1972–1991	136
5	The Second Wave of Rebellion: Tigrayans, Oromos, Afars, and Somalis, 1973–2008	185

Part III Rebel Fragmentation in the Broader Horn

6	The Long War in Somalia: The Somali National Movement, Islamic Courts Union, and Al-Shabaab, 1981–2013	211
7	Concluding Thoughts	282

Appendix: Narrative of Fieldwork and Description of Data Sources	289
References	295
Index	307

Figures

1.1 Percentage of rebel organizations in sub-Saharan Africa that fragmented, 1946–2006	*page* 20
2.1 Outline of argument and causal mechanisms	47
2.2 Number of active Ethiopian rebel organizations, 1960–2008	58
2.3 Ethiopian rebel organizations, fragmentation by decade, 1960–2008	59
2.4 Ethiopia provincial map, geographic distribution of case studies	62
2.5 Fragmentation by Ethiopian rebel organization, 1960–2008	63
3.1 Provincial map of Eritrea	72
3.2 Jebha areas of operation, by district, March 1967	97
3.3 Jebha areas of operation, by district, November 1967	97
3.4 Jebha areas of opration, by district, January 1974	106
3.5 Jebha areas of operation, by district, March 1975	106
3.6 Jebha areas of operation, by district, January 1981	117
3.7 Jebha areas of operation, by district, March 1982	117
4.1 Shaebia areas of operation, by district, February–March 1973	156
4.2 Shaebia areas of operation, by district, summer 1973	157
6.1 Map of Somali regions	212

Tables

2.1	Cross-tab, fragmentation, and gain/loss by rebel year	*page* 60
2.2	Baseline model of rebel fragmentation	61
2.3	Ethiopian rebel organizations	61
3.1	Jebha – gains, losses, and the onset of fragmentation over time	134
4.1	Shaebia – gains, losses, and the onset of fragmentation over time	183

Acknowledgments

This is a book about the politics of armed rebellion in the Horn of Africa. That I would write a book on this subject – instead of on parliaments in Western Europe, the political economy of development in China, or any number of other topics that concern political scientists – probably should come as no great surprise. My parents were young Eritrean refugees who fled the violence and insecurity that characterized their country's long armed struggle for independence. Although I would not set foot in Eritrea until I was ten years old, a few years after that struggle had been won, my earliest childhood memories are of the revolution. I still remember, for instance, the long drives from our New England home to Washington, DC, where our family took part in protests designed to publicize the Eritrean cause; the birthday parties and weddings where my parents and their friends would loudly discuss the latest battlefield developments; or the Eritrean festivals in one American city or another, in which my young friends and I would reenact the bravery and fortitude of Eritrea's independence fighters for an audience of gleeful Eritrean adults. Although the circumstances of my American birth sheltered me from the burdens of war in Eritrea, the long armed struggle left an indelible mark on my political consciousness and social sensibilities. It could really be no other way.

Graduate school at Princeton is where I channeled these experiences into an actual intellectual project. My decision to focus on the issue of factionalism and fragmentation within organized rebellion was really driven by two considerations. First, as a good social scientist, I noticed that there was a lacuna in the academic literature on civil war and political violence that needed to be filled. Second, the years after 2001 were a time in which Eritrea's liberator turned ruling party – the Eritrean People's Liberation Front/People's Front for Democracy and Justice – had begun to lose its luster. This is not the place to litigate the policies and performance of the PFDJ, or explore why Eritrea has been mired in interlocking social, economic, and political crises in the years since 2001. And to be clear, all those that fought in the Eritrean struggle – including many of those who paid with their lives – have this author's deep respect and esteem. The important issue is that the post-2001 moment was one in which many Eritrean intellectuals began to question what they thought they knew about the long independence struggle, and the organization that had been at its center. Old, sanitized narratives, about the purity of the EPLF, its unity and coherence, and the unquestioned integrity of its leadership, were challenged. And many began to call for a more honest, and perhaps more subversive, historical rendition of the independence struggle. Had it not been for this emerging political frame, and the revisionism about an armed struggle that had shaped my political consciousness for so long, I am not sure factionalism and fragmentation would have been the themes that informed this book.

However I might have arrived at this book's motivating questions, I owe huge debts to so many who helped me write it. In the interest of brevity, it is not possible to mention the countless family and friends who have, in one way or another, supported this project. I have learned, in the truest sense, that it takes a community to write a book.

First, I am hugely grateful to all of the interviewees who were kind enough to share some of their time with me, broker introductions to other informants, and provide me access to useful research materials. It was a privilege to hear their stories and learn from their lived experiences. I am particularly grateful to Gunter Schroeder for sharing with me a treasure trove of interview material he collected in the 1970s, 1980s, and 1990s.

At Princeton, I owe my biggest debt to my mentor, Prof. Jennifer Widner, who more than any other person taught me what it means to be a social scientist. Members of my dissertation committee – Mark Beissinger, Amaney Jamal, and Keren Yarhi-Milo – were also incredibly supportive and provided invaluable guidance on turning a doctoral thesis into a book manuscript. My friends and fellow graduate students Kristen Harkness, Jing Chen, and Vinay Jahawar also read significant portions of this project, and for that I am grateful. Finally, there is my dear friend Alden Young, who has probably heard and seen more versions of this book than he cares to remember. His perceptive intellect is spread across this book's pages.

I spent a year at Penn State as a postdoctoral fellow further revising my dissertation project into a book. Douglas Lemke was my mentor at State College, and he has been an encouraging voice my entire academic career. D. Scott Bennett was chair of the political science department, and played a big role in bringing me to Penn State. His successor, Lee Ann Banaszak, also provided some much-needed positivity along the way, as did the director of African Studies, Kidane Mengisteab. The good people at the Africana Studies Center – Lovalerie King, Tracy Beckett, and Dawn Noreen – made sure my fellowship year at Penn State was productive and smooth.

I have had the pleasure of serving as a faculty member at Boston University's Pardee School of Global Studies during this book's most critical stages. This has been a wonderful professional home with fantastic colleagues, and I could spend many pages thanking them all. I owe a particular debt of gratitude to our dean, Adil Najam; our associate dean, Bill Grimes; the director of our African Studies Center, Tim Longman; and my ever-supportive faculty mentor, Houchang Chehabi. Dino Christensen, my colleague in the Department of Political Science, was kind enough to organize a seminar in which I was able to present the book's main findings and solicit feedback. My thanks also go to a wonderful cohort of junior (and some now senior) faculty at Boston University: Manjari Miller, Noora Lori, Kaija Schilde, Jeremy Menchik, Renata Keller, Cornel Ban, Julie Klinger, and Min Ye.

Outside of Princeton, Penn State, and Boston University, many friends and colleagues have shaped my thinking on conflict and rebellion in Africa and the Horn. Will Reno was kind enough to visit me at Penn State and share his thoughts on the project. Terrence Lyons, Christopher Day, Awet Weldemichael, Dan Connell, Joe Woldense, Jennifer Riggan, Jason Mosley, Costa Pischedda, Christopher Clapham, Ruth Iyob, Rashid Abdi, Laura Hammond, Ken Menkaus, Lee Cassanelli, Adan Abakor, Harry Verhoeven, Maimuna Mohamud, Peter Krause, Mia Bloom, and Jonathan Fischer have, in one form or another, made helpful observations and interventions that have had some bearing on this book. My interaction with some of these friends and colleagues was facilitated by my engagement with the Rift Valley Institute, a first-rate research organization that works on the Horn of Africa (among several other regions). Thus I owe its senior staff – in particular, John Ryle, Mark Bradbury, and Cedric Barnes – special thanks. Pythias Temesgen, my dear friend and godfather to my son, has read much of the manuscript and brought a critical eye to many of its main arguments. These individuals join a broad array of conference and research talk attendees that engaged my work and offered productive critiques.

Research support for this work has come in a variety of guises. Beyond Princeton, Penn State, and Boston University, I have benefited from the support of the Lynde and Harry Bradley Foundation and the Woodrow Wilson International Center for Scholars. Brian Shevenaugh, Patricia Egessa, and Maddie Powell all provided invaluable research assistance. My editor at Cambridge, Maria Marsh, has done a superb job guiding this book manuscript to publication, as have several others at

Cambridge: Julie Hrischeva, Shubhangi Tripathi, and Theresa Kornak. Rohan Boltan did great work in putting together the index, as did Amy Sherman in helping to review the proofs. The suggestions from three anonymous reviewers were also invaluable. Lastly, I would be remiss if I did not acknowledge the support of the journal *Terrorism and Political Violence*, which granted me permission to use portions of a previously published article in Chapters 2 and 3 of this book (Woldemariam, 2014).

Of course, this book would not have been possible without the support of my loving family. My mom and dad, Saba Hadgu and Habte Woldemariam, have been the core guiding inspirations throughout my life. I owe them so much. My sister Selam Woldemariam read portions of the manuscript and made some important writing suggestions, while my other siblings Yonas and Leah provided moral support and plenty of laughs. I would also be remiss if I didn't mention my extended family in Minnesota – aunts, uncles, and cousins – that have been important pillars of my life. It's so large a group that I will not list them all here by name out of the sincere fear that I might leave someone out. They know I love them all dearly.

My wife, Adiam Belay, has been my rock – patient, supportive, and always able to put me at ease about my work and life when I am most anxious. I could not have finished this book without her love. I also owe her family some important debts. And then there is my son Adam, who came along just as I brought this book to a close. I'm glad to have concluded this chapter in life just in time to start a new one with him.

Finally, there is my grandfather, Hadgu Muhur. Sadly, he passed away as I was working on this book. He is greatly missed. He was an author in his own right, publishing some important Tigrinya-language texts on religion. I like to think I am continuing a family tradition.

Acronyms

ARDUF	Afar Revolutionary Democratic Unity Front
ARPCT	Alliance for the Restoration of Peace and Counter-Terrorism
ARS	Alliance for the Reliberation of Somalia
EDU	Ethiopian Democratic Union
EFLNA	Eritreans for the Liberation of North America
ELF	Eritrean Liberation Front
ENDF	Ethiopian National Defense Forces
EPLF	Eritrean People's Liberation Front
EPRDF	Ethiopian People's Revolutionary Democratic Front
EPRP	Ethiopian People's Revolutionary Party
EPRP	Eritrean People's Revolutionary Party
FGS	Federal Government of Somalia
ICU	Islamic Courts Union
JVA	Juba Valley Authority
NIF	National Islamic Front
OLF	Oromo Liberation Front
ONLF	Ogaden National Liberation Front
SALF	Somali Abo Liberation Front
SNF	Somali National Front
SNM	Somali National Movement
SPM	Somali Patriotic Movement
SRRC	Somalia Reconciliation and Restoration Council
SSDF	Somali Salvation Democratic Front
TFG	Transitional Federal Government (Somalia)
TLF	Tigray Liberation Front
TNG	Transitional National Government (Somalia)
TPLF	Tigray People's Liberation Front
USC	United Somali Congress
WSLF	West Somali Liberation Front

Part I

Theory and Concepts

1 Organized Rebellion and Its Intractable Problem

Darfur, 2003–2010

Since 2003, Minni Minawi has been an important, if somewhat polarizing, fixture of Darfur's armed rebellion. Born in North Darfur in 1968 to the Awlad Digayn clan of the Zaghawa, Minni had an eclectic career prior to joining the militant Darfuri nationalist organization, the Sudanese Liberation Army (SLA). The soon-to-be rebel commander worked early on as a primary school teacher in Darfur, transitioned to being a customs officer in Chad, and finally settled as an English instructor in Nigeria. With no real military experience to speak of, his rise to prominence within Darfur's armed political field is striking. Yet what he lacked in military expertise, he compensated for with natural rhetorical skill and political acumen.

In 2001, a relative who was prominent in nationalist Darfuri circles gave Minni USD 5,000 to join the incipient rebellion in Darfur. As one of the few available cadres who were literate, Minni was appointed the secretary of Zaghawa strongman Abdallah Abbakar Bashar, who would become the SLA chief of staff. In January 2004, Abdallah was killed in fighting with the Sudanese government. This was a critical turning point in Minni's career, as he engineered a process through which he was installed as Abdallah's replacement over and above the skepticism of many better-trained Zaghawa fighters. This move placed Minni at the apex of Zaghawa politics in Darfur.

As chief of staff of the SLA, Minni's direct superior was Abdel Wahid-Nur, who represented the other major component of the SLA coalition – the Fur, Darfur's other large, non-Arab ethnic grouping. With large political ambitions, Minni was not content with playing second fiddle. Differences between the two men would soon boil over, triggering a rupture between the Zaghawa and the Fur that fueled intense violence in mid-2004.

In an about-face that would become his political trademark, Minni solidified the SLA's fragmentation by signing the Darfur Peace

Agreement (DPA) in 2006 – in effect, transforming this antigovernment rebel into an ally of the central government in Khartoum. Not only were Minni's forces refitted as a progovernment militia, he also became a state functionary, replete with offices, vehicles, and salaried employees to the cost of USD 1 million a month. Khartoum appointed Minni the highest-ranking central government official in Darfur and senior assistant to the president – the latter post making Minni the fourth in line to the Sudanese presidency. Minni even tried his hand at electoral politics – although his forces remained an armed presence throughout Zaghawa-populated areas of North Darfur – winning several parliamentary seats in the 2006 elections.

These were good years for Minni, as the largesse of the central government allowed him to thrive politically. His willingness to make peace earned him the grudging acknowledgment of the international community. Yet Minni's warm embrace of Khartoum, and the rise to national prominence it promulgated, quickly came to an end. Despite the trappings of his new office, the reality was that his position was more symbolic than substantive. When the incentives for keeping Minni around changed, the central government in Khartoum acted. After the 2010 general elections, Minni's post in the national government was not renewed. Minni moved to the South Sudanese capital of Juba as relations with the central government appeared to unravel, and in December he declared the DPA "dead," seamlessly switching allegiances back to Darfur's antigovernment rebels. The central government in Khartoum responded by declaring Minni a "legitimate target" and began ruthlessly attacking his forces in Darfur. The dramatic turn of events triggered another round of rebel fragmentation in which Minni was again to feature prominently, although this time he was less an agent of fragmentation and more its victim.

The collapse of the alliance with Khartoum caused a three-way rupture within Minni's forces that he found impossible to contain. One faction of his organization broke ranks, staying in Khartoum and negotiating the terms of its disarmament with the government. A second group in North Darfur defected to a rival Darfuri insurgent group named the Justice and Equality Movement (JEM), which remained steadfast in its opposition to Khartoum. The third group, led by his longtime chief of staff, Juma Mohammed Hagar, and field commander Mohamadein Osman "Aurgajo," remained loyal. Over time, a fourth faction would emerge and defect from Minni's forces.

Today, Minni's rebel organization, which is fittingly called the SLA-Minni Minawi, forms part of an anti-Khartoum rebel alliance called the Sudan Revolutionary Front (SRF). It is through this alliance that Minni has made amends with many of the former rebel colleagues he had so unceremoniously betrayed, and been forced to reconcile with some of those who had been quick to reject Minni's authority when the DPA collapsed in 2010.

If Minni appeared to be a political chameleon, or perhaps more pejoratively the consummate opportunist, his behavior was by no means unique. The seeming fluidity with which Minni forged, and more importantly for the purposes of this book, broke political and military allegiances, was echoed by many of his subordinates. As is clear, many Minni loyalists have broken ranks with their leader and defected to the government or other militias, or struck out on their own – most prominently after the signing of the DPA, but also following Minni's rupture with SLA–Abdel Wahid and in more recent years as Minni has struggled to regain the credibility lost by joining forces with the central government.[1]

The twists and turns of Minni's political career, and the political itinerary of many of those who served under him, illustrate a broader pattern of behavior in the Darfur rebellion. Factionalism and fragmentation among Darfur's rebel forces was not the exception but the rule, a seemingly endemic feature of Darfur's ever-shifting political map. Indeed, when the rebellion broke out in 2003, there were two clearly defined organizations that had emerged to challenge the authority of the central government – Minni's SLA and the JEM of Dr. Khalil Ibrahim. Seven years later, there were nearly two dozen factions vying for influence within Darfur's armed political arena, the product of a seemingly endless process of fission that had rendered the region's politics a maze of temporary loyalties and alliances of convenience. Meanwhile, Darfur's armed struggle – notwithstanding periodic signs of life – hangs in limbo.

The Puzzle of Rebel Fragmentation

Darfur's recent politics underscore what is seemingly an intractable problem of organized rebellion – that of factionalism and fragmentation within rebel ranks. In civil wars around the world, rebel organizations fight against states and their nonstate rivals, while at the same time waging an ongoing but often covert internal battle to maintain their organizational coherence and unity.[2] And just as rebels often fall short in

---

[1] Information on Minni Minawi is drawn from Tanner and Tubiana (2007), de Waal (2007), and Flint and de Waal (2008). Also see a profile published by *Sudan Tribune*, which can be found at www.sudantribune.com/spip.php?mot190 (Accessed August 20, 2015).

[2] This book treats the terms "rebel" and "rebellion" as synonymous with the terms "insurgent" and "insurgency," respectively.

their struggle against external adversaries, they sometimes fail to surmount internal challenges as well. In Afghanistan, Syria, Somalia, Iraq, Sri Lanka, and Colombia, rebel organizations have regularly exhibited factionalism and fragmentation, with dramatic and wide-ranging effects.

This book attempts to explain factionalism and fragmentation within organized rebellion. Its laboratory is Africa, specifically the Horn, which has been home to the some of the world's most intractable civil wars. However, as will be clear, the book's lessons are not regional but global. As such, this book is firmly situated within the recent body of social science scholarship that has sought to unpack the causes and consequences of insurgent factionalism and fragmentation in contemporary civil wars. Drawing an analytical distinction between factionalism and its variants, this study provides a careful treatment of what I argue is one of the more significant manifestations of rebel factionalism – "rebel fragmentation." This phenomenon can be defined as the splitting of rebel organizations into politically distinct, mutually exclusive entities, where these entities create a new rebel organization, join an existing organization, or join forces with the incumbent government. At its core, this book asks, and answers, the following central question: Why, and under what conditions, do rebel organizations fragment?[3]

In answering this question, this study yields a number of testable, falsifiable hypotheses. I evaluate these hypotheses through a multimethod approach, using historical data from one of Africa's longest, and bloodiest, conflicts, the Ethiopian civil war. The analysis of the Ethiopian civil war, which examines the conflict and its key rebel participants between the years 1960 and 2008, is complemented by a rigorous analysis of the civil war in neighboring Somalia.[4]

The argument contained in the following pages can be summarized as follows. Rebel organizations are coalitions that depend on cooperation among differentiated, heterogeneous units. In the anarchic context of war, where in the famous words of Hobbes (1981), the life of man (or woman) is "solitary, poor, nasty, brutish and short," immediate concerns over survival predominate. Thus cooperation within rebel organizations

---

[3] This book's operative definition of "factionalism" within rebel organizations conceptualizes the phenomenon in terms of its real-world manifestations. Formally, I define factionalism as a clearly identifiable manifestation of a breakdown of cooperation within a rebel organization, which may include phenomena such as coups, extrajudicial killings, extrajudicial purges/arrests, fragmentation/organizational splitting, and insubordination." These events are characterized by their extralegal nature, and sit outside the bounds of the normal, political processes of a rebel organization. I will provide a more rigorously defended definition of "rebel fragmentation" in the following chapter.

[4] The Ethiopian conflict is ongoing (although the insurgency is now low intensity), and 2008 is the year in which this study began.

depends on the *perception* that continued participation in the organization is the best way for constituent units of a rebel organization to maximize the core imperative of survival.

Yet this perception depends on the overarching military situation a rebel organization faces. In settings where a rebel organization is losing territory, often through a set of major shocks, the incentives to cooperate are reduced, as battlefield losses suggest that the collective enterprise that is organized rebellion no longer guarantees the survival of the organization's constituent units. Put differently, losing territory creates a basic commitment problem, prompting an organization's constituent units to question the cooperative bargain that is at the heart of the rebel organization. All things equal, fragmentation is more likely in such contexts.

Yet victory has its costs as well. If the constituent units of a rebel organization participate in the organization because they believe that it is the best way to guarantee their survival in war, then it follows that the reduction of security threats (or at the least the perceived reduction), and the resulting dissipation of survival concerns, bodes ill for the internal coherence of rebel organizations. I argue that there is little that reduces security threats more rapidly than battlefield victory and gaining territory. With a core raison d'être for the organization removed, the basis for cooperation is eroded, and the constituent units of a rebel organization behave in ways consistent with the pursuit of their own *individual* interests. All things equal, fragmentation is more likely.

The implication of this very simple argument, of course, is that rebel organizations are in a double bind, as the inevitable ebb and flow of war, and constantly shifting battlefield geography, produce internal pressures that can contribute to organizational fragmentation. Somewhat counterintuitively, it is only battlefield stalemate that can preserve organizational cohesion – a concept I call "cohesive stalemates."

The History of an Intractable Problem

Why is the issue of rebel factionalism and fragmentation an important topic of inquiry? On one level, it is important because some of the prominent practitioners of insurgent or revolutionary warfare have told us it is. Concerns over internal cohesion, and by extension, rebel fragmentation, have been a central preoccupation of some of the twentieth century's most famed theorist-practitioners of insurgent warfare.[5] These concerns

---

[5] The classic literature on insurgent warfare is largely a twentieth-century creation. Owing to the ideological ferment of the time, it owes its emergence to the efforts of theorist/practitioners rooted in leftist traditions of revolutionary warfare.

were sometimes directly stated, but often implied, manifesting themselves in various ways: in ruminations about the dangers of enemy infiltration; fears over the impact of ideological, class, or tribal differences on internal unity; or the urgency of politically indoctrinating rank-and-file fighters.

Consider the following. Vladimir Lenin, the Marxist ideologue who led the Russian revolution, wrote in his now famous 1902 treatise "What Is to Be Done?" that an ideologically astute core of "professional revolutionaries" was critical to propelling the Russian workers' movement to victory. This professional class, better known as the "vanguard," was to feature heavily in the organizing logic of later rebel movements that sought to model themselves on Lenin's successful revolutionary project. In Lenin's view, this professional class was necessitated by a number of factors, none greater than the fear of movement fragmentation. This concern is best signaled by Lenin's identification of "agents provocateurs," "demagogues," and the "two opposite extremes" of "unsound economism and the preaching of moderation, and equally unsound 'excitative terror...'" as core impediments to the unity of the revolution (Christman, 1987, pp. 141–159).[6] Four years later, in his treatise on guerrilla warfare, Lenin expressed similar concerns, postulating that the ideological diversity of revolutionary movements could leave them

---

[6] These ideas are littered throughout Lenin's essay. On "agents provocateurs," Lenin writes, "We must also warn the workers against traps often set by police, who at such open meetings and permitted societies spy out the 'hotheads' and who, through the medium of legal organizations, endeavor to plant their *agents provocateurs* in the illegal organizations" (Christman, 1987, p. 140). On the threat of demagogues, Lenin writes, "...I shall never tire of repeating that demagogues are the worst enemies of the working class, because they arouse bad instincts in the crowd, because the ignorant worker is unable to recognize his enemies in men who represent themselves, and sometimes sincerely represent themselves, to be his friends. They are the worst enemies of the of the working class because in this period of dispersion and vacillation, when our movement is just beginning to take shape, nothing is easier then to employ demagogic methods to sidetrack the crowd, which can realize its mistake only by bitter experience" (Christman, 1987, pp. 146–147). On ideological tensions within the Russian workers' movement, between moderates and extremists, Lenin writes, "It is precisely at the present time, when no such organization exists yet, and when the revolutionary movement is rapidly and spontaneously growing, that we already observe two opposite extremes... This is not surprising because, apart from other reasons, the 'economic struggle against the employers and the government' can never satisfy revolutionaries, and because the opposite extremes will always arise here and there. Only a centralized, militant organization that consistently carries out a Social-Democratic policy, that satisfies, so to speak, all revolutionary instincts and strivings, can safeguard the movement against making thoughtless attacks and prepare it for attacks that hold out the promise of success" (Christman, 1987, p. 159).

"frayed, corrupted, and prostituted."[7] Writing in 1930, even Lenin's Russian comrade Leon Trotsky, in his meticulous account of the Russian revolution, fatalistically acknowledged the pervasiveness of infighting and fragmentation, admitting that "such tragic 'accidents' are one of the inevitable overhead expenses of a revolution" (Trotsky, 2008, p. 382).[8]

Mao Tse-Tung, the Chinese rebel whose victory over the Nationalists became the blueprint for insurgent armies around the world, largely shared Lenin's preoccupation with the issue of internal fragmentation. Arguing that "Victory in guerrilla war is conditioned upon keeping the membership pure and clean," Mao worried that "the enemy may take advantage of certain people who are lacking in conscience and patriotism and induce them to join the guerrillas for the purpose of betraying them." As such, he advocated the swiftest of countermeasures: "The traitors who are in our ranks must be discovered and expelled, and punishment and expulsion meted out to those who have been influenced by them" (Mao Tse-Tung, 2000).[9] That same year, in another widely distributed essay titled "On Contradictions," Mao – much like Lenin before

---

[7] On this subject, Lenin's exact words were, "It is said that guerrilla warfare brings the class-conscious proletarians into close association with degraded, drunken riff-raff. That is true. But it only means that the party of the proletariat can never regard guerrilla warfare as the only, or even as the chief, method of struggle; it means that this method must be subordinated to other methods, that it must be commensurate with the chief methods of warfare, and must be ennobled by the enlightening and organizing influence of socialism. And without this latter condition, all, positively all, methods of struggle in bourgeois society bring the proletariat into close association with the non-proletarian strata above it and below it and, if left to the spontaneous course of events, become frayed, corrupted and prostituted." See "V. I. Lenin: Guerrilla Warfare," which can be found at www.marxists.org/archive/lenin/works/1906/gw/ (Accessed May 25, 2015).

[8] This quote was brought to my attention by a working paper written by Boston College's Peter Krause, which was presented at Rand's Insurgency Board on September 8, 2016. It was titled "Winning the 'War of Position': Measuring and Explaining Insurgent Organizational Success."

[9] Written in 1937 as the communists were embroiled in arduous resistance to Japanese invasion, Mao's solution to the cohesion problems – as it was for most Marxist revolutionaries – was political education. On this, Mao says, "First of all, political activities depend upon the indoctrination of both military and political leaders with the idea of anti-Japanism. Through them, the idea is transmitted to the troops. One must not feel that he is anti-Japanese merely because he is a member of a guerrilla unit. The anti-Japanese idea must be an ever-present conviction, and if it is forgotten, we may succumb to the temptations of the enemy or be overcome with discouragement. In a war of long duration, those whose conviction that the people must be emancipated is not deep rooted are likely to become shaken in their faith or actually revolt. Without the general education that enables everyone to understand our goal of driving out Japanese imperialism and establishing a free and happy China, the soldiers fight without conviction and lose their determination" (Mao Tse-Tung, 2000).

him – suggested that ideological tensions could be an additional source of dangerous internal "antagonism" that would require, in his words, "serious struggle against erroneous thinking."[10]

The Argentinian insurgent leader Che Guevara, whose final bid as a rebel ended with his demise in a shallow Bolivian grave in 1967, advised that a guerrilla should be "closed-mouthed... and never permit himself a single useless word, even with his own comrades in arms," since the enemy could introduce spies into insurgent ranks that could undermine the rebellion (Guevara, 1961). Later, in writing about his disastrous 1965 Cuban-backed campaign in the Congo, Guevara bemoaned the political infighting of his Congolese counterparts. In a letter to Fidel Castro that same year, he excoriated the Congolese leftists he had come to support, arguing that their lack of unity had caused them to surrender major towns without a fight. Although acknowledging his own initial "totally unwarranted optimism" about the prospects of leftist revolution in the Congo, these divisions had caused Guevara to glumly concede that "on our own, we cannot liberate a country that has no desire to fight" (Gott, 1996, pp. 29–30).

General Vo Nguyen Giap, who along with Ho Chi Minh was a leading architect of Vietnamese resistance to the Japanese, French, and American occupations, argued that within its ranks, insurgent armies needed to "energetically combat expressions of bourgeois and other nonproletarian ideologies." Although Giap believed that Vietnam's arduous years of resistance had melded the insurgency into an "unbreakable monolithic block," he argued that maintaining cohesion required continuing vigilance: "We must always take care to strengthen the monolithic solidarity within the army."[11]

Writing around the same time as Giap and Guevara, Amilcar Cabral, the Guinean insurgent so instrumental to the decolonization of Lusophone Africa, also intellectually grappled with the challenges of insurgent fragmentation. In a famous address titled "A Weapon of Theory," Cabral acknowledged a core dilemma. While the "petty bourgeoisie,"

---

[10] On this issue, Mao Tse-Tung (2010) writes, "At present the contradiction between correct and incorrect thinking in our Party does not manifest itself in an antagonistic form, and if comrades who have committed mistakes can correct them, it will not develop into antagonism. Therefore, the Party must on the one hand wage a serious struggle against erroneous thinking, and on the other give the comrades who have committed errors ample opportunity to wake up. This being the case, excessive struggle is obviously inappropriate. But if the people who have committed errors persist in them and aggravate them, there is the possibility that this contradiction will develop into antagonism."

[11] See "Giap: People's War," which can be found at www.nelsonmandela.org/omalley/index.php/site/q/03lv03445/04lv04015/05lv04154/06lv04158.htm (Accessed September 4, 2015).

endowed with a "revolutionary consciousness," must lead the revolution, this group would always revert to its base class interests, undermining the working class and thwarting the true political transformation that was in the interests of the majority. To eliminate this veritable Trojan horse, Cabral famously argued that the petty bourgeoisie leaders needed to commit "class suicide" and be reborn as "revolutionary workers." In practice, this meant that insurgent leaders must voluntarily give up the trappings of their class status, lest they pollute the purity of the movement. For Cabral, then, the concept of "class suicide" was the solution to the ongoing problem of forging a unity of aim and action in the midst of a movement wracked by contradictions of wealth and status.[12]

Predictably, insurgent fragmentation has not only been the preoccupation of some of the twentieth century's most famed theorist-practitioners of rebellion. It has also been a phenomenon of great interest to counterinsurgents – not as a condition to avoid, of course, but as a weakness to exploit. David Galula, the French officer who was captured by Mao's Chinese communist forces in 1947 and would later serve with French forces in Algeria, acknowledged that "among guerrillas, as among any human group, can be found a variety of thoughts, feelings, and degrees of commitment to the insurgent's cause." Given these internal differences, Galula urged caution, warning that "treating them as a bloc would surely cement their solidarity." Instead, the task of the counterinsurgent should be to "divide their ranks, to stir up opposition between the mass and the leaders to win over the dissidents" (Galula, 1964, p. 89).

More recently, David Kilcullen, a widely read theorist-practitioner of contemporary counterinsurgency, has argued that in the post-9/11 globalized threat environment, those who have waged armed rebellions against US and coalition forces in contexts as diverse as Iraq, Afghanistan, and Somalia were "accidental guerrillas." By "accidental," Kilcullen meant that these rebels were motivated not by hatred of the United States, Takfiri ideological leanings, or the transnational programmatic aims of Al-Qaeda's global jihad but by profoundly localized feelings of threat provoked by US interventions throughout the Muslim world. In this setting, organizations like Al-Qaeda have exploited these fears, and grafted themselves onto local struggles whose aims and purposes were quite different from those of transnational militant jihadism. The task of the counterinsurgent, then, was to break this alignment and co-opt those who were not committed to the global jihadist project (Kilcullen, 2009). In effect, it was to use all tools at the disposal of

---

[12] For a copy of Cabral's speech, delivered in Havana in January 1966, see www.marxists.org/subject/africa/cabral/1966/weapon-theory.htm (Accessed September 8, 2015).

the State to promote the factionalism and fragmentation of organized rebellion.

Although couched in a wide variety of terms, this review makes clear that the practitioners who shaped the canon of insurgent and counterinsurgent warfare recognized that the internal cohesion of organized rebellion was never a given. Instead, unity was a delicate political condition that had to be carefully monitored, maintained, or, from the perspective of Galula and Kilcullen, subverted. More importantly, the subtext of this collective body of work was that cohesion mattered in significant ways. Indeed, why would these figures spill so much ink on an inconsequential challenge? Yet for all their insight, Lenin, Galula, and their intellectual descendants never really identified the specific consequences of a breakdown of cohesion, nor the downstream implications of one of its more significant manifestations, rebel fragmentation. It is to this issue that I now turn.

Theoretical and Practical Importance

Rebel fragmentation is a critically important issue for those interested in the phenomenon of civil war. The preoccupation of classic theorists of insurgent warfare with this issue is but one indicator of its importance. Yet in what specific ways does fragmentation matter to civil wars?[13] Broadly speaking, rebel fragmentation – or something very close to it – is an important causal variable that can explain a wide range of civil war outcomes.

The most obvious effect of rebel fragmentation is on the survival of rebel organizations, and by extension, their eventual success or failure. Social science analysis is not necessary to decipher this fact, as this basic intuition is an unstated assumption in most of the canon on insurgent warfare. Rebels cannot win if they cannot police fragmentation and remain coherent political actors. Fragmentation, as I have defined it, means the departure of skilled manpower and equipment, and the subsequent enhancement of the relative capabilities of a rebel organization's adversaries. It also involves the leakage of critical intelligence that can be exploited by a rebel organization's enemies. Perhaps most critically, fragmentation can reduce the morale of rebel troops, lowering their level

---

[13] For an excellent review of recent social science on this question, see K. Bakke, K. G. Cunningham, and L. Seymour, "The Problem with Fragmented Insurgencies," May 13, 2015, which can be found at www.washingtonpost.com/blogs/monkey-cage/wp/2015/05/13/the-problem-with-fragmented-insurgencies/ (Accessed September 20, 2015).

of preparedness and overall battlefield effectiveness. Sometimes, fragmentation can trigger a cascade of further defections that bring organized rebellions close to implosion. These deleterious impacts can be felt immediately or manifest themselves further down the road, but these effects are real and consequential.

Recent research has also shown that the fragmentation of rebel organizations impacts not only the success and failure of individual insurgent groups but also the ability of the overall "movement" to realize its political objectives. Peter Krause (2014, 2017), for instance, has argued that successful armed nationalist movements – which are often incubators of numerous rebel organizations with similar political objectives – require a single armed actor to consolidate it's hegemony. The benefits of hegemony are significant, since according to Krause, "hegemonic movement structure incentivizes the pursuit of shared strategic goals; reduces counterproductive violent mechanisms and foreign meddling; and improves the movement's coherence in strategy, clarity in signaling, and credibility in threats and assurances to yield strategic success" (Krause, 2014, p. 1). Fragmentation, however, subverts the possibility of establishing movement hegemony, because it increases the roster of insurgent organizations fighting for a particular cause.

Rebel fragmentation can also shape the intensity of civil war violence, both between contending armed actors and between these actors and civilians. Since rebel fragmentation can produce multiple contending armed groups, it may trigger a competitive dynamic in which these organizations attempt to "outbid" one another by increasing the scale and intensity of their operations against the state (Kydd & Walter, 2006; Cunningham, Bakke, & Seymour, 2012; Lawrence, 2010, 2013; K. G. Cunningham, 2013).[14] Violence against civilians may also increase, as proper conduct toward civilians requires that rebel fighters maintain a discipline and restraint that breaks down as the hierarchy of command erodes and rebel organizations fragment (Weinstein, 2005a, 2007; Humphrey & Weinstein, 2006).

The duration of civil wars is also impacted by rebel fragmentation. The splintering of rebel organizations increases the number of "veto players" in civil wars – parties whose acquiescence is required to negotiate and implement a peace agreement – and thus extends their duration (D. Cunningham, 2006, 2011). Civil wars with multiple veto players

---

[14] Much of the work on outbidding is drawn from an expansive literature on terrorist organizations, which are a category of armed actor that overlaps, but is analytically distinct from rebel or insurgent organizations; see Findley and Young (2012) for research that disputes outbidding arguments. Nemeth (2014) argues that outbidding logic is mediated by ideology.

last longer because the set of all agreements that all parties will accept is smaller, the risk of overestimating victory is higher, the incentive to be the last holdout is greater, and multiple players encourage shifting alliances.[15] This is a perfectly intuitive argument: the more parties that need to be reconciled in a political agreement, the harder it is to find a deal that satisfies all of them. Longer civil wars, of course, mean more violence, destruction, and human suffering. A related line of research focuses more narrowly on the specific context of broken peace processes, and demonstrates that rebel fragmentation can produce "spoilers" who sabotage peace negotiations because the realization of an agreement would jeopardize their fundamental interests (Stedman, 1997; Pearlman, 2009, 2011). Since peace processes often represent a shift in the allocation of benefits, and are therefore contentious and likely to create internal disagreement, rebel leaders require an ability to impose the agreement on the various constituent units of the organization. Yet fragmentation means rebel leaders lack this basic enforcement capacity, and disgruntled rebel commanders have the ability to use violence to subvert the terms of the peace agreement, leading to its failure and a continuation of war.

The lack of enforcement capacity endemic to rebel organizations that have undergone fragmentation also has serious implications for the behavior of the state. Interactions between the state and fragmented rebels are characterized by severe commitment problems since the state is unlikely to commit to an agreement (or negotiations) with rebel organizations that lack the mandate to fulfill their end of the bargain. Moreover, insofar as rebel fragmentation implies weakness, why would states negotiate with a rebel organization in decline? This can lead the state to double down on counterinsurgency and a military solution by increasing its investments in the political and economic tools of war. States may even introduce a strategy of "divide and conquer," using petty inducements such as amnesty or money to further divide the rebels before dealing them a crushing military blow. Complicating these intuitions, however, is recent research that has shown that in some settings, fragmentation may not induce states to "divide and conquer," but "divide and concede" in ways that constitute a real recognition of the political ambitions of rebel organizations (K. G. Cunningham, 2011). Whatever

---

[15] Findley and Rudloff in an unpublished 2011 paper titled "Combatant Fragmentation and the Dynamics of Civil Wars" disagree with this view, arguing that the effects of rebel fragmentation are minimal, and when effects can be identified, fragmentation leads to negotiated settlements. This is largely due to the fact that fragmentation contributes to parity between competing sides.

the direction the effect on state behavior runs, there is little doubt that rebel fragmentation has real impacts on state behavior.

The fragmentation of rebel movements is also deeply implicated in the politics of state failure. State failure quite obviously has many important correlates, however the concept might be defined.[16] Yet the most acute examples of state failure – 1990s Somalia, Zaire, Liberia – are part of a familiar and consistent pattern: a civil war begins with a challenge to state power from one or two rebel organizations, state power erodes and collapses, and these organizations fragment and yield splinter organizations of varying strength that violently compete with one another. The result is that neither the original organizations nor their offspring can effectively seize the state, leading to a complex spiral of increasingly fragmented violence that becomes far more difficult to contain than the initial civil war.[17] By contrast, current governments in Uganda, Rwanda, Ethiopia, and Eritrea are examples of rebel organizations that maintained their coherence and succeeded in effectively consolidating control of collapsing states. Indeed, many of the intellectual icons of insurgent warfare – like Lenin and Mao – were icons precisely because they fell into this latter group. Christopher Clapham (1998) articulates this distinction well, writing of the difference between what he calls "state-consolidating insurgencies" and "state-subverting insurgencies," wherein some rebel organizations have the capacity to reconstitute and reproduce state power, while others are little more than a disintegrative force. Clapham's insights are connected to those of Jeremy Weinstein (2005b), who suggests, among other things, that the capacity of certain rebel groups to cohere and impose a new political order is elemental to the "autonomous recovery" of collapsed states wracked by civil war. The lesson here is that if we care about the contemporary phenomenon of state failure, we need to seriously consider the problem of political factionalism and fragmentation within armed nonstate actors who seek to replace incumbent governments.

The existence of a number of rebel organizations that successfully seized the mantle of state power raises additional considerations about the postwar behavior of these groups. An interesting research program has emerged in recent years exploring the myriad transitions insurgent groups make into peaceful politics, and connects their postwar foreign and domestic politics to their wartime behaviors, practices, and institutions (Sadri, 1997; Jones, 2013; Southall, 2013; Woldemariam, 2015,

---

[16] One of the key texts on the concept of state failure is a volume edited by Robert Rotberg (2003).
[17] See Christopher Day and Michael Woldemariam (2017), "From Rebelling to Ruling: Insurgent Victory and State Capture in Africa" (unpublished paper).

2016; Huang, 2016; Lyons, 2016a; Zukerman-Daly, 2016).[18] In this context, rebel factionalism and fragmentation can be an important analytic dimension of understanding the downstream behavior of rebels once they have transitioned into political parties, whether they govern or simply participate in the official political process. Fragmentation during wartime can often presage factionalism and fragmentation in the postwar period, impacting everything from the rebel organization's survival prospects as a party to its programmatic impulses. Even when postwar fragmentation doesn't occur, the legacy of wartime splits can have huge effects on how rebels-turned-political-parties organize themselves internally and externally, either because it shapes their historical memory or, more intuitively, because it impacts which constituencies remain part of the organization in peacetime.

It is worth emphasizing that considerations over rebel fragmentation's impact on rebels' peacetime political behavior is not a minor consideration. Countless rebel organizations in Africa have transitioned into opposition parties, and as of December 2011 there were a total of fourteen African states governed by political parties that were once rebel organizations.[19] The domain of these ruling regimes was vast, occupying more than 10 million square kilometers, or about one-third of Africa's total landmass. In population terms, this meant about 280 million Africans out of a total continent-wide population of just over 1 billion were under the charge of such regimes.[20] And of course, beyond this book's African laboratory, there have been many other regimes that had their start as rebel organizations, including the notable cases of China, Vietnam, and Cuba.

Rebel Fragmentation: A Common Occurrence or a Rare Phenomenon?

As the preceding section makes clear, rebel fragmentation is an important causal variable in civil war and post–civil war contexts. Yet even if we are able to identify a host of theoretical and practical reasons why rebel fragmentation is important, we have little sense of the prevalence of the phenomenon. Certainly, the vignette drawn from the conflict in

---

[18] Also see unpublished paper by Christopher Day and Michael Woldemariam titled "From Rebelling to Ruling: Insurgent Victory and State Capture in Africa."
[19] These states are the following: Chad, Central African Republic, Ethiopia, Eritrea, Uganda, Rwanda, Congo, Côte d'Ivoire, Angola, Mozambique, Zimbabwe, Namibia, and South Africa.
[20] Population statistics were computed by the author in 2013, but the general point still holds.

Darfur at the beginning of this introductory chapter suggests that rebel fragmentation is an all too common phenomenon. Further afield, observations from non-African contexts such as in Syria and Afghanistan tend to confirm this view. Yet we require a more systematic snapshot.

Toward this end, I have compiled an original dataset on patterns of rebel fragmentation in post–World War II sub-Saharan Africa, excluding the North African countries of Egypt, Libya, Tunisia, Algeria, and Morocco. The dataset, which includes the full sample of African rebel organizations between the years 1946 and 2006, is designed to measure exactly if and when rebel organizations fragmented.

In identifying the "full sample" of African rebel organizations, I use data provided by the Uppsala Conflict Data Program (UCDP)/ Peace Research Institute Oslo (PRIO) Armed Conflict Dataset (Gleditsch et al., 2002; Harbom, Melander, & Wallensteen, 2008), which defines rebel organizations, or what they call "opposition organizations," as formally organized, nongovernmental opposition, which uses armed force. In addition, these entities must have been involved in "consciously conducted and planned political campaigns rather than spontaneous violence," and participated in military confrontations with the government resulting in twenty-five battlefield deaths annually.[21]

This leaves us with a base sample of 139 rebel organizations in sub-Saharan Africa that have operated between the years 1946 and 2006. However, on closer examination it is clear that the UCDP/PRIO count is not exhaustive. This is particularly true in civil wars that involve multiple rebel organizations, where identifying *which* organizations actually participated in military confrontations leading to twenty-five annual battlefield deaths can be a challenge. The result is that UCDP/PRIO often excludes smaller rebel organizations participating in long-running civil wars populated by multiple rebel organizations.[22]

In order to correct for this omission, I include thirty-two additional rebel organizations across ten countries that in my estimation, and according to UCDP/PRIO's own inclusion criteria, should be included in the dataset.[23] The data, while informative, suggest that the

---

[21] The codebook for the UCDP/PRIO Armed Conflict Dataset (2009 version) from which these quotations are drawn can be found at www.prio.org/Global/upload/CSCW/Data/UCDP/2009/Codebook_UCDP_PRIO%20Armed%20Conflict%20Dataset%20v4_2009.pdf (Accessed October 26, 2017).

[22] To be fair, an exhaustive list of all of rebel organizations is not the real focus of the UCDP/PRIO dataset. Rather, UCDP/PRIO's data are geared toward identifying the precise onset and duration of particular conflicts.

[23] These organizations are the following: Angola (FLEC, FLEC-Platform), Burundi (Palipehutu – FNL – Rwasa Faction, Palipehutu – FNL – Mugabarabona Faction, CNDD – FDD – Ndayikengurukiye Faction, CNDD – FDD – Nkurunziza

distribution of the sample is uneven across countries, a function of the concentration of protracted civil wars in a few historically volatile African countries, each of which yielded a significant number of competing rebel organizations. In fact, rebel organizations from three countries – Chad, Uganda, and Sudan – make up more than a full third of the total sample.

With the complete sample of African rebel organization established, we now turn to the more problematic issue of measuring rebel fragmentation across this population. Many scholars of civil war recognize that historical data on rebel organizations are rarely available, yielding scant source material for coding. Even in cases where the data may be present, it is of dubious quality. These problems are compounded when the rebel organizations of interest are older and operating in countries or regions without the capacity to generate proper records.

In addition, while rebel fragmentation has been defined as the simple occurrence of an organizational split, measuring the phenomenon creates certain conceptual dilemmas. The core of the problem emanates from the fact that individuals and small groups exit rebel organizations at recurring intervals in what are the normal processes of war. For instance, the rebel officer who squabbles with his superior may join a rival organization, departing with three or four of his colleagues. Yet can this relatively minor event be counted and compared alongside the fairly dramatic (and consequential) political ruptures I seek to investigate here – events that involve tens, hundreds, and even thousands of rebel fighters?

The answer to this question is probably not. Grouping dissimilar events in this way under the banner of "fragmentation" would only complicate the construction of clear theory and produce biased conclusions. Moreover, we would find ourselves with almost nothing to explain, as fragmentation would be occurring virtually all the time. How then do we distinguish between the departure of individuals and very small groups from rebel organizations, which are part of the normal noise of civil war, and fragmentation of significant size and scope? Were we trying to measure fragmentation across a few cases, the analyst could use his/her professional judgment and knowledge of these small number of cases to identify consequential instances of fragmentation (as is done in case

---

Faction), Central African Republic (APRD, FDPC), Chad (Second Liberation Army, FROLINAT Originel, FAO, Volcan Force, FNTR), Democratic Republic of Congo (RCD – Goma, CNDP), Liberia (ULIMO, ULIMO – J, ULIMO – K), Mali (FPLA, ARLA, Ganda Koi), Niger (Tamoust Liberation Front, ARLN, ORA), Sudan (NMRD, SLM/A – Abdel Wahid Faction, SLM/A – Abdel Shafi Faction, SLM/A – Unity), Uganda (FRONASA, Ugandan People's Army, Uganda Freedom Fighters, Popular Resistance Army).

study portions of this study). However, this is not a workable proposition across 171 organizations.

One option would be to employ inclusion criteria consisting of strict numerical thresholds in identifying instances of fragmentation. So, for instance, if an organizational split results in the departure of more than twenty rebels, we could code this as fragmentation. Or, since some organizations are quite small, we could use a figure based on the proportion of the organization that splits. Yet numerical estimates of splinter groups, much less rebel organizations as a whole, are notoriously difficult to come by. Moreover, it is hard to develop a compelling theoretical rationale for why a split that includes twenty rebels, and not seventeen, should be coded as fragmentation.

The other alternative, which I favor for the purposes of this dataset and *drop in the subsequent analyses in the following chapters*, is to code fragmentation only for those splits that result in the creation of a new rebel organization. This would exclude fragmentation that results in a splinter group joining government forces or an existing rebel organization. The rationale behind this temporary narrowing of focus is that it allows us to employ a "capacity threshold," in coding fragmentation by including *only those splinter groups that have demonstrated the independent ability to engage in military hostilities with the government*. Such a threshold could not be applied to groups that split and join the government or another rebel organization, since separating the actual military capacity of these splinter groups from the entity they have joined is virtually impossible. The important point is that by making this coding decision, we differentiate between splinter groups of consequence – i.e., those that actually have some independent military capacity from those that are marginal.

The dataset tracks rebel organizations through the duration of their operational life, from their first armed engagement with government forces to their final engagement. Information used to code fragmentation is drawn from a wide variety of publicly available sources, including newspapers, books on particular civil wars and rebel groups, documents published by rebel organizations and governments, and the reports of nongovernmental organizations (NGOs) and international organizations.

The data are striking. As Figure 1.1 indicates, more than one-third of Africa's rebel organizations have fragmented at least once – in this case defined as a split that results in the establishment of a new, militarily functional rebel organization.[24] Even with such a high bar for what

---

[24] This result is roughly confirmed by actor-level data released in 2010 by the Uppsala Conflict Data Program. An updated version of "UCDP Actor Dataset 2.1–2010, Uppsala Conflict Data Program" can be found at www.ucdp.uu.se/downloads/

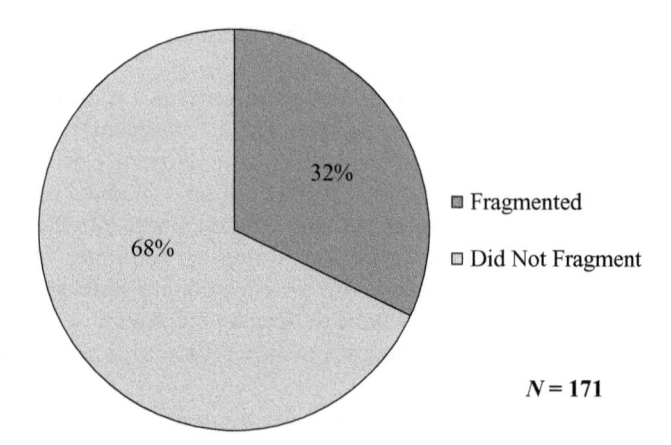

[Figure 1.1: Pie chart showing 32% Fragmented, 68% Did Not Fragment, N = 171]

Figure 1.1 Percentage of rebel organizations in sub-Saharan Africa that fragmented, 1946–2006.

constitutes fragmentation, there is a one-in-three chance that an African rebel leader will be unable to prevent the fragmentation of his organization.

Moreover, the data indicate that of the one-third of African rebel organizations that fragmented at least once, a full 20 percent fragmented multiple times, suggesting that for some organizations the affliction of fragmentation is endemic.

Clearly, the fragmentation of rebel organizations is not rare. Were the criteria for counting the occurrence of fragmentation revised to include splits that result in groups joining an existing rebel organization or the government, fragmentation would likely occur within well in excess of 60 percent of the sample.

While this finding suggests the importance of the forthcoming analysis, the possibility does exist that the fragmentation of rebel organizations is unique to a particular period of African postcolonial history. Several analysts have argued that there are important distinctions to be had between rebel organizations that emerged during the Cold War and

(Accessed October 25, 2017). The author's understanding is that this actor-level data is closely related to UCDP's Non-State Actor Dataset, whose codebook can be found at www.pcr.uu.se/digitalAssets/55/a_55112-f_NonStateActorCodebook.pdf (Accessed October 26, 2017). To its credit, the actor-level data managed to identify several African rebel organizations that I was unable to identify, thus enlarging the potential sample of African rebel organizations. In any case, the UCDP actor-level data that became available after my data was collected goes through 2009, while my data stop in 2006, a fact that in part accounts for the UCDP's larger sample; a global dataset put together by Christia (2012) also finds a rate of rebel fragmentation consistent with my own findings.

those that emerged afterwards, such that rebel organization operating in "new civil wars" are more interested in private loot, suffer from a lack of popular support, and tend to perpetrate gratuitous violence against civilians.[25] Rebels operating in "old civil wars" have exactly the opposite characteristics. As Kalyvas (2001) has noted in a critical commentary on the issue, "most versions of the distinction between old and new civil wars stress or imply that new civil wars are characteristically criminal, depoliticized, private, and predatory; old civil wars are considered ideological, political, collective, and even noble. The dividing line between old and new civil wars roughly corresponds to the end of the Cold War." A logical extension of this argument is that post–Cold War rebel organizations tend to be less internally disciplined, and thus more prone to fragmentation.

Yet a cursory examination of my data – which can be done by splitting the sample of rebel organizations into Cold War and post–Cold War cohorts (eighty-eight and eighty-three rebel organizations respectively) – suggests that the occurrence of rebel fragmentation is not temporally bounded, and has been a consistent feature of civil wars over time. In fact, somewhat counterintuitively, a slightly larger percentage of Cold War–era rebel organizations fragmented.

The Way Forward

Having demonstrated the prevalence of rebel fragmentation in postcolonial Africa, and motivated the topic more generally, we can turn to the theoretical and empirical portions of the book. The road map of this book is as follows.

Chapter 2 provides a theoretical framework for explaining the occurrence of rebel fragmentation. As noted in the preceding pages, the framework puts the territorial ebb and flow of war front and center. The chapter goes on to introduce the laboratory for investigating the book's core claims, the Ethiopian civil war, and provides descriptive statistics on patterns of rebel fragmentation across that conflict. It concludes by providing a basic statistical test designed to establish a relationship between rebel fragmentation and territorial losses and gains and provide a point of departure for the selection of seven cases for qualitative, historical analysis.

Chapters 3, 4, and 5 are the empirical core of this book, and narrate the experiences of the seven rebel organizations that have faced the

---

[25] Kaldor (1999) provides a general picture of this body of work, although her book is concerned with war more generally.

periodic challenge of factionalism and fragmentation. Chapters 2 and 3 are particularly important, and provide detailed analysis of two cases that demonstrate the proposed theory in a particularly lucid fashion. These two cases hail from Ethiopia's restive former province of Eritrea: the Eritrean Liberation Front (ELF) and the Eritrean People's Liberation Front (EPLF). Throughout much of this book, I will use the popular or colloquial names for the ELF and EPLF, lest readers be confused by the similar acronyms. The colloquial name name for the ELF is *Jebha*, and literally means "front" in Arabic, while the EPLF's colloquial name is *Shaebia*, which means "peoples" in the same language. In regular conversation, most Eritreans and Ethiopians would refer to these two organizations using these terms.[26]

The remaining five case studies explored in Chapter 5 are drawn from other regions of Ethiopia proper, and designed more as "shadow cases," although they succinctly provide compelling support for this book's central argument.

Chapter 6 seeks to establish the external validity of the book's main argument by tracking the evolution of three major participants in the Somali Civil War (1978–2014), the Somali National Movement (SNM), the Islamic Courts Union (ICU), and Al-Shabaab. The study's conclusion summarizes the main findings of the book, identifies the importance of the arguments made, and reflects on avenues for future research.

The book builds on years of careful research in Ethiopia, Somalia, Kenya, Sudan, Europe, and North America, and a wide variety of materials, including interviews, archives, and a vast secondary literature. As such, the forthcoming analysis provides a theoretically innovative, historically rich perspective on rebel fragmentation in the Horn of Africa that both builds on and revises conventional thinking about organized rebellion's intractable problem.

---

[26] Arabic speakers from Eritrea and Sudan will often refer to Jebha as "Jebha Tahrir," which means "Liberation Front."

2 A Theory of Rebel Fragmentation

Chapter 1 introduced the book's main research question, outlined its broad contours, and demonstrated its practical importance using data on patterns of rebel fragmentation across African civil wars. I now turn to the task of explanation. This chapter opens by defining core concepts such as "rebel organization" and "fragmentation." Having completed this basic conceptual work, the chapter goes on to summarize existing research on the topic at hand and outline a theory with a clear causal mechanism linking "independent variables" to the outcome of interest, rebel fragmentation. It concludes with a discussion of case selection, motivating the analysis of the Ethiopian civil war, and particular groups that participated in it, through an investigation of original statistical data.

Core Concepts

What Is a Rebel Organization?

To measure the fragmentation of rebel organizations, we must be explicit about what we take a rebel organization to be. Without a clear delineation of what our unit of analysis is, we may violate the assumption of unit homogeneity that is vital to comparative work in the social sciences (King, Keohane, & Verba, 1994). I find it useful to follow the definition of rebel organizations provided by the Uppsala Conflict Data Program (UCDP)/Peace Research Institute Oslo (PRIO) Armed Conflict Dataset, not only because the use of UCDP/PRIO criteria makes the data I present throughout this book more readily comparable to other work but also because the criteria UCDP/PRIO employs in defining rebel organizations are intuitive and complete.[1]

---

[1] Note that these criteria are essentially the same as in the Uppsala Conflict Data Program's (UCDP) actor-level dataset. See an updated version of "UCDP Actor Dataset 2.1–2010, Uppsala Conflict Data Program" at www.ucdp.uu.se/downloads/ (Accessed October 25, 2017). The author's understanding is that this data (and its definitions) are closely related to the UCDP's Non-State Actor Dataset, whose codebook

Although they were briefly introduced in Chapter 1, it is worth developing the rationale for my use of UCDP/PRIO criteria further.

First, a rebel organization must be "a nongovernmental group of people having announced a name for their group" who are "formally organized." The metric "nongovernmental" is important because it allows us to distinguish rebel organizations from progovernment militias, while the metric "formally organized" distinguishes rebel organizations from spontaneous forms of rebellion that lack formal structures and direction – riots, for instance.

Second, a rebel organization should have used "armed force to influence the outcome of a stated incompatibility." The metric "armed force" is crucial because it differentiates rebel organizations from political parties and other organizations that oppose incumbent governments through nonviolent means.

Third, a rebel organization's military activities must be part of "consciously conducted and planned political campaigns rather than spontaneous violence." The key word here is "political," as a well-defined set of political goals allows analysts to draw a distinction between rebel organizations and networks of organized crime whose primary imperative is profit. And of course, the exclusion of "spontaneous violence" underscores the point made earlier about the need to draw a distinction between formally organized and unplanned violence.

Fourth, a rebel organization must be involved in a military event resulting in at least twenty-five battle-related deaths. The casualty bar is a necessary one because it suggests that the activities of the rebel organization are of significance, that the organization maintains a certain capacity, and that it is not a rebel organization in name only.[2]

Collectively, these four criteria precisely define our population of interest. While we could think of other relevant markers of rebel organization, the foregoing metrics are precise and logical, with each exclusion rule grounded in our intuitive, conventional understandings of what armed organized rebellion is, and is not.

What Is Fragmentation?

The outcome (or dependent variable) this book seeks to explore is rebel fragmentation, defined as an *event where a segment of a rebel*

---

can be found at www.pcr.uu.se/digitalAssets/55/a_55112-f_NonStateActorCodebook.pdf (Accessed October 26, 2017).

[2] The codebook for the UCDP/PRIO Armed Conflict Dataset (2009 version) from which these quotations are drawn can be found at www.prio.org/Global/upload/CSCW/Data/UCDP/2009/Codebook_UCDP_PRIO%20Armed%20Conflict%20Dataset%20v4_2009.pdf (Accessed October 26, 2017).

organization formally and collectively exits that rebel organization and either a) establishes a new rebel organization, b) joins an existing rebel organization, or c) joins the incumbent government.[3] I view rebel fragmentation as a clearly identifiable manifestation of a breakdown of cooperation within a rebel organization, and thus a category of factional events that include other phenomena such as coups, extrajudicial killings, extrajudicial purges/arrests, and insubordination. These events are characterized by their extralegal nature and sit outside the bounds of the normal political processes of a rebel organization.

What is the logic behind this definition? By bracketing elements that fragment into three identifiable categories, I exclude actors that exit a rebel organization simply to lay down their arms and leave the political sphere altogether. Such behavior, though quite common in civil war, would more appropriately be labeled *desertion* rather than fragmentation.

Furthermore, the preceding definition describes fragmentation as the *formal exit* of a segment of a rebel organization and thus the product of intentional action. By defining fragmentation in this way, we avoid conflating the emergence of particular organizational forms within a rebel organization with its fragmentation. Consider the following: units of a rebel organization may be forced to decentralize and operate independently of one another because of increases in state surveillance and repression, as existing levels of coordination and communication may jeopardize security.[4] To the outside observer, this reduction in coordination across rebel units may be interpreted as the rebel organization having fragmented, but to the parties involved this is a tactical maneuver that has little to do with any underlying factional dispute.

Rebel fragmentation as defined here is also a *collective action* and involves a number of individuals who *coordinate* their efforts with the objective of exiting a rebel organization. This is an important point, because defining fragmentation in this way excludes spontaneous occurrences in which a large number of individuals, at random, exit an organization at similar points in time for their own personal, private reasons.

Notably, the foregoing definition includes all instances of fragmentation, however large or small. Analytically, I treat the exit of a group of 50 the same as that of a group of 500. Some may find this to be problematic, as certain instances of fragmentation are likely to be insignificant to the overall strategic picture and not comparable to larger fragmentation events. Yet distinguishing between insignificant and significant or minor and major cases of fragmentation is a difficult task. While one could

---

[3] Note how this definition expands the definition of rebel fragmentation used in my Africa-wide dataset. Italics are used here for emphasis, as this definition is foundational to this book.
[4] An excellent example of this would be Joseph Kony's Lord's Resistance Army.

employ a strictly numerical threshold, coding fragmentation as having occurred in instances where upwards of 10 or 20 percent of the rebel organization has exited, the collection of these kinds of reliable troop estimates over a large number of cases is highly implausible – a point that has been made earlier.

Another possibility is to define fragmentation in terms of its effects. For example, if we can reasonably argue that the exit of a rebel group has led to a reduction in the operational capacity of the group from which it exited, then this can be included as a case of fragmentation. If not, then the fragmentation is probably so insignificant as to be irrelevant and not comparable to larger cases of fragmentation. Yet however clever this measurement criterion may seem, it involves making causal claims about the connection between fragmentation and operational capacity, a venture that, given the complexity of war – and when carried out over several or more cases – will likely lead to major inaccuracies.

Of course, the historical record itself tends to mitigate the likelihood of including marginal cases of fragmentation. Newspapers, online media, archives, original interviews, and ethnographies are unlikely to capture the minor, insignificant cases of fragmentation – where, for instance, three low-level combatants decide to exit and join another rebel organization. Written and oral history tends to act as a filter, keying the analyst in to events that are consequential, rather than those that are not.[5]

In the subsequent analysis, I measure fragmentation on an annual basis, investigating whether fragmentation has occurred within a particular rebel organization within a given year. As fragmentation can sometimes, but not always, be an extended process, I code it as occurring in the year in which that process begins. By "begins," I mean the first observable manifestation of factionalism that evolves into an instance of fragmentation. So, if hypothetically, the Palestine Liberation Organization (PLO) officially split into two organizations in 1977, but the factional infighting and violence that sparked that split began in 1976, I would code 1976 as the year of fragmentation. By contrast, many cases of fragmentation occur in such a way that fragmentation is rapid, instead of the outgrowth of a drawn-out process of factional infighting.

The Social Science of Rebel Fragmentation: Blind Spots and Recent Advances

Until recently, the social science of civil war had little to say about the issue of factionalism and fragmentation within rebel organizations

---

[5] In the context of the subsequent analysis of Ethiopia's civil war, the smallest positive case of fragmentation coded was at about twenty individuals, while the largest was at about 2,000.

(Kalyvas, 2004; Blattman & Miguel, 2010). Traditionally, there were few theoretically compelling, empirically tested models that could help us understand, explain, and interpret such explosions of internal conflict within rebel organizations.

This omission raises an obvious and important question: Why did this stark gap in the literature on rebel organizations and civil wars exist? As the introduction to this book has shown, rebel factionalism and fragmentation are prevalent in contemporary civil wars and central to understanding a whole range of civil war outcomes. Moreover, some of the twentieth century's leading practitioners of insurgent and counterinsurgent warfare acknowledge factionalism and fragmentation as a central concern. Logically, these phenomena should have garnered much more attention from social science researchers of political violence and civil war.

The reason for the long-standing paucity of social science research on issues of rebel factionalism, I would argue, is attributable to several factors that have either made factionalism a difficult topic of inquiry from a data collection standpoint or masked the prevalence – and thus the importance – of the phenomenon in civil wars. First, the strategic imperatives of rebel organizations require that they feign unity. After all, rebels are not politicians operating in open political systems, where life and liberty are protected by widely accepted rules of the game. The world of the rebel is anarchic, and the only security that rebel organizations possess is that derived from their own capacities. In such an environment, where one misstep could have permanent and fatal consequences, rebel organizations have incentives to misrepresent the true nature and significance of their internal divisions, lest opponents exploit these divisions for immediate military or political advantage. Factionalism becomes hard to explore because rebel organizations purposely render it difficult to observe.

A second issue is related to the fact that much of the writing on rebel organizations focuses on those that have achieved victory, or at the very least, achieved a broad degree of operational success (Lewis, 2012, 2016). I refer here to the journalistic, historical, and anthropological accounts written by *observers* of particular rebel organizations and civil wars, which are an important entry point for social scientists seeking to theorize and explain civil war phenomena (Kalyvas, 2004).[6] This bias

---

[6] More generally, social science that is built upon the comparative case method routinely leverages the descriptive work of non–social scientists. Some of the most widely cited works in comparative politics and international relations are empirically grounded in the journalistic, historical, or anthropological accounts of particular cases. This cross-fertilization, though profitable, can produce a number of analytic challenges (Goldthorpe, 1991; Lustick, 1996).

toward an analysis of "victorious" or "successful" rebel organizations is a simple reflection of the fact that such groups tend to be of lasting political consequence: they often become ruling-parties, or succeed in having their ideas and interests integrated into the political system (Lyons, 2016a, 2016b, 2016c). Those that fail, or succumb to the vagaries of war relatively quickly, do not have the same obvious long-run political impacts. As a consequence, they attract far less scholarly and journalistic attention. There are, for instance, many more historical works on Fidel Castro's wildly successful rebellion in Cuba than on Che Guevara's failed insurgency in Bolivia; more writing on the Vietcong than on the Karen rebels in Burma; and more analyses of Mao's Red Army than on Muslim militants in southern Thailand. Alone, this bias toward telling the story of rebels that have been "winners," or at least those that have been operationally potent, seems to have little bearing on the lacunae in research on rebel fragmentation, until one considers the fact that successful rebel organizations are probably less likely to have suffered from factionalism and fragmentation. To outside observers, this "selection effect" renders rebel factionalism and fragmentation a seemingly less relevant feature of civil war dynamics – a reality that helps explain the notable absence of research on such topics.[7]

The bias toward an analysis of victorious rebel organizations creates a related problem for the analysis of rebel factionalism. This problem stems largely from the subconscious effects of analyzing organizations and movements that were so wildly successful. Consider for a moment the African context, which is this book's primary focus, and several of the most prominent African rebel organizations that were victors, or partial victors, in the military struggles in which they participated – the Eritrean People's Liberation Front–People's Front for Democracy and Justice (EPLF–PFDJ, Eritrea), Tigrayan People's Liberation Front (TPLF, Ethiopia), Rwandan Patriotic Front (RPF, Rwanda), South West Africa People's Organization (SWAPO, Namibia), and the National Resistance Movement (NRM, Uganda). The historiography of each of these organizations contains deep biases in the way the historical experiences of these rebellions were remembered and conveyed to broader audiences. The reason is that victory implies military prowess, organizational capacity, and perseverance borne of unity of aim and effort. These

---

[7] Kalyvas (2004, p. 24) has persuasively made the case that there is also an "urban bias" in analyses of civil war and political violence. One consequence is that "many general histories treated as 'evidence' in social science studies promote versions of the past that emphasize fixed and unchanged identities and ignore or deny the presence of intragroup conflict."

"implied traits of victory," in turn, lead to a subconscious elevation of the organization's virtue above its many faults – in the eyes of combatants, supporters, and those who seek to tell the organization's story. As catastrophic pathologies that do not comport with healthy, productive armed rebellions, internal wrangling and factional episodes scarcely receive mention in the public and scholarly historiography because they are out of sync with what victorious organizations eventually achieved. Put differently, because factionalism and fragmentation do not intuitively fit the narrative of "successful" rebel organizations, these phenomena are purged from the historical record.

It is worth pointing out that as victorious rebel organizations that transformed themselves into ruling parties, the aforementioned movements had every incentive to sanitize their history in ways that created the legitimacy necessary to govern. As history is often "written by the victors," these rebels-turned-ruling-parties were able to construct "official" or "authorized" narratives that swept the dirty laundry of factional infighting under the rug. Historical narratives that diminished the internal divisions of organized rebellion, in this sense, were not only a result of a subconscious process but also part and parcel of an endeavor in purposeful mythmaking by emergent governments and their allies. Robert Southall (2013, p. 71), the noted scholar of Southern Africa's liberation movements, concurs with this view, arguing that such "reinventions of history" were deliberately designed to promote "the victorious and now ruling party and its claim to perpetuity."[8]

Even where rebel organizations have been less successful, years of ideological indoctrination and the inculcation of the party line leave members with a distorted historical narrative and a limited perspective on their organization's past shortcomings, thus biasing the work of historians and other observers. As such, a Guevara-like romanticism about these organizations persists. Social scientists who seek to tap the written history of an organization, and the historical memory of an organization's members, can find these prevailing narratives to be obscuring and a major barrier to inquiries of rebel factionalism and fragmentation.[9]

To make these claims more concrete, it is worth considering the broad orientation of the literature on a rebel organization that will feature heavily in the following pages – the Eritrean People's Liberation Front (EPLF or *Shaebia*). The EPLF was the most formidable of the insurgent fronts

---

[8] To read more about these dynamics in the context of the RPF's Rwanda, see the work of Reyntjens (2004, 2006), among many others.
[9] Kalyvas (2006) echoes this view, citing what he has called "partisan bias" in ethnographic accounts of civil war, where narratives of the conflict – ostensibly balanced – take on a political hue designed to validate one side or another.

that fought in the Ethiopian civil war, and its eventual victory over the Marxist regime of Mengistu Hailemariam paved the way for its emergence as the ruling party of an independent Eritrea. Not surprisingly, the EPLF has been the focus of great scholarly and journalistic attention, relative to some of the other rebel participants in the Ethiopian–Eritrean conflicts. Yet beyond a few notable exceptions, the internal politics of the EPLF, and its factionalism and fragmentation, remains an unexplored dimension of the organization's history. This is despite the reality – as this book will show – that the EPLF went through several very serious and consequential internal crises. Indeed, as one EPLF central committee member told the author with respect to these ruptures, "The 'true' history of the EPLF has never been told."[10] Patrick Gilkes, a scholar-journalist of the Horn of Africa, argues that this stark gap owes its origins to the influence of stylized rebel narratives on external observers. According to Gilkes (2003), "Much, indeed, of the writing on Eritrea has been at the level of polemic or a product of the 'guerrilla groupie.' A surprising number of eminent scholars and journalists have taken the leading Eritrean movement, the EPLF, at its own evaluation, and its historical claims as fact. The results have impoverished the literature on Eritrea, and have created a distorted national mythology."[11] Yosief Ghebrehiwet, a leading if somewhat controversial Eritrean intellectual, summarizes the issue even more succinctly, writing that analyses of the Eritrean conflict, and the EPLF more specifically, are wrapped in a "romantic obsession with the revolutionary past, magnifying whatever was good in it beyond proportion, while discounting anything else that mars that picture."[12]

The biases Ghebrehiwet and Gilkes refer to are not restricted to the historical record of victorious or successful rebel organizations in Ethiopia, Eritrea, or Africa. Perhaps the most well known and most thoroughly romanticized rebel organization is Mao's Red Army. Sun Shuyun's *The Long March: The True History of Communist China's Founding Myth* carefully investigates the historical edifice surrounding the Red Army's finest hour – Mao's 1934 strategic retreat across China that purportedly saved the communist revolution. In Shuyun's words, "the Long March is a story on par with Moses leading the Exodus out of Egypt.

---

[10] Author's interview, Shaebia commander, May 28, 2009.
[11] See also "Eritrea: Historiography and Mythology," by Patrick Gilkes, posted on February 7, 2011, available at http://asmarino.com/articles/908-eritrea-historiography-and-mythology.
[12] Quote is taken from Ghebrehiwet's widely read "Romanticizing Ghedli." "Ghedli" effectively means the "the struggle" or the "revolution." The article is available at https://dissidentdiaries.files.wordpress.com/2013/06/romanticizing_ghedli.pdf.

We can hardly escape it... the Long March remains the sun in the sky" (Shuyun, 2006, pp. 2–3).

Yet with striking clarity, Shuyun does much to reappraise the Long March, as well as the Red Army's exploits more generally. Her research "uncovers shocking stories of starvation, disease, and desertion, of ruthless purges ordered by Party leaders, of the mistreatment of women, and of thousands of futile deaths."[13] Clearly, Mao's Long March was not what it seemed. Notably, the pages of Shuyun's book are littered with examples of power struggles between Mao and many of the Red Army's leading commanders – internal factionalism and fragmentation that have been effectively written out of the standard histories of the Red Army as a rebel organization.

One should note that the work of Gilkes, Ghebrehiwet, and Shuyun – by its very existence – forces us to acknowledge that what we are talking about are only general tendencies within what is a large body of scholarship spanning multiple disciplines. A number of historians, anthropologists, and journalists, many of whom are cited in this book, have been able to capture the contentious internal dynamics of rebel organizations.[14] Some scholarship on particular rebel organizations and civil wars is collectively nuanced and more attuned to rebel factionalism and fragmentation.[15] Yet this work notwithstanding, the analytic barriers to the systematic, social scientific study of the internal politics of rebel organizations has long left scholarship on this topic somewhat marginalized.

A final point needs to be made. While the deliberate effort to misinform for strategic purposes and the myriad implications of an analytic bias toward successful rebel organizations are important reasons for the seeming blind spot in the social science of civil war on questions of rebel factionalism and fragmentation, these factors were compounded by a third, but particularly obvious issue: civil wars are a tough setting for field research. The insecurity of contemporary civil wars, even when researchers are not directly targeted, is a serious constraint to on-the-ground data collection. While in recent years social scientists have increasingly turned toward focused field research to address questions of

---

[13] Quote is drawn from the book's inner flap.
[14] See, for example, Pool (2001), on the EPLF.
[15] For instance, the literature on Hamas, a good example of which is Tamimi (2008). See also the literature on Mozambique's Renamo as reflected by Vines (1991). Kalyvas (2001) has argued that the romanticization of rebel organizations has been bounded by time, such that pre–Cold War organizations that operate in "old civil wars" are described in a more positive light than those that operate in "new civil wars." For a good example of this kind of analysis, see Jeffrey Gettleman, "Africa's Forever Wars: Why the Continent's Conflicts Never End," *Foreign Policy*, February 11, 2010.

armed conflict and political violence (Wood, 2006; Thaler, 2017), much of the first-generation civil war scholarship relied on quantitative datasets or the aforementioned work of journalists, historians, and anthropologists. The problem here was that field research was precisely the sort of scholarly tool that could have helped overcome many of the previously described obstacles to analysis of rebel fragmentation (Kalyvas, 2004). On-the-ground observation and close contact with combatants, though no silver bullet, could have helped identify rebel fragmentation as a phenomenon with real import to civil war dynamics, and one capable of being systematically studied.

The Analytic Turn in the Study of Rebel Fragmentation: Static versus Time-Variant Explanations

Given this somewhat bleak intellectual backdrop, recent advances in the social scientific analysis of rebel factionalism and fragmentation have been remarkable. These advances, in my view, have been enabled by the "micro" turn in the social science of political violence and civil war and the increasing quantity of studies informed by field research in conflict or postconflict contexts (Kalyvas, 2008). In many ways, these advances build on an earlier intellectual tradition that has explored the topic of factionalism and fragmentation within political organizations/entities more generally.[16] Many of these new excellent studies, some of which were referenced earlier, treat rebel factionalism and fragmentation as independent variables (Pearlman, 2009; Cronin, 2009; Lawrence, 2010; K. G. Cunningham, 2011, 2012) rather than as outcomes to be explained in their own right.

The existing literature on the causes of rebel factionalism and fragmentation, meanwhile, can be usefully separated into two strands. The first strand consists of explanations and approaches that explore how the core structural, ideological, and institutional characteristics of specific organizations shape their propensity for factional infighting and fragmentation over the course of their lifespans. Generally speaking, these kinds of explanations build on the intellectual traditions of "path

---

[16] One could look at Riker's famous work on "minimum-winning coalitions" (Riker, 1962). See also an edited volume by Steffen Schmidt et al. on the relationship between factionalism and the development of politically clientelistic societies (Schmidt, Scott, Landi, & Guast, 1977). See also Bayart (1993, pp. 207–228) on the relationship between factionalism and African political development, and a voluminous literature on factionalism in the Chinese Communist Party (Teiwes, 1990; Huang, 2006; Shih, 2007). The social movement literature also deals with the factionalism and fragmentation of social movements (Turner & Killian, 1972; Harrison & John, 1978).

dependency" and "historical institutionalism," and focus on the early, founding characteristics of rebel organizations, and how they leave profound legacies shaping an organization's downstream behavior. This approach is primarily geared toward explaining variation in factionalism and fragmentation across insurgent organizations, since the causal variables identified vary at the level of the organization but tend to be constant within an organization over time.

Weinstein's pathbreaking study of rebel organizations – a classic illustration of this first explanatory strand of factionalism and fragmentation – argues that the character and conduct of a rebel organization is best explained by its resource base (Weinstein, 2005a, 2007). In this story, resource-rich movements have the ability to attract members through short-term payoffs, while resource-poor movements are forced to rely on social endowments – shared beliefs, common expectations, norms of behavior, and trust. Given that the startup costs of building a movement around social endowments are high, leaders who have the option of turning to material resources in organizing rebellion will do so. The result is that resource-rich movements tend to attract "opportunistic joiners" while resource-poor movements tend to attract "activists" and "investors."

There are two additional explanations of rebel fragmentation that build upon the structuralist orientation of Weinstein's work. Staniland (2012b, 2014) argues that the founding social networks of organized rebellion are a critical variable in the downstream cohesion and unity of rebel organizations. Organizations built upon close-knit, vertically bonded social ties are likely to avoid factionalism and fragmentation throughout their lifespans. Where the founding social ties within the organization are weak or coalitional in nature, fragmentation will frequently be the result. Kalyvas and Balcells (2010), for their part, shift the discussion to the role of founding ideology and argue that rebellions organized initially along Marxist lines tend to possess the institutional resources capable of suppressing internal discord.

Time-variant explanations of rebel cohesion, which can explain the "when" of rebel fragmentation, have also produced interesting insights. Along these lines, recent work suggests that shifts in state behavior may directly affect the fragmentation of rebel organizations. Shapiro (2008, 2013) describes how increases in state repression exacerbate principal–agent problems in terrorist organizations, as survival necessitates decentralization.[17] Though terrorist leaders prefer centralized

---

[17] "Terrorist" organizations can be considered, in most cases, a subset of rebel organizations that rely on attacking civilian targets in the pursuit of broad strategic objectives;

command structures and tight monitoring, state repression makes these sorts of organizations highly insecure. Thus there is a trade-off between organizational survival and the effective control of subordinates, and by extension the deterrence of fragmentation.

Scott Gates (2002) argues that increases in geographic distance exacerbate principal–agent problems in rebel organizations. Using formal theory, Gates suggests that organizations that operate over increasingly expansive and difficult terrain face greater barriers in inducing compliance from their membership, as the costs of employing sanctions are higher. Furthermore, Gates suggests that ethnically heterogeneous organizations – and heterogeneity is a variable that can vary over time – are unable to rely on shared identities and norms in facilitating cohesion and encouraging behavior consistent with the goals of the organization. Olson (1965, 1982) describes a similar phenomenon when he argues that the effective use of social selective incentives – and thus the possibilities of collective action and cooperation – depend on the homogeneity of the group in question.

Ethan Bueno de Mesquita (2008) also uses formal theory to explain the timing of fragmentation, and like Shapiro, focuses on terrorist organizations. Importantly, Mesquita restricts his analysis to the emergence of splinter groups that are more "extreme" than the original terrorist faction. The argument proposes that both improvements in the economy and increases in opportunities for democratic politics promote extremism and hard-line politics within a terrorist organization's leadership, and thus diminish the likelihood of an extremist splinter. This is because such changes reduce the ability of terrorist organizations to attract more moderate supporters, and therefore decreases the marginal costs of more extreme positions. Furthermore, when potential splinter leaders can offer material benefits to supporters, and the costs of splintering are low (i.e., because the original terrorist leader does not have the ability to sanction a splinter element), fragmentation is more likely to occur.

Another argument that deals directly with the issue of rebel fragmentation – and is consistent with the time-variant, nonstructuralist tradition – is authored by Stephen Stedman, who suggests that the source of fragmentation lies in peace processes that yield what Stedman has called "spoilers" (Stedman, 1997, p. 1). Spoilers, in this formulation, are "parties who believe that peace emerging from negotiations

---

thus what defines terrorist organizations are the tactics they employ (Crenshaw, 1981). However, because our definition of rebel organizations requires operations against military targets, not all terrorist organizations could be considered rebel organizations.

threatens their power, worldview, and interests, and use violence to undermine attempts to achieve it." In such a story, elements within rebel organizations recognize that they have more to gain from continuing war, and as a result break with a leadership that sues for peace or attempts to cut a deal with the government. While in policy circles, "spoiler" arguments have gained wide currency, and find significant support in recent peace processes in Darfur and Burundi, the explanation has little to offer in cases in which rebel fragmentation does not occur in the context of a peace agreement. A related but somewhat more tractable argument is that rebel factionalism and fragmentation are driven by state efforts to appease and mollify certain segments of rebel organizations, efforts that can occur both within and outside the context of a peace process.

Nicholai Lidow (2016), meanwhile, employs econometric techniques and data from the Liberian civil war to explore how external sponsors, and the resources they provide, can shape the timing of rebel factionalism and fragmentation. The argument is a fairly simple one: access to external resources allows rebel leaders to pay off commanders and ensure their loyalty. In this context, the loss of external support can lead to increasing indiscipline and factional infighting.[18]

Recent research by Lee Seymour (2014) provides yet another twist, and argues, based on longitudinal data from the Sudanese civil war, that rebel fragmentation – or what he calls "side-switching" – is conditioned by two factors. The first is the provision of material support that defecting insurgent factions can use in localized struggles against rivals within their own camp; the second is the provision of patronage that encourages defection to "the side providing material advantages" (Seymour, 2014, p. 94).

Battlefield Performance and Rebel Fragmentation: Right Approach, Incomplete Predictions

Within this second strand of explanation – which, again, is about the timing of rebel factionalism and fragmentation – is another line of thinking that situates patterns of organizational infighting firmly within the shifting military contexts that insurgent organizations face. It is this conceptual approach that is the point of departure for my own argument.

---

[18] In a recent article, Henning Tamm (2016) complicates this picture by arguing that shifts in the *nature* of external support – in particular, when an external sponsor decides to no longer favor the incumbent leader over his rivals – can lead to factionalism and fragmentation. Another recent paper, by Lounsbery (2016), argues that while rebels may coalesce in the midst of external intervention, such interventions have no direct effect on rebel fragmentation.

Kalyvas's (2008a) analysis of "ethnic defection" in civil wars is an early articulation of this perspective, and argues that ethnopolitical rebel organizations incur defections in territory they have just lost, as civil war allegiances follow shifts in power and territorial control. The logic of the argument is as simple as it is powerful: in civil war, there are no permanent friends, only permanent interests. When the tide of war begins to imperil the survival and well-being of the constituent units of an ethnic rebellion, they easily break previous solidarity in favor of new commitments. Kalyvas's conclusions are echoed by scholars who argue more generally that effective state repression undermines the cohesion of insurgent organizations.

Fotini Christia's (2012) excellent book on alliance formation in civil war builds on the work of Kalyvas and is one of the most systematic analyses of rebel factionalism and fragmentation available. Embedded within a broader analysis of "interorganizational" alliance dynamics in multiparty civil wars, Christia argues that rebel organizations succumb to factional infighting when they incur significant military losses. This is because losses precipitate survival concerns among the organization's constituent units, thereby prompting direct challenges to the supremacy of the leadership. An added layer of the argument is that the incentives to launch an organizational split are particularly high when battlefield losses are symmetric across the organization's constituent units, since no subgroup will be powerful enough to successfully launch an organizational takeover. Conversely, when the losses are uneven across subgroups, organizational takeovers are the preferred course of action.[19]

Christia's theory of organizational fragmentation is explicitly contrasted with her claims about the fragmentation of interorganizational alliances, and it is here that the argument takes an intriguing turn. Battlefield gains at the level of the interorganizational rebel coalition create a series of pernicious commitment problems over postwar spoils that drive weaker organizations to defect from the coalition. In other words, alliances between rebel organizations fall apart in the wake of battlefield victory. Yet interestingly, Christia insists that the causal logic of this argument does not apply to the internal fragmentation of rebel organizations. Although readily acknowledging that the internal dynamics of rebel organizations resemble the coalitional politics of interorganizational rebel alliances (as I do in this book), Christia concludes that

---

[19] For more commentary on the importance of Christia's work as well as a discussion of some critiques, see Roundtable on Alliance Formation in Civil Wars, H-Diplo/ISSF Roundtable Reviews, 2013, www.h-net.org/~diplo/ISSF/PDF/ISSF-Roundtable-6-2.pdf.

battlefield gains do not have the same deleterious effects on the internal cohesion of rebel organizations. This is due to the "identity ties," shared "trust," and "preexisting institutions" that reduce commitment problems within rebel organizations in the wake of military success. In fact, Christia takes this line of thinking one step further, asserting that in contrast to interorganizational rebel coalitions, "battlefield wins will foster intra-group [organizational] cohesion by convincing sub-groups that they are on the winning side" (Christia, 2012, p. 8).[20]

Although Christia's claims are compelling, and supported by a wide array of evidence from the Afghan and Bosnian civil wars, the analysis is encumbered by two major problems. First, the claim that battlefield gains reinforce internal organizational solidarities is readily contestable on historical grounds. Casual reflection suggests that there is a nontrivial number of rebel organizations that have fragmented in the wake of battlefield success: the Somali National Movement (SNM) in Somaliland, Charles Taylor's National Patriotic Front of Liberia (NPFL) in Liberia, and Mozambique's Frente de Libertaçäo Moçambique (FRELIMO), to name a few. Second, even if we acknowledge that the constituent units of rebel organizations possess shared affinities that do not exist at the level of an interorganizational rebel alliance, how can it be argued that battlefield success has opposite effects on the internal dynamics of rebel organizations? One is hard-pressed to think of a good theoretical reason why battlefield success would have a salutary effect on the cohesion of rebel organizations, but a fragmentary effect on interorganizational rebel alliances.

In this book, I suggest that while the literature is correct in its general observation that battlefield outcomes matter to the internal cohesion of rebel organizations, and right to point to the fragmentary effects of battlefield losses, it omits important predictions. Organizational cohesion is structured not only by the perceived viability of rebel organizations (in the eyes of its constituent units) but also by the existence of a common, unifying threat. Two key predictions flow from this assertion. First, battlefield gains will often (but by no means always) provoke factionalism and fragmentation within rebel organizations, as is the case with battlefield losses. This is because military success reduces the scale and severity of external threats, creating preference divergence over unresolved differences, and commitment problems over the internal distribution of

---

[20] In other words, Christia would argue that military gains have deleterious effects on organizational coalitions such as Syria's Supreme Military Command, or Afghanistan's Northern Alliance, but not Turkey's PKK or Lebanon's Hizbollah, which are discrete, unified rebel organizations.

power and future spoils. Intuitively, this makes sense: in the face of external threats, divergent preferences remain submerged in the pursuit of collective self-defense, while disputes over the division of postwar spoils are postponed.[21] What this means more broadly is that there is little reason why Christia's predictions about the fragmentation of interorganizational rebel alliances cannot be extended to the fragmentation of rebel organizations.

A second conclusion is that battlefield stalemate is the only durable basis of organizational cohesion, because static military contexts allow the constituent units of rebel organizations to believe that two conditions are true: the organization appears viable, because it is not losing, but is perceived as vulnerable to external threats, because it is not winning. In other words, stalemate produces an equilibrium that enhances organizational solidarity and cooperation, by creating perceptions that incentivize collaboration and deter infighting. It is the context most likely to preserve organizational cohesion. I refer to this core empirical claim as a "cohesive stalemate."

We now turn to a more involved elucidation of this book's main theoretical arguments.

The Challenge of Battlefield Performance: Organizations, Coalitions, and Elites

The framework I employ begins with the assumption that rebel organizations are amalgamations of identifiable groups that possess distinct interests. To a greater or lesser degree, they are coalitions united by the pursuit of a common goal – the violent contestation of state power – rather than an identical set of preferences.[22]

At the apex of each of these groups – respective coalition members, if you will – is a class of elites who command the loyalty of rank-and-file subgroup members. Though the source of their authority differs, these elites engender allegiances that provide a capacity to mobilize those around them. Similar to what Charles Tilly has called "political entrepreneurs," who "specialize in activation, connection,

---

[21] As will become clear in the forthcoming pages, I argue that the precise causal mechanism that links military/battlefield success to rebel fragmentation is one of "preference divergence." I see the mechanism of "commitment problems" being more relevant in the context of battlefield losses, although one cannot rule out the possibility of "equifinality" – the idea that a given outcome can be reached by many potential means.

[22] This view of rebel organizations as internally complex and heterogeneous has increasingly come into vogue in both academic and policy circles, and draws its intellectual inspiration from behavioral theories of the firm first developed by economists in the early 1960s. For an example of this work, see Cyert and March (1963).

coordination, and representation" of particular intraorganozational constituencies, these individuals are the focal points of collective action, and thus cooperation in war hinges on their behavior (Tilly, 2003).[23]

The fragmentation of a rebel organization logically represents the rupture of an existing coalition, or in game theoretic terms, the *breakdown of a cooperative equilibrium* where an equilibrium is defined as "any state of affairs which no actor has an individual incentive to disturb" (Reeve, 2003). Whereas at $t+1$ the constituent units of a rebel organization are able to adhere to the cooperative status quo, at $t+2$ they cannot, since it is no longer in the interests of one or more of the constituent units to do so.

The obvious question that follows from these representations – and the most important to this chapter – is *why and how the conditions that sustained the cooperative equilibrium within a rebel organization in one period no longer obtain in the next*. Without a theory of these shifting "conditions," one cannot construct a theory of the breakdown of a cooperative equilibrium, and hence, fragmentation.

Two implications follow from the recognition that explaining rebel fragmentation requires a careful discussion of changes in the conditions that underpin the cooperative equilibrium within a rebel coalition. First, path-dependent arguments that focus on the initial conditions that rebel organizations confront in explaining behavior downstream are ill suited to investigating the collapse of the cooperative equilibrium within a rebel organization. While path-dependent arguments would be useful in understanding differences in the propensity of certain kinds of rebel groups to fragment, they cannot explain variation in fragmentation

---

[23] Of course, careful readers will note that the focus on organizational elites seems arbitrary and assumes more than it explains: surely, the motives and behavior of rank-and-file combatants are in many ways unique, and distinct from, the organizational elites who lead them. Can we assume away a unity of thought and action between elite and rank-and-file combatants? Robert Michels (Michels, 1968), the well-known theorist of political organization, was the first to underline the most persuasive grounds for this assumption. To Michels, almost all political and social organizations converge on "oligarchy," where a select few dominate decision-making processes. The reason for this state of affairs, Michel contended, is that in large political organizations members must delegate decision-making authority to elites in the interests of efficiency: since mass participation in decision making would be unwieldy and chaotic, "oligarchy" is the only way to manage an organization's affairs. In the context of rebel organizations, the implication of Michel's argument is clear: rebels cede authority to subgroup elites who make strategic decisions on their behalf. Focusing on elite behavior within rebel organizations is warranted, the logic goes, because no organization – particularly military organization – can function without the full delegation of decision-making authority to a subset of leaders. Thus in war, the politics of coalition construction and destruction is an elite-level game in which rank-and-file combatants are marginal players.

across time within groups since the causal variables they identify do not change temporally.[24]

Second, the model proposed is partial in that framing fragmentation as a breakdown of a cooperative equilibrium places analytic primacy on the "motives" and "incentives" to fragment, rather than the "capacity." This is an important point. While rebel organizations can be viewed as a coalition of groups that voluntarily contract into a cooperative arrangement for the production of a joint good, they are "organizations" nonetheless; they possess hierarchies and the ability to sanction members who seek to disrupt the cooperative equilibrium. Thus, the fragmentation of rebel organizations is not simply about how the incentives to cooperate may change, but also about the failure of power, threats, and coercion to enforce the organizational status quo. In other words, a complete theory of fragmentation would focus not only on the demand to fragment but also its supply.

Gains, Losses, and the Shifting Incentives to Cooperate

So what exactly drives the breakdown of cooperative relations within rebel organizations?

Theories of punctuated equilibrium posit that environmental shocks are the central cause of dramatic organizational and institutional change.[25] Such shocks produce "revolutionary" moments where the structures and processes of organizations, hitherto static, go into rapid and dramatic flux. This study picks up on this general theme, by focusing on how military shocks create contexts conducive to factional infighting, fragmentation, and the rapid reordering of rebel groups.

My core claim is that organizational performance affects the cohesion of rebel organization in novel and unique ways. More specifically, I argue that, *ceteris paribus*, rebel organizations are most susceptible to fragmentation at two critical moments: the first when they have incurred *significant* military losses, and the second when they have achieved *significant* military gains. The implication is that periods of military stalemate, or particularly slow, marginal battlefield change, tend to promote organizational cohesion and underpin organizational stability.

The language of "gain" and "loss" is not without import, for the argument proposes that what triggers cooperation breakdown is not so much

---

[24] For the best example of this sort of work in the civil war literature see Reno (2007) and Weinstein (2007).

[25] See Gersick (1991) for a good review and application of this literature to organizations. The literature on punctuated equilibrium is vast. For a well-known application in American politics, see Baumgartner & Jones (1993).

the military position a rebel organization occupies in absolute terms – say, near victory or failure – but rather the change in military position relative to some recent reference point or identifiable status quo. This is critical if one is trying to predict exactly where in the evolution of a conflict rebel organizations fall apart.

Gains and the Origins of Preference Divergence

So what are the causal mechanisms linking situations of gain and loss to the dependent variable of interest, fragmentation? My theory suggests that the mechanisms differ depending on whether a gain or a loss has been incurred.

To understand the basis of the argument we need to address the critical issue of actor preferences. My starting point is the work of Realists in the field of international relations, who argue that states have a hierarchy of preferences and seek to satisfy their core preference above, and sometimes at the expense of, all others. Arthur Stein (1990, p. 90) typifies the insights of this perspective when he suggests that states have lexical preferences where actors "maximize in sequence rather than make trade-offs... Thus they will choose an option that maximizes the main objective regardless of how it does on secondary ones..."

For Realists and the states they theorize about, this "main objective" is survival (Waltz, 1979; Mearsheimer, 2001). Given the nature of the international system where "self-help" and "anarchy" are organizing principles, survival concerns must be paramount, since failure to guarantee this objective can be fatal. For our purposes here, Realism's key intuition is this: in insecure environments, where existential threats loom large, actors will strive to secure immediate survival above all else.

The intuition of international relations Realists about hierarchical preferences is echoed in comparative politics. James Scott, in writing about the dynamics of peasant rebellion in south east Asia, notes that the political economy of peasant life is characterized by pervasive uncertainty about crop yields (Scott, 1976). The precarious nature of food supply, in turn, leads the peasantry to a "security first" outlook in which they spurn risky innovation that could lead to large improvements in aggregate yields in favor of lower yields that guarantee survival. As with states in the Realist version of international politics, environments characterized by systemic insecurity produce a behavioral logic wherein the management of security risk becomes an objective that supersedes all others.

Somewhat fortuitously, the idea of hierarchical preferences is the implicit basis of much of Realist theory about why alliances form and why they fall apart. Since survival is at the top of the hierarchy of objectives, states "balance against threats," and thus "the internal cohesion of an alliance depends to a large extent on the intensity and duration of the threat" (Walt, 1987). With a coalition's raison d'être gone – guaranteeing security in an insecure environment – it becomes difficult for that coalition to cohere.

Yet how is this relevant to understanding fragmentation within rebel organizations? My sense is that ideas of hierarchical preferences and uncertainty about survival are useful in thinking about the conditions that sustain cooperation in a rebel organization. Since civil wars are anarchic environments where self-help is the rule, it may be the case that the constituent units of a rebel organization – and by extension the leaders of these distinct units – are in a position analogous to that of states in the international system. What this means, if we follow the comparison to its logical conclusion, is that when rebel organizations face insecurity and uncertainty about short-term, immediate survival, its constituent units have incentives to ensure they maintain a united front. Since the primary objective of members of a rebel coalition is survival, the constituent units will put their divergent preferences on a whole range of issues aside to face the common challenge.

Of course, wars can, and often do, turn quite rapidly. As rebel organizations incur military gains, often quite rapidly through a set of major shocks, the conditions that sustained cooperation begin to shift. Surging militarily, rebels no longer perceive grave uncertainty about immediate survival. As a result, the hierarchy of objectives within a rebel organization is reordered. With immediate survival guaranteed in the minds of rebels – a basic objective that everybody in the rebel coalition could unite around – other issues about which rebels have heterogeneous preferences increase in importance and dominate the issue arena. Under such circumstances, the incentives to cooperate have been significantly altered. No longer preoccupied with the common concern for survival, constituent units of a rebel organization begin to take actions that undermine cooperation in ways that heretofore they had not – approaching potentially divisive issues with greater vigor and intensity, bargaining harder, and even resorting to coercion. *Ceteris paribus*, consensus gives way to division, and the cooperative equilibrium collapses.

In this scenario, the fragmentation of a rebel organization is one of preference divergence. Yet, critics may ask, preference divergence over what? The model is agnostic about what sorts of issues drive preference divergence precisely because the issues in contention vary across groups and within groups over time. As the forthcoming comparative analysis will show, by dint of history and circumstance, the lines of cleavage within rebel organizations are often different; ideology, ethnicity, religion, and personality conflicts can all be raw material that determines the anatomy of a particular rebel organization. Yet the underlying issues over which preference divergence emerge are less important than the recognition that this divergence happens at certain moments and not others.

Losses and the Origins of Commitment Problems

The notion that actors within rebel organizations attempt to maximize outcomes on the core objective of survival has implications for fragmentation in situations quite different from those in which rebel organizations have achieved significant military gains. However, the mechanism here is one of credible commitment rather than preference divergence.

What do we mean by credible commitment? Problems of credibility tend to emerge in situations in which one or more parties to a formal or informal agreement cannot reliably commit to performing the obligations that agreement entails in the future. According to Shepsle (1991), commitments can be credible in two possible ways. First, commitments can be *imperatively* credible if the participants are unable to do otherwise because either they will be coerced to do so by an external authority or they lack the means and resources to ignore obligations. Second, and more important for the argument here, commitments can be *motivationally* credible if the participants expect to receive sufficient rewards for them to honor the commitment at the time of performance – thus the commitment is incentive compatible and self-enforcing.

The constituent units of a rebel organization contract into an organizational arrangement on the understanding that in the production of violence for the pursuit of broad political objectives, they are maximizing on the core objective of survival in an insecure and uncertain environment. Thus at their core, rebel organizations are institutions that manage risk. Yet cooperation of this sort also entails possible costs. While rebel organizations and the coalitions that underpin them provide collective security, when they fail the future survival of its members can be imperiled.

Simply put, rebel organizations must be credible in demonstrating that they have a reasonable chance of surviving into the future. Seen in this light, the consequences of significant military losses for rebel organizations are obvious. With expectations about the future substantially altered, the constituent units of a rebel organization calculate that continuing to cooperate under the status quo will likely lead to their individual demise in the next period. As a consequence, they seek to challenge the cooperative status quo, with fragmentation the frequent outcome. Since a rebel organization can collectively no longer credibly commit to providing the basic benefit it was contracted to provide – survival – the risks of continued cooperation become prohibitively high.

Such an argument does not necessarily mean that those who challenge the status quo do better than if they had continued to observe the cooperative equilibrium. In a world of perfect information, they would always do better. However, in the context of war, in which incomplete information about capabilities is widespread – what Karl von Clauswitz famously called the "fog of war" (Clauswitz, 1968) – what rebels believe to be the best course of action in preserving their survival and managing risk may not be.

Stalemate and the Origins of Cooperation

The implication of the arguments I have offered here is that there is a static, stalemated middle ground where rebel organizations tend to cohere. I call this a "cohesive stalemate." Yet what exactly differentiates, at the micro level, the stalemated military context from situations of gains and loss I have described? How does it affect the behavior of rebels?

The idea here is that stalemated contexts – and I make no distinction here between those produced by active combat or an extended lull in fighting – are uniquely positioned to provide the basis for cooperation because they allow two conditions to be true: (1) organization members perceive that there is significant insecurity and are *uncertain* about survival, and (2) organization members perceive that there is a *reasonable* chance that the organization can continue to provide the benefits it was contracted to provide if the constituent units of a rebel organization abide by the cooperative status quo.

Since survival is at the top of the hierarchy of objectives, cooperation in such contexts makes perfect sense: rebels can realize the obvious gains of cooperation, with the recognition that this cooperation will not imperil their survival in the future. Cooperation is thus incentive compatible and self-enforcing.

The obvious implication of such arguments is that there is a connection between the maintenance of cooperation in war and the origins of cooperation in war. Indeed, it would seem to make sense that the conditions that sustain a cooperative equilibrium will be similar to the conditions under which it originates.

As has already been suggested, rebel organizations and the coalitions that sustain them emerge because they allow potential organization members to maximize on the core objective of survival. Why? Applying the tenets of organizational economics, civil war theorists have recognized the value of organization in capturing the benefits of economies of scale and reducing transaction costs (Weinstein, 2007). My contention here is that rebels with heterogeneous preferences tend to coalesce under a hierarchical organizational framework when they are uncertain about future survival, but consider the new organizational framework to have a reasonable chance of surviving into the future. While the early evolution of a rebel organization does not resemble the situation of stalemate I have described, such contexts evoke similar perceptions about the uncertainty of immediate survival, but with the plausibility that if the coalition stays united it can survive.

In fact, many observers of civil wars note that insurgents, in the early days of war, have the strategic advantage because they are first-movers; they can pick targets at their choosing, without having to deal with a military that is sufficiently deployed and prepared (Kalyvas, 2006). Therefore insurgents feel as though there is a legitimate chance at success. At the same time, having never truly encountered the long arm of the state in its most serious and violent manifestations, there is uncertainty about the true military potential of the organization and ambiguity about the immediate survival of its members.[26] Such an environment would seem to be fertile ground for cooperation, as it engenders similar incentives to periods of military stalemate.[27]

Gains, Losses, and Absolute Values

One should note that the theory I have outlined is fundamentally a theory about perceptions and expectations – in particular, rebels'

---

[26] This point is echoed by Che Guevara in his discussion of early "guerrilla strategy": "At the outset, the essential task of the guerrilla fighter is to keep himself from being destroyed" (Guevara, 1961, p. 15).

[27] My thinking about the origins of rebel cooperation in war is partly informed by Staniland (2014), who argues that most rebel organizations are built on peacetime networks, which are then refitted for the purposes of warfare. Such networks may include local associations, sports teams, political parties, etc. I would add here, however, that the creation of rebel organizations usually involves the bridging of *distinct* and *separate* networks. In other words, there is a coalitional dynamic at the founding point of most rebel organizations. This is because a single peacetime network usually lacks the capacity to seamlessly transform into a viable armed group on its own, since the demands and requirements of war are different from those of peaceful politics. Coalition building is thus necessary in the early, preparatory stages of organized rebellion. In this way, rebel organizations can usually be judged as coalitions from the outset. This idea will be illustrated in the forthcoming case studies.

perceptions of military gains and losses, and their expectations about the future of the organization. When rebels incur losses they believe that the organization cannot survive, and when they achieve gains, they conjecture that problems of acute insecurity have been resolved. But it is important to note that a theory of perceptions and expectations that hinges on the language of gains and losses implies that what shapes rebels' behavior is change relative to some reference point or status quo, rather than where a rebel organization sits in absolute terms. In other words, in explaining the timing of fragmentation it matters less whether a rebel organization is close to winning or losing, but rather *whether it is incurring a gain or loss at a given time.*

Yet does this make sense? Shouldn't the absolute position of a rebel organization affect perceptions and expectations about the nature of external threats and the sustainability of the organizational status quo? My response is simple, but also counterintuitive. Military stalemates – no matter where an organization may sit along the continuum of victory to defeat – convey very specific information to the constituent units of a rebel organization. On the one hand, the ability to maintain the military status quo reflects organizational viability both now and in the future, and thus prevents the emergence of commitment problems; yet on the other hand, the inability to make positive progress suggests that the organization still faces very real collective threats, thus minimizing preference divergence. Simply put, stalemated military contexts have unique properties, and provide the conditions that make cooperation durable, irrespective of an organization's absolute or overarching military position.

This intuition is consistent with prospect theory, in which a key principle – as reflected in the work of Kahneman & Tversky (1979) and later echoed by political scientists like Jervis (2004) and McDermott (2004) – is that an actor's absolute position is not as important in their calculation of utility and welfare as a recent change in position.

Furthermore, it would seem to make sense that gains and losses convey important information about the future prospects of rebel organizations, because military change indicates the direction an organization is trending. Since in and of itself, absolute military position says little about trends, rebels look to the direction of military change in forecasting and making crucial decisions about cooperation.

Thus, a rebel organization that is close to defeat, but stalemated, will be less likely to fragment than an organization whose overall position is better but is incurring a significant loss. Similarly, a rebel organization that is on the verge of victory, but stalemated, will be less likely

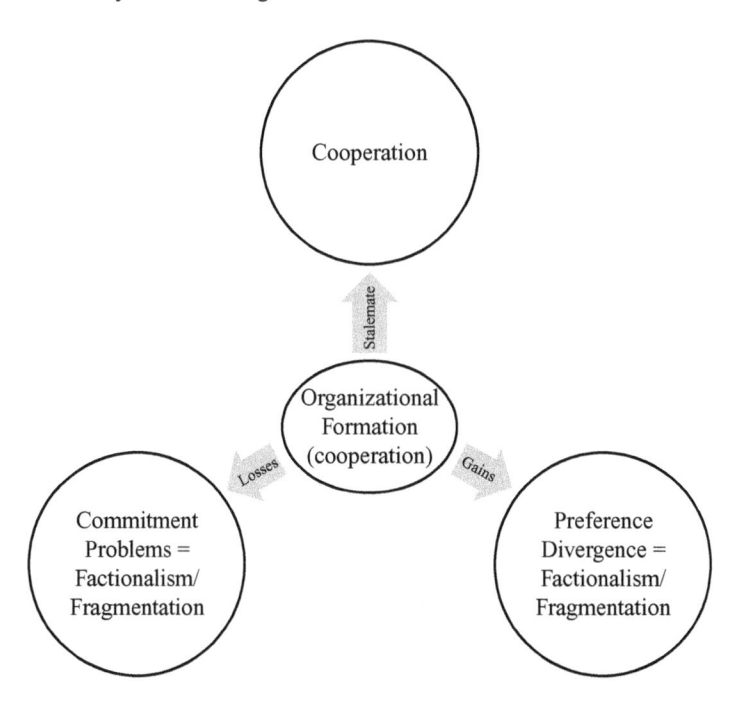

Figure 2.1 Outline of argument and causal mechanisms.

to fragment than an organization that is doing moderately well but has experienced significant recent gains.[28]

Having laid out my argument, which is visually depicted in Figure 2.1, the central hypotheses of the theory of gains and losses are as follows:

H1: Gains and losses will be associated with fragmentation.

H2: Stalemate will be associated with organizational cohesion.

Corollary Arguments

Fragmentation as a Second-Order Effect

Having mapped out the main argument of this book, I now offer theoretical extensions. While these corollary arguments *will not be systematically*

---

[28] The importance of relative change in battlefield position versus the absolute battlefield position is reflected in Kilcullen's (2010) discussion of the "win/loss ratio" as a metric in counterinsurgency warfare. According to Kilcullen, the win/loss ratio tells us little about performance in war since rebels usually lose most engagements. In Kilcullen's view, what is more important is relative change in the win/loss ratio.

tested, they do find some support in the case study portions of the following chapters.

Although the framework outlined in the preceding pages offers a clear set of hypotheses and causal mechanisms, the theory is incomplete in important ways. More specifically, since fragmentation is defined as only one possible manifestation of factionalism, we need to identify exactly why rebel fragmentation occurs, instead of alternative noncooperative behaviors – such as coups, purges, extrajudicial killings – designed to alter the status quo organizational arrangement. In other words, given a desire to alter the cooperative status quo, why do rebel elites choose fragmentation from a full menu of modes of contention that would allow them to alter organizational power dynamics and achieve their political ends?

Fragmentation is generally not the preferred option for rebel elites who seek to change the status quo organizational arrangement. Whether the context is one of gain or loss, "exit" from a parent organization in the "fog" of civil war entails significant uncertainty, and thus great risk. For those that are considering the creation of a new rebel organization, the potential viability of the new enterprise can be hazy and indeterminate. For others that are inclined to defect to an existing rebel organization or the incumbent government, the payoffs can be difficult to validate ex ante. Indeed, after successfully wooing a particular splinter group, the receiving rebel organization or government may renege on its commitments. Moreover, having come to a political impasse with members of their own organization, what assures a defecting splinter group that relations will be any better with their new comrades-in-arms?

Given the primacy of survival concerns in civil war, the uncertainty surrounding fragmentation outcomes produces a "risk aversion" toward the fragmentation option among those who seek to alter the cooperative status quo within a rebel organization.[29] Fragmentation is simply not the optimal strategy, because it provides few guarantees of survival in the anarchic environment of war.

The result is that dissatisfied rebels pursue alternative strategies for altering the organizational status quo, including coups, extrajudicial killings, purges, or outright insubordination. Like fragmentation, such strategies reflect a breakdown of cooperation in war, triggered by military shocks. *Yet in contrast to fragmentation, such efforts involve altering the organizational status quo while remaining within the organization.* While

---

[29] James Scott's (1976) notion of risk aversion is the logical extension of the "security first" principle mentioned earlier, which Scott uses to explain the fairly conservative agricultural techniques of the southeast Asian peasantry.

internal coups, the killing of fellow combatants, and insubordination are all risky forms of collective action, they are associated with relatively less uncertainty than leaving the organization altogether, since dissatisfied rebel elites, through experience, are aware of all of the organization's properties – its strengths, weaknesses, and possibilities. Whatever the political, economic, or tactical motives in challenging the organizational status quo may be, it is better for disaffected rebels to change their organization by imposing their preferences on it than to take the radical and uncertain step of abandoning it. Put simply, in a world of pervasive insecurity, it is better to stick with the devil you know instead of the devil you don't. Thus, information problems render fragmentation the worst form of collective challenge to the organizational status quo.

This claim loosely echoes Hirschman's famous argument about the firm in *Exit, Voice, and Loyalty*, in which the opportunities for organizational "exit," or lack thereof, condition the willingness of disaffected members of an organization to employ "voice" internally. Since "voice" is a "residual of exit," Hirschman argues, "the role of voice would increase as the opportunities for exit decline, up to the point where, with exit wholly unavailable, voice must carry the entire burden of alerting management to its failings" (Hirschman, 1970, p. 34). As exit is inherently risky for rebels, circumstances dictate they employ other measures of changing the organizational status quo.

So if dissatisfied rebels prefer alternative extralegal actions that allow them to change the organization, instead of leaving it, then why does fragmentation occur? The reason is simple. The factionalism triggered by the ebb and flow of war often yields "losers," who, in order to avoid the severe sanctions of "winners," exit the organization. Fragmentation is thus the preferred option for those who have survived a power struggle, but lost it at the same time. A failure to fragment at this juncture would mean that the concerned rebels would be at the mercy of the internal rivals who have just defeated them.

The claim is an interesting one. Fragmentation is almost never the intentional result of purposive action, but the unintended, path-dependent consequence of a bid to alter the organizational status quo through coups, killings, insubordination, purges, or other extralegal, noncooperative behaviors. In other words, fragmentation is a second-order effect of military shocks.[30]

---

[30] My argument here is similar to Staniland's (2012a) claims about "fratricidal flipping." However, Staniland does not provide a theory of why fratricide occurs when it does. Moreover, Staniland's theory explicitly focuses on insurgent defections to the government only.

> *H3:* Fragmentation is precipitated by factional struggles – as evidenced by coups, extrajudicial killings, and insubordination – and is not the result of purposive action. Rather, it becomes a matter of necessity for the "losers" of factional struggles in order to survive.

Factionalism, Fragmentation, and "Cycles of Contention"

Not all of the constituent units of a rebel organization respond to gains and losses in the same way. A few, what we may call "early risers," elect to mobilize their resources and engage in factional infighting, in an effort to alter the organizational status quo, while the vast majority elect to remain spectators. Yet according to Sidney Tarrow, while the claims of early risers are often "narrow and group specific," they can trigger a "cycle of contention" that can involve increasingly broad swathes of an organization. This diffusion occurs for three reasons: the efforts of early risers "demonstrate the vulnerability of authorities to contention, signaling to others that the time is ripe for their own claims to be translated into action"; "they challenge the interests of other contenders, either because the distribution of benefits to one group will diminish the rewards available for another, or because the demands directly attack the interests of an established group"; and finally, because "they suggest convergence among challengers (or their opponents, I may add) through the enunciation of master frames" (Tarrow, 1998, p. 144).

Yet unlike Tarrow, who situates the contagious and diffusive properties of contention within the context of national political systems, the object of the analysis in this book are small rebel organizations, often consisting of no more than a few thousand combatants. The difference is crucial, since information tends to flow relatively quickly in smaller entities, and as a result, the diffusion of contention, i.e., factional infighting, tends to be magnified.

The result is that while factionalism tends to start small, and involve a narrow set of actors, it can gather momentum, incorporating broader sectors of an organization, producing monumental and sometimes cataclysmic results – *although this need not occur in all cases*. The implication is that fragmentation, which is itself the outgrowth of factionalism, can be temporally clustered, and involve multiple distinct and identifiable constituent units of a rebel organization fighting among one another and in some cases exiting in close sequence. Since different sectors of a rebel organization are often sucked into the factional fight, it follows that there can be multiple "losers," and thus multiple dissatisfied groups that are compelled to exit.

H4: Factional struggles within rebel organizations are initially triggered by territorial gains and losses, but can then be characterized by a process of diffusion that often yields multiple splinter elements fragmenting in close temporal sequence.

Alternative Explanations

With a theory of rebel fragmentation carefully mapped out, it is important to amplify what the alternative variables or explanations would be. Indeed, the only way to appropriately test the explanation outlined earlier is to evaluate it against the best possible alternatives.

There were several considerations used in identifying alternative variables. First, I attempted to build on the existing literature identified in previous sections. Second, I attempted to include for analysis alternative variables that are intuitive, even if they were absent from the existing literature. Since I have theoretically framed fragmentation as the breakdown of a cooperative equilibrium, and thus an issue of longitudinal variation within rebel organizations, I have focused on variables that vary across time within rebel organizations. Finally, I targeted alternative variables that theoretically are likely to have some explanatory power in the case analysis to follow in the upcoming chapters. For instance, Seymour's (2014) intuition that advantage in local rivalries triggers rebel fragmentation assumes that the rebel organizations in question are composed of a patchwork of locally rooted militia. However, that was not the case for the vast majority of rebel organizations that fought in the Ethiopian civil war, and Seymour's argument (excellent though it is) is therefore excluded from systematic analysis.[31]

These imperatives have led me to target several alternative variables for careful analysis, which will be carefully measured in the following chapters. Briefly, they include the following:

1. *State repression,* which can lead to organizational decentralization and can reduce the ability of leaders to observe and sanction possible defectors
2. *Peace negotiations and/or government efforts to co-opt rebels,* which for insurgents may increase the economic and political benefits of ending conflict, and drive a wedge between those who sue for peace and those rebels who become "spoilers" or seek to continue the war

---

[31] It should be noted that I also do not explore alternative arguments about the effects of "leadership decapitation" (Jordan, 2009, 2014; Johnston, 2012). While this variable has not been directly linked to rebel fragmentation, it is intuitive. However, both the Ethiopian and Somali civil wars – which are the empirical cores of this book – had strikingly few cases of leadership decapitation.

3. *External support*, which provides the resources needed for rebel leaders to deter and punish defectors
4. *Organizational structure*, as organizational decentralization can provide the autonomy that potential splinter elements require in successfully fragmenting
5. *Organizational size and complexity*, as the increasing number of organizational members, and the increasing number of social cleavages that divide them, creates the structural conditions that enable fragmentation
6. *A rebel organization's absolute position*, since rebels may make decisions about cooperation based on where they sit in absolute terms, rather than the experience of any recent gains or losses. In other words, crossing some threshold along the continuum from victory to defeat may trigger rebel factionalism and fragmentation.

While these variables may effect fragmentation through their impact on rebel gains and losses, in and of themselves, I will show that they have no independent effects on rebel fragmentation. I now move to a discussion of measurement of the key independent variable.

How Do We Measure Gains, Losses, and Stalemate?

The independent variable of interest – a tripartite measure of gains, losses, and stalemate – is measured as a function of shifts in "territorial control" or "operational reach," with the former the relevant metric in cases where an organization fights a conventional war and the latter the relevant metric in contexts where guerrilla warfare is the primary tactic.[32] The variable is measured at the conclusion of each year in which a rebel organization effectively operates, and evaluates the ebb and flow of war by placing a rebel organization into one of the three aforementioned categories.[33] In coding along these dimensions, I investigate whether in a given year there is evidence that a rebel organization has seen a significant contraction or expansion of the territory they control or are able to effectively operate within.[34] By "significant," I mean a gain or loss in territory that involves an expansion or contraction in the aggregate number

---

[32] "Operational reach," for the purposes of this discussion, can be defined as territory in which a rebel organization demonstrates the ability to consistently launch attacks.

[33] The reader may note that there is a noticeable similarity between the three substantive military contexts I describe and Mao's "three stages of guerrilla warfare" – there may be connections I have not completely thought through, but the similarity is entirely accidental.

[34] To be clear, if the group primarily employs guerrilla warfare, one obviously cannot look at territorial control as a relevant metric. This is why I look at "operational reach" if they primarily rely on guerrilla warfare.

of districts a rebel organization controls or operates within. Furthermore, since the expansion or contraction into large cities or towns is also a "significant" territorial exchange, these are also coded as gains or losses.[35] Territorial exchanges that do not meet this threshold are excluded and coded as stalemate.[36]

In defining gains and losses as shifts of districts or population centers, we focus on territorial exchanges that are likely to be of strategic and political consequence, and as such, those most likely to affect the perceptions and expectations of combatants. The downside of the measure, of course, is that while it allows us to distinguish periods of stasis and marginal territorial change from periods of more dramatic change, it does not capture the relative size of change beyond the minimum threshold. Such a measure, for instance, could be captured by a moving percentage of formally disputed territory controlled by a rebel organization. However, data availability – particularly in the context of African civil wars of the 1960s and 1970s that this study explores – make this kind of precise data almost impossible to collect. However, to the extent possible, the subsequent case studies, and in particular the grayscale district-level maps of war zones, make an effort to describe and quantify the precise magnitude of territorial change.

Another key implication of this measure is that it conceives of gains and losses as military outputs rather than inputs. Inputs, in common military parlance, would include things like manpower, war material, financial capital, etc. Intuitively, it would make sense to conceive of gains and losses as encompassing fluctuations in these metrics. Yet following Biddle (2004), who demonstrates that historically, using raw military inputs (what he calls "capabilities") to predict war outcomes is statistically no better than flipping a coin, I see no reason to assume that inputs such as manpower and war material are reliable predictors of war outcomes

---

[35] In the context of the subsequent analysis, this would include all population centers above roughly 5,000 people (2005 estimates), but in practical terms there is a high level of colinearity between district-level exchange and the exchange of towns and cities.

[36] In coding the territorial ebb and flow of war at the district level in the Ethiopian and Eritrean context, I rely on a range of sources: archival material, news reports, secondary sources, and interviews. A small sample of some of the archival material can be found in the appendix. Interviews were generally more important for organizations and time periods in which existing documentary evidence was sparse. Admittedly, this is an imperfect science, and the quality of data for certain years does raise real concern. To the extent that any miscoding does occur, it is likely because I may have missed a district-level shift in a given year, and thus coded a gain or loss year as a stalemate. That said, I am fairly confident that the few gain or loss years missed were relatively marginal in significance and scale (that is likely why they were missed), and wouldn't undermine the broad argument about the varying cooperative incentives created by military contexts of gain, loss, and stalemate.

or military effectiveness. Therefore, there is little reason to expect that such variables have a decisive effect on the expectations and perceptions of rebels about cooperation in war. Given the inherent uncertainty of war – and the often tenuous connection between means and ends – I argue that the best way for rebels to interpret battlefield developments is through actual military outcomes – i.e., territorial exchange. Of course, this is not meant to suggest that military inputs such as men and material do not impact battlefield outcomes, but rather that their only effect on expectations and fragmentation is indirect and/or at the margins, often through their impacts on territorial gains or losses. In any case, such factors cannot be ignored, but rather should be treated as alternative variables against which we weigh our own explanations.

A final consideration should be addressed with respect to the specification of our independent variable. Using territorial gains or losses as a relevant indicator of consequential battlefield developments assumes that both rebels and the government have a strategy in which territorial exchange is actually a key metric of success and failure – i.e., that these parties actually attempt to control territory or maximize operational reach. Yet tactical and strategic considerations may dictate that parties to a conflict not contest territory or maximize operational reach and control (Kilcullen, 2010).

Addressing this concern requires that we discuss the empirical cases against which we will test our hypothesis. Clearly, if the metrics of gains and losses I employ are to be substantively meaningful, they must account for the strategic imperatives of those engaged in war. In the case of Ethiopia – the country from which the bulk of the data for this book has been drawn – all of the rebel organizations that were analyzed, as well as the three separate Ethiopian governments they fought against, evidenced a strong strategic and tactical commitment to expanding their territorial control or operational reach.[37] The basic reason for this focus on territory was that civilians were the "center of gravity" of conflicts in resource-poor environments like Ethiopia.[38] Without moving into and controlling territory, rebels could not hope to obtain, and deprive their enemies of, the material resources that civilians can supply. Unable to extract rents from mineral resources and lacking access to lucrative illicit economies, Ethiopia's rebels cared deeply about territory

---

[37] Ethiopia – along with its one-time province of Eritrea – comprises more than 600 districts, or *woredas*. In the Eritrean context, these districts would be referred to as *sub-zoba* administrations. *Zoba* is the Tigrinya word for "zone."

[38] Civilians as the "center of gravity" in counterinsurgency is phrasing borrowed from the US Army and Marine Corps Counterinsurgency Field Manual (2007).

precisely because the people who occupied the land were central to their war effort.[39]

It should also be said here that the majority of the rebel organizations that fought in Ethiopia's long civil war had strong ideological commitments to expanding their territorial footprint. There were a number of reasons for this. Ethiopia's civil war was dominated by the "national question" and the status of Ethiopia's non-Amhara nationalities, because the consolidation of the modern Ethiopia state under Emperor Menelik at the end of the nineteenth century had placed Amhara elites – their politics, symbols, and culture – firmly at the apex of a state premised on a blend of coercive assimilation and ethnic exclusion (Keller, 1981). As the student intellectual Wallelegn Mekonnen famously noted in 1969, this contributed to a sociopolitical system in which, "in short, to be an Ethiopian you will have to wear an Amhara mask" (Smith, 2013, p. 66). By the 1960s, the resulting discontent took form in a variety of rebel organizations espousing ethnonational agendas that ranged from autonomy to outright independence. Like most organizations with such aims, territory, and an ideologically grounded, emotional affinity to the concept of a "homeland" became a powerful dimension of political struggle. As Monica Duffy Toft (2003, p. 1) argues, it is in exactly such contexts that "territory takes on a meaning that far exceeds its material and objective description. It becomes not an object to be exchanged but an indivisible component of a group's identity." This meant that for many rebel organizations that participated in the Ethiopian civil war, the acquisition of territory wasn't simply a strategic necessity, but an ideological and emotional requirement of rebellion. A powerful indication of this attachment to territory is that those areas "liberated" from the enemy were often administered in a manner illustrative of the new political order the rebels sought to establish. Put differently, these territories served as laboratories of the future. Thus the rebels went beyond simply extracting resources from local civilian populations in areas they controlled or could operate within, to bearing the costs of providing critical public services, even when such efforts had no obvious military rationale.[40]

The other ideological force behind the commitment of many Ethiopian rebel organizations to territory was largely a product of global political currents of the 1960s and 1970s. Insurgent movements across the so-called Third World were swept up by the clarion call of

---

[39] It should be said that the centrality of civilian support is central to Marxist notions of effective insurgency – see Guevara (1961) and Tse-Tung (2000).

[40] See Mampilly (2011) for more on how separatist rebellions have incentives to control territory and govern it in a coherent way; also see Stewart (2017) for a new argument on the strategic incentives separatist rebel groups have to control and administer territory.

Marxism–Leninism, and many (but certainly not all) armed challengers to the Ethiopian state were no different. Since Marxism–Leninism, and its Maoist variant, carried with it a particular idea of how society ought to be transformed amidst the traditionalism of rural society – particularly on the important issue of land tenure – many Ethiopian rebel organizations devoted significant energy to the task of local administration and state building. The acquisition of territory, in this sense, mattered a great deal, since it enabled the proliferation of the rebellion's program of social change at the local level.

It should be noted that the Ethiopian state, across three distinct regimes, also maintained a profound ideological commitment to the control of territory. The Imperial Ethiopian Government of Emperor Haile Selassie (1930–74) spent much of its tenure preoccupied with extending the boundaries of the Ethiopian state, and it was thus deeply sensitive about ceding territory to its internal and external opponents. The cabal of military officers that would replace the monarchy, known as the *Derg* (1974–91), were Marxists committed to the project of radical social transformation at the local level, as evidenced by sweeping land reforms just a year after they took power. Their socialist revolution, designed to liberate Ethiopian society from the feudal chains of the old order, thus required preserving the state's writ across the country. Finally, the Ethiopian People's Revolutionary Democratic Front (1991–present), Ethiopia's present-day rulers, have presided over a high-modernist "developmental state" that shares some of socialist inclinations of their predecessor regime, and thus the general commitment to territoriality.

Data on Ethiopia's Civil Wars: Statistical Analysis and Case Selection

The first portion of this study relies on original cross-sectional, longitudinal data on a complete sample of rebel organizations from the African country of Ethiopia. As suggested by the annual measurement of key independent and dependent variables, I use "rebel year" as the unit of analysis in evaluating the relationship between rebel fragmentation and territorial gains and losses. The organizations were identified using the UCDP/PRIO Armed Conflict Dataset, and new data from the UCDP Actor Dataset, which defines rebel organizations along the lines identified earlier.[41] However, I included one additional organization, Osman Saleh Sabbe's Eritrean Liberation Front–People's

---

[41] The reader should note that the sample of Ethiopian organizations under analysis in this chapter is larger than that included in my Africa-wide dataset. This is because of

Liberation Forces, since I believe the group met this book's working definition of a rebel organization but was omitted by these existing datasets. Organizations are analyzed through the duration of their operational life, and once they lose the capacity to operate within Ethiopia, they drop out of the analysis. The goal of targeting a sample of rebel organizations from a single country is to control for variables at the country level that may affect the fragmentation of rebel organizations, and thus complicate and distort the causal effect of territorial gains and losses we seek to capture.

Yet why locate this study in Ethiopia? Given that several African countries have experienced protracted civil wars that yielded a critical mass of rebel organizations – and thus sufficient sample size for analysis – on what basis have we selected Ethiopia over other possible cases? Are we cherry-picking cases, or is there a deeper rationale for case selection?[42]

Historically, there are few African countries that have had as many rebel organizations as Ethiopia. According to the UCDP Actor Dataset, only Uganda, Chad, Sudan, and the DRC have had more rebel organizations than Ethiopia, which has fourteen. More importantly, since rebel year is our unit of analysis, the sheer longevity of Ethiopia's rebel organizations – the average lifespan of an Ethiopian rebel organization in the postcolonial period – 15.8 years for a total of 223 rebel years– suggests that we are maximizing our sample size and thus our analytical leverage.[43]

In addition, unlike the cases of Uganda, Chad, Sudan, and the DRC, Ethiopia has been engaged in continuous – if at times low-intensity – civil war since as early as 1960. This means that our data is not bounded temporally, and covers the full range of postcolonial African history. As a result, we can be sure that the conclusions being drawn are broadly representative of patterns across historical periods, and unbiased by trends particular to one historical period or decade. Figure 2.2 displays the number of rebel organizations active per year – i.e., the distribution of the sample across time, while Figure 2.3 displays the distribution of rebel fragmentation years by decade.

Now that we have described and motivated the sample, we need to actually demonstrate that there is a correlation between the key independent variable and the outcome we seek to explain. Using a

the release of new data in 2010 – the UCDP Actor Dataset – which I was able to make use of.

[42] It should be noted that there are a few strong recent studies that have used the Ethiopian and Eritrean case to explore civil war dynamics. These works take up research questions related to, but distinct from those explored in this book. See Pischedda (2015) and Krause (2018).

[43] The longest-surviving organization in the sample is the Oromo Liberation Front, which operated for thirty-six years.

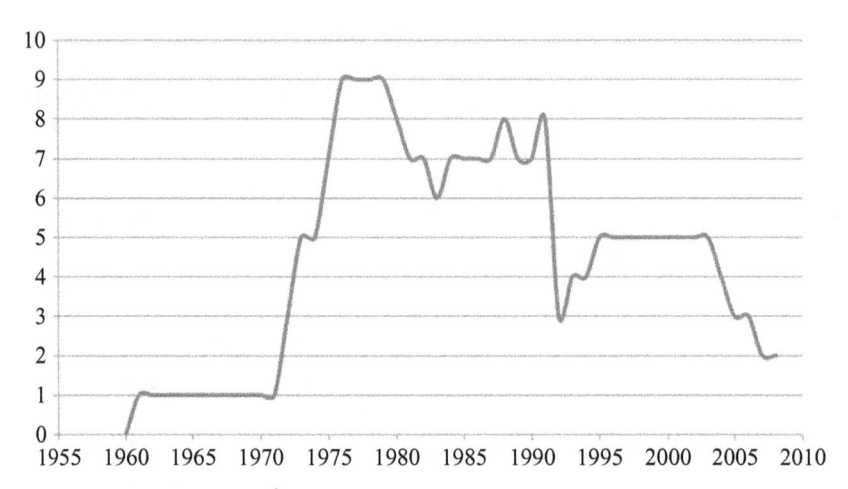

Figure 2.2 Number of active Ethiopian rebel organizations, 1960–2008.

two-by-two matrix, Table 2.1 shows the extent to which years in which a rebel organization fragmented, and years in which these organizations experienced a gain or loss, covary.[44]

This cross-tabulation is instructive, and demonstrates clearly that territorial gains and losses, in the Ethiopian context, are very close to a necessary but not sufficient condition for rebel fragmentation. While it is true that many instances of territorial gain and loss are not associated with fragmentation – rebels would never win wars if every battlefield victory led to their own fragmentation – only a mere three out of twenty-seven total fragmentation years were also years in which there was territorial stalemate.[45]

Yet the correlation between territorial gains and losses and rebel fragmentation raises another issue: since fragmentation itself is a key source of losses in war, how do we know that there is not an endogenous

[44] Although not reflected in the cross-tab, the gain/loss years are unbalanced, as 40 percent of gain/loss years consist of gain years, and 60 percent of loss years. This is not surprising, as traditionally, rebel organizations face steep power disparities. It is also important to note that the correlation between gain/loss years and fragmentation is not being driven by either gains or losses: fourteen cases of fragmentation occur in loss years and ten occur in gain years.

[45] The fact that there are many instances of territorial change that do not result in fragmentation will be addressed to some extent in the conclusion of the book. At this point, suffice it to say that territorial gains and losses can explain a significant portion of the temporal variation in the fragmentation of a rebel organization, but certainly not all of that variation. This book is designed to explain a particularly important dimension of rebel fragmentation in war, but not all of its facets. In any case, it is rare that one book can explain 100 percent of the variation in a given political phenomenon.

A Theory of Rebel Fragmentation

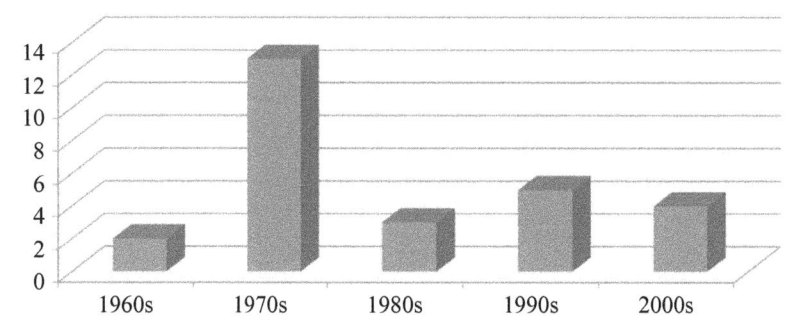

Figure 2.3 Ethiopian rebel organizations, fragmentation by decade, 1960–2008.

feedback effect driving our results? It may be the case that an initial instance of fragmentation spurs a chain of loss that causes fragmentation several years later. Given the possible endogenous relationship between our X and Y variables, there is no reason to think that an organization's fragmentation at T1 and T5 are independent of one another.[46]

In order to account for this sort of endogeneity across rebel years, I analyze the data statistically using a random effects logistic regression model with rebel year as the unit of analysis. Fragmentation takes a value of 0 or 1, while stalemate versus gain/loss is also framed as a dichotomous 0 or 1 variable. Crucially, a dichotomous measure of prior rebel fragmentation is included in order to investigate whether the correlation between fragmentation and gain/loss years is robust, or whether it is being driven by the endogeneity I identified. Table 2.2 presents these results.

The results suggest that despite endogeneity concerns, gains and losses remain a robust predictor of rebel fragmentation.[47] In fact, prior fragmentation actually reduces the likelihood that fragmentation will occur in later rebel years. Yet while this exercise provides a useful point of departure, by itself, it does not validate the causal claims we seek to make. With only one control in the model, it is likely that other confounding variables are driving our results. Furthermore, this sort of cross-sectional, longitudinal time series analysis is suspect with an N of

---

[46] Obviously, my discussion of "cycles of contention" and "diffusion" of factional infighting suggests that factionalism and fragmentation are endogenous within "rebel year," as various groups respond to the initial eruption of factionalism and fragmentation. The statistical exercise in this section refers to endogeneity across "rebel years." In this case, fragmentation events would not be immediately and directly linked, but related through the more long-term effects of territorial loss.

[47] This conclusion is also suggested by the distribution of fragmentation years across cases in Figure 2.5. If endogeneity across rebel years were a concern, then the distribution of fragmentation years would be highly uneven.

Table 2.1 *Cross-tab, fragmentation, and gain/loss by rebel year*

	Stalemate	Gain/Loss
Fragment No	120	76
Fragment Yes	3	24

just over 220. And even with a larger sample, the challenges of coding certain cases, largely due to gaps in available information, make the data itself less than 100 percent reliable. Finally, our efforts ignore the sort of endogeneity that results from "simultaneity" bias: since our unit of analysis is the rebel year, one cannot be sure whether territorial gains and losses occurred before fragmentation, or whether fragmentation occurred before territorial gains and losses.

In order to resolve these issues, I subject a subset of these rebel organizations to careful process tracing in which a conscious effort is made to both elucidate the causal mechanisms that link independent variables to outcomes and carefully weigh competing explanations.[48] This subset of organizations consists of seven organizations out of the total sample of fourteen. In selecting case studies for more thorough analysis, I attempted to maximize variation on the key independent and dependent variable. Thus, several rebel organizations that did not experience significant territorial gains or an episode of fragmentation were automatically dropped from consideration (see Table 2.3).

The second core imperative used in case selection was to maximize the representativeness of the cases selected both temporally and spatially. Thus, collectively, the case studies encompass the full range of postcolonial Ethiopian history – 1960 to the present – and a broad cross-section of geographic regions (northern, southern, and southeastern Ethiopia) and operational environments (arid lowlands, fertile plains, mountainous regions, and heavily forested terrain). Figure 2.4 visually depicts the geographic distribution of the case studies.

The final imperative in case selection was to obtain a sufficient level of cross-sectional variation on our outcome variable – fragmentation – even though our primary focus is on temporal variation within cases. While this imperative is somewhat at odds with our effort to obtain as much temporal variation on our X and Y variables as possible, selecting only organizations with multiple cases of fragmentation may bias our

---

[48] For more on "process tracing," see Eckstein (1975) and George & Bennett (2005).

A Theory of Rebel Fragmentation

Table 2.2 *Baseline model of rebel fragmentation*

Variable	Full Model
Gain/loss	2.440901***
	(.6318165)
Prior fragmentation	−.3343384
	(.4498132)
N	221
Constant	−3.445373

*** Significant at the .01 level, ** significant at the .05 level, and * significant at the .10 level

results, since (1) there may be something systematically different about how the causal chain we have identified operates in high-fragmentation organizations, and (2) it minimizes the possibility of examining outliers or "off-the-line" organizations – those that experience gains and losses but not fragmentation – that may reveal significant insight

Table 2.3 *Ethiopian rebel organizations (shaded cases not selected)*

Organization Name	Years Operational	Variation on X and Y Variables?
Eritrean People's Liberation Front	1972–91	Yes
Eritrean Liberation Front	1961–82	Yes
Tigray People's Liberation Front	1975–91	Yes
Oromo Liberation Front	1973–2008	Yes
West Somali Liberation Front	1973–88	Yes
Ogaden National Liberation Front	1984–2008	Yes
Afar Revolutionary Democratic United Front	1993–2004	Yes
Afar Liberation Front	1975–91	Yes
Al-Ittihad	1991–2003	Yes
Eritrean Islamic Jihad Movement[49]	1988–2006	Yes
Eritrean Liberation Front–People's Liberation Forces	1975–79	No
Ethiopian Democratic Union	1975–79	No
Ethiopia People's Democratic Movement	1980–91	No
Ethiopian People's Revolutionary Party	1972–80	No

[49] The Eritrean Islamic Jihad Movement is an odd case, in that it was founded before Eritrea's formal independence in May 1993, but is primarily remembered as a stiff opponent of the newly established government in Asmara.

Figure 2.4 Ethiopia provincial map, geographic distribution of case studies.[50]

and possible refinements of our theory. Figure 2.5 visually depicts rebel organizations included in the full sample along with the number of years in which they experienced fragmentation. Note that two of the cases selected – the TPLF and the WSLF – experienced only one instance of fragmentation.[51]

Thus in summary, we have used a method of case selection that maximizes sample size, maximizes variation within and across cases, is representative, and offers ample opportunity for investigation of outliers. Although no method of case selection is perfect, the guide to case selection we provide here is transparent and precisely articulated.

---

[50] Please note that this is a map of Ethiopia prior to Eritrea's independence in 1993.
[51] The general inspiration for this case selection strategy is drawn from Gerring (2001).

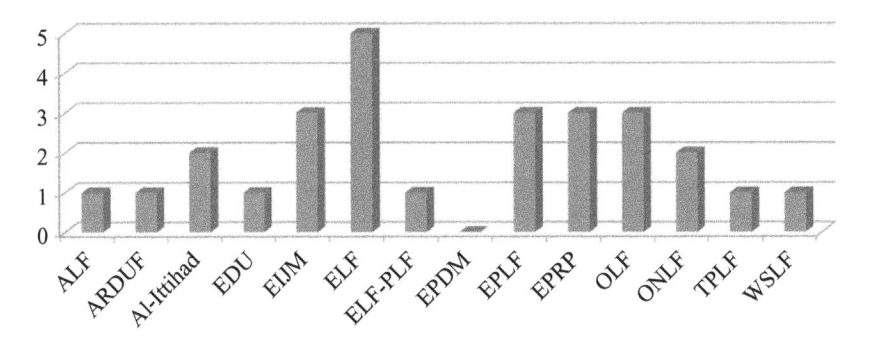

Figure 2.5 Fragmentation by Ethiopian rebel organization, 1960–2008.

Scope Conditions

There are obvious implications of the case selection strategy pursued in this book, and in this section I discuss these implications with reference to the scope conditions of my argument. While the gold standard for this sort of study would be to produce a truly global explanation for rebel fragmentation, the proposed theory is more medium range, and makes a set of claims about a distinct subset of rebel organizations and civil wars.

One aspect of my case selection strategy that *does not* necessarily affect the scope of my argument is the decision to look at an African case. Some may argue that the failure to examine other cases outside of Africa renders my results Africa specific. This would be true only if there were reasons to think that African civil wars and rebel organizations systematically differed from those in other parts of the world on some meaningful dimension. Yet there is no theoretical reason to think this would be the case, and the literature on African civil wars makes no claims about African exceptionalism in this regard. Indeed, on the key outcome variable of interest, data collected by Findley & Rudloff suggest that Africa is no more or less likely than other regions of the world to have civil wars in which at least one of its rebel participants splits into two or more distinct organizations. In their sample, 54 percent of African civil wars have witnessed rebel fragmentation, while in Asia this figure stands at 59 percent.[52]

But there are other ways in which my case selection strategy limits the scope of my theoretical claims. First, because Ethiopia is an environment that has few high-value natural resources, and more importantly,

---

[52] Note that my Africa-wide dataset (introduced in the first chapter), and the UCDP Actor Dataset, differ from Findley and Rudloff's data in that the unit of analysis is the rebel organization, not the civil war. See M. Findley and P. Rudloff (2011), "Combatant Fragmentation and the Dynamics of Civil Wars" (unpublished paper).

virtually no easily lootable natural resources, it is hard to generalize my theoretical claims to civil war contexts in which diamonds, gems, timber, and illicit drug crops are present. This is because there are strong theoretical reasons to believe that in such cases, it is not the gain or loss of territory that is important, but the gain or loss of territory that has strategic natural resources that can materially sustain either the rebel organization or the government. Thus, we cannot necessarily expect general shifts in territory to trigger rebel fragmentation in contexts like Colombia, Liberia, Sierra Leone, DRC, and present-day Afghanistan. However, in resource-poor environments like Ethiopia, Darfur, Somalia, Yemen, and Western Sahara, the argument would be more tractable.

Second, it is hard to know whether my theory could explain rebel fragmentation in democratic states. While Ethiopia has gone through three different governments since 1960 – Haile Selassie's monarchy, the Marxist Derg, and the EPRDF coalition led by Meles Zenawi and later Hailemariam Deselegn – there is little variation on regime type, as all were nondemocracies.[53] This is important, because democratic politics can reveal societal and state preferences, thus reducing the information and credibility problems that drive uncertainty about negotiated settlements between states or within states suffering from civil wars. Thus, in democratic states we could expect government efforts to split rebel organizations through the provision of economic and political incentives to be more successful than in nondemocratic states. As a consequence, shifts in territory may be a relatively less important factor in explaining rebel fragmentation among, for instance, India's Maoists and Sri Lanka's Tamil Tigers, where democratic governments have had a more reasonable expectation of peeling of disgruntled rebel factions.

A third issue to consider is the political goals of the organizations being analyzed. As noted before, a peculiar reality of Ethiopia's civil wars was that the conflict was deeply tied to the "national question" and the political status of Ethiopia's major non-Amhara communities. Nearly all of the organizations within this dataset, and all of the organizations selected for deeper case study analysis, were ethnonationalist rebel organizations that levied political claims on behalf of a particular ethnic or national community. These groups were bound together by a common ascriptive identity, rather than a set of programmatic aspirations or ideologies (although ideologies like Marxism certainly played a mobilization role). Therefore, is my theory's application limited to rebel organizations that are ethnonationalist in orientation?

---

[53] The EPRDF had the highest polity score of the three regimes, scoring a 2.

A Theory of Rebel Fragmentation 65

I would argue that the theory does have broader applicability, because the selection of ethnonationalist organizations means that my theory is being tested against "least-likely" or "hard" cases. Assuming a similar level of interest in territory, ethnonationalist rebel organizations systematically differ from those that are more programmatic or ideological in nature in that when they incur shifts in territory, they should theoretically be *less likely to fragment*. This is because such organizations are based on ethnic and nationalist attachments, where social pressures – or what Olson (1982) has called "social selective incentives" – can be mobilized to police defection and fragmentation. Instead of limiting the scope of my argument, then, my selection of ethnonationalist organizations ensures that the scope of my conclusions remains fairly broad.[54] In any case, my in-depth analysis of Somali Islamist movements in Chapter 6 – designed as an external validity test – addresses this specific concern over scope conditions.

Conclusions: A Note on Method

Having outlined a theory of rebel fragmentation, tested its plausibility through cross-sectional, longitudinal data on the complete sample of Ethiopian rebel organizations from 1960 to 2008, and then used that data to identify appropriate cases for closer analysis, we are now prepared to move forward. The subsequent case studies use an eclectic range of sources, but are primarily based on fieldwork conducted in Ethiopia, Sudan, Kenya, and Ethiopian and Eritrean diaspora communities in the United States and Europe from 2008 to 2016. More than eighty-five structured and unstructured interviews were conducted with a range of individuals – in Tigrinya, Amharic, and English – including ex-combatants of various ranks, ex-government officials, and civilians of varying partisan stripes who lived through the conflict. Participants were identified using snowball sampling, and although not representing a purely scientific sample, reflect a broad cross-section of Ethiopian and Eritrean society (Cohen and Arieli, 2011).[55] I have also utilized

---

[54] As a practical matter, under Reno's (2011) well-known typology, most of the organizations discussed in this book (the EPLF, ELF, TPLF, SNM, etc.) would qualify as "reform rebels" – that is, organizations grounded in a well-articulated ideological program geared toward revolutionary transformation of the state. I would conjecture that it is exactly these kinds of organizations that are least likely to fall victim to fragmentation.

[55] One of the primary reasons that the sample is not broadly scientific is that the mortality rates of early combatants were high. Thus, there are few participants from the 1960s. Because of IRB regulations and the sensitivity of the topic at hand, all identifying information is removed from citations and quotes based on interviews. The exception here

thousands of pages of archival material from the National Archives in Washington, DC, the National Archives in the United Kingdom, and the Institute of Ethiopian Studies, data that have been complemented by a trove of original rebel documents, news reports, and other secondary sources. I have also benefited from access to interviews conducted by Eritrea analyst Gunter Schroeder with Eritrean and Ethiopian insurgents in the 1970s and 1980s. These interviews were provided to the author by Schroeder himself, and were invaluable to the analysis that follows.

By design, the three upcoming chapters that focus on the Ethiopian civil war serve different purposes. Chapters 3 and 4 are extraordinarily detailed analysis of the ELF and EPLF, and include a careful consideration of alternative explanations. These chapters are the empirical core of the book. Chapter 5 involves analysis of a further five organizations, which are designed more as "shadow cases" that can confirm the findings of the preceding chapters.

As highlighted in the opening chapter of the book, Chapter 6 seeks to test the lessons learned from the investigation of the Ethiopian civil war against data from the Somali civil war. This analysis involved substantial additional fieldwork in Somaliland in October–November 2010 and January–February 2014, Mogadishu in January–February 2014, and Kenya in the summer of 2012. My research strategy in the Somali context roughly maps onto what was done in the Ethiopia/Eritrea analysis, with roughly forty interviews conducted with a range of relevant informants: government officials, veterans of particular rebel organizations of interest, employees of nongovernmental organizations (NGOs) who interfaced with these organizations, etc. In addition, I marshal a wealth of other primary and secondary material to make my case.

In terms of the manner in which the evidence is presented, I proceed in the following fashion. First, I provide deep historical background on the circumstances that gave rise to each of the rebel organizations explored in this book. Without proper context, these organizations, and the coalitional dynamics within them, cannot be properly understood. Second, I motivate the assumption that these organizations should in fact be treated as coalitions at their inception, by describing the different constituent units that formed the original coalition, and elucidating the security and survival dynamics that brought this diverse configuration of interests together. Third, I chart the military history of these organizations, with a special focus on the territorial ebb and flow of war,

---

is part of the research for Somaliland, where research protocols were different. A justification for these protocols and further information on interviewees can be found in the appendix.

and causally link these developments to factional infighting and fragmentation – across this book, I explore twenty-two distinct moments of factional infighting and fragmentation. Finally, I unpack moments of factional infighting and fragmentation, in order to illustrate my key corollary arguments: that factionalism and fragmentation can *sometimes* be characterized by a process of diffusion, and that fragmentation is a bid for survival on the part of those who have lost factional struggles. Deliberately, I provide as much descriptive information as possible so that readers understand that the narratives that follow have not been massaged to "fit" this book's prevailing theoretical model. In other words, I put the data on the table, and let it speak for itself.

While reconstructing any violent conflict is difficult, these sources provide an interesting window into the internal politics of organized rebellion and, as I will show, compelling support for the theory I have proposed.

Part II

Rebellion in Ethiopia and Eritrea

3 The Eritrean Liberation Front
Jebha in Action, 1960–1982

This chapter seeks to test the theoretical claims outlined earlier in this book through careful process tracing. It focuses on the historical evolution of one strategically selected rebel organization, the Eritrean Liberation Front (Jebha), charting the relationship between the ebb and flow of war and periods of factional infighting and organizational fragmentation. As readers will note, this chapter will pay careful attention to historical detail, in an effort to allay concerns that history has been massaged to fit the book's "preconceived" theoretical model. Integrating a trove of newly collected material on Jebha's operations with a careful consideration of existing histories of the organization, the analysis focuses on key events and moments of variation on which the book's argument turns, while remaining careful to place these events in their appropriate social and historical context. If the book's underlying theory is correct, we should observe a number of important patterns.

As the previous chapter suggested, we should observe that the coalitions that are rebel organizations are formed in the context of deep security concerns, as various constituent units seek to minimize risk in war and guarantee survival. Given this underlying logic of organizational formation, in which security concerns drive politically disparate rebelling constituencies to collaborate under a presumably viable organizational umbrella, factional infighting should be triggered by both territorial gains and losses. The former provokes preference divergence and the latter commitment problems. By extension, periods of territorial stalemate should be associated with moments of relative cohesion.

We should also expect to see support for the book's corollary arguments. Fragmentation, when it occurs, should be the result of factional infighting in which the losers of these disputes exit in a bid for survival. Also, we should expect to see that *some cases* of factional infighting are characterized by a process of diffusion, as segments of the organization not involved in the initial dispute are mobilized in response to emerging divisions. *On some occasions*, this can lead to multiple factions fragmenting in close and rapid succession.

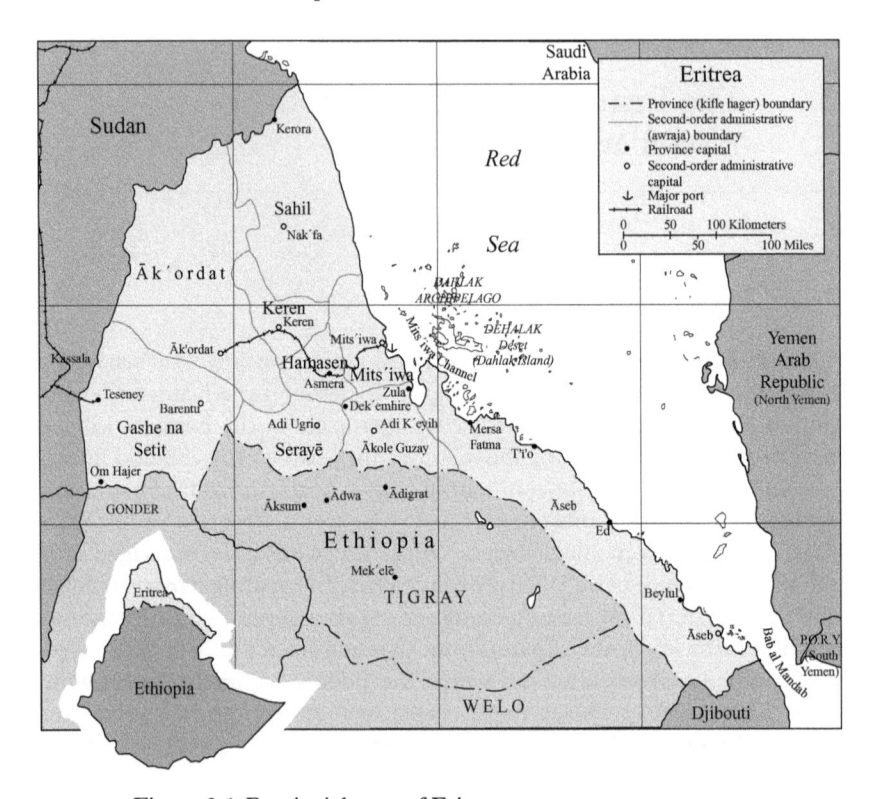

Figure 3.1 Provincial map of Eritrea.

The chapter begins by discussing Jebha's historical background, and then moves into the heart of the analysis. It concludes by carefully considering some alternative causal explanations, in an effort to determine if the observed variation is being driven by factors outside of the scope of our main argument.

Background to Rebellion

When the secessionist war in Eritrea came to a conclusion on May 24, 1991, it had been the longest-running conflict in postcolonial African history. This is a distinction the Eritrean conflict still holds if one were to consider South Sudan's long secessionist conflict as two separate wars (see Figure 3.1 for old provincial map of Eritrea).[1] Although the insurgency initially appeared to consist of little more than sporadic

---

[1] As many students of African history will know, South Sudanese nationalists waged armed rebellion from 1955 until 1972, when a peace agreement brokered in the Ethiopian capital of Addis Ababa ended the first phase of the Sudanese civil war. Conflict was reignited in 1982 and did not formally conclude until 2005 (Johnson, 2003).

banditry, in the end its protagonists would be engaged in the largest mechanized battles on the African continent since World War II.[2]

Any measure of the cost of the war illustrates its scope and scale. Gebru Tareke estimates that Ethiopia's civil wars, of which Eritrea was the central front, killed between 800,000 and 1 million people, roughly 2 percent of Africa's second-largest country (Tareke, 2009, p. 132).[3] This excludes the famine of 1984–85 – of which the war was the principal cause – in which another 1 million people died. If one assumes that a total of 2 million people died as a consequence of the war, this would make the number of conflict-related deaths in Ethiopia twenty times larger than that of the Yugoslav civil wars, roughly double that of the Iran–Iraq conflict, and a little more than equal to that of Afghanistan between 1979 and 2001.[4]

As one might expect, Eritrea's long rebellion produced a steady stream of refugees. Although small numbers of political dissidents began to leave Eritrea in the 1950s, it was not until 1967 that the conflict produced large-scale displacement.[5] By 1985, neighboring Sudan was home to nearly a half a million Eritrean refugees, many of whom were forced to remain within a network of UN High Commissioner for Refugees (UNHCR)–maintained refugee camps in eastern Sudan.[6] The figure of half a million excludes the thousands who utilized Sudan as a transit point for onward migration to North America, Europe, and the Arab world (Kibreab, 1985, 1987). The effects of this mass displacement largely persist, as Eritrea remains the quintessential diasporic nation – an estimated one-third of its 6 million people currently reside beyond the country's recognized borders.[7]

---

[2] In a telling commentary to the BBC in the late 1980s, the British historian Basil Davidson described the Ethiopian's government's defeat at Afabet, Eritrea, in 1988 as "one of the biggest victories ever scored by a liberation movement since Dien Bien Phu in 1954" (Connell, 1993, p. 228).

[3] Journalist Peter Gill refers to the 1984 famine as an event of world historical proportions, writing that it was "... the greatest humanitarian disaster of the late 20th century. The face of aid was transformed, and the face of hunger was Ethiopian" (Gill, 2010, p. 2).

[4] PRIO Battle Deaths Dataset, 2005, which can be found at www.prio.no/CSCW/Datasets/Armed-Conflict/Battle-Deaths/ (Accessed October 29, 2017).

[5] See review produced by Awate.com of an Arabic-language Al Jazeera documentary on Eritrean migration, which can be found at http://awate.com/aljazeera-the-tragedy-of-the-eritrean-refugees-in-sudan/ (Accessed August 28, 2014).

[6] Indeed, eastern Sudan still possesses a huge number of Eritrean refugees. Many estimate that the city of Kassala, which sits on the Sudanese side of the Eritrean–Sudanese frontier, is 50 percent Eritrean. Author's interview, longtime Eritrean refugee in Sudan whose household served as temporary quarters for Eritrean refugees, August 5, 2008.

[7] It should be noted that a large percentage of the Eritrean diaspora comprises those who have left the country since 2001. Scholars estimate that this recent migration is in excess of 400,000 people, who are largely fleeing Eritrea's indefinite, low-wage national service, and more generalized political repression. See Kibreab (2009, 2017). For more work on the politics of the Eritrean diaspora see Hepner (2011) and Bernal (2014).

The economic costs of the conflict were not minor either, although they pale in comparison to its excruciating human toll. Gayle Smith, a journalist who covered Ethiopia's internal conflicts in the 1980s, conjectured that at the height of the secessionist war in 1982, the Ethiopian government was spending USD 1.5 million a day in fighting the insurgents.[8] By the late 1980s, Ethiopia was maintaining sub-Saharan Africa's largest military, a situation that would have been untenable were it not for the huge infusion of assistance from the Soviet Union. When the military government of Colonel Mengistu Hailemariam finally lost power in May of 1991, it had accumulated a foreign debt of USD 9 billion in its failed bid to find a military solution to Ethiopia's civil wars (Tareke, 2009, p. 137).

For the Ethiopian economy more generally, the costs of war were devastating. In 1990, a grim World Bank report described the "crippling cost of internal security" and Ethiopia's "catastrophic" decline in per capita income. In the critical sector of agriculture, where 90 percent of rural Ethiopians sustained their livelihoods, the crisis appeared even more severe, as yields in critical areas of food consumption were failing to meet domestic demand, creating a heavy dependence on imports that was exhausting Ethiopia's already meager foreign currency reserves.[9]

The major actors in the complex Eritrean drama – besides the central government – were two rebel organizations, the Eritrean Liberation Front (Jebha) and the Eritrean People's Liberation Front (Shaebia).[10] Although both organizations were firmly committed to Eritrean self-determination, up to and including secession, they had a contentious relationship. Jebha was the first organization to emerge in 1960, and was the standard-bearer for Eritrean independence until several splinter groups coalesced into Shaebia in February 1972. Shaebia's emergence was a significant moment in the trajectory of the war, launching both Eritrean nationalist organizations into a bloody contest for supremacy from 1972 to 1974. Despite its numerical superiority, Jebha was unable to eliminate its younger rival, and a somewhat uneasy détente between the two organizations ensued until 1980, when another dispute within

---

[8] Smith would later become the head of the US Agency for International Development (USAID) in the administration of US president Barack Obama. Gayle Smith, "Ethiopian Conflicts: All Is Not Quiet on the Northern Command," *New York Times*, July 6, 1983, p. A22.

[9] World Bank, "Ethiopia's Economy in the 1980s and Framework for Accelerated Growth," *World Bank Report No. 8062-ET*, March 14, 1990, p. 1–2.

[10] To reiterate, *Jebha* is the Arabic term for "front," while *Shaebia* is the Arabic term for "peoples." These colloquial names for the ELF and EPLF respectively are used throughout this book.

the nationalist camp resulted in Jebha's demise. Having unceremoniously eclipsed its parent organization, Shaebia defeated the Ethiopian military conclusively in 1991, and after a UN-monitored referendum, declared an independent Eritrea. For the most part, this chapter focuses on Jebha and leaves the relations between the two insurgent organizations untouched, except when these relations tell us something about Jebha's shifting military position. However, most histories of the Eritrean conflict focus a great deal on the dynamic between the two groups (Erlich, 1983).

The origins of the secessionist conflict in Eritrea can be found in the arrival of the Italians on the Red Sea coast in the latter half of the nineteenth century. Prior to the Italian colonial state of Eritrea, "Eritrea" did not exist as a political or administrative entity. While most parts of lowland and coastal Eritrea, predominantly populated by Muslim tribes, had links to Ottoman, Egyptian, and Sudanic political authorities, the central highland plateau – populated predominantly by Orthodox Christians – had historical links with an expanding Ethiopian monarchy to the south. In a sense, Ethiopia's coastal province of Eritrea, like other parts of Sahelian Africa, was the meeting point of two very different cultural entities: one Arab and Islamic, the other African and predominantly Christian. Importantly, these different cultural heritages mapped onto two very different modes of social organization and production, with the Muslim lowlands predominantly pastoral and the Christian highlands a sedentary, rain-fed agricultural economy.[11] These different political, cultural, and economic legacies largely outlasted the Italian period, and, as I show, were crucial to understanding Jebha's internal politics.

Owing to a delayed process of internal state formation that did not fully crystallize until the 1860s, the Italian state was relatively late to the colonial game. Italian capital was the first to venture into Eritrea, when the Rubattino Shipping Company purchased the Bay of Assab, a strategic port nestled into the extreme end of the Eritrean panhandle. With the completion of the Suez Canal in that same year, the company sought a Red Sea port that could serve as a coaling station for its vessels. The central government in Rome would purchase the port in 1882, and

---

[11] Obviously, this is a very simplified account. Eritrea's social and ethnic demography is far more complex – the territory technically has nine ethnic groups. Moreover, some "lowland" communities, like the Kunama, are agricultural communities. For more complete accounts see Negash (1987) and Pool (2001). The foregoing comments were only meant to contextualize what many believe to be the major cleavage in Eritrean politics. However, many other lines of cleavage had been relevant at different points in time, particularly *awraja*, or provincial/ regional differences.

with the diplomatic support of the British, extend its political administration up the coast to Massawa, and further inland into the Christian highlands.[12]

Yet the Italians would not be content with the possession of their new Red Sea colony, viewing it as a strategically located stepping stone into the territory's large southern neighbor, Ethiopia. These dreams were quashed in 1896, at the battle of Adwa, in a humiliation that Italy, and the Western world, would remember for some time.[13] In a decision that remains mired in controversy, and had far-reaching effects, Ethiopian emperor Menelik chose not to press his military advantage by asserting claims to Eritrea, and instead recognized Italian sovereignty over Eritrea in return for Rome's unqualified acknowledgment of Ethiopian independence.[14]

With control over Eritrea reassured, the Italians devoted their attention to the administration of their colonial possession. Under the supervision of trailblazing governor Fernando Martini (1897–1907), the political and administrative foundations of the colonial state were put in place. Martini eschewed the policies of early administrators who envisioned Eritrea as a settler colony, believing that the land alienation such policies would cause was politically untenable within Eritrea, and could complicate Italy's relationship with Eritrea's Ethiopian kinsmen to the south. Instead, Martini and his successors pursued a policy of what Tekeste Negash (1987) has called "rational imperialism," structuring the colony as an outlet for Ethiopian goods, and more importantly, a source of soldiers for Italy's colonial army. Given the political challenge of raising a colonial army within Italy in the post-Adwa era, the Eritrean *Ascaris* (as they came to be known) were to prove critical to Italy's campaigns of colonial subjugation in Libya and Somalia.[15] From the

---

[12] The British had been compelled to establish a colony in what is now Somaliland, in order to protect the livestock trade that supported the strategic port of Aden. Having established a political stake in the Horn, the British were keen to prevent the expansion of their French competitors out of the colony they had established in Djibouti. Italian control of Eritrea accomplished this at minimal cost to the British Crown.

[13] For the most comprehensive history of the battle, see Pakenham (1992, pp. 470–486) and Jonas (2011).

[14] On this very issue, Pakenham (1992, p. 485) muses: "Why had Menelik thrown away the initiative just when he had the chance of driving the Italians into the sea?" The simple answer, in Pakenham's view, was that *"The price of victory had been excruciating."* For Menelik, war fatigue made a further offensive against the Italians a grim and unlikely possibility.

[15] According to Negash (1987, p. 51), by 1935, nearly 40 percent of active Eritrean men were soldiers. Italian historian Guilia Barrera (2003, p. 84) sums up the logic of Ascari recruitment in this way: "By using Eritreans, and not Italians, as cannon fodder, the Italian government was able to continue its expansionist colonial policy in Somalia and

perspective of Eritrea's own political development, the Ascari experiment was to prove significant, both in sustaining the colony's economy (as Ascari wages supplemented the incomes of rural families) and in generating the early beginnings of an Eritrean national consciousness.[16]

The rise of the fascist regime of Benito Mussolini in 1922 altered Italy's Eritrea policy in some fundamental ways. The major shift was the reemergence of an overtly racist native policy that sought to resettle Italians in Eritrea at the expense of native Eritreans, who would be confined to reserved areas. Racialized barriers to employment and education were also hardened, while miscegenation and racial mixing were effectively criminalized. Interestingly, this racialized colonial project was associated with a period of rapid urban and industrial growth of the colony, developments that were in part fueled by Mussolini's decision to invade Ethiopia in 1936.

The proponents of Italy's fascist colonial project would never fulfill their bold aspirations, since the British would put an end to Italy's East African empire in 1941. Despite an almost sixty-year colonial interlude, marked by deep social, political, and economic transformations, scholars remain divided on the precise impact of the colonial period on the trajectory of Eritrean nationalism.[17] These disagreements aside, Tekeste Negash (1987) was largely correct when he argued that Italian colonialism had done little more than to create "an inchoate consciousness of a separate identity" among the Eritrean body politic. Colonialism had certainly forged new boundaries of identity and community within the colony, but as the fragmentation of Jebha would soon illustrate, it had done little to establish a common politics that could transcend the territory's long-standing sectarian divides.[18]

Eritrea was administered by the British after World War II, and following a UN-mandated inquiry into the future status of the territory, was federated with Ethiopia in 1952. The British Military Administration (1941–52) was a period of great political tumult, as the future status of Eritrea hung in the balance. Although no referendum was held on the

Libya without running the risk of the political backlash that the death of Italian soldiers could have caused."

[16] As I will point out in subsequent pages, one of the founders of Jebha, Idris Hamid Awate, was a former Italian Ascari.

[17] For more on these different schools of thought, which characterize much of the writing on Eritrea, see Sorenson (1993) and the opening pages of Dirar (2007). The debate over the impact of Italian colonialism was a contentious issue in the post-Italian period, as evidence of Italian impact could validate the claims of Eritrean nationalists that sought to dissociate Eritrea from the political, social, and economic linkages that had bound the territory to Ethiopia in earlier periods.

[18] Of course, this is a claim that one could make about the impact of colonialism in most African countries (Herbst, 2000, Chapter 3).

issue, several political parties mobilized on different sides of the debate: the Muslim League and its allies rejected union with Ethiopia, while the Unionist Party and the aggressive *Mahber Andinet* youth league, encouraged by the very powerful Orthodox Church, supported the idea.[19] In this "era of competing nationalisms," those who mobilized on behalf of an independent Eritrea faced long odds (Reid, 2011, p. 116). Cold War politics meant that the United States and its Atlantic allies would decisively support Ethiopian claims to Eritrea. Just as important was the reality that there was simply no precedent for an independent Eritrea, as the critical moment of African decolonization would not occur for at least another decade. An independent Eritrea would have effectively made the Red Sea territory the first of Europe's African colonies to achieve independent statehood, at a moment when much of imperial Europe was not yet resigned to the independence of its African subjects.[20] Swimming against prevailing political tides, opponents of the Federation accepted the decision of the UN with varying degrees of enthusiasm.

In retrospect, most recognize that the Federation was destined to fail. The lengthy Italian colonial period, and the British administration that had followed it, had created new political and economic institutions in Eritrea: it had acquired an assembly, political parties, labor unions, a well-trained bureaucracy, commercialized agriculture, and a manufacturing sector that was the most substantial in the Horn of Africa. By contrast, Emperor Haile Selassie's Ethiopia – one of only two African countries to have never been colonized – had legal slavery until the mid-twentieth century, was feudal, and desperately poor. Furthermore, royal absolutism and federalism were a contradiction in terms.[21]

Piece by piece, Haile Selassie destroyed the Federation, formally incorporating the territory as Ethiopia's fourteenth province in 1962

---

[19] A third option, endorsed by British administrators, was to partition the colony, with the western portions being attached to Sudan and the central highlands attached to Ethiopia. A fourth option, entertained by some within Eritrea, was an irredentist plan to create an independent "Greater Eritrea" that incorporated the Tigrinya-speaking highlands of Ethiopia.

[20] Author's interview, Eritrean academic, May 29, 2010. According to the interviewee, "discussions on Eritrean independence were too early for us."

[21] On this point, Negash (1997, p. 32) quotes Eritrean intellectual and Shaebia cadre Araia Tseggai (1988), who wrote: "The new Eritrean government – a democratically elected government with a democratic constitution – would not coexist with Ethiopia's absolutist and archaic monarchy. With its labor unions and independent political parties, Eritrea was an anathema to the Ethiopian entity." Moreover, on p. 34, Negash (1997) quotes another well-known Shaebia intellectual (at least at the time), Bereket Habteselassie (1989), who writes that the Federation was undone by "the fear and uncertainty of a feudal regime harnessed to a modern bourgeois democratic government."

amidst recriminations from several opposition parties.[22] The culmination of this process was a dubious decision taken by the Eritrean Assembly to dissolve itself in November of that year.[23] The sitting president of the Assembly, Hamid Farej Hamid, refused to attend the vote, perhaps wanting to avoid being seen as an accomplice to a process that was marred by bribery and intimidation. While much of Eritrea's highland Christian population was persuaded on grounds of shared religious and cultural heritage,[24] the Imperial Ethiopian Government (IEG) had systematically applied coercion and bribery across the territory long before the controversial dissolution of the Assembly. Opponents were jailed and killed, while others fled to neighboring countries. Many Eritrean elites were cowed into submission.[25]

For Eritrea's Muslim lowlanders complete union with Ethiopia was an uncomfortable proposition, and a quick glance at the makeup of Ethiopia's governing class illustrates why. Of the top twenty-six officials within the Imperial Ethiopian Government in 1973 – ministers, commanders of the armed services, provincial governors – not one was a Muslim. Of the 101 government officials who sat directly below those with major government portfolios – deputy ministers, administrators, division commanders – only three were Muslims.[26] This, by the way, was in a country that was 50 percent Muslim and had more Muslims than every Arab country except for Egypt, Morocco, and Algeria (Woldegiorgis, 1989, p. 73).

The IEG's provincial administration in Eritrea largely reproduced the pro-Christian bias at the center. In 1965, for instance, both the governor-general and his deputy were Christians, as were seven of the eight provincial governors. So were the commissioner of police and his deputy. So were the seven top-ranking military officers in the province. So were all

---

[22] My assessment of this period is drawn from a large literature. See Habteselassie (1980), Gebremedhin (1989), and Iyob (1995). For a somewhat different interpretation see Negash (1997). Perhaps the most controversial moves in this period were the replacement of the Eritrean flag, seal, and coat of arms with those of the Ethiopian crown, and the May 1960 move to introduce Amharic as the official language of the territory.

[23] For a vivid recounting of the vote, see Wrong (2005).

[24] Author's interview, provincial bureaucrat, October 11, 2009. In this and prior discussions the interviewee had provided his recollection of events as early as the 1950s. In any case, these events are a matter of public record. It is also important to note that leading Christian politicians of the era, including Asfaha Weldemichael, Demetrios Gebremariam, and Tedla Bairu, supported the efforts of the IEG in this period.

[25] See Issayas Tesfamariam interview with Nicole Saulsberry, November 7, 2002, www.shabait.com.

[26] See Telegram 51 from Addis Ababa to State, date unclear, RG 59, Central Files 1970–73, "Potential Leaders Biographic Reporting List – 1973-74."

five of the governor-general's cabinet, and both members of his secretariat. One could go on and on.[27]

Given the public face of Ethiopia's administration in Eritrea and its overt discrimination against Muslims, it was no surprise that the rebellion that began in September 1961 found its home in the Muslim communities of western Eritrea.

Jebha as a Coalition in Struggle: Origins and Early Rebellion, 1958–1961

The details surrounding Jebha's precise origins remain somewhat contested, with published works weaving a number of diverging narratives of the group's emergence. Based on previously untapped material, my historical analysis both reinforces and departs from existing histories in ways that are likely discernible only to students of Eritrean and Ethiopian historiography.

Most scholars agree that the organization was formed in Cairo in July 1960 by a collection of Muslim exiles who were disenchanted with Haile Selassie's willful disregard for the Federation and felt that the only reasonable response was armed resistance. Less recognized is that Jebha's founding core was diverse, in terms of social background and ethnic identity. As my theory suggests, what bound this organizing cohort together were the shared security concerns that emerged from their individual commitments to armed struggle. Without collaboration, in the form of a presumably viable organization to which they were all a party, the aspiring revolutionaries would be defeated long before they had built momentum or achieved their goals.

By the late 1950s, the idea of armed resistance had begun to germinate among distinct but overlapping networks of individuals within Eritrea's lowland Muslim political class, both within Eritrea and in its growing diaspora. Cairo was home to 400–500 Muslim Eritrean students to whom the regime of Gamal Abdel Nasser had generously extended scholarships, and soon, a fledgling Eritrean student movement had emerged, imbued with the radical Nasserism and pan-Arab ideology of its Egyptian benefactors.

Set against the emerging radicalism of this community was a growing politics of resistance within Eritrea. Ethiopia's creeping dismemberment of the Federation had generated an underground opposition movement called *Mahber Showate*, or in the lowlands, *Harakat*. The organization's large support base was Eritrea's urban intelligentsia and

---

[27] Statistics computed by the author. Data drawn from Imperial Ethiopian Government, Governate General of Eritrea, Officials List, 1965.

educated classes. By 1960, Harakat could claim nearly 65,000 underground cell members, and a vast network of supporters within the highest rungs of the IEG's Eritrea administration.[28]

Yet Harakat was decidedly secular and nonsectarian in approach, a seemingly admirable quality that would lead to its downfall. While its founding leadership had been Muslims who organized themselves out of Sudan's Red Sea town of Port Sudan, it had successfully absorbed much of Eritrea's Christian community. More importantly, it remained committed to nonviolent resistance. To the ethnically diverse but religiously homogeneous students in Cairo, many of whom had once held pro-Harakat loyalties, such an organization could not be an effective vehicle of national self-determination. What was required was a pan-Arab vanguard, committed to the language of violence, which could wrest Eritrea from the clutches of Haile Selassie and his Christian highland collaborators.

While the Cairo students had no shortage of fervor, they lacked the means to put their project into action. Literally hundreds of miles from the Eritrean heartland, with few strategic assets and little diplomatic support, armed resistance would be a futile endeavor. The students needed allies; more specifically, they required partners that would garner them the international and domestic support necessary to constructing an effective rebel organization.

Into this void stepped Idris Mohammed Adem, a former president of the increasingly handicapped Eritrean Assembly, who had been unceremoniously forced from power in 1956. Increasingly drawn to an openly defiant nationalist stance, Adem had spurned a number of overtures that Haile Selassie had hoped would placate the aggrieved politician. When this strategy proved unsuccessful, the emperor employed the hammer: Adem was deprived of his vehicle and home in the Eritrean capital of Asmara, an action that forced him to retire to his hometown of Agordat.[29] Eventually, fearing for his life, Adem would flee Eritrea in March 1959 with another Muslim nationalist icon of the era, Ibrahim Sultan.

On his arrival in Egypt, the students found Idris Mohammed Adem to be the ideal front man for their organization. To the students, Adem would provide "a presentable, mature face to the Arab world," since

---

[28] It is widely known that Eritrea's chief of police at the time, Tedla Ogbit, was a member of Harakat (Kibreab, 2008, p. 151).

[29] Haile Selassie had invited Idris Mohammed Adem to Addis to take up the post of palace adviser. Absorbing potentially disruptive local elites into the imperial center was a strategy of state building Haile Selassie pursued throughout his tenure. Interview with Idris Mohammed Adem, conducted by Gunter Schroeder, March 15, 1989, Khartoum, Sudan.

he was a known quantity with sufficient stature to attract support in Arab capitals such as Cairo, Riyadh, Damascus, and Baghdad. Standing alone, none of the potentially supportive Arab governments would have taken the youthful students seriously. Sultan was a powerful and highly regarded statesman; he founded the Eritrean Moslem League in 1946 and played a critical role in the emancipation of Eritrea's Tigre serfs. Yet he was older and less radical in disposition than Idris Mohammed Adem. Indeed, in these early days, it was not even clear whether Ibrahim Sultan would fully endorse armed struggle.[30]

Through a series of meetings in 1959 and 1960, the outlines of Jebha began to emerge. A secret discussion was held in a picnic area on the outskirts of Cairo at Jebel Meqattan in late 1959 that gave way to the official announcement of the organization in July of 1960.[31] For Adem, an alliance with the students was a necessary burden. The former president of the Eritrean Assembly was in a difficult position, having fled the country – and his natural support base – in great haste and with little preparation. Under duress, he had navigated his way through Sudan, where the regime at the time did not look fondly on Eritrean dissidents, to find sanctuary in Cairo.[32] Once there, he dealt with a steady stream of threats from Ethiopia's intelligence apparatus. Haile Selassie himself had warned the exiled politician "not to wear himself out standing against the might of Ethiopia," a statement that could only be interpreted by Adem as an all too credible effort in intimidation.[33]

Thus, the uncomfortable uncertainties of exile weighed heavily on Adem's strategy of armed resistance. The exiled politician understood all too well that the support of the students in Cairo and other parts of the Arab world would be critical to getting rebellion off the ground: both as an important source of funding and critical leverage that could be

---

[30] For good biographical details on Sheikh Ibrahim Sultan Ali, please see "Ibrahim Sultan Ali: A Liberator Who Passed Away on Revolution Day 20 Years Ago Today," by Woldeyessus Ammar, which can be found at www.ehrea.org/Ibrahim0Sulta20Ali.pdf (Accessed September 23, 2014).

[31] The official announcement of Jebha's creation was through a newsletter penned by Adem.

[32] At the time, Sudan was led by the military regime of Ibrahim Abboud, who had taken power via coup in 1958. His government was known to arrest Eritrean dissidents and extradite them to Ethiopia. As will be clear, later governments tended to be more tolerant of Eritrean dissidents.

[33] Interview with Idris Mohammed Adem, conducted by Gunter Schroeder, March 15, 1989, Khartoum, Sudan. Other pro-independence politicians, such as Woldeab Woldemariam, fled to Cairo during this period. Woldeab actually survived more than four attempts on his life. Woldeab ran a Tigrinya-language weekly titled *Nai Eritrea Semunawi Gazeta*. Although he was born in Eritrea, Woldeab's family was of Tigrayan origins, a fact that unionist politicians used to slander him during the period of the British Military Administration (BMA). See Issayas Tesfamariam interview with Nicole Saulsberry, November 7, 2002, www.shabait.com.

deployed in lobbying governments in the region. Without foreign backing and the arms it would provide, Adem would be unable to effectively mobilize potential supporters within Eritrea. Meanwhile, Ibrahim Sultan's presence in Cairo created added incentive for Adem to formalize his linkage with the students, as the two were locked in a competition for support among Cairo's Eritrean Muslim community. If Adem failed to attract the allegiance of the students, it would be a missed opportunity that his rival would surely exploit.[34]

The students selected Adem as chairman of the newly minted Jebha and one of their more enigmatic peers, Said Hussein, as a deputy who would serve as key operational commander.[35] A high committee of six students would function as the organization's executive body, and be charged with getting the rebellion off the ground.[36]

Yet Adem recognized that this exile group was not sufficient to launch armed struggle. First, it lacked a direct connection to capable fighting forces on the ground. Second, as a member of the Tigre/Beni Amer tribe that hailed from Eritrea's western lowlands, the exiled politician did not possess ties of kinship to the critically important Muslim constituencies that hailed from Massawa–Hirgigo, an important town nestled at the center of Eritrea's long Red Sea coast. As an ethnic Saho, Said Hussein had links to these communities, but he was young and lacked the stature to fully utilize them.[37] Adem knew cultivating support in coastal areas would be vital to securing any future flow of arms and fighters across the Red Sea from the Arab world.

Adem was able to resolve the first challenge by exploiting ties of kinship among his Beni Amer tribesmen. Idris Hamid Awate, a fiery Beni Amer strongman who had served as an Ascari with the Italians in Rome during World War II, and become well known for his bandit activities

---

[34] The competition between Ibrahim Sultan and Idris Mohammed Adem has been highlighted in the work of Venosa (2011, 2012, 2014), whose analyses hinge on previously unexamined interviews with Ibrahim Sultan, among others. Venosa argues that much of Eritrea's Muslim nationalist camp "was divided along opposing ideological grounds," owing to competing religious traditions in the western lowlands: the first, the Khatimiyya tariqa, a more moderate, Sufi tradition, and the second, Wahabist doctrine supported by King Faisal in Saudi Arabia. Ibrahim Sultan, as leader of the Muslim League (and Harakat sympathizer), subscribed to the former, while Idris Mohammed Adem subscribed to the latter (Venosa, 2011, p. 347).

[35] Said Hussein was a critical figure in these early days, likely owing to some of his training with the Palestinian *Fedayeen*.

[36] This group was responsible for an attack on the Ethiopian Embassy in Cairo in 1960, months before Jebha actually became operational on the ground in Eritrea. Interview with Abdel Karim Ahmed, conducted by Gunter Schroeder, January 7, 1988, Kassala, Sudan.

[37] The Saho area diverse ethnic group that resides in the provinces of Akele Guzai and Semhar, including the Massawa area. The group contains both Muslims and Christians.

during the British period, was to be Adem's key local partner.[38] While Adem and Awate had established a rapport in the years before Adem had left, and even once broached the subject of armed struggle, it was local Beni Amer traditional leaders, whom Adem knew well, who would serve as the broker between the two men and a key initial source of support for Awate.[39]

From Awate's perspective, the link to Adem and the exile community was absolutely essential. As Awate's early communications with his supporters make clear, access to arms and ammunition was a key concern of the Beni Amer strongman. Automatic weapons were of particular interest, given the paucity of such weaponry in Eritrea at the time. Adem's patronage meant that Awate could access the steady corridor of support from the Arab world without which his rebellion would be stillborn.[40]

A more pressing issue for Awate was that he had been prematurely forced into the field by Ethiopia's security services. Organized rebellion requires careful preparation and planning – so that insurgents can acquire arms, cultivate support, and gather intelligence – but Awate did not have this luxury. Realizing that the Beni Amer strongman was on the precipice of rebellion, Ethiopian security forces sought to preempt his efforts by ordering his arrest. Tipped off by collaborators in the area, Awate fled to the remote countryside of western Eritrea.[41] Nonetheless, his home was raided, two wives arrested, and property seized.[42] The

[38] Awate's father was a Nara, a Nilotic ethnic group that resides in the western lowlands. His mother was a Beni Amer, and it is his Beni Amer heritage that was central to his political affiliation. The Beni Amer are a Tigre tribe, all Muslim and pastoral, who reside on both sides of the Eritrean and Sudanese border. Most of the early fighters were drawn from among this tribe.

[39] Idris Adem cites three critical figures: Sheikh Mohamed Ibn Dawud, Sheikh Suleiman Mohammed El-Amin, and Adem's cousin, Sheikh Mohammed Al-Hussein Kelai. Interview with Idris Mohammed Adem, conducted by Gunter Schroeder, March 15, 1989, Khartoum, Sudan.

[40] A particularly good example of Awate's preoccupation with accessing arms is his first interaction with Abdulla Idris, who was only fifteen years old at the time, and would go on to play a key role as Jebha military commander in later years. According to Abdulla, who was serving as a go-between for Awate and Eritrean officers in the Sudanese military, Awate told them "not to send anyone, trained or untrained, before securing for them a piece of equipment [gun], and that he was in need of equipment and ammunition, and that they should secure for him ammunition, especially for the Abu Ashra [M1 rifle]." Interview with Abdulla Idris, conducted by Awate Team, which can be found at www.awate.com/awate-archives-interview-with-abdella-idris/ (Accessed January 10, 2014).

[41] Awate had been tipped off by the police commissioner of Tesseney, Captain Mohamed Saleh Suba, who acted through his subordinate, Kidane Tewedros. Tewedros appears to have been a member of Harakat. Interview, Adem Mohamed Hamid "Gendifel," conducted by Gunter Schroeder, January 7, 1988, Kassala, Sudan.

[42] Interview with Idris Mohammed Adem, conducted by Gunter Schroeder, March 15, 1989, Khartoum, Sudan. According to Adem's recollections, he was frustrated by

simple reality, often missed in conventional narratives of Jebha's early emergence, was that Awate was a man on the run. It was this vulnerability that created scope for cooperation between the fiercely independent local militant and external allies.

The second challenge was resolved by Idris Mohammed Adem's skillful enlistment of Osman Saleh Sabbe, a figure who was to become the most prominent spokesman of the Eritrean nationalist cause in the 1970s. It was in Jeddah, Saudi Arabia, in early 1961, that Adem persuaded Sabbe to join the nascent Jebha movement. As a member of the Saho/Assuarta tribe who hailed from the Massawa–Hirgigo area, Sabbe was Jebha's perfect bridge to Eritrea's coastal regions.[43] Moreover, he had served as a schoolmaster in the Massawa–Hirgigo area for several years, and was thus a known quantity who had developed a vast network of support amongst Massawa's students that could be easily mobilized.[44]

Interestingly, Sabbe was embarking on his own venture in rebellion, which is why he was in Jeddah. Named *Al Urwa al Wutqa* ("the firm bond"), Sabbe's organization was designed to serve as an Ethiopia-wide political platform for uniting Ethiopia and Eritrea's aggrieved Muslims. Like Adem, Awate, and Sultan, Sabbe's activities had attracted the ire of Ethiopian security services. In 1959, under threat of capture, Sabbe was smuggled out of Eritrea by his collaborators, arriving in Yemen by sea. From Yemen, he slipped into Saudi Arabia, where he planned to build support for his new organization.

Yet Sabbe's organizational efforts faced an uphill climb. The Saudis were not keen on his residency within the country, as King Faisal had sought to cultivate the veneer of cordial relations with Emperor Haile Selassie. Sabbe was thus pressured to leave. The government of Pakistan initially seemed willing to accept the beleaguered exile, but on hearing of Adem's overtures, insisted Sabbe join forces with Adem. With

---

Awate's premature departure to the field, hoping that he would wait for equipment and arms.

[43] The Assuarta are a subdivision of the Saho. Some notable sources refer to Sabbe as a "Tigre/Assuarta," which is incorrect. He was not a Tigre.

[44] The evidence for Sabbe's centrality to early Jebha operations is robust. Idris Adem himself later acknowledged that Sabbe's arrival hastened the inclusion of large numbers of recruits from the Massawa area. Moreover, Sabbe was responsible for securing the flow of weapons from across the Red Sea. A key player in Sabbe's strategy of securing arms was Captain Ahmed Sheikh Feres, a close personal friend who also hailed from the Massawa–Hirgigo area. As a trained seaman who captained a variety of commercial vessels in the Red Sea basin, Ahmed Feres was responsible for procuring arms abroad and smuggling them into Eritrea by ship. He would be arrested in 1965 by the IEG, but later escape in 1975. "Eritrea: Ahmed Sheikh Feres' Death Kept Secret for Four Years," which can be found at http://awate.com/eritrea-ahmed-sheikh-feres-death-kept-secret-for-four-years/ (Accessed September 10, 2014).

Sabbe's range of options quickly shrinking, the budding revolutionary chose the path of least resistance – to fold his own efforts into Jebha's larger project of armed struggle. Adem decided that Sabbe would best serve the organization as an external representative in Somalia, where Jebha was allowed to establish its first external office in 1961 under the name of the Eritrean–Ethiopian Friendship Society.[45]

The final element of Jebha's early organization was a collection of Eritrean officers in the Sudanese military who defected to Jebha ranks in late 1961. By the late 1950s, Sudan's armed forces were home to two separate brigades of Eritrean soldiers – based in Kassala and Gedaref. The presence of Eritreans within the Sudanese military was due to the settlement of many of Eritrea's western lowlanders in eastern Sudan, who were drawn across the border for the purposes of education and business. This population, in turn, was viewed by British authorities as a useful pool of recruits since they were presumably independent of domestic political forces within Sudan. Mohammed Idris Haj, Omar Izaz, Abu Tiyara, Tahir Salem, Abu Rijeila, and Adem Gendifel were among this critical batch of fighters who resigned their posts in the Sudanese military to join Jebha ranks, and most of this cohort would make up the backbone of the organization's commander core throughout the 1960s.[46] Many of these soldiers had distinguished records of military service dating back to World War II, and brought with them the critical military expertise that would prove essential in Jebha's early operations.[47]

Many standard accounts of Jebha's early emergence do not treat the contingent of Sudanese–Eritrean soldiers as part of Jebha's initial organizing core. Previously unexamined evidence suggests that this view is incorrect, as it is clear that Adem had absorbed this network into Jebha in the preparatory phase of rebellion. Throughout the 1950s, Eritrean soldiers in the Sudanese military became increasingly drawn into the orbit of Eritrean nationalist politics. As Eritrean Muslims, they were not immune to popular anger directed at Haile Selassie's slow erosion of the Federation. Many of the soldiers that would join Jebha had initially become members of Harakat, which further politicized them. In 1956 they established their own small secret nationalist organization called to advance the Eritrean cause.

[45] Interview with Idris Mohammed Adem, conducted by Gunter Schroeder, March 15, 1989, Khartoum, Sudan.
[46] Interview with Abu Tiyara, conducted by Gunter Schroeder, March 23, 1989, Kassala, Sudan. Interview, Adem Mohammed Hamid "Gendifel," conducted by Gunter Schroeder, February 9, 1991, Kassala, Sudan.
[47] Abu Tiyara had fought with the British against the Germans at the Battle of El-Alamien in 1942.

Yet it was decolonization in the Sudan that truly pushed Eritrean soldiers into the arms of the budding armed nationalist organization. The conclusion of British rule in 1956 was the end of a golden era for Eritrean soldiers in Sudan, as it was followed by fairly transparent efforts by the postcolonial state to Arabize the Sudanese military. Eritrean soldiers soon faced discrimination in promotion and appointments. Some were deployed to fight the emerging insurgency in the swampy, disease-ridden districts of southern Sudan, an assignment that most regarded with dread.

Since many of the disgruntled soldiers were fellow Beni Amer, Adem had carefully maintained relations with this network through much of the late 1950s. In fact, it had been these soldiers who had coordinated his treacherous journey out of Eritrea, through Sudan, and onward to Egypt. For the soldiers, an alliance with Adem was attractive for many of the same reasons that Awate was drawn to the exiled politician. As the soldiers began to consider the prospects of infiltration across the Eritrean-Sudanese frontier, they recognized that an external patron and a steady supply of arms were essential to their early survival. The concern over access to arms was particularly acute given that the soldiers had calculated that they would need to leave the arms and ammunition currently in their possession in Sudan, lest they provoke the wrath of Sudanese officials.

The preceding historical discussion conveys a clear and unalterable reality: from its earliest days, Jebha was a security-based coalition in armed struggle. Of course, there were ideological and identity-based affinities that tied the organizing units of Jebha together. All were driven by the marginalization of Eritrea's Muslims, and most were imbued with the ideological imprint of the radical pan-Arabism of the era. Yet they were a diverse group, in terms of social background, organizational roles, and ethnic affiliation. These differences were put aside in order to forge a unity that would allow them to survive the difficult challenges of armed rebellion.

Adem was the beleaguered exile with the stature to attract the support of Arab governments. The zealous but inexperienced Cairo students were a critical reservoir of popular support through which to raise funds and lobby governments. Sabbe, as a Saho/Assuarta from the Massawa-Hirgigo area, added access to the strategically vital coastal smuggling routes. He was also facing the uncertainties of deportation and his own flailing venture in subversion. Awate and the Sudanese-Eritrean soldiers were to serve as the muscle of the operation, and the essential local link. What they needed were the weapons that only the exile community could provide.

As will become obvious, this coalition would grow and evolve, as would the internal cleavages that structured the organization's politics. Yet as long as the weight of serious security concerns existed, and the organization appeared to retain its viability, intraorganizational cooperation would persist.

From Organizing to Action, from Action to Fragmentation: Jebha, 1961–1967

Almost thirteen months after Jebha formally announced its existence from the distant confines of Cairo, the insurgents went operational within Eritrea. On September 1, 1961, Awate and a band of thirteen of his kinsmen attacked Ethiopian police forces at a place called Mt. Adal, west of the town of Agordat. The attack was a bold, if somewhat inauspicious beginning to armed rebellion. The initial battle lasted for nearly seven hours, despite the fact that between Awate's thirteen kinsmen there were only four guns.[48]

Awate was largely isolated in the rural hinterlands of Barka in the first months of the rebellion, although the beneficence of several Beni Amer elders was critical to his group's survival. After several weeks the Beni Amer strongman encountered a small group of local bandits led by Ibrahim Mohammed Ali, whom Awate successfully pressed into the service of the cause. By early 1962, the group of Eritrean soldiers in Sudan, with great difficulty, had made contact with Awate's mobile contingent and deployed into Eritrea. They were joined by Said Hussein from Cairo, who, as noted before, would serve as the link between the leadership in exile and the fighters in the field.

From Jebha's early beginnings, accessing ever-increasing amounts of territory was central to the organization's strategy of rebellion. Again, this fact is consistent with a key argument of this book: that territory is a key metric of gains and losses for insurgents. The significance of territory was tied to Jebha's belief that access to civilian populations was the only durable basis for the development of organizational resources. The more territory in which Jebha could operate, the more taxes it could levy and the more young men it could recruit. One Jebha officer underlined this logic, explaining that expanding Jebha's operational reach went beyond access to populations:

Of course, territory was important. You must develop contacts with the people. Freedom fighters cannot survive without mobilizing the people and politicizing

---

[48] Drawn from "Hamid Idris Awate: The Spirit of Defiance," which was posted to the Eritrean website www.awate.com.

them. But it went beyond that. Expanding our presence throughout the country also spread out the Ethiopian security forces; it made things harder for them. It was also symbolic, and said to our allies "we are strong and we can win." Not just our internal allies but our international ones too.[49]

Yet Jebha often found that it was not always easy to move from theory to practice. Life was hard for the first group of fighters. Few in number, and lacking adequate armaments, the early Jebha contingents sought to avoid major confrontations with the Ethiopian police and the few army regulars in the province. As one early fighter noted,

We were short of literally everything. We were few in number; carried very few rifles; had no ammunition stock and space for movement was very limited and we had to suspect most people in the villages. For security reasons, we were covering very long distances in a single day, mainly in Barka, Gash, and Setit. We were nowhere and everywhere at the same time... The first three years were terribly difficult.[50]

Where Jebha fighters engaged enemy forces, it was usually in the form of ambushes designed to capture caches of arms and ammunition. For example, during an operation at the end of 1963 Jebha commandos hijacked a bus and drove it into the town of Haicota, where they took the Ethiopian police station by surprise. In the end, the rebels escaped with thirty-two guns and twelve hand grenades. Other, less daring ventures were an ambush of an Ethiopian convoy in Telay in mid-1963, where seventeen guns were captured, and an ambush at Anseba that same year, where twenty-three more guns were seized. Although such early successes seem trivial in retrospect, they were vital to the early survival of the relatively isolated Jebha contingent.[51]

The operational challenges Jebha faced in its early days were compounded by a number of factors. The flow of weapons from abroad,

---

[49] Author's interview, Jebha fighter, September 25, 2009.
[50] See *Eritrean Newsletter*, issue no. 44, September 1981, "Interview with Mohammed Ibrahim Bahdurai."
[51] Much of the discussion of the early operations of the ELF/Jebha is drawn from "From the Experiences of the Eritrean Liberation Army," which was posted to the Eritrean website www.nharnet.com. Another copy of this document can be found at http://snitna.com/From_the_Experiences_of_the_Eritrean_Liberation_Army_ELA.pdf (Accessed October 30, 2017). Most of the information from this document, in turn, is drawn from an Arabic-language book published by Jebha leaders Abdulla Idris and Mohammed Hasab, *Experiences of the ELA: 1961–1981*. For other good accounts see Markakis (1987, pp. 104–145). One should note that both Markakis (1987) and Tareke (2009) dispute the official Jebha accounts, and argue that Idris Awate had no formal links with the external leadership until after the rebellion started. My sources suggest that these views are incorrect.

funneled from sympathetic Arab governments (at this point, mostly Syria) through Idris Mohammed Adem, remained intermittent, largely because the Sudanese government was a reluctant collaborator.[52] Since the early fighters almost all hailed from the western lowlands of Gash, Setit, and Barka, and thus were mostly confined to those zones, land routes via Sudan were the only route of resupply.[53] The organization also suffered some key personnel losses. Awate fell ill and died in May 1962, a secret Jebha did not disclose for three years so as not to cause alarm among its broader network of supporters. Said Hussein had infiltrated the Eritrean capital of Asmara on a clandestine mission, only to be captured and placed in prison, where he would languish for thirteen years.

The losses of these key human assets would cause significant shifts in Jebha's early organization, in ways that would profoundly shape the lines of internal cleavage and competition within the group. Said Hussein's capture, in addition to attrition among student supporters in Cairo, allowed Adem to dissolve the old high council and forge a new, more centralized leadership body called the Supreme Council in mid-1962. This body was effectively run by three people – Adem, who continued on as chairman; Sabbe, who left Mogadishu and joined the leadership in Cairo; and Idris Glawedos, a law graduate who would replace Said Hussein as the operational link to the field. The new Supreme Council was to dominate the affairs of Jebha for the next five years, and was carefully calibrated to maintain representation among three critical geographic constituencies within Eritrea's Muslim community: Adem the Tigre/Beni Amer from Barka; Sabbe the Saho/Assuarta from the coast; and Glawedos, a Tigre/Beit Juk from Eritrea's secondmost populous city, Keren.[54]

Awate's death also prompted changes to leadership in the field. Some of the soldiers who had arrived from Sudan had sought to take over command of the field units in the wake of Awate's death. Abu Tiyara, the steely veteran of El-Amanein, was at the forefront of this effort. Yet as a Tigre/Marya, his claim to leadership caused some unrest among Awate's Beni Amer kinsmen. In December 1962, Sabbe held a meeting

---

[52] According to Sabbe, the first shipment from abroad came from funds raised from Eritreans in Jeddah. The equipment purchased was limited: 5 British rifles, 7 pistols, 500 bullets, and 10 hand grenades. The supplies were moved across Sudan via diplomatic passports provided by Somalia in April 1962. Interview with Osman Saleh Sabbe, conducted with Gunter Schroeder, April 4, 1983, Khartoum, Sudan.

[53] This would of course change when Jebha established itself in the coastal regions of Semhar.

[54] Keren also sits on the very edge of the Christian highlands, and was thus a critical entry point into this densely populated zone.

with the fighters in the field, which at that juncture numbered no more than fifty. It was the first direct consultation between the leadership in exile and the armed units. Sabbe's goal was to resolve existing tension by appointing a new field commander, and in so doing, stamp the Supreme Council's authority over units in the field.[55] Mohammed Idris Haj was appointed field commander and Taher Salem the external coordinator of military activities in Sudan. However, Mohammed Idris Haj would be killed in battle shortly thereafter, paving the way for Abu Tiyara to serve as field commander for a short period. In what must have seemed like an unending game of musical chairs, Abu Tiyara would be replaced by Mohammed Dinai, a Beni Amer, who would run field operations until changes to the structure of the organization in 1965.[56] Obviously, for an organization still in its infancy, the challenge of losing a key leader was incredibly difficult to surmount.

Despite these operational challenges, morale among Jebha's early recruits was high.[57] Not only were the fighters in the early batch deeply committed to the cause but they were also buoyed by the Ethiopian administration's clumsy response to the outbreak of hostilities. Dismissing the rebels as *shifta*, the Ethiopian government decided to deploy only provincial police to deal with the attacks, instead of regular army units who were better equipped to deal with the demands of counterinsurgency (Erlich, 1983, p. 35).[58] Thus, while Jebha's early operational challenges underscored the very real security threat the rebel organization faced, the government's slow response made the organization a perfectly viable enterprise. The combination of threat and viability – as this book suggests – created scope for sustainable intraorganizational cohesion and cooperation.

As Jebha began to make a name for itself among the relatively friendly Muslim communities of the western lowlands, recruitment began to

---

[55] The meeting was held at a place called Bargashish, in the western lowlands. Osman Saleh Sabbe claims that as a Saho/Assuarta from the coast, he was not party to what was an intra-Tigre dispute. He was therefore able to operate as a successful mediator. Interview with Osman Saleh Sabbe, conducted by Gunter Schroeder, December 12, 1980, Khartoum, Sudan.

[56] Interestingly, all of these men were part of the contingent of Sudanese soldiers that defected to Jebha. However, they came from different tribal backgrounds, suggesting that issues of tribal balance were central to the appointment of leaders. Even at this early stage, Jebha's internal politics were a messy, tumultuous affair.

[57] As a general point, nearly all of the Jebha fighters I interviewed revealed themselves to be deeply committed to the cause of Eritrean self-determination. Unlike Renamo or the Tamil Tigers, there was no forced recruitment. Somewhat paradoxically, a movement that suffered from significant episodes of factionalism had a membership that was highly dedicated to the cause.

[58] *Shifta* is the Amharic word for "bandit."

increase. Three groups were particularly important during this phase. The first was another detachment of soldiers from the Sudanese army, who brought with them yet more of the formal military expertise that Jebha desperately needed. A second contingent was a group of Muslim Eritrean policeman who defected to the rebels and brought with them not only technical expertise but also an intimate understanding of the enemy and its strategy.[59] Finally, Jebha would also benefit from the demise of Harakat, which was hastened by a full military altercation between the two groups in May 1965. Having just deployed armed units within Eritrea for the first time in its history, Harakat stood little chance against Jebha's more seasoned complement of Sudanese veterans. The group was quickly destroyed, and over time a few of its members decided to join Jebha's ranks (Kibreab, 2008, pp. 151–152).

By the end of 1963 Jebha had 250 men under arms, and by the end of 1964, they had around 800. Additionally, the leadership in Cairo had achieved ever-increasing success in attracting external aid, particularly from Baathist regimes in Syria and Iraq, which was then funneled to fighters in the field by land and sea.[60]

By 1965, Jebha began to successfully recruit beyond the pastoral communities of the western lowlands. Among the new sectors to join the nationalist organization were urban, predominantly Muslim recruits from the coastal area of Massawa–Hirgigo, and an increasing number of left-leaning Christian students from the highlands. As mentioned before, the former group's inclusion was largely driven by the efforts of the Massawa schoolmaster Osman Saleh Sabbe, as evidenced by the fact that many of these new recruits were his former students. Many within this diverse cohort were given the opportunity to train abroad, in the Arab world, China, and even Cuba, and would become critical players in the factional cataclysms that were to come.

In order to accommodate this new diversity, Jebha sought to reorganize along ethnic and tribal lines in 1965 and 1966. Using Algeria's *Front de Liberation Nationale* (FLN) as a model, the Cairo triumvirate – which had now relocated to Khartoum after running afoul of Egyptian president Gamal Abdel Nasser and a favorable change of regime in Sudan in 1964 – established five zonal commands, in which commanders and recruits from the ethnic and tribal constituencies residing within these zones were given responsibility for operations (Markakis,

---

[59] "From the Experiences of the Eritrean Liberation Army," which was found at www.nharnet.com; and Markakis (1987).
[60] "From the Experiences of the Eritrean Liberation Army," which was found at www.nharnet.com; and Markakis (1987).

1987; Iyob, 1995; Pool, 2001).[61] The fifth zone was created several months after the first four, and was by design dominated by Christian highlanders. Coordinating the activities of these five zones was a newly established body called the Revolutionary Command, based in Kassala and led by Idris Glawedos.

There is probably no decision in Jebha's long history that is as popularly maligned as its choice to establish the zonal commands. Although designed to promote the effective use of local resources while enhancing the operational flexibility of local commanders, Jebha's restructuring effectively tribalized the organization, discouraging coordination across zonal units and undermining the development of solidarity across Jebha's ethnic and tribal groupings.[62] Perhaps more worrying was that the creation of these zones exacerbated tension within the Supreme Council, as Adem, Sabbe, and Glawedos were pulled into patron–client relationships with the zones from which they hailed. Adem was closely tied to the first zone, which was based in Barka and dominated by the Beni Amer. Sabbe was tied to the fourth zone, which encompassed the provinces of Semhar and Danakil, since the former province contained his home town of Massawa. Glawedos was linked to the second division, which had operational control over Senhit and Sahel and included his birthplace of Keren. By contrast, zone 3, which was based in Akele Guzai and dominated by the Saho, lacked an external patron. The same was true of the Christian zone 5, centered in Hamasien and Seraye. As a result of their free-floating status, both these zones became the site of a competition for influence between Adem, Sabbe, and Glaewedos. The bottom line, it would seem, is that the institutional arrangement created new points of conflict within the leadership over the control and distribution of military, economic, and human resources.[63]

[61] Officially, Jebha's leaders had mandated that only 30 percent of each zone's membership would be composed of recruits from outside the zone, but in practice, this policy was ignored.
[62] As implied, there were very compelling reasons for the establishment of zones based on tribe/ethnicity. A major problem, according to one interviewee, was that local communities would generally only provide support to Jebha fighters who were their tribal kinsmen, and to a lesser extent, coreligionists. A particularly poignant example he gave was an occasion where his unit required assistance in carrying a wounded highland Christian fighter to a location for medical treatment. The fighter was named Mebrahtu, which is a common Christian name. Recognizing that the local Muslim community had refused to help carry wounded Christian fighters in the past, they told the locals that his name was Mohammed, which is quite obviously a common Muslim name. The name change worked. Author's interview, Jebha fighter, April 22, 2009.
[63] Gaim Kibreab (2008, p. 154) is exceedingly blunt on this point, arguing that the zones "degenerated into nepotism and patronage similar to mafia-type organizations... military commanders and their patrons in the Supreme Council used recruitment as a means of shoring up their power base and channeling resources to their 'clients' in the field..."

But it was battlefield shifts that were to turn tension into open discord. As growth and internal differentiation progressed, the Ethiopian government became increasingly alarmed. The very limited expansion of Jebha activities into the economically vital highland Christian plateau, which was linked to Jebha's recruiting successes among historically pro-Ethiopian Christian communities and its successful "extortion" of local merchants and wealthy farmers, was a particular cause for concern, and spurred the Ethiopian government to action.

In 1965 Governor-General Asrate Kassa assembled a paramilitary force composed exclusively of Christian Eritreans called Commandis 101. Trained in the latest counterinsurgency techniques at an Israeli-run military academy in the highland town of Dekemhare, the Commandis became a formidable force, consistently bearing the brunt of counterinsurgency responsibilities in the rural parts of the province, while regular military units – comprising mostly soldiers from Ethiopia proper – remained garrisoned in the major towns.[64] The Commandis's close connection with Christian communities in the highlands made them very effective, and their presence rendered it virtually impossible for Jebha to establish a highly effective presence on the highland plateau until 1974 when the monarchy collapsed.[65]

While the emergence of the Commandis signaled that tougher times were on the horizon for Jebha, it was a major Ethiopian Army offensive in March of 1967 that nearly crippled the young insurgency and unleashed an orgy of factional conflict within Jebha's ranks. What the Ethiopians had long treated as a problem of policing now became an issue of full-fledged counterinsurgency. Consistent with this strategic shift, the government redeployed two extra brigades of army regulars to the province, and launched a series of crisp offensives that were as brutal as they were effective. Jebha units acquitted themselves poorly, as the five zonal commands were so decentralized that they were unable to coordinate any meaningful resistance. Attempting to exploit Jebha's organizational weaknesses, the Ethiopians employed infantry, armor, and aerial bombardment to strike and isolate each zone, moving west from the highlands through Gash-Barka, and then northeastward toward Keren

---

[64] Ethiopian efforts to build the Commandis units appear to have grown out of an earlier experiment with Kunama militias. The Kunama are Nilotic, Christian agriculturalists, who live in the fertile plains of Gash-Barka. The Kunama are historical competitors of the Beni Amer, and given the prominence of the Beni Amer in Jebha's early organization, this group became willing counterinsurgents for the IEG.

[65] Airgram 18 from Asmara to State, March 2, 1970, RG 59, Central Files, "Eritrean Commando Police Now at Full Strength." Also, author's interview, Jebha intelligence officer, September 11, 2009.

in an attempt to strangle retreating Jebha units. Confused and bewildered, Jebha cadres fled in a haphazard and disorganized fashion, leaving the predominantly Muslim communities that had given them food and shelter to face government troops that heretofore they had never really encountered in great numbers.[66]

The result was predictable. The Ethiopians created strategic hamlets of 3,000 inhabitants each to cut the rebels off from the population. They burned villages and massacred civilians, causing more than 20,000 civilians to flee to Sudan, the first refugee wave of many that would follow over the course of the next twenty-four years. The discontent among the population was palpable, especially among women. As former Jebha cadre Haile Woldense recalls:

So the first protests came from the mothers. This is very important. The mothers were saying: "We are feeding the fighters while leaving our children hungry. But when the enemy came, rather than at least not be inside to give a pretext for the enemy to burn the village, the worst thing the ELF (Jebha) fighters were doing was they stayed in the villages, fired some shots, and then escaped. And they wouldn't even try to do some fighting so the elderly, the children, and the mothers could get out."

And of course a lot of people went to the Sudan and they were saying that the fighters had not performed well. There was no support. (Connell, 2005, pp. 48–49)

For an organization that had traded on its popular appeal in the western lowlands, this was a devastating development. Yet the poor showing in combat was not all Jebha's fault. The Ethiopian offensive, either by intention or happenstance, coincided with the Six Day Arab–Israeli War of June 1967, in which Jebha's Iraqi and Syrian allies were thoroughly trounced. The result of developments in the Middle East was twofold: not only were Jebha's Arab benefactors no longer in a position to offer the support that they had provided previously but in addition the Israelis were able to close shipping lanes in the Red Sea. Ominously, Jebha was incurring acute shortages of supplies at precisely the moment that they could least afford them.[67]

Even Jebha sources signal that 1967 was a tough year. In an otherwise effusive historical publication, Jebha writers noted that in 1967, "the

---

[66] Fantahun Ayele's (2014, pp. 23–25) history of the Ethiopian military provides an analysis of the campaign, and actually describes it as five distinct operations executed in close sequence.

[67] INR Memo, George C. Denney to Acting Secretary, April 1, 1968, RG 59, Central Files, "Ethiopia: Kagnew and the ELF." Also see Airgram 174, Asmara to State, October 9, 1968, RG 59, Central Files, "The ELF and Kagnew: An Assessment." See also Lefebvre (1996).

very continuation of the revolution was in danger ... Fighters in the field, who had little food and arms supplies, were being overwhelmed with desperation."[68] Detailed American declassified intelligence reports from the period largely echo these observations, noting that Ethiopian military efforts during 1967 had been a "consistent success story" and that Jebha had seen "a loss of momentum." These reports go on to say that, given the success of the 1967 offensive, the Ethiopian military would phase out of the province the majority of army regulars – some 6,000 in all.[69] To Ethiopian authorities, the insurgency in Eritrea had been dealt a severe blow.

In territorial terms, Jebha's losses were significant. On the eve of the offensives of March 1967, Jebha's guerrilla army effectively operated in about half of the country – in Sahel, Barka, Gash-Setit, Seraye, and parts of Hamasein province. After the Ethiopian offensives, Jebha units were forced to operate in a small, largely uninhabited corner of land in northern Sahel bounded by the Sudanese border to the west and the Red Sea to the east. While Jebha had lost popular support and credibility, its territorial losses were crushing. What had been an organization with national scope was now confined to a dusty outpost in a remote, strategically irrelevant district that had more hyenas than people. Figures 3.2 and 3.3 are district-level maps that give an indication of the size of Jebha's territorial losses in 1967.

In the wake of the Ethiopian offensive, the breakdown of credible commitments and cooperation amongst Jebha's membership was almost immediate, and largely played out along sectarian lines.[70] Osman Hishal, deputy commander of zone 5, summarily executed twenty-seven Christians for failing to perform their duties during the Ethiopian offensive.[71] For Hishal, and many Muslim lowlanders like him, the influx of Christians into Jebha raised the prospect of penetration by the Ethiopian authorities. The successful Ethiopian offensive, and the territorial losses it wrought, represented Christian collusion with the Ethiopian government. The uncomfortable reality that Christian highlanders had been the backbone of the unionist camp in the 1940s, 1950s, and 1960s, and prior defections of high-profile Christian fighters in 1965, helped to fuel

---

[68] See Jebha publication the *Eritrean Newsletter*, issue no. 44, September 1981, "Diary of the Revolution."

[69] Airgram 174, Asmara to State, October 9, 1968, RG 59, Central Files, "The ELF and Kagnew: An Assessment."

[70] INR Memo, Thomas Hughes to Secretary, April 8, 1969, RG 59, Central Files, "Ethiopia: ELF takes a Radical Turn" – the memo draws a direct connection between military failures of 1967 and the outbreak of "internecine fighting."

[71] According to Osman Saleh Sabbe, the specific offense was fleeing from the site of an arms store.

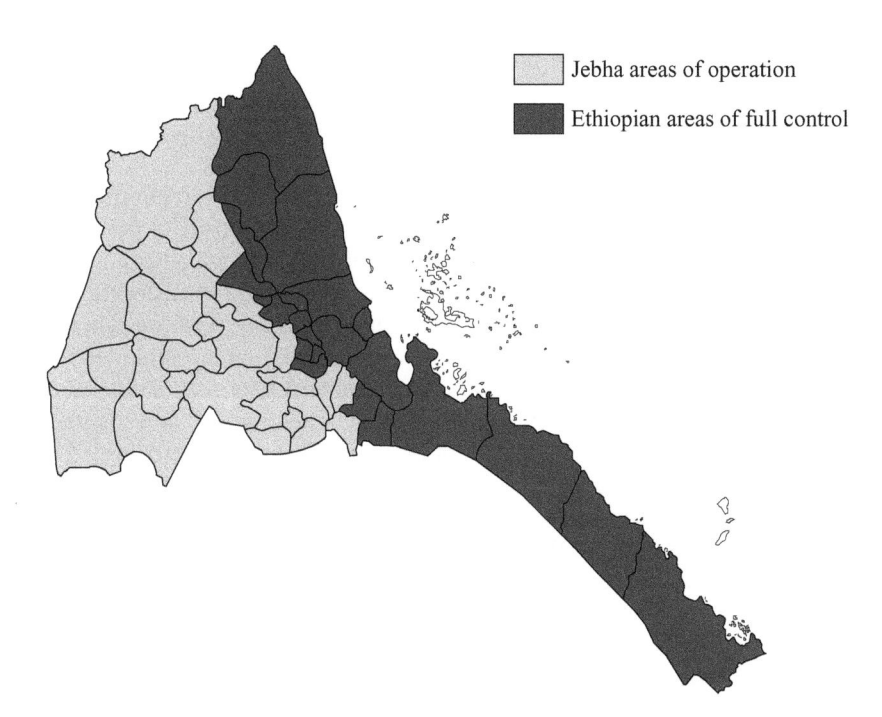

Figure 3.2 Jebha areas of operation, by district, March 1967.

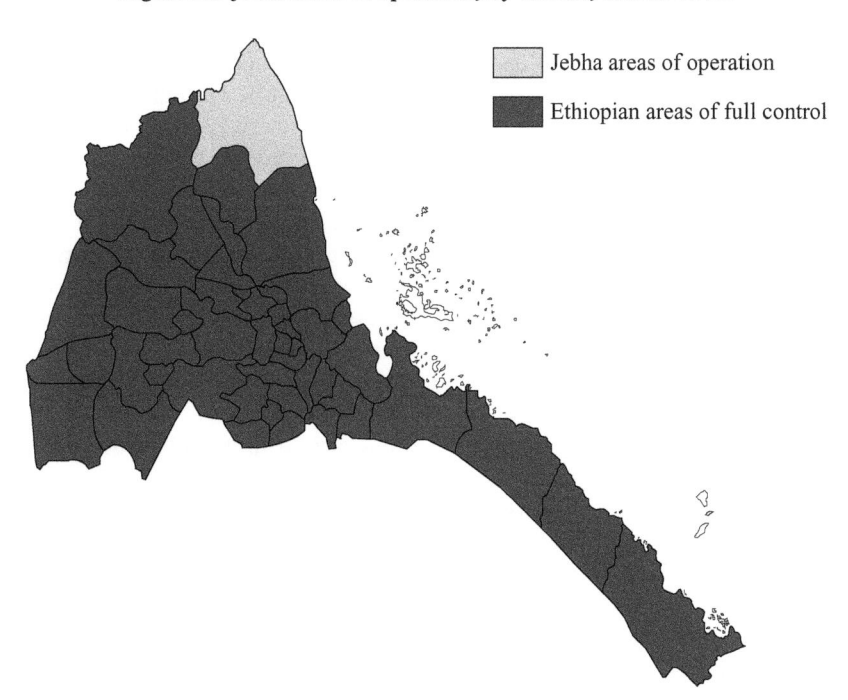

Figure 3.3 Jebha areas of operation, by district, November 1967.

these sentiments. Significantly, the executions were carried out without the approval of the zone's commander, Woldai Kahsai, who himself was a Christian (Markakis, 1987).

The summary executions served as a trigger, as factional conflict diffused to broader sectors of the organization, creating a veritable "cycle of contention." Fearing for his life, Woldai Kahsai, who was in the Sudanese–Eritrean border town of Kassala at the time, took a contingent of Christians and defected to the Ethiopian consulate. For the remaining Christian cadres within zone 5, the defection of their commander was too much to bear. In an effort to build a coalition Christian cadres successfully appealed to many new arrivals from zones 3 and 4, and together these constituencies began to demand reform. Criticisms were leveled at the external leadership in Khartoum, who were accused of absenteeism, at the zonal command structure for lacking coordination and tribalizing the organization, and at the nationalist program for being Arab-centric and tending to exclude Christians. Calls for reform evolved rapidly into open insubordination as units in the field began to make efforts to reorganize independently of the external leadership.

What followed in the months ahead was an incredibly complex set of maneuvers between the external leadership, their supporters in the field, and the reformers, which would yield fragmentation. Since this period is essential to understanding the emergence of Shaebia, a detailed recounting is provided in the next chapter. Politically attuned and ever resourceful, the triumvirate of Adem, Glawedos, and Sabbe attempted to resist reforms that would inevitably reduce their power. What happened next remains a subject of serious disagreement. In a series of meetings in 1968 and 1969 that were designed to reform the organization, the reformist camp appears to have split. Some claim the Supreme Council was able to mobilize support and successfully infiltrate the ranks of the reformers, although this is not entirely clear. Many were purged and killed, even though the leadership made major concessions that ceded real authority to an interim body made up of units in the field. Interestingly, as this process played out, open splits emerged among the external leadership as well.

Indeed, the direct challenge to the Cairo triumvirate's power had driven a wedge between the leaders, as each employed different strategies in dealing with the dissidents and attempted to use the chaos to augment their individual power. For Sabbe, who by now was Jebha's most prolific fundraiser abroad, the leadership's marginalization was too much to bear. In 1969 he broke with the Supreme Council, as his fight for control of the organization appeared to be a losing cause, and created what he called the General Secretariat in Amman, Jordan. At this point, Sabbe actively began to encourage others to defect from Jebha ranks.

In the field, the losers of the factional disputes at the meetings of 1968 and 1969 exited the organization in a bid for self-preservation – much as Sabbe had done. A group of Christians under the direction of Abraham Tewolde set out for the Ala plains in the eastern part of the highlands, while a collection of younger cadres from the Massawa–Hirgigo area, many foreign trained, joined up with Sabbe's network in Sudan and Yemen. Yet another faction led by Adem Saleh of the Beni Amer set off for the Obel River to reorganize. Even a group of Marya tribesmen, led by the veteran Abu Tiyara, was forced to fragment amidst the violent power struggle. It was these diverse and disenchanted elements that would form the nucleus of Shaebia in 1972.[72]

The episode of 1967–68 is telling in many respects. For Hishal, who triggered the factional infighting, Jebha could not go on as it once did. Whereas he and others like him had been willing to cooperate with their Christian comrades in better times, the debacle of 1967 broke down the credible commitments between these groups. The response of the Christians and their allies was primarily a direct reaction to these killings, but in part a recognition that the organization was failing. Their criticisms of the decentralized zonal system were a telling indication of the latter. In any case, once the initial breakdown of cooperation occurred, factional infighting spiraled out of control, diffusing and incorporating broader cross-sections of the organization as the various constituent units of Jebha began to jockey for power in the pursuit of their own interests. For the losers of this factional fight, fragmentation became a survival strategy and the end result.

Although this factional moment was complex, involving a range of decisions and strategic calculations that should be examined more closely, one thing is clear: Jebha's performance failures were a key driver of factional infighting, and one cannot understand the events of 1967 without accounting for the context of territorial loss in which they occurred.

Slow Recovery, Stalemate, and Unity: Jebha, 1969–1973

After the military failures of 1967–68, and the torrent of factional infighting that it produced, Jebha began a slow, halting recovery. Though the Ethiopian offensive had drastically curtailed Jebha's operations in many

---

[72] The preceding four paragraphs are drawn from a range of historical works (Markakis, 1987; Iyob, 1995; Pool, 2001).

parts of the country, in the long term, it had done little to permanently damage the guerrilla army's structure. In addition, supplies from Arab supporters resumed at higher levels in the years after the 1967 Arab–Israeli War, serving to sustain and enhance Jebha's operations (Lefebvre, 1996).

Under the Palestine Liberation Organization's (PLO) advisement, Jebha began to expand its tactical repertoire. Intent on capturing headlines, Jebha destroyed Ethiopian commercial jetliners as far afield as Karachi, Rome, and Frankfurt in 1969 and early 1970. Vital transport routes like the Asmara–Massawa and the Asmara–Tessenei roads became hazardous to travel, as Jebha did its utmost to exact an economic price for Ethiopia's occupation. Foreigners were kidnapped or detained, including the US counselor in Asmara, and in November 1970 the IEG's most senior military commander in the province – Teshome Ergetu – was killed in ambush on the Asmara–Keren road.[73] Jebha activity became so significant that the United States, which had a large signal installation in Asmara, began to worry about the security of more than 2,000 American personnel who operated the facility.[74] Surprised by Jebha's staying power, the Ethiopians declared martial law over the province in 1970, and in 1971 replaced the civilian governor-general with a military man and a known hardliner, General Debebe Hailemariam.

After the 1st National Congress at Arr in 1971, composed of 500 delegates elected by the field units themselves, Jebha reorganized the zonal commands into a more centralized administrative structure.[75] Idris Mohammed Adem was rehabilitated and elected chairman, although he remained abroad and real decision-making authority was vested with senior commanders on the ground. In a conciliatory move, a Christian was appointed as his deputy. With a new, more rational system of command and organization, and between 1,500 and 2,000 trained fighters,

---

[73] Because Jebha had split by this point, it is unclear that they were responsible for all of these attacks. For example, from the American documents, we know that Ali Said Abdella, Mussie Tesfamichael, and Yohannes Sebahtu were all involved in the airplane attacks. However, it is widely known that these individuals would later become part of the leadership of the splinter elements that coalesced into Shaebia in 1972. Furthermore, Erlich (1983) claims that it was dissident factions that killed Teshome Ergetu in 1971. Press clippings from the period reveal that Jebha was often unwilling to claim credit for these attacks. In any case, it was obvious by this point that Jebha, as the major rebel organization in the province, had recovered from the low point of summer 1967.

[74] This was the reason the Americans were writing so many reports about insurgent activities. Scarcely a month went by during this period where dispatches did not indicate fear at the prospect of direct Jebha attack on America assets in the province. However, such attacks never materialized.

[75] This is an important point that should be discussed more. Jebha essentially went from a loose coalitional structure to a highly centralized Leninist organizational structure.

Jebha seemed rejuvenated. Yet despite these new realities, Jebha faced far from a rosy scenario: the splinter groups of 1967–68, despite numerous conciliatory gestures, refused to rejoin. With their hand forced, Jebha leaders attempted to "liquidate" these splinter elements in 1972, declaring in the 1st Congress Political Program that "the Eritrean field can only tolerate one nationalist organization."[76] Despite its resource advantages Jebha was unsuccessful, and instead of directing the balance of its forces against the Ethiopians, began a costly war with its conationalists.[77]

Also of critical importance during this period was the Sudanese closure of overland routes into western Eritrea, and Jebha offices in Kassala and Khartoum. Prompted by Ethiopia's support of a peace agreement that ended the first phase of the Sudanese civil war in 1972, Sudan's actions caused great hardship for Jebha cadres, as Sudan had evolved into a key conduit for Arab arms, a rear base for Jebha's military operations, and home to the now tens of thousands of Eritrean refugees who served as important Jebha supporters. Indeed, Sudan's actions were symptomatic of its wider ambivalence about Jebha, and indicative of the tumultuous relationship it would have with the Eritrean nationalist movement throughout the late 1970s and 1980s.[78]

In any case, the position of the Ethiopian military in the province was simply too strong to be challenged. Backed by their erstwhile American and Israeli supporters, the chance that the Ethiopian military would incur significant losses at the hands of an increasingly bold, but outgunned band of rebels was remote.[79] At the same time, the Ethiopians seemed unable to make any major military breakthrough, if in fact there

---

[76] ELF 1st National Congress Political Program; the term "liquidate" was used by most interviewees, distasteful as it might seem.

[77] See Pool (2001) for the dynamics of this conflict, as well as Markakis (1987). Also, author's interview, Shaebia commander, May 28, 2009 – commander noted that during the 1972–74 war between Jebha and Shaebia, the Ethiopians barely launched any attacks against the rebels, and were largely content to watch the rebels fight among themselves.

[78] Another reason for Sudanese animosity was that in July 1971, the Sudanese Communist Party (SCP) attempted a coup against their onetime ally, President Gaafar Nimeiry. The coup failed, and Nimeiry believed that Jebha had been complicit in the plot. This view was fueled by the fact that a number of Jebha fighters had been members of the SCP, and many SCP members that fled in the wake of the failed coup ended up in Eritrea under Jebha protection. The clear effect of the coup is highlighted by a letter from the senior Jebha cadre, Fessehaye Gebrezghi, to the British Embassy in Khartoum, in which he expresses fear of being deported by the Sudanese to Ethiopia, and British diplomatic support in the matter. The actual letter is enclosed in a British diplomatic cable from Khartoum to Addis, and to the British, constituted "the first direct evidence we have had that the Sudanese are taking action against members of the ELF in the Sudan." See "Eritrean Liberation Front," EJ Anglin, British Embassy Khartoum, to British Embassy Addis Ababa, September 6, 1971, FCO 31/540.

[79] See Lefebvre (1991) for the best and most complete discussion of this support.

was one to be had. American intelligence assessments from the period, in a telling series of memos, describe what can only be interpreted as a stalemated military situation in the early 1970s, noting that the insurgents "lack the ability to win a decisive victory" but that the Ethiopian army had no chance to "break the stalemate without substantially expanding and improving its counter insurgency efforts."[80]

British diplomatic assets in Eritrea seemed to concur with American assessments of the military balance in this period. For instance, in September 1970 officials at the British Embassy in Addis wrote that the situation in Eritrea "showed no signs of dramatic change" and concluded:

> All in all, life in Eritrea continues much as usual and although, over the last couple of months, there has been a fair catalogue of incidents, none of them appears to add up to anything but a temporary high point in the continued fluctuation of ELF terrorism on the one hand and Government reprisals on the other.[81]

Moreover, the following year, when Britain's Deputy Ambassador to Ethiopia visited Asmara and spoke with senior political and military officials in the province, the Ambassador wrote, "The consensus opinion of those to whom I spoke is that now a stalemate exists..." Such evaluations were common fare among British diplomats and security experts through the end of 1973.[82]

Such assessments were reflected in territorial terms. While Jebha had made some initial, very slow recoveries in western Eritrea, and was able operate in Barka, Gash-Setit, and parts of Semhar along the Asmara–Massawa road by 1970, these shifts were a pittance compared to the losses it had incurred in 1967–68. Furthermore, between 1970 and 1973, there was no perceptible change in the territory over which Jebha was able to operate. Interestingly, as this book predicts, this period was characterized by an absence of factional infighting or fragmentation within Jebha ranks, a fact that is more striking when one considers the potentially divisive organizational elections held at Arr in 1971.

In this context, it is clear that territorial stalemate served to underpin cooperation within Jebha ranks. While Jebha cadres and the elites

---

[80] INR Research Study, T. Murphy, May 10, 1973, RG 59, Central Files, "Ethiopia: Eritrean Liberation Front Persists Despite Weakness." The report also went on to say that "the ELF is not likely soon to jeopardize Ethiopian control over Eritrea, but the movement is not dead." See also INR Research Study, A. Palmer, February 24, 1972, RG 59, Central Files, "Ethiopia: Status of Eritrean Liberation Front."

[81] "Eritrean Liberation Front," J. S. Wall, British Embassy Addis Ababa to Hogger, East African Department, Foreign Office, September 30, 1970, FCO 31/540.

[82] "Visit by DA to Asmara," British Embassy Addis Ababa to Foreign Office, June 28, 1971, FCO 31/540.

who led them had reason to believe that the organizational status quo was sustainable, the threat to their collective security remained large. Such fertile conditions for cooperation, however, were about to quickly change.

The Ethiopian Revolution, Gains, and Fragmentation: Jebha, 1974–1977

The Ethiopian Revolution of 1974 substantially altered the dynamics between Jebha and the Ethiopian government. Although not generally appreciated by the literature on Eritrea, the revolution not only transformed the Ethiopian state but also permanently altered the trajectory of the Eritrean cause, putting in motion forces that changed the scope and intensity of nationalist rebellion.

The literature on the Ethiopian Revolution is vast, and it is not necessary to recount all of it here.[83] In short, following a set of army mutinies (the first in Eritrea), a series of strikes in Addis Ababa, and student protests, the monarchy of Haile Selassie was overthrown. A cabal of junior military officers called the Derg, ostensibly Marxists, took power in the chaos of mass upheaval.[84] In many ways, Haile Selassie's ouster was not hard to anticipate. By 1974, he was over eighty years of age, and largely bereft of the guile and charisma that had sustained him in power for decades. Rapid economic modernization had created new social classes and rising expectations for political change among the intelligentsia and the military. A crushing famine in 1972 had deeply damaged the IEG's reputation. The old monarch became increasingly detached from the day-to-day operations of state, leaving a leadership vacuum that loomed large as the first open challenge to the monarchy emerged. Haile Selassie's heir, Crown Prince Asfaw Wossen, had suffered a stroke in 1973 and was largely irrelevant. Meanwhile, palace factionalism among the monarchy's leading ministers undermined any rear-guard action to save the regime. Suffice it to say, the causes of the revolution were deep and complex and the insurgency in Eritrea was only one factor among several.

Somewhat ironically, the military's takeover exacerbated political instability in Addis Ababa, sparking a series of battles between the Derg and the student movement for control of the government, as well as a sequence of major confrontations within the Derg. Under siege by its external and internal opponents, the military became paralyzed

---

[83] For classic analysis of the Ethiopian revolution see Clapham (1990) and Keller (1991).
[84] *Derg* means "committee" in Amharic.

and unable to prosecute the war in Eritrea. By the beginning of January of 1975, classified US diplomatic cables were reporting that "few observers now believe that a military solution is possible in Eritrea. In fact, although we think it premature, many here view Eritrea as already slipping from Ethiopia's grasp."[85]

As the central authorities in Addis began to devour themselves, Jebha managed to strike a tactical alliance with its splinter groups, which by then had been consolidated into Shaebia. The insurgents took the initiative, and began to expand from one district to the next. In early 1975 the nationalist organizations made real breakthroughs, not only penetrating the Christian highland plateau, but attacking the provincial capital of Asmara – Eritrea's largest city and the second-largest urban center in Ethiopia. For three days at the end of January, the city was on fire. In the streets, the rebels fought running battles with government forces.

Although Jebha failed to seize the city, the Asmara raids signaled a major transformation in the direction and scale of the war. The Ethiopian response in the aftermath of the fighting was as tragic as it was consequential. Angry government soldiers went on a rampage, dragging people out of their homes and murdering them. Youths were garroted with piano wire and disappeared. Stores and businesses were looted. The social and political order in Eritrea's cities and towns was beginning to break down.[86]

In the months ahead, terror became the mainstay of the Ethiopian Army in Eritrea. The degree of brutality that the Marxist military regime was willing to apply – particularly on the Christian highland plateau – was like nothing Eritrean civilians had seen during the Haile Selassie era.[87]

That many of Eritrea's youths faced pervasive insecurity in government-controlled urban areas at precisely the time that the government seemed to be teetering on the brink of collapse triggered mass defection to the rebels.[88] While Muslims had always gravitated toward the secessionist movement, Christian youths flocked to Jebha in ways that had never been seen before. In 1975, an organization that was no more than 2,000 people took in nearly 10,000 recruits. The years 1976–77 saw a similar spike in recruitment. Jebha's training camps and

---

[85] Airgram from Addis to State, January 10, 1975, RG 59, Central Files, "Embassy Quarterly Report."
[86] For a systematic accounting of these atrocities see de Waal (1991).
[87] Author's interview, provincial bureaucrat, October 11, 2009.
[88] Goodwin's (2001) comparative analysis of revolutions makes exactly this sort of argument.

infrastructure could barely keep pace with the expansion in numbers.[89] In his memoirs, former Derg Governor of Eritrea Dawit Woldegiorgis (1989) captures the sentiment of the time quite clearly when he writes:

> More men and women fled to join the movements. With indiscriminate death all around, it was either stay and die, or flee and fight. Anywhere from 300 to 800 people slipped out of the cities each month to join the rebels. Only the aged, the sick, the weak, and those with connections to the military in Asmara were left behind. Out of a total population of over 200,000 in 1974, Asmara dwindled to less than 90,000 people in 1977. Many of those remaining spent their nights in the churches for fear that they would be dragged out of their beds and killed by the death squads. The rest of the major towns were also virtually abandoned.

Another individual, who actually made the decision to join Jebha during this tumultuous period, puts it even more succinctly when he says:

> The way the Ethiopians were treating the public provided a good ingredient to leave and join the revolution. They were torturing people; younger people were the main targets, killing them in the streets. So I decided to join the revolution and fight for my country, instead of dying in the streets like my other friends.[90]

Many of the urbanites who joined Jebha during this period were relatively well educated and brought with them valuable technical skills – clerks, accountants, doctors, and mechanics. Heavy equipment and trucks were captured from retreating government forces, a shift in logistics that allowed Jebha to seamlessly transition from guerrilla warfare to conventional combat. By 1977, the two nationalist organizations had captured nearly 90 percent of Eritrea and every major town except Asmara, Barentu, and Massawa, although Jebha controlled only a little more than half of the province. Figures 3.4 and 3.5 visually depict these territorial changes. Combined, Jebha and Shaebia outnumbered the 20,000 Ethiopian combat troops stationed in Eritrea (Connell, 1993). Fortuitously, or perhaps by design, the Somali regime of Siad Barre took the opportunity to wage an offensive of its own against the Ethiopian government, penetrating deep into the Ethiopia's southeastern province of Ogaden. Meanwhile, separate insurgencies had spontaneously appeared in nearly all of Ethiopia's other thirteen provinces. "We were controlling everything," a Jebha fighter remembers. "The Ethiopians were in shock."[91]

---

[89] Author's interviews, Jebha fighters, April 22, 23, and May 3, 2009. Many of these fighters indicated that Jebha officials often asked new recruits to wait before leaving home to join Jebha camps, because the organization simply lacked the capacity to absorb all of them so quickly.
[90] Author's interview, Jebha fighter, April 22, 2009.
[91] Author's interview, Jebha fighter, May 3, 2009.

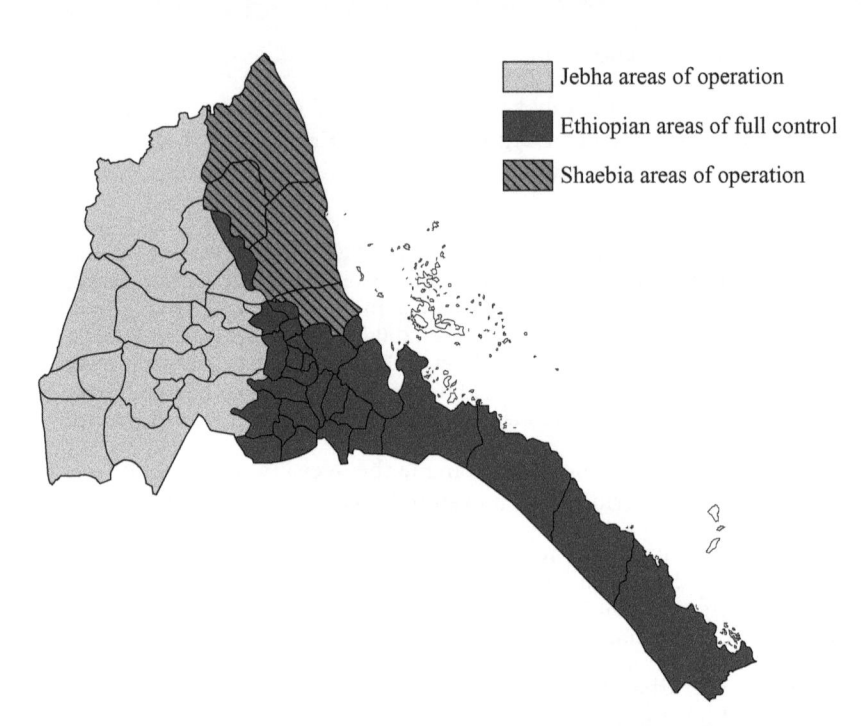

Figure 3.4 Jebha areas of operation, by district, January 1974.

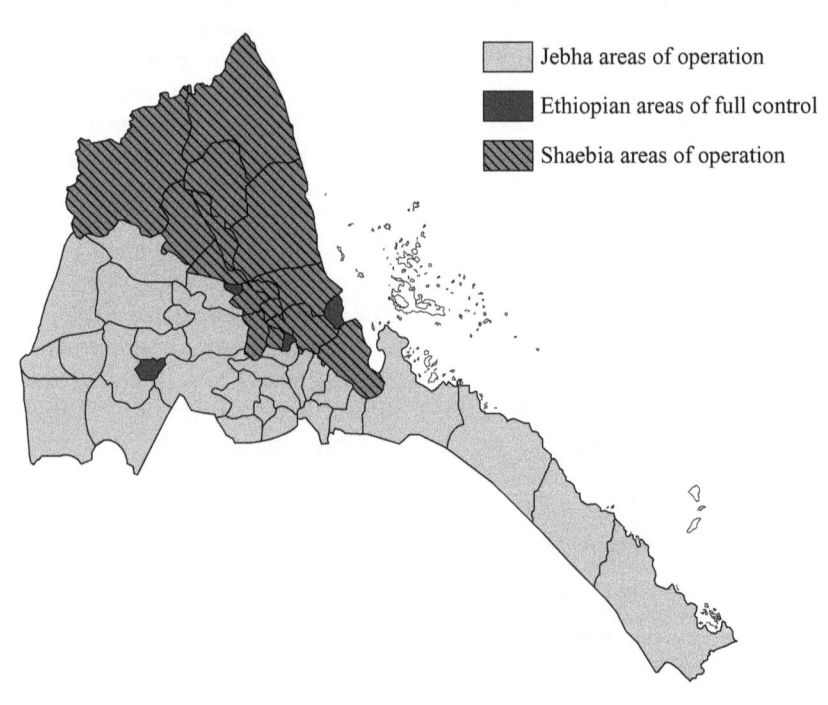

Figure 3.5 Jebha areas of operation, by district, March 1975.

It was ironic that as Jebha was achieving significant territorial gains, it descended into bloody factional infighting. Success seems to have reduced security concerns and driven preference divergence among the organization's various constituent units. The trigger was the 2nd National Congress in May 1975, where Vice-Secretary General Herui Tedla Bairu – an individual popular in Christian circles whose father had been a prominent unionist and former Ethiopian Ambassador to Sweden that later defected to Jebha – lost his post in an election marked by rancor and recrimination.[92] Herui had earned the disfavor of many of the more hardline Muslim elements of the leadership, some of whom were linked to the Iraqi Baathist party, for his overtures to Shaebia on issues of nationalist unity. As vice-chairman of Jebha, and a Christian highlander, Herui had positioned himself as a critical bridge to the disaffected Christians who sat at the core of Shaebia's leadership. As such, he became the main architect of the loose détente that emerged between the nationalist organizations in 1975. Yet this effort was viewed with deep suspicion within Jebha. In the context of ever-increasing nationalist successes, Herui's lowland Muslim detractors believed he was attempting to forge a union between the two nationalist organizations that would augment his power and permanently marginalize Muslim lowlanders within Jebha ranks.

Herui's other problem was that he had been a key cog in a campaign to introduce rigorous political education into Jebha ranks. Given the ideological ferment of the times, "political education" meant training in socialist and Marxist theory. Herui had pushed this program not out of deep ideological conviction, but because the organization's Shaebia rivals were heavily promoting themselves as socialists, and were slowly emerging as the more politically "sophisticated" of the two movements to the new generation of relatively well-educated Christian and urban recruits who were flooding the nationalist camp.[93] Yet Jebha's Muslim old guard, particularly the Tigre tribesmen from the western lowlands, regarded Marxism as anathema to their deeply held conservative religious beliefs. Herui's turn to political education, in their view, constituted a direct threat to the Islamic, historically pan-Arab character of the movement.[94]

---

[92] Author's interview, Jebha fighter, June 10, 2009.
[93] There were other senior Jebha officials who backed this effort, many of whom had links to the Sudanese Communist party. Ibrahim Totil, who was of the Nara tribe, and Azien Yassin are two commonly cited figures. It should be said, however, that these two figures retained their leadership positions after the 1975 congress that ousted Herui.
[94] Author's interview, journalist who was in communication with Jebha leaders in the 1970s and 1980s and conducted multiple field visits, September 4, 2014.

With the prodding (and perhaps threats) of the Iraqi representative at Jebha's 2nd National Congress, Abu Ala, Jebha's leadership organs voted Herui out of power.[95] Herui himself claimed that the whole process was rigged, arguing that ballots were thrown out and that the elections should have been direct instead of tiered, as had been the case during the organizational elections of 1971. Interestingly, many of the actors that sought to oust Herui from the leadership in 1975 as Jebha was surging had been among those who supported his candidacy in 1971 in the hope that he could attract Christian support.[96] The incentives to cooperate seemed to have changed.

Added to this combustible mix was the issue of the political status of the thousands of new, mainly Christian recruits who were swelling Jebha's ranks. By this point, most of these recruits were in three major training camps in Jebha rear bases in Barka, and were demanding that they be given equal representation at the Congress and allowed to elect delegates. Yet many in the leadership argued that as newcomers, these recruits should not be granted equal voting status with older, mostly Muslim members. In the end, the votes of these new recruits were counted at one-third of those of older members. While substantially affecting the outcome of the 1975 elections, the feeling that Christian influence was being deliberately limited was widespread. Christians now recognized that they were a majority within Jebha ranks, but believed their power did not correspond with their large numbers.[97]

Voted out of power, Herui was upset. His critics paid him no heed, accusing him of being a sore loser. The elections, they asserted, had been fair, and Herui had simply become unpopular. Moreover, they argued that the rotation of leaders was an emerging trend within Jebha that needed to be cultivated. In these same elections, Chairman Idris Mohammed Adem had himself been replaced by Ahmed Nasser, a young left-leaning former student many considered to be a compromise candidate between the Muslim hardliners and left-leaning Christian cadres.[98] Had Herui let the issue rest, the conflagration that was to

---

[95] Author's interview, Jebha intelligence officer, September 11, 2009. Also see Medhanie (1986).
[96] Author's interview, Jebha intelligence officer, May 19 and September 11, 2009.
[97] This view was further fueled by the fact that the 2nd National Congress yielded a leadership body in which Christians were a clear minority. By this time, Jebha had two primary leadership bodies: the Revolutionary Council and the Executive Council. In the former, only thirteen of forty-one were Christian highlanders. In the latter, only three of nine were highlanders. Interview with Herui Tedla Bairu, conducted by Gunter Schroeder, December 24, 1980, Khartoum, Sudan.
[98] Beyond his ideological leanings, Nasser was also considered a compromise candidate because he was a Saho Assuarta who had been educated in the Asmara area, and thus while a Muslim, had no real link to the old guard western lowlanders who had historically dominated the organization. Author's interview, journalist who was in close

come may have been averted.[99] Instead, he went to the training camps and sought to mobilize support among Christian cadres, accusing the leadership of willfully trying to suppress Christian aspirations. He also dispatched loyal cadres to various units to drum up and coordinate support. Facing severe sanctions from the Jebha's Central Committee, Herui fled to Sudan and founded a new group called the Eritrean Democratic Movement (EDM), or *Magu*. According to one Jebha fighter Herui's decision to splinter was the unambiguous result of a stark choice: "He could either leave or be imprisoned. That was the situation. His actions after the election, with the playing of the religious card, had crossed a red line. The leadership had no appetite for reconciliation."[100] As this book has suggested, Herui's fragmentation was a second-order effect of a power struggle that he had lost. Fragmentation was pure survival.[101]

As theorized in the previous chapter, Herui's actions generated a cycle of contention, as factional infighting rapidly spread to other sectors of the organization not involved in the original dispute.[102] Responding directly to Herui's departure, Christian fighters in the field began to challenge the leadership on a whole range of issues. Chief among these was the relationship between Jebha and Shaebia and the issue of nationalist unity, which many Christian members deeply desired.[103] The agitation, with the support of several Christians in the leadership organs of Jebha, rapidly spread through several units, forcing the leadership to hold open seminars to defend their policies.[104] This was to no avail, as truculent

communication with Jebha leaders in the 1970s and 1980s and conducted multiple field visits, September 4, 2014.

[99] Herui Tedla Bairu himself referred to Nasser as a "second-rank cadre." In his view, Nasser held no real power. Instead, he was a front man for an organization dominated by Abdulla Idris, a Beni Amer executive committee member who by this time headed the all-powerful military committee. Fairly or not, Abdulla Idris is viewed as a key player in blocking Christian aspirations within Jebha. Interview with Herui Tedla Bairu, conducted by Gunter Schroeder, December 24, 1980, Khartoum, Sudan.

[100] Author's interview, Jebha intelligence officer, December 12, 2009.

[101] Although his statements must be interpreted with some caution, Sabbe generally confirms this paragraph's depiction of the origins of the 1975–76 internal crisis. Interview with Osman Saleh Sabbe, conducted by Gunter Schroeder, January 16, 1985, Khartoum, Sudan.

[102] Herui himself acknowledges his role in sparking this infighting. See Saleh A. Younis interview with H. Tedla Bairu, January 1, 2001, which was found at www.awate.com.

[103] As alluded to earlier, Shaebia had a large Christian base, and many, if not most, of its core leaders were Christian highlanders. Many of Jebha's Christian cadres were thus sympathetic to Shaebia. The issue of unity between the two fronts was put front and center by events in 1975–76 that will be discussed more in the following chapter. A unity agreement between the two fronts brokered by Osman Saleh Sabbe – by this time part of Shaebia – had collapsed. Sabbe's forces broke with Shaebia, and began coordinating its activities with Jebha. Since Sabbe was perceived as a Muslim conservative, this enraged many of the Christian fighters.

[104] According to Markakis (1987, p. 288) these leaders were Christian members of the revolutionary council – Fisseha Gebremichael, Tareke Beraki, and Ande Gebremichael.

fighters demanded a fresh Congress to debate many of the major policy issues Jebha now faced, and published a manifesto formally declaring themselves the "Revolutionary Democrats." Exemplifying the wide division that was now emerging within Jebha ranks, opponents of the insurrectionists responded by giving them the pejorative title of *Fallul*.[105]

By the summer of 1977, as Jebha seized major towns like Adi Keih, Agordat, and Mendefera, Fallul had become open insubordination. The leadership embarked on a clear effort to isolate and contain the emerging wave of dissension, including cutting off supplies to disorderly units and reassigning troublesome fighters. When this failed to stem Fallul's activity, Chairman Ahmed Nasser and military chief Abdulla Idris decided to take lethal action against the rowdy elements, launching an attack on the primary unit dominated by Fallul members, Brigade 149. By July 1977, Brigade 149 was deployed in the area of Tekreret, not far from Agordat in Barka province. The group's leaders were operating under the assumption that they would shortly meet with Jebha leaders to find a resolution to their concerns. Instead, Jebha's leadership surrounded the brigade and attacked, in what Gaim Kibreab (2008, p. 303) calls an act of "cold and unprovoked murder." A number of Christian cadres were killed. In the ensuing chaos, the military committee, headed by Abdulla Idris and dominated by Beni Amer, executed eleven survivors, in what was widely interpreted as a sectarian slaughter. More executions would likely have taken place were it not for the intervention of the head of the internal security committee, Melake Tekle, a Christian highlander. More than 800 survivors were then detained and tortured, some of whom would be convicted of insubordination and languish in Jebha prison camps for years. An additional fifteen Jebha senior cadres associated with Fallul were arrested, and suffered a similar fate.

The attack on Brigade 149 reverberated through the organization. However, it failed to resolve the situation, as by this late hour Fallul had mushroomed into a much larger phenomenon. In response, Fallul killed two members of the leadership in an ambush in Danakil – Abdul Kadir Ramadan and Ali Mohammed Ibrahim.

All-out war ensued, yet, outmaneuvered and unable to mobilize a critical mass of support, Fallul's play for power largely failed. The central problem was that key Christian commanders like Seyoum Ogbemichael had refused to support the dissidents.[106] Facing complete destruction at the hands of the leadership and its supporters, the scattered Fallul elements fled to the Ala plains. Surrounded by both Jebha and Shaebia

---

[105] *Fallul* is the Tigrinya word for "anarchists."
[106] In fact, it was Seyoum Ogbemichael who coined the well-known jibe against Fallul, "Learn your ABCs, Fallul, and return to the battlefield."

forces, they defected to Shaebia in the summer of 1977 largely out of desperation, nearly 2,000 in all.[107] Fragmentation, in this case, was a clear bid for survival.

The Fallul uprising had important, if somewhat unexpected, ripple effects as contention diffused further. A group of old-line Muslim conservatives began to organize a countermovement to Fallul and a leadership that was believed to have done little to properly contain it. The group, later given the title *Yemin*, was led by Said Hussein, one of the original Cairo founders of Jebha, who had the bad luck of being captured by Ethiopian security forces in 1963–64.[108] Said Hussein was finally freed during Jebha's Sembel and Adi Quala prison break operations in 1975. On returning to Jebha ranks, he was stunned by the altered character of the movement – the Cairo triumvirate was gone, the pan-Arab tilt of the organization had been minimized, and the leadership and rank-and-file were increasingly dominated by a growing number of Christians. The emergence of Fallul was an alarming indication of what Jebha's future orientation might look like, and provoked Said Hussein and his sympathizers to action.

The dissident movement actually began as a clandestine effort within Jebha, yet the need to survive would soon trigger Yemin's fragmentation. A key figure within the group was the aforementioned Ibrahim Idris, son of now former chairman and Jebha founder Idris Mohammed Adem. Ibrahim and his collaborating network were arrested by Jebha internal security in 1978, a fact that caused Said Hussein and others to seek an exit strategy that would allow them to confront Jebha's leadership from the outside. With the internal network crumbling, clandestine resistance within Jebha would now prove impossible.[109] As an ethnic Saho, Said Hussein was able to obtain the active support of his coethnic, Osman Saleh Sabbe, who by now was at odds with both Jebha and Shaebia. With Sabbe's assistance, the Yemin trekked across the border to Sudan, where they were then taken by boat to Yemen. Sabbe provided arms and ammunition, and the group crossed the Red Sea in an effort to link up with sympathizers in the Danakil and overthrow Jebha's leadership.[110]

---

[107] Most of the information in the preceding five paragraphs is drawn from author's interview, Jebha intelligence officer, May 19 and September 11, 2009, and Saleh Younis interview with H. Tedla Bairu, dated January 1, 2001, and posted at the website www.awate.com (Accessed October 25, 2009). See also Markakis (1987) and Medhanie (1986).

[108] There was a dissident movement of the same name in Shaebia. It will be discussed in the following chapter. *Yemin* means "rightists" in Tigrinya.

[109] Ibrahim Idris, and collaborators like Hamed Turki and Mohammed Ismail Abdu, were subjected to severe torture. Interview with Mohammed Said Nawud, conducted by Gunter Schroeder, July 28, 1986, Khartoum, Sudan.

[110] Yemin was also known as the "*Minifere* rebels." The Minifere are a Saho tribe, and all of Yemin's members were drawn from it. Kibreab (2008, p. 307) argues that it is possible

According to Ahmed Nasser, Jebha chairman at the time, Yemin's subterfuge was no small affair: "The reactionary groups dropped north of Assab and had been in the possession of thousands of individual arms, 36 wireless communication sets and supplies that would suffice them for months in addition to the great sums of money they brought with them in order to bribe the citizens." It seems Fallul had triggered a countermovement whose size and scale rivaled the initial factional rupture.

Fortunately for the leadership, Jebha security forces had managed to infiltrate Yemin. Part of the reason that the dissidents had chosen to enter Eritrea through the Danakil was that they had been coordinating their activities with Ali Isaq, an Afar member of the leadership. Afar clans, of course, dominate the Danakil. Ali Isaq, however, became a turncoat, and informed Jebha's leadership about the looming putsch.[111] As a result, Yemin was intercepted on arrival in Danakil in mid-1978. If there were any doubts about the survival concerns that had motivated Yemin's initial fragmentation, their treatment on eventual capture laid such questions to rest. To a man, the group and its leaders were summarily executed by Jebha forces, in what one of its chief organizers abroad, Mohammed Said Nawud, dubbed an act of "crime." Jebha chairman Ahmed Nasser later confirmed that Jebha sought no compromise with the Yemin dissidents, noting that they had been a "reactionary project" and that Jebha had responded "by resolutely liquidating these elements on May 22, 1978."[112]

The EDM and Fallul episode is instructive. That Herui Tedla Bairu – and by extension some of the Christian interests he represented – was deliberately excluded from the leadership in 1975 by those who had been eager to include him in 1971 raises many questions. What changed? As Jebha began to make serious gains in 1975, the pro-Baathist elements in the leadership saw little incentive to maintain the cooperative status quo. At the same time, Herui was becoming increasingly aggressive on the issue of unity with Shaebia and took steps (including holding private meetings with Shaebia leaders) that many hardliners could not countenance.[113] It was pure preference divergence.

---

that Said Hussein was moved by Saho grievances rather than religious motives; also see interview with Mohammed Said Nawud, conducted by Gunter Schroeder, July 7, 1986, Khartoum, Sudan.

[111] Interview with Mohammed Said Nawud, conducted by Gunter Schroeder, July 7, 1986, Khartoum, Sudan, and Kibreab (2008, pp. 305–309).

[112] Quotes drawn from interview with Ahmed Nasser in *ELF Information Bulletin*, Vol. 3, No. 1, June-August 1978, which can be found at www.ehrea.org/responses.htm (Accessed October 29, 2017). Also see "Ten Fighters Executed in the Dankalia," which can be found at www.ehrea.org/ExecutedDankalia.htm (Accessed October 29, 2017).

[113] Author's interview, Jebha intelligence officer, May 19 and September 11, 2009.

For others who were later dragged into the dispute, brinkmanship and provocation had different sources. Fallul was a direct response to Herui's departure, as its Christian members saw an opportunity to challenge a leadership that was increasingly seeking to marginalize them. Yemin, in turn, was a direct response to the threat that Fallul's mobilization posed to conservative Muslim elements within Jebha ranks. After the initial rupture between Herui and the Baathists within Jebha's leadership, factional infighting and fragmentation diffused to other sectors of the organization, and in this case led to multiple splinter factions.

Nearly twenty-five years later, Herui himself summed up the core dynamic of my theoretical argument best, commenting that "the first error was made, I believe, when we did not assess our situation properly. We were slightly blinded; we were victims of our own success."[114]

As the war went, so went cooperation.

Soviet Intervention, the Shaebia Defeat, and Fragmentation: 1977–1982

By the beginning of 1978, the high tide of the Eritrean nationalist victories was beginning to recede. Two factors were decisive in this reversal. The first was that after a massive upheaval of the Ethiopian revolution, the Ethiopian state began to gain some coherence. Factional infighting and a brutal series of purges within the Derg had led to the emergence of Major Mengistu Hailemariam as the unquestioned leader of Ethiopia. Leftist movements like the Ethiopian People's Revolutionary Party (EPRP) and MEISON, which had challenged the Derg's power in Addis Ababa, were wiped out in a notoriously bloody campaign called "The Red Terror." Between 1976 and 1978, more than 10,000 opponents of Mengistu and the Derg – mostly students and young professionals – were killed (de Waal, 1991, p. 101).

The other important issue was massive communist bloc military and economic support. Believing that Ethiopia's existing patron, the United States, was unwilling to provide the necessary armaments the Derg required in prosecuting both a war in Eritrea and deterring a Somali invasion, the Derg slowly began to cultivate a relationship with the

---

[114] Saleh Younis interview with H. Tedla Bairu, January 1, 2001, which was found at www.awate.com (Accessed October 25, 2009). To be clear, while Herui would agree that Jebha's success was central to its fragmentation, his comments in this interview also suggest that the absorption of new recruits was the fundamental causal mechanism. I agree that it was important issue in the context of the 1975 crisis, although that does not invalidate my claim about the importance of territorial exchange in this context or more generally.

Soviets in 1975.[115] Indeed, American diplomats had repeatedly told Ethiopia's leaders throughout the 1960s that their Military Assistance Program (MAP) to Ethiopia would involve the full outfitting of a 40,000-man army, and no more. American reluctance to up the ante is probably why the Haile Selassie regime scrapped a program of national conscription even though the size of its armed forces was believed to be insufficient to counter existing security threats.

Negotiations were stop-and-start, but Soviet support came online after Mengistu's state visit to Moscow and the signing of a military cooperation agreement on December 14, 1976. The first real effects of Soviet military support were seen during the Somali invasion of the Ogaden in 1977. After the seizure of nearly the entire province of Ogaden and the major regional hub of Jigjiga by Somali forces, the Ethiopians, with Soviet and communist allies, began to turn the tide. The intervention of communist forces could not have come at a more important time, as Somali forces were less than 200 kilometers from the Ethiopian capital, Addis Ababa. By March 1978, Jigjiga had been retaken and Somali forces were in full retreat.

Westad's (2007, pp. 276–277) authoritative account describes the overwhelming scale of the communist bloc intervention in Ethiopia:

Via an air bridge starting in September 1977 and lasting for the following eight months, the Soviets sent more than $1 billion worth of military equipment. In late September two South Yemeni armored battalions arrived to take part in the fighting. Fidel Castro sent 11,600 Cuban soldiers and more than 6,000 advisers and technical experts, who were crucial in defeating the Somalian advance. Most spectacularly of all, almost one thousand Soviet military personnel went to Ethiopia in 1977–78 to help organize the counter-offensive. By early 1978, when the tide of the war turned in favor of the Mengistu regime, General of the Army Vasilii I Petrov, deputy commander of USSR ground forces, was in charge of Ethiopian military planning. Altogether, it was the most important Soviet-led military operation outside the area of the Warsaw Pact since the Korean War.

With the defeat of the Somali invasion, the Derg and its new communist bloc allies turned toward Eritrea, which by now was effectively controlled by the combined forces of Jebha and Shaebia.[116] The offensive, anticipated by British intelligence, kicked into gear in May of 1978. Using a newly constructed airbase in the city of Mekele, the Ethiopian

---

[115] Stephen R. David (1991) makes exactly this point in using the Derg's Ethiopia as a key case of what he calls "omni-balancing," where states ally with foreign patrons in order to balance not only against external threats but also against domestic challengers.

[116] Believing the Eritrean nationalist forces to be leftist in orientation, Castro and the Cubans refused to participate.

air force began a campaign of saturation bombing (de Waal, 1991, p. 113). Many of the sorties were run by Soviet, South Yemeni, and Libyan pilots. In July a ground offensive began, and proceeded northward in three prongs from the adjoining province of Tigray. Jebha, which controlled a corridor of territory stretching the entire length of Eritrea's southern border, was left exposed. In the face of a greater number of well-equipped troops, newly fitted armored columns, and improved air support, Jebha had no chance against the Ethiopian offensive. Badly mauled, Jebha was forced into full retreat. "The Ethiopians were using new weapons," a Jebha fighter recalled. "We had to adjust."[117]

The "adjustment" that Jebha chose to pursue was to accompany Shaebia in its withdrawal to its Sahel base area, where the mountainous terrain would allow the rebel organizations to mount a last stand and neutralize the advantages of Ethiopia's mechanized forces.

The virtual encampment of Jebha forces with Shaebia in the latter's remote base area in northern Eritrea was the high-water mark of cooperation between the two nationalist rebel organizations. A series of meetings and agreements between the leadership of the two organizations in 1977 presaged this development, and laid the basis for joint leadership bodies that could coordinate affairs not only in the military realm but in the political, economic, and social realms as well.[118] Between 1979 and 1980, the combined forces of Jebha and Shaebia stifled three separate Ethiopian attempts to seize the Sahel base area, creating a virtual stalemate in the Eritrean theatre that the Derg was unable to break.

But the relationship between the two rebel organizations was beset by problems from the outset. The retreat of the Ethiopian state in the mid-1970s created friction over what territories each respective group would occupy. Shaebia's seizure of Keren, Eritrea's second-largest city and a vital artery to the western lowlands, was regarded as a serious breach by Jebha's leaders. At El Abared, a valuable agricultural plant that employed thousands of workers in the Eritrean highlands, surrounding Jebha and Shaebia forces were at a standoff as neither side could agree on how the resources from the plant would be divided. The uneasy standoff was broken when Shaebia forces unilaterally attacked the plant and seized it, much to Jebha's chagrin.[119]

---

[117] Author's interview, Jebha fighter, May 3, 2009.
[118] See the "Hawashait Communique" of May 31, 1977, the "ELF-EPLF Unity Statement" of October 20, 1977, and the "Khartoum Unity Statement" of January 21, 1979.
[119] Author's interviews, Shaebia clandestine operative who was stationed within plant, December 2009 January 2010.

Further tensions emerged from efforts, under the auspices of Ethiopian allies East Germany and the Soviet Union, to broker a peace agreement with the Eritrean rebel organizations. Secret negotiations (which were not that secret) were held with Jebha and Shaebia leaders separately, fueling rumors and mutual suspicion between the two nationalist fronts that the other would make a separate peace with the Ethiopians at the expense of their conationalists. When Shaebia units accused Jebha forces of allowing Ethiopian troops to penetrate rebel defenses in Sahel unmolested in the summer of 1980, and seize the key border depot of Karora, the writing was on the wall (Pateman, 1990a, pp. 137–138).[120]

In August 1980, Shaebia attacked Jebha forces in Sahel. A Jebha cadre who was wounded in the fighting confirmed that it was Shaebia who began hostilities, noting, "I took the first bullet."[121] Despite cool relations, Jebha was taken by surprise. By early 1982, Jebha had been completely driven out of Eritrea, and was situated in three major encampments in adjoining areas of Sudan: the villages of Karakon, Tadai, and Rasai. This loss of territory is depicted in Figures 3.6 and 3.7.

The result of the fighting was a devastating development for an organization that had started the nationalist struggle and been its standard bearer for years. How had Jebha come to a situation in which its much smaller offspring was able to militarily expel it from the Eritrean field?

First, it was not clear that Jebha was the numerically superior organization by 1980. By virtue of its pro-Christian tilt, Shaebia was able to make relatively larger territorial gains on the strategic and densely populated Christian plateau. Since young recruits made decisions about which rebel organization to join based almost entirely on who was operating in their area, this meant that Shaebia grew more rapidly. This was particularly the case when the nationalist fronts began seizing Eritrea's major urban centers in 1977.

The second issue was the complete breakdown of military discipline within Jebha ranks. The departure of Fallul in 1977 weakened Jebha while augmenting Shaebia's capabilities. It also began to create a permissive culture in which military hierarchy became increasingly meaningless. "In the EPLF [Shaebia], if someone gave an order it was accepted by subordinates. In the ELF [Jebha], that order was debated," a Jebha

---

[120] For other work by Pateman, see Pateman (1990b).
[121] Author's interview, Jebha fighter, June 10, 2009. Fighter was held in Shaebia prisons for more than a year. Shaebia has never really provided a compelling story about why the fighting in Sahel began.

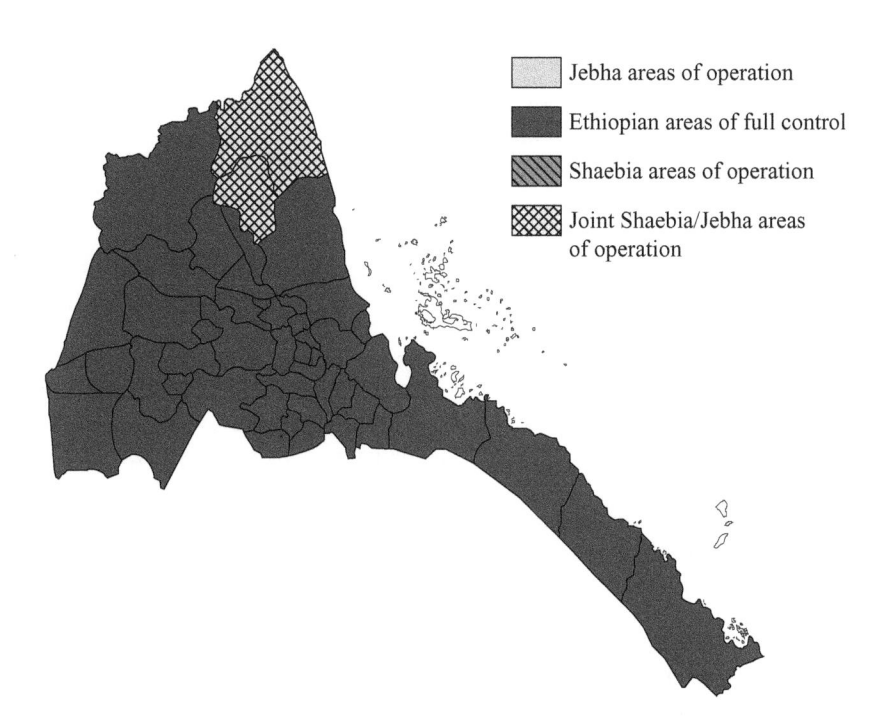

Figure 3.6 Jebha areas of operation, by district, January 1981.

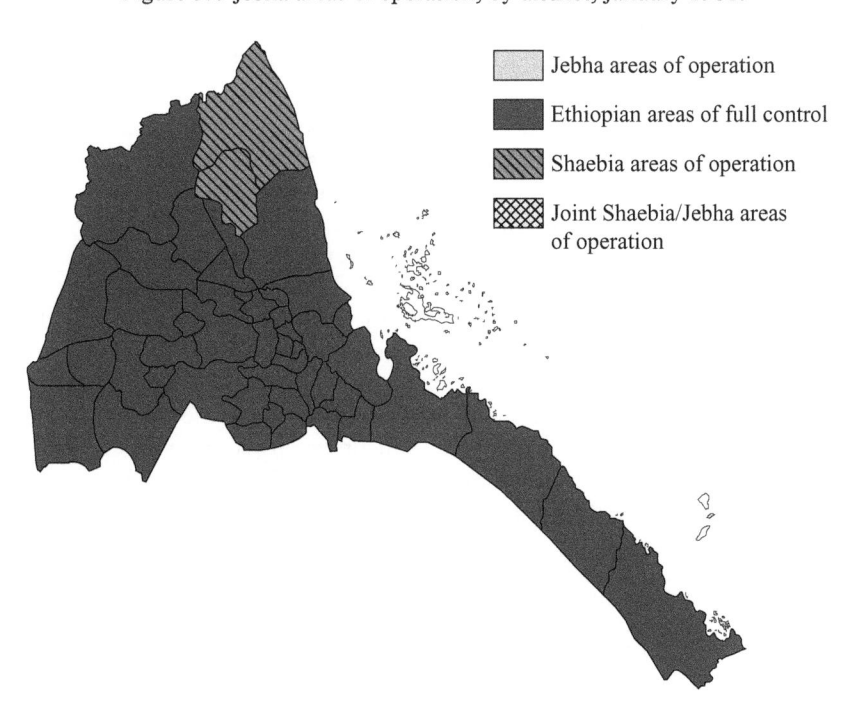

Figure 3.7 Jebha areas of operation, by district, March 1982.

intelligence officer remembered.[122] "You could say anything you wanted," a rank-and-file Jebha fighter confirmed.[123]

The breakdown of military discipline – which undermined Jebha's military effectiveness – began to erode the morale of many older fighters, leading many to return to civilian life. By the late 1970s, the average fighter had served in Jebha for four years. In 1974, the average fighter had served for a decade.[124] This trend, in turn, compounded the organization's military problems.

Other factors were at play as well. As mentioned earlier, Jebha's control of Eritrea's entire southern border during the 1978 Soviet-backed Ethiopian offensive left it with little time to maneuver. As such, its capabilities were badly damaged. Yet what was Jebha's loss was Shaebia's gain, since Jebha's occupation of Eritrea's southern border placed a buffer between Shaebia and oncoming Ethiopian mechanized units. As such, Shaebia units had adequate time to conduct a phased withdrawal to their Sahel base area, preserving the fighting capacity of its units while taking whatever resources they could from the areas of Eritrea they had formerly occupied.

Finally, Shaebia was able to obtain the support of the Tigray People's Liberation Front (TPLF), which had strained relations with Jebha over the administration of particular territories along the border of Eritrea and Tigray. Thousands of *Woyane* fighters – as the TPLF was commonly known – were deployed against Jebha positions. In the end, the TPLF's intervention was a fatal blow.[125]

Military failure had a devastating effect on Jebha, eroding credible commitments between the organization's constituent units and unleashing a cycle of factionalism and fragmentation that hastened Jebha's final demise. Internal tensions within Jebha were already high, as the organization's leadership had failed to hold an organization-wide congress since 1975. Although, in fairness, the failure to hold a congress was a function of the rapidly shifting military situation between 1975 and 1980, the perception that the leadership was attempting to maintain its power into perpetuity was overwhelming.

In any case, Jebha leaders held a meeting to discuss the organization's future. With thousands of fighters still under arms in three camps in Karakon, Tadai, and Rasai, Jebha retained significant potential. A decision was made to redeploy Jebha's entire force back into Eritrea in order

---

[122] Author's interview, Jebha intelligence officer, May 13, 2009.
[123] Author's interview, Jebha fighter, June 10, 2009.
[124] Author's interview, Jebha intelligence officer, May 13, 2009.
[125] Author's interview, TPLF Politburo member, later EPRDF minister, May 19, 2012; author's interview, TPLF Central Committee member, May 6, 2015.

to continue the armed struggle. But it was here that things became difficult. Given the recent military failures, Jebha's executive committee decided to resign so that a new leadership could be selected. This was designed as a confidence-building measure. However, many of the same faces remained, including Jebha chairman Ahmed Nasser and Abdulla Idris, the chief military commander. Inexplicably, not a single Christian was selected for the newly constituted leadership body. The decision to exclude Christians, through what were widely believed to be surreptitious means, reflected a clear breakdown in credible commitments within the organization, and a final erosion of a cooperative ethos between some of its primary constituent units.[126]

It is important to understand that for many old-line Muslim conservatives, who believed that their community had played the signal role in the nationalist movement from its earliest days, Jebha's recent ills were a result of sabotage by Christian highlanders. A nefarious highland Christian alliance that included Shaebia, Fallul and other infiltrators still in Jebha's midst, and the TPLF, had bled Jebha from within and without. The conservatives, who would be led by Abdulla Idris of the Beni Amer, sought to cleanse the movement of this scourge.

The failure to guarantee Christian representation on the executive committee was decisive, and triggered a factional fight that diffused, leading to an open rupture between Jebha's main political and military leaders. Abdulla Idris, who remained Jebha's military chief, had direct command over forces at the Rasai camp, and began to redeploy his units back into Eritrea. Ahmed Nasser, who was tasked with mobilizing and redeploying the forces at the other two camps, was met with firm resistance by disaffected Christians, who were the majority within these camps and once again felt marginalized within Jebha ranks. Moreover, many believed that the leadership's plans to redeploy back into Eritrea were foolish and unsustainable. "It was too late. Most of the fighters felt the situation was such that we couldn't reorganize," one reluctant fighter recalled.[127] Without an agreement with Shaebia, many believed, redeployment would be suicide.

The situation was compounded when the Sudanese, alarmed by large numbers of armed fighters within their borders, gave Jebha an ultimatum: if they did not return to Eritrea they would be disarmed. The reluctant fighters under Nasser's purview did not budge, and were

---

[126] Author's interview, Jebha fighter, April 22, 2009; according to this fighter and others, Jebha leaders brought in Sudanese tribesmen to pose as Jebha fighters, and used these votes to sway the outcome.
[127] Author's interview, Jebha fighter, April 22, 2009.

disarmed by Sudanese forces, which was a massive blow to Jebha's military capabilities.

These developments permanently soured relations between Abdulla Idris and the Ahmed Nasser camp. In private communications, Idris implored Nasser to move the remaining forces at Karakon and Tadai back into Eritrea as quickly as possible. Nasser seemed unable, and perhaps unwilling, to deliver. The looming dispute within the leadership was reinforced by differences of competency and evaluations of self-worth: Idris was military man, while Nasser was a political leader. Abdulla Idris was also viewed as more conservative, with deep sectarian loyalties to his Beni Amer tribal group, while Nasser was regarded as the more cosmopolitan leftist.

In any case, Idris demanded a leadership meeting at a place called Rasai on the Eritrean–Sudanese border. Nasser and his supporters resisted, largely because Idris had managed to retain his arms and equipment by redeploying across the border, while the Sudanese had taken the weapons of the units under Nasser's command. An awkward stand-off ensued, until finally, the leadership's met at Abdulla Idris' base area in Rasai in March 1982.

The ensuing chain of events was not entirely unexpected, as Ahmed Nasser and his colleagues were walking into a clear trap. In what amounted to a military coup, Abdulla Idris arrested Nasser and vice-chairman Ibrahim Totil on March 25, 1982. A close ally of Nasser, Jebha internal security chief Melake Tekle, was killed under circumstances that are not entirely clear. Abdulla Idris described his coup as a bid to save the organization and guarantee its survival: "The organization was in a state of anarchy and chaos from the irresponsible actions from some of the leaders. Because of this, the Eritrean Liberation Army moved to bring an end to mishandling. It stood for a historical uprising to save the organization, to guarantee its continuity, and to carry out its role in the struggle."[128]

Yet Idris's bold play for power failed, as the recalcitrant Christian fighters at Karakon and Tadai – which remained the majority of Jebha's fighting force – refused to mobilize and follow him back into Eritrea. With

---

[128] "Awate Archives: Interview with Abdullah Idris," April 30, 2011, which can be found at www.awate.com; interview with Tekle Melekin (who was arrested at the Rasai conference), conducted by Gunter Schroeder, August 6, 2005, Frankfurt, Germany. Abdulla Idris has since published an Arabic-language book explaining in some detail Jebha's troubles in 1982 and the rationale for the Rasai coup. It was published in 2016 and is titled *Highlights of the Experience of the Eritrean Liberation Front*. Dr. Mohamed Kheir Omer has kindly provided a review of the book that can be found on his website, at https://hedgait.blogspot.com/search?q=book+idris (Accessed May 4, 2017).

little alternative, Idris returned to Eritrea with units under his command that continued to support him – mostly Muslim conservatives, many of whom hailed from the Beni Amer – effectively fragmenting the organization.

Nasser and Ibrahim Totil were eventually released, but the rupture with Abdulla Idris now exacerbated the factional fight within the remaining forces they commanded within Karakon and Tadai. A group of mostly leftist Christians that collectively became known as *Sagem* seized the opportunity created by Abdulla Idris's botched coup and challenged Ahmed Nasser's authority, demanding he step down in order for a new leadership to be selected. However, Ahmed Nasser retained the support of the majority of the organization by arguing that the leadership could not be removed by extraconstitutional means; i.e., a congress needed to be held. Having failed to seize executive authority within the organization, Sagem was forced to split. Factionalism and fragmentation diffused still further when Sagem was joined by Vice-Chairman Ibrahim Totil, who brought fighters from his mostly Nara ethnic group along with him. A large component of Sagem would later join Shaebia at its Second Congress in 1987.

The factional fight and ensuing fragmentation of 1982 heralded the end of Jebha as an effective fighting force within Eritrea and solidified the dominance of Shaebia in the nationalist movement. A humiliating string of territorial losses eroded credible commitments between Jebha's constituent units, as reflected in the purge of Christians from the leadership. This initial dispute between Christian and Muslim members of the leadership over the election of a new leadership body diffused, creating a rupture between Ahmed Nasser and Abdulla Idris. Abdulla Idris's failed coup led to his fragmentation, but in turn reinforced factional wrangling within the units that remained under Nasser's command. The eventual result was the fragmentation of Jebha into three groups, none of which had the individual capacity to continue the armed struggle (although each group did try).

Kibreab (2008, p. 312), in writing about these events, interprets them in a way entirely consistent with this book's main arguments about battlefield losses and rebel fragmentation:

The ELF [Jebha] had suffered a substantial loss of social trust subsequent to its withdrawal to Sudan, reflected, inter alia, in the wearing out of glue that previously interconnected the fighters across the social and political cleavages of ethnicity, religion and region and ideology. As a result, even those who rejected the old line could not agree to carry on fighting together.

Once again, as the war went, so went cooperation.

Alternative Arguments

Of course, it is difficult to ascertain whether the historical arguments made in this chapter are valid without carefully weighing alternative hypotheses. In this section, I evaluate several competing explanations that could plausibly account for variation on the dependent variable of interest, fragmentation. It should also be noted that while some of the alternative variables discussed may affect fragmentation by shaping the possibilities of gains and losses, taken alone they cannot explain the variation on the dependent variable we observe.

State Repression and Counterinsurgency Strategies

A number of researchers have argued that state repression and counterinsurgency operations impact the internal cohesion of rebel organizations, although there is a difference of opinion regarding the exact nature of this causal relationship. Shapiro (2008, 2013) argues that high levels of state repression force insurgents to decentralize their operations, thus reducing a rebel leadership's control over their subordinates. More intuitively, it also seems as though increases in state repression boost the likelihood that potential dissident factions believe that the rebellion cannot succeed, and therefore encourages fragmentation.

If these theories are correct, we would expect increases in the coercive resources that the Ethiopian government deployed against Jebha to be correlated with the organization's fragmentation. Using standard, but very blunt measures of state repression – measures of numerical preponderance – it is clear that significant increases in the coercive capacity of the Ethiopian state do not explain the three incidences of cooperation breakdown cited in this chapter. Ethiopian troop levels and military expenditures increased most dramatically in the mid-1970s, after Haile Selassie's ouster and the Derg's consolidation of authority in 1974–75. The size of the Ethiopian military rose from 45,000 in 1974 to 50,000 in 1975, to 65,000 in 1976, to 225,000 in 1977, to a whopping 250,000 in 1978. These increases were unprecedented in modern Ethiopian history, and were enabled by the introduction of a conscription program. Up until that point, under the imperial administration, troop levels and military expenditures had been fairly consistent, at least from the period beginning in 1960, which is the year Jebha emerged. While the 1980s did not see a similar sort of spike in troop numbers as was witnessed in the mid- to late 1970s, the Ethiopian military would later top out at 300,000 men under arms in 1986–87, from where its numbers would decline as morale began to lag, the conscription program began to collapse, and the Derg's overall military effort began to crumble. In terms of military expenditures, there was a corresponding increase in the mid-1970s that closely parallels increases in the size of the Ethiopian armed forces: the Ethiopian state spent nearly 50 million in 1974, roughly 75 million in 1975, 120 million in 1976, 135 million in 1977, and just over 200 million by 1978. The 1980s would see a further, although ultimately unsustainable climb in military expenditures: in 1990 alone, the Derg's military expenditures skyrocketed to 1.3 billion.

The first real effect of these increases in the Eritrean theatre was not felt until June of 1978, during the Derg's First Offensive. This was because the Derg chose to concentrate its early efforts on combating the Somali threat on its eastern flank, before turning to fight the insurgents in the north. As such, these increases, and their military effects, cannot explain much of the variation on the dependent variable. Jebha's fragmentation in 1967–68, and the emergence of EDM/Fallul during 1975–77, largely predated the huge increases in the coercive resources of the Ethiopian state and their significant military effects in the Eritrean theatre in 1977–78. Furthermore, Jebha's disintegration into three groups in 1982 occurred a full four years after the effects of this dramatic increase became apparent on the battlefield.

Interestingly, many have argued that battlefield outcomes and state power have less to do with numerical preponderance and more to do with military technology.[129] In the Ethiopian context, this would mean that major increases in the technology employed by the Ethiopian military, rather than numerical preponderance, should roughly correlate with Jebha's fragmentation.

Although a full discussion of the equipment employed by the Ethiopian military is beyond the scope of this book, a good proxy for variation in technology employed by the Ethiopian state over time would seem to be arms transfers from the major producers of military technology during the Cold War, the United States and the Soviet Union.[130] Yet trends in arms transfers do not explain much of the variation on the dependent variable. Consider the following. The decisive increase in arms transfers and military technology, like increases in troop numbers and military expenditures, occurred in the mid-1970s, and was tied very directly to the Derg's decision to switch Cold War partners and embrace the Soviets. In 1974, Ethiopia received only 14 million in arms

---

[129] Biddle (2004, pp. 16–17) collectively calls these explanations "Dyadic Technology Theory."

[130] See Westad (2007) for what might be the most well sourced account of superpower involvement in Ethiopia. Also see Patman (1990), Woodroofe (2013), and Yordanov (2016).

transfers from the United States, and nothing from the Soviets. By 1975, US arms transfers would increase to 39 million, and yet again, arms transfers from the Soviets stood at virtually zero. In 1976 the situation began to change. By 1977, as arms transfers from the United States were phased out, the Soviets provided the Derg more than 1 billion in weapons. Although this number would level off in the late 1970s and 1980s, and collapse as the Cold War drew to a close, Soviet arms transfers for much of the 1980s would continue to surpass by hundreds of millions of dollars the value of US weapons transfers to Ethiopia in the pre-1974–75 era. In any case, the massive spike in Soviet arms transfers to Ethiopia in the late 1970s, which again was first felt in the Eritrean theatre in 1977–78, can really explain only one episode of Jebha's fragmentation, which is 1982, and even here, there is a significant lag between cause and effect.[131]

However, there are strong reasons to think we should take a closer look at state repression. Biddle (2004) persuasively argues that numerical preponderance and technology are poor predictors of war outcomes because they tell us nothing about how effectively coercive resources are used. Furthermore, it seems self-evident that numerical preponderance is endogenous to the performance of the government's counterinsurgency operations: if the state has failed to curb the activities of the rebels, or the rebels are surging, state authorities are forced to ramp up their coercive capacities. Lastly, the Ethiopian state has historically had many internal and external opponents, so increases in numerical preponderance may be an artifact of developments not entirely related to the insurgency in Eritrea.

A better, albeit imperfect measure of state repression would be to look at major Ethiopian government offensives against Jebha between 1960 and 1982, and examine the extent to which fragmentation occurred during, or directly following, such offensives. Of course, not all offensives achieve a degree of success, but if theories about state repression are true, fragmentation should be preceded by a major government offensive that has achieved some success.

My research suggests that there were roughly four major offensives against Jebha in Eritrea, occurring in 1967, 1970, 1976, and 1979. The 1979 operation actually involved five distinct operations in close temporal sequence. Many of these offensives have been mentioned in this chapter, but a comprehensive list can be found in Woldemariam (2011,

[131] Data on troop strength, expenditures, and arms transfers are taken from publicly available databases to ensure consistency across time: these include the Correlates of War dataset and data provided by Stockholm International Peace Research Institute (SIPRI).

pp. 140–141), along with relevant details on each operation, its eventual outcome, and whether the offensive was followed by Jebha's fragmentation. Examining these data, it seems clear that the occurrence of major government offensives does not explain Jebha's fragmentation – particularly the events of 1975–77. The 1976 offensive, the Derg's hastily prepared "Peasants' March," came after the Herui Tedla Bairu/Fallul factional episode was already in motion. In any case, the offensive was a dismal failure that had no appreciable negative impact on Jebha's military situation. In fact, as discussed earlier, Jebha was surging in this period.

Of course, successful counterinsurgency efforts are not composed solely of coercion. Some governments have successfully split rebel organizations by offering political or economic incentives that persuade particular segments to defect or provide an issue of contention within rebel ranks. Such arguments are closely related to theories about "spoilers" and peace negotiations that split rebel organizations between those that seek to cooperate with the government, and those that want to continue war (Stedman, 1997). Yet in the Eritrean context, these sorts of explanations are not convincing. First, the Ethiopian government had virtually no official contacts of any consequence with Jebha until the monarchy was overthrown in 1974. Until that point, the Ethiopian government communicated with Jebha largely indirectly through community elders who would relay messages between the two sides.[132] In fact, until the mid-1970s, the Ethiopian government largely denied that there was even an insurgency in the province of Eritrea. Therefore, it does not seem likely that serious government efforts to split the rebels could have been made before 1974, and thus such efforts could not explain the splits of 1967–68.

Even after the precipitous demise of the monarchy in 1974, and despite the rhetoric of the new Marxist military government in Addis Ababa, few actual efforts were made to encourage defection from Jebha through the provision of political or economic incentives. In fact, data from Minorities at Risk's discrimination dataset shows there was minimal variation in the degree to which the political institutions of the Ethiopian state discriminated against Eritreans over the course of Jebha's operational life.[133]

Indeed, the opening of secret talks between Jebha and the Ethiopian government in the first half of 1978, under the auspices of Eastern Bloc

---

[132] For instance, in cases where the government and Jebha were seeking to negotiate the release of foreigners whom Jebha had detained.
[133] Minorities at Risk data can be found at www.mar.umd.edu/mar_data.asp.

countries, failed to generate any agreement that would divide Jebha precisely because the Ethiopians were unwilling to budge on virtually any of Jebha's core demands – which oscillated between full autonomy and a plebiscite on an independent state that would guarantee Ethiopian access to the sea.[134] The Cuban vice-president Carlos Rafael Rodriguez, in declassified conversation with East German officials on February 13, 1978, largely concurred with this perspective:

> We also completely agree with the view that the Ethiopian leadership apparently does not have a clear concept, either on a general solution of the national problem in Ethiopia nor on the specific problems in Eritrea. They have until now not really seriously believed in it and have not seriously concerned themselves with it but instead only considered the demand for a peaceful solution as [in itself] a kind of political solution.
> They probably still have the thought in the back of their minds that a peaceful solution of the Eritrean problem will mean a capitulation by the Eritrean movements, which means that the military solution would be the preparation for a further peaceful strategy.
> One can certainly not neglect the military measures in this matter, but the Ethiopian comrades still do not have the deep recognition of the necessity of a political, i.e., peaceful solution of the Eritrean problem."[135]

The reluctance of the Derg to make real concessions to Jebha was due to a number of factors. Obviously, as the murder of General Aman Andom indicates, a process of "outbidding" made the public countenance of concessions to Jebha particularly dangerous (Horowitz, 1987) for any member of the Derg. During ongoing power struggles within the Derg, Mengistu repeatedly played the Ethiopian nationalist card against opponents that were perceived (correctly or incorrectly) as being keen to make concessions regarding Eritrean autonomy, thus signing away the country's sovereignty. Mengistu himself, in private conversations with the Soviets, said that any concessions on Eritrea on his part "would throw him to the nationalist wolves" (Westad, 2007, p. 281).

---

[134] SED Department of International Relations, "Information on talks of Ahmed Nasser (ELF-RC) in the USSR Solidarity Committee, June 7–8, 1978, SAPMO-BArch, DY30 IV 2/2.035/127, which can be found at the Cold War International History Project Virtual Archives.

[135] SED CC, Department of International Relations, "Report on Conversation with [Vice-president] Carlos Rafael Rodriguez, Member of the Politburo of the CP Cuba, in Havana," February 16, 1978, SAPMO-BArch, DY30 IV 2/2.035/127, which can be found at the Cold War International History Project Virtual Archives. As the East German and Soviet documents from 1978 attest, it was a commonly held perception among Eastern Bloc countries that the Derg was looking for a military solution in Eritrea, and was unwilling to make any meaningful concessions.

However, an honest history should note that the Ethiopian government periodically offered amnesty to enemy combatants.[136] Yet in practice, these efforts were open-ended instead of time-bound, and as such, cannot explain temporal variation in fragmentation. Furthermore, it is doubtful whether amnesty, in the absence of extra political or economic benefits, would be sufficient to trigger defection among those who have taken such high risks to obtain political or economic benefits through war.

Another point to consider, and perhaps the most compelling rebuttal against arguments about state efforts to politically co-opt the rebels, is that if these sorts of theories are true, we would expect all splits of rebel organizations to result in defection to the government. However, we know from the historical analyses that this is not the case. In fact, of the eleven identified groups that split from Jebha, only one group defected to the government.

External Support and Control

Another explanation for the occurrence of factional infighting and fragmentation within rebel organizations is the presence of a strong external backer who can enforce cooperation and provide leaders with the material tools necessary to forge (and sometimes coerce) organizational unity. If such a theory were true, we would expect shocks in external support to correlate roughly with the fragmentation of Jebha.

Yet the reality is that this is a weak explanation in the Eritrean context. Although it is difficult to accurately assess the degree to which states materially supported Jebha, a brief historical commentary is illuminating.

There were a broad collection of state and nonstate actors that provided material support to Jebha over its twenty-two-year armed confrontation with the Ethiopian government.[137] The historiography of the war in Eritrea often understates the degree of external support that the rebels received, yet given the extent to which the revolution became an extension of Arab–Israeli conflicts, intra-Arab rivalries, and Cold War politics, the external dimension is hard to ignore.

---

[136] Airgram, Asmara to State, May 4, 1970, RG 59, Central Files, "ELF Defections." Also, interview with Jebha fighter, May 3, 2009, described incessant Ethiopian radio broadcasts and loudspeakers across the front lines designed to encourage defection. Not surprisingly, the tactic was ineffective.

[137] See INR Research Study, Alison Palmer, February 22, 1971, RG 59, Central Files, "Ethiopia–Foreign Aid to the Eritrean Liberation Front." The report implicates nearly sixteen countries in supporting ELF at one point in time or another.

Early support for Jebha came from Egypt, which allowed radio broadcasts and the leadership to organize openly in Cairo. By 1963, the Egyptians, who for political reasons opposed the dismemberment of Ethiopia, withdrew their support, only to be replaced by the recently transformed radical Baathist states of Iraq and Syria (Erlich, 1983).[138]

Throughout the 1960s, the Iraqis and Syrians were Jebha's most committed supporters, channeling much of their financial and military aid to the field through Jebha's external leadership and providing Jebha members with valuable training in their military academies. During the 1960s, Jebha radio broadcasts from Damascus and Baghdad railing against imperial Ethiopia's oppression of its Eritrean minority were the primary mediums through which the Eritrean struggle was publicized on the international stage. For the Arab Baathist states, the war in Eritrea pitted a Muslim minority against a Christian-dominated empire, and thus on grounds of religious affinity, was deserving of Arab support. If this were not reason enough to support Jebha, the Arabs had the strong suspicion – which was correct – that the Ethiopians had a secret, albeit very close security partnership with the Israelis (Lefebvre, 1996).

For its part, neighboring Sudan, by virtue of ethnic kinship with Eritrea's western lowlanders – particularly the Beja and Beni Amer tribes that occupy eastern Sudan and much of adjoining parts of Eritrea – border issues, and pressure from its Arab neighbors, also supported the cause of Eritrean nationalism, allowing Jebha to establish its executive in Khartoum and a field command in Kassala.

Despite the fact that Ethiopia devoted substantial time and energy to stopping the flow of personnel and arms from radical Arab states into Eritrea, such efforts were largely unsuccessful. Recognizing that Eritrea's 700-mile Red Sea coast was simply too long to police effectively, Jebha's Arab supporters would drop shipments of arms along the coast – with the friendly regime of South Yemen as the conduit – where they would be picked up by Jebha militants who were waiting at predetermined locations. On many occasions, Jebha would use local fishermen to ferry weapons to the coast and successfully avoid the interdiction efforts of the Imperial Ethiopian Navy.[139]

This was by no means the only way that men and material were moved by the rebels into Eritrea in the 1960s and early 1970s. Overland routes through Kassala were often utilized, as were direct overland routes from

---

[138] Because the official position of the Organization of African Unity (OAU) was that Africa's colonial borders were sacrosanct, Egypt feared alienating its African partners by supporting Eritrean nationalists. Furthermore, because of concerns over the Nile, Egypt did not want to encourage South Sudan's secession by legitimizing the practice.

[139] Airgram, Addis to State, June 14, 1971, RG 59, Central Files, "Dhow Activity in Eritrean Waters."

Port Sudan, where much of the arms and munitions from the Arab world destined for the rebels arrived.[140] Furthermore, at the primary Eritrean port of Massawa, Jebha leader Osman Saleh Sabbe had constructed a clandestine network of customs officials who allowed crucial supplies to slip through to the rebels (Pool, 2001).

Even in cases where neighboring states were reluctant to support Jebha – Sudan during the Abboud administration, Sudan's Nimeiry regime during the years 1971–72, and North Yemen – the inability of these governments to control their own borders, as well as private pressure from more committed Arab states, rendered this reluctance inconsequential.[141]

As previously noted, the Arab–Israeli War of 1967 crippled, at least temporarily, the militaries of Jebha's most significant benefactors in Damascus and Bagdad. Coupled with the closure of the Red Sea by Israel, Jebha faced a real shortage of arms and equipment, a shortage that coincides nicely with Jebha's first split.

Yet by the end of the 1960s, the flow of external support resumed, with new additions. A revolution in Libya that brought Muammar Gaddafi to power provided yet another external patron in the region. US intelligence also reported PLO involvement in Eritrea in the early 1970s, and attributes the rise in urban terrorism, hijackings, and kidnappings during this period to this support. Even the Chinese provided material support to the rebels in Eritrea, including the training of more than thirty Jebha cadres in mainland China in 1967.[142]

After the 1967 war, it does not seem that Jebha incurred any significant loss of external support. The one exception was the loss of Libyan support after the departure of Osman Saleh Sabbe from Jebha ranks in 1968–69, although continuing Syrian and Iraqi support more than compensated. Although the commitment of certain external sponsors was idiosyncratic (the Sudanese), and Cold War realignments wrought significant changes in external backing (South Yemen in 1976), there were always states in the region that were willing to fill the void. In fact, the loss of support from several radical Arab states after the overthrow of the Ethiopian monarchy created new opportunities, bringing a number of conservative Arab states to Jebha's aid.[143] Indeed, by the late 1970s and early 1980s, there was a growing significance of Saudi petro-dollars in

---

[140] Author's interviews, Jebha intelligence officer, May 19 and September 11, 2009, and Shaebia intelligence officer, August 11, 2009.
[141] Airgram, Sanaa to State, January 24, 1973, RG 59, Central Files, "Ethiopia-Yemen: IEG efforts to prevent YARG assistance to Eritrean Liberation Front."
[142] Future leaders of Shaebia Issais Afeworki and Ramadan Mohammed Nur, who were part of Jebha at this point, both went to China during this period.
[143] Telegram, Jidda to State, February 24, 1975, RG 59, Central Files, "Ethiopia, Saudi Arabia, and the United States."

the Eritrean field, much of it encouraged by the Reagan administration (Lefebvre, 1996). Thus, it is hard to see how a loss of external support could explain Jebha splits in 1975–77 and 1981–82.

To drive this point home further, declassified dispatches from US embassy officials in Khartoum reported interesting information in March of 1975, directly prior to the divisive Jebha Congress of May 1975 that began the organization's fragmentation:

> According to a diplomatic colleague, whose own source is a regional arms dealer, GOS (Government of Sudan) has permitted shipment of substantial quantity of arms to transit Sudan on the way to Eritreans. Specifically, source reported that 51 tons of anti-tank and anti-aircraft rockets and small arms, originating in Syria and Iraq, have recently arrived in Khartoum by air. Packing crates, which arrived labeled 'vegetables,' were allegedly relabeled 'school supplies' to better account for weight by Sudanese security forces before arms permitted to continue to destination in Eritrea.
>
> While story is inconclusive, it echoes earlier reports of same tonnage of arms arriving in early December (1974), and lends weight to Ethiopian conviction that GOS is indeed assisting in supplying arms and ammunition to Eritreans."[144]

If this were not evidence enough, the participation of Abu Ala, Iraqi director of the Department of Palestinian Affairs and Liberation Organizations, in the Jebha Congress of 1975, suggests that external support, or lack of it, was not the relevant causal factor in Jebha's fragmentation at that time.

Organizational Structure, Centralization, and Control

It is also reasonable to assume that rebel organizations that possess fairly decentralized command and control structures are more likely to fragment. Thus shifts in organization toward more decentralized administrative structures could map onto incidences of fragmentation and be driving my results. Since there is no consensus in the literature on how to measure organizational centralization/decentralization, and the concept is often misused in studies of civil war,[145] I prefer to outline Jebha's institutional evolution.

When Jebha launched the armed insurrection in September 1961 in Eritrea's Barka province, it was led by a self-appointed Provisional Executive Committee of three who were based in Cairo: Idris Mohammed

---

[144] Telegram 50, Khartoum to State, March 13, 1975, RG 59, Central Files, "Arms Shipment to Eritrea."
[145] Johnston (2008) makes a similar point in his discussion of insurgent organizational structure in Liberia and Sierra Leone.

Adem, Idris Glawedos, and Osman Saleh Sabbe. While there is little information about Jebha's early organization, communication between the Cairo triumvirate and fighters in the field was likely limited, and as such, fighters probably operated with a broad degree of autonomy.

In 1962, the Provisional Executive Committee was replaced by the Revolutionary Command (RC), which consisted of the Cairo three as well as a twelve-member executive committee composed of Eritrean exiles from Sudan, Egypt, and Saudi Arabia. In 1965, the growth of the organization in the field from a small band of fighters to nearly 1,000 required a more formal structure. After meetings held in Khartoum in which Adem, Sabbe, and Glawedos were confirmed as leaders of Jebha, the three moved their operations to Khartoum while also opening a field command in Kassala that oversaw military affairs. The leaders of Jebha decided that the best mode of organization in the field would be zonal structure, largely decentralized, and based on the experience of the FLN in Algeria. Initially, Jebha consisted of four zones, each of which drew their leadership and rank-and-file membership from the geographic area in which they operated. The predictable result was that the zonal system tended to reproduce the ethnic, religious, and regional divisions of Eritrean society. In 1966, an increasing influx of Christians from the central plateau necessitated a fifth zone, dubbed the "Christian zone." By virtue of kinship, Adem, Sabbe, and Glawedos had particularly strong kinship links with the first, fourth, and second zone, respectively, and ties of patronage bound these leaders to each of these zonal commands quite closely.

Yet ties of patronage and kinship with the external leadership notwithstanding, the zonal system largely lacked coherence. Zonal leaders treated the areas in which they operated as personal fiefdoms, and operated independently of one another. More importantly, the zonal system created a competitive dynamic, a trend that was only exacerbated by rivalries among the external leadership.

It was in this context that Jebha fragmented in 1967, and thus organizational decentralization would seem to be a good explanation for the breakdown of cooperation. However, a discussion of what Jebha's organization looked like on the eve of the divisive congress of 1975 suggests that this sort of explanation is inadequate in explaining the breakdown of cooperation that ensued.

By 1971, Jebha had gone through a major transition, the result of which was a radically different organizational structure based on Leninist principles of democratic centralism. Recruitment, training, and personnel issues were now centralized. A two-tiered leadership was elected by a fighter's congress, with a Revolutionary Council of thirteen and an executive committee of nineteen. Importantly, the executive organs were now in the field in close proximity to the units they commanded. A secretary-general was empowered with day-to-day responsibilities for management while a set of committees in the executive bodies was set up for centralized policymaking. Furthermore, Jebha set up a secret internal Marxist party to enforce discipline and ideologically train new members.[146]

Thus Jebha was relatively centralized on the eve of the explosion of factionalism in 1975, a situation that persisted through the factional events of 1982. Thus, a theory of organizational centralization versus decentralization would not seem to explain much here.

Organizational Size and Complexity

One of the more compelling competing explanations has to do with organizational size and complexity. Building on Olson's famous insight that collective action is difficult in groups that are large and/or socially differentiated (Olson, 1965, 1982), it may be the case that Jebha's size and social complexity affected its fragmentation.

However, Jebha's aggregate size is a weak explanation for its fragmentation. Jebha fragmented when it was both relatively large, and relatively small. On the eve of the factional cataclysm of 1967, its forces numbered roughly 1,700. Meanwhile, lower bound estimates of Jebha's troop strength just prior to its fragmentation in 1975 and 1982 are roughly 18,000.[147] Clearly, then, there is no real correlation here.

Nor was a rapid and dramatic increase in membership, relative to the size of Jebha at a particular point in time, responsible for fragmentation. While, as discussed before, the fragmentation of 1967–68 and 1975–77 coincided with rapid increases in membership, the fragmentation of 1982 did not.

Finally, while increases in Jebha's diversity would seem to be central to the story of its fragmentation, Jebha likely became a less diverse organization after the departures of Herui Tedla Bairu and Fallul in 1975 and 1977, respectively. How then does one explain the events of 1982? Indeed, the new equilibrium reached after the factional cataclysms of the

---

[146] The "secret" party was actually open knowledge. It was called the Labor Party. This section is drawn from a wide range of sources. See Markakis (1987) and Medhanie (1986), also author's interview with Shaebia intelligence officer, August 11, 2009. A fantastic primary source document that details Jebha's organizational structure is a 1977 booklet produced by its information office in Beirut titled "The Eritrean Revolution: 16 Years of Armed Struggle."

[147] These are best estimates, and a rough average of numbers provided by available non-Jebha sources.

mid-1970s was built on a slightly narrower ethnic, religious, and ideological base.

Absolute Position, Victory, and Defeat

A final issue to consider is whether processes of factionalism and fragmentation are triggered by where a rebel organization sits in absolute terms, rather than change in position, i.e., significant territorial gains or losses. In particular, it may be that gains and losses are masking the effect of being near victory, or near total defeat. One could well argue that as a rebel organization approaches either of these points, it hits a threshold beyond which cooperation becomes very difficult.

In order to get a handle on this issue, I measure Jebha's annual military position in absolute terms by placing the organization in one of five categories annually: Jebha is given a 1 if it occupies less than 20 percent of the province, a 2 if it occupies roughly 20 to 40 percent, a 3 if 40 to 60 percent, a 4 if 60 to 80 percent, and a 5 if 80 to 100 percent. If Jebha is still in its guerrilla phase, I look at effective operational reach, rather than control. Woldemariam (2011, p. 155) has a visual depiction of these data over time.

If absolute military position was the relevant causal variable, and gains and losses masked its effect, we would expect Jebha to fragment in category 1 and category 5 – near defeat and near victory, respectively. At the very least, we would not expect to see fragmentation in the middle category 3. Yet the data demonstrate that this is simply not the case. While two cases of fragmentation (1967 and 1982) occurred when Jebha was in category 1, the 1975 episode occurred when it was category 3, owing in large part to the fact that its rival, Shaebia, controlled much of the other half of the province. Therefore, it is hard to argue that my theory of relative gains and losses masks the effect of being on the brink of victory, or the precipice of defeat.[148]

Conclusions

The historical material presented in this chapter has argued the following. Jebha's territorial losses of 1967 precipitated commitment problems, which in turn triggered overlapping sectarian and ideological struggles

---

[148] Of course, this chart does not nail this point very well, since Jebha does not demonstrate the full variation on levels of absolute control. It may be the case that as Jebha passes category 3 it hits a threshold above which intraorganizational cooperation is difficult. However, the six other cases I use help validate this argument much better. Indeed, not every case can perfectly highlight every nuance of the argument.

Table 3.1 *Jebha – gains, losses, and the onset of fragmentation over time*

Year	Gain/Loss/ Stalemate	Onset of Fragmentation
1961	Stalemate	No
1962	Stalemate	No
1963	Gain	No
1964	Stalemate	No
1965	Stalemate	No
1966	Gain	No
1967	Loss	Yes***
1968	Loss	Yes*
1969	Gain	No
1970	Gain	No
1971	Stalemate	No
1972	Stalemate	No
1973	Stalemate	No
1974	Gain	No
1975	Gain	Yes*
1976	Gain	Yes*
1977	Gain	No
1978	Loss	No
1979	Loss	No
1980	Stalemate	No
1981	Stalemate	No
1982	Loss	Yes***

* An asterisk is used to denote the number of groups that split.

within Jebha that spread across the entire organization and fragmented it into several components. The rapid territorial expansion of 1975, and the preference divergence that was associated with this expansion, provoked factional infighting within Jebha's leadership that eventually led to the fragmentation of Fallul and the Yemin countermovement. Jebha's 1982 expulsion out of Eritrea caused yet another round of factional infighting that began as a dispute between Chairman Ahmed Nasser and the troops at Karakon and Tadai, but eventually resulted in Abdulla Idris's fragmentation and the permanent split of Jebha into three distinct groups. By contrast, periods of territorial stalemate – for instance, 1971–73 – were devoid of any organizational factionalism and fragmentation. The underlying relationship between territorial gains and losses is summarized visually in Table 3.1.

The discussion of alternative explanations, for its part, is not meant to be conclusive. In the interest of space, I have highlighted those that are most theoretically compelling. However, what this chapter has tried to demonstrate is that the occurrence of factional infighting and fragmentation is contingent on organizational performance in unique and novel ways. Careful historical analysis of Jebha – using original interviews with ex-combatants, grayscale coded district level maps, and archival sources – demonstrates how territorial shifts can both erode credible commitments and drive preference divergence. The counterintuitive conclusion of this narrative is that territorial stalemate, or periods of slow, marginal battlefield change, promote cohesion and are the only sustainable basis for cooperation in war. No range of alternative variables, I argue, can account for variation in Jebha's fragmentation across time.

We now turn to an analysis of Jebha's nationalist rival, Shaebia, which was itself the product of the factional cataclysms of 1967–68.

4 The Eritrean People's Liberation Front
Shaebia in Action, 1972–1991

This chapter, like the previous chapter, seeks to test this book's theoretical claims through careful process tracing. The chapter focuses on the history of another strategically selected rebel organization, the Eritrean People's Liberation Front (Shaebia), and charts the relationship between the ebb and flow of war, periods of factional infighting, and organizational fragmentation within Shaebia ranks. If my theory is correct, we should expect to see a number of things.

The historical evidence should show that the coalitions that are rebel organizations were formed in the context of deep security concerns as various constituent units sought to minimize risk in war and guarantee survival. Factional infighting should be triggered by both territorial gains and losses, as the former tends to provoke preference divergence and the latter triggers commitment problems. Periods of territorial stalemate should be associated with relative cohesion.

We should also expect to see support for my corollary arguments as well. Fragmentation, when it occurs, should be the result of factional infighting in which the losers of these disputes exit in a bid for survival. Finally, we should expect to see that *some cases* of factional infighting are characterized by a process of diffusion, as segments of the organization not involved in the initial dispute are mobilized in response to emerging divisions. *On some occasions*, this can lead to multiple factions fragmenting in close sequence to one another.

The chapter begins by focusing on Jebha's factional cycle of 1967 in an effort to understand how contention spread, why specific constituent units were forced to fragment, and why several of the splinter elements that emerged out of this crisis coalesced into Shaebia in 1972. To be clear, I further unpack the dynamics of 1967 fragmentation of Jebha in this chapter, rather than the last, because it is central to understanding the context of security and survival that led to the emergence of its offspring, Shaebia. The chapter then moves on to further describe Shaebia's formal emergence, charts the ebb and flow of war, and links these battlefield developments to Shaebia's own moments of factional infighting and fragmentation. It concludes by carefully considering some alternative possible causal explanations.

Background to Rebellion

The Eritrean People's Liberation Front, which to reiterate, I refer to by its colloquial name, Shaebia, was itself the product of rebel fragmentation. As described in the previous chapter, Jebha's military failures in 1967 produced factional cataclysms that splintered the organization into several components. In 1972, these splinter groups coalesced to form the nucleus of a new nationalist rebel organization called Shaebia. Yet Shaebia's formation was more complex than indicated earlier, and the outcome of a long and protracted process that is crucial to understanding the organization and the trajectory of its internal politics.

As has been noted, a series of organizational conferences were held from 1967 to 1969, in an attempt to bring Jebha in line with the demands of the organization's internal critics.[1] Even in the wake of the debilitating defeats of 1967, most critics of Jebha's leadership had no intention of fragmenting the organization. The focal point of the reform movement, or *Eslah*, as it was called by sympathetic Jebha members, was the Christian elements of the fifth zone, which were commanded by Abraham Tewolde after the departure of Woldai Kahsai in 1967.[2] As a consensus emerged for organizational reform within the fifth zone – largely in response to the excesses of deputy commander Osman Hishal and Woldai Kahsai's departure – the fifth zone's newly minted political commissar, Issais Afeworki, was to play a key role in broadening the reform coalition beyond the Christian, mostly urban university students who were its early supporters.

Given Issais Afeworki's centrality to Shaebia's development – he would evolve into its most important political figure and the president of an independent Eritrea once the war was won – a few background notes are in order. Issais had been an engineering student at Addis Ababa University, who at the young age of twenty-one had quit school in order to join Jebha's ranks in Sudan. His father was a civil servant in the Ethiopian Tobacco Monopoly and Ministry of Land Reform, and an ardent unionist.[3] His uncle, Solomon Abraha, had been appointed deputy minister of the interior and governor of the Ethiopian province of Wollo by Emperor Haile Selassie. Described by one Western journalist

---

[1] There were three distinct conferences held in the western towns/villages of Aradib, Anseba, and Adhoba.
[2] *Eslah* is the Arabic term for "reform."
[3] Details drawn from Markakis (1987, p. 286) and the author's interview with senior Eritrean civil servant and Shaebia clandestine operative, June 13, 2009.

as "imposingly tall," "fiercely intelligent," and "naturally austere," Issais had been deeply critical of Jebha's ills for some time, and had the talent to broker an alliance between Jebha's disparate disaffected communities (Wrong, 2005, p. 373).

Selected as one of five Jebha cadres to receive political training in China in 1967, Issais Afeworki struck up a close friendship with Ramadan Mohammed Nur, a Muslim Jebha recruit from the Massawa area who would soon become the political commissar of the fourth zone when the two men returned to Eritrea in 1968. Both had acquired a leftist ideological orientation in China, although their three colleagues on the trip to China did not become similarly disposed. The relationship between the two men was important in mobilizing the fourth zone for the cause of reform. The fourth zone's commander, Mohammed Ali Omaro, sensed the growing opportunity to reorder power relations within Jebha, and thus supported the cause of organizational reform, throwing his weight behind the efforts of the fifth.[4]

But contention diffused still further, as the factional fight rapidly expanded in scope. The third zone, which was responsible for the highland Christian provinces of Akele Guzai and Seraye, was a natural ally in the budding reform efforts of the fourth and fifth zones. While the zonal command comprised primarily Muslim fighters, it operated in many Christian communities, which required that the unit develop an outwardly tolerant attitude toward Christians in order to survive. In fact, most Christians who joined Jebha prior to the fifth zone's creation in late 1966 elected to join the third zone owing to its reputation for tolerance. In addition, the majority of the zone's fighters were drawn from the Saho ethnic group, which was composed of substantial numbers of both Christians and Muslims. Finally, the third zone lacked the patronage of a coethnic on the Supreme Council, and was thus open to challenging the leadership.[5]

Fortuitous circumstances were also responsible for the third zone's support for the nascent reform movement, when the zone's commander,

---

[4] Omaro would become a Shaebia battalion commander and Eritrea's ambassador to Kenya, and later Nigeria. He was arrested in 2013 for his connection to an attempted coup – known as the *Forto* incident – that resulted in the seizure of Eritrea's Ministry of Information. As will be related later, both Ramadan and Issais Afeworki would serve as secretaries general of Shaebia, the only two individuals to occupy the organization's top post. There were a few important cadres in the fourth zone who had received training in Cuba and were ideologically prepared to embrace Ramadan's appeals. They include Ibrahim Afa, who would become a top political figure in Shaebia before his death in 1986.

[5] Haile Woldense, at that time part of the reformist elements in the fifth zone, makes this general argument (Connell, 2005, p. 32).

Abdel Karim Ahmed, was suspended for leaving his unit to get married in Sudan. His deputy, Hamid Saleh, and the zone's political commissar, Ahmed Mohammed Ibrahim, recognized the potential of the growing reform coalition, and embraced the calls of the fourth and fifth zones. Together, the three zones forced an impromptu meeting at Aradib in June of 1968 that was attended by representatives from all of the five zones as well as the heads of Jebha training and support units. The meeting provided for an expression of internal grievances – the absenteeism of an unelected external leadership, the dysfunctional zonal operational system, and debilitating sectarianism – and called for another conference that would take a broader set of decisions regarding reform.[6] The meeting was conducted without reference to the Revolutionary Command in Kassala or the Supreme Council in Khartoum.

Jebha's leaders abroad, Adem, Sabbe, and Glawedos, were not amused by what was a clear and open challenge to their authority. They countered by appealing to tribal solidarities and familial attachments in a bid to mobilize support within Jebha ranks. This effort was partially successful, and the first and second zones, dominated by Adem's Beni Amer and Glawedos's Bilen, respectively, refused to participate in another reform meeting.[7] What began as a narrow dispute, triggered by commitment problems between Hishal and his Christian subordinates, had turned into something much larger.

After some delay, the third, fourth, and fifth zones met again at Anseba in September 1968, and merged into what was called the Tripartite Unity Force. The body was led by a committee of twelve, comprising the commanders, deputy commanders, and political commissars of each of the three zones, in addition to the commanders of Jebha's training and

---

[6] The formal decisions of the Aradib meeting were to (1) call for a second Jebha-wide conference to take reforms further; (2) call on the 2nd division, which was based in the Keren area, to organize the conference; (3) call on the Revolutionary Command in Kassala to move its operations to the field; (4) call on the support unit to join the 1st division since the unit was underresourced; and (5) call on the 1st, 2nd, and 3rd divisions, which resided in Jebha strongholds in the west and the coast, to provide assistance to underresourced zones. See "From the Experiences of Eritrean Liberation Army," which was found at www.nharnet.com.

[7] To be fair, it appears that the second zone was in no position to attend the meeting given the military defeat it had suffered at Hal Hal on September 8th. Its commander Omar Ezaz was killed, in addition to forty-five other fighters. The first zone sent emissaries to the meeting to ask for a delay, as they had done on several occasions before, but were ignored. See "From the Experiences of the Eritrean Liberation Arm," which was found at www.nharnet.com. Haile Woldense argues that Hal Hal was a poorly conceived attempt by the first and second zones to demonstrate their military capacity to the organization's internal critics in the other zones (Connell, 2005, p. 51).

reserve units.[8] At this juncture, the Supreme Council, concerned that events were moving beyond its control, signaled its willingness to participate in a further round of reform meetings. However, Jebha's leaders placed a set of conditions on the forthcoming negotiations. First, they sought to guarantee that there would be no change in the status of the Supreme Council. Second, they argued that if a united command was set up, representatives from the first and second zones should retain a clear majority. Third, they demanded that new recruits be barred from joining the organization, in order to prevent Ethiopian infiltration. Since most new recruits were Christian, and were routinely accused of pro-Ethiopian sympathies, this demand was interpreted as a thinly veiled sectarian attempt to limit growing Christian influence within the organization. Presaging what was to come, a consensus on the proposed meeting's agenda could not be reached. Nevertheless, all parties agreed to meet at Adhoba in western Eritrea in late summer of 1969.

From August 10 to 25, 1969, 162 representatives of the five zones met to map out Jebha's future, debating a variety of organizational reforms. It is here that events become unclear. Apparently, divisions had begun to emerge within the Tripartite Unity Force prior to the conference, and although the group was collectively pushing reform, it could never really agree on a program of concrete action. Jebha sources contended that Issais and Ramadan had opposed the Adhoba meeting, and pushed for the Tripartite Unity Force's twelve-man committee to supplant Jebha's existing leadership wholesale.[9] But many sectors of the Tripartite Unity Force did not believe in such radical change, fearing it could undermine their own standing in the organization. This led supporters of Issais and Ramadan to claim that these more moderate elements functioned as a Trojan horse inserted into the reform movement by the Supreme Council and their supporters in the first and second zones.[10]

The Supreme Council sought to exploit these differences. Glawedos returned from Kassala to further mobilize opposition within the first and second zones against the reformist forces. In this effort, Jebha's leadership was only partly successful, as the resulting decisions of the Adhoba conference reflected some tangible change in the political status quo.

---

[8] The members of the committee, or the "Provisional Revolutionary Command," were its chairman, Mohammed Ahmed Abdu, a Syrian-trained commander from the third zone, and the following: Abdulla Idris Mohammed Ali Omaro, Ramadan Mohammed Nur, Abraham Tewolde, Issais Afeworki, Abu Tiyara, Ahmed Mohammed Ibrahim, Mohammed Abdalla Taha, Omar Damer, Abdalla Yusuf, and Hamid Saleh.

[9] Drawn from "From the Experiences of the Eritrean Liberation Army," which was found at www.nharnet.com.

[10] The ELF source is "From the Experiences of the Eritrean Liberation Army," available at www.nharnet.com, and the opposing view is Haile Woldense (Connell, 2005, p. 51).

First, the zonal system was abolished, and a unified command structure was created under the operational leadership of a thirty-eight-member council called the *Kaida al-Amma*. Mohammed Ahmed Abdu, chairman of the Tripartite Unity Force, became chairman of this new body. An eighteen-member committee was created to investigate the failures of the organization and its leadership. Other committees were established in order to oversee Jebha's assets (including those overseas) and make preparations for a national congress in one year's time.

Yet the leadership extracted some key concessions. The Supreme Council retained its status as the organization's executive body pending the proposed national congress. Also, the first and second zones were given a slight majority in the Kaida al-Amma, with twenty seats to the Tripartite Unity Force's eighteen. Rather than being selected by a general meeting of the five zonal commands, as the reformists seemed to prefer, the representatives of the first and second zones would be selected by the two zones. Furthermore, the Supreme Council was able to place a temporary hold on the admission of new fighters into the organization, in what was a clear effort to prevent the incorporation of new (often Christian) recruits that might be sympathetic to the reformists' agenda (Kibreab, 2008, pp. 160–161).

Predictably, the seeming compromise that was achieved at Adhoba satisfied no one. Many within the Tripartite Unity Force felt that the Adhoba meetings had not gone far enough in reforming and restructuring Jebha. Christians in the fifth zone, in particular, worried that the old-line, Arab-centric leadership, retained its influence. The Supreme Council, and its allies in the field, interpreted Adhoba as the first step toward their complete marginalization.

It was the Kaida al-Amma, large, unwieldy, and deeply divided, that was to be the site of conflict in the days and weeks following Adhoba. A complete breakdown occurred in December 1969, when the body inexplicably announced that it was suspending the Supreme Council because of its failure to visit units in the field. The decision was the straw that broke the camel's back, sparking violence between those who sought to defend the status quo, those who sought to radically alter it, and those who, like Chairman Mohammed Ahmed Abdu, attempted to retain Kaida al-Amma's coherence and reimpose order. While the diffusion of contention had initially strengthened the reformists' hand, the ongoing "cycle of contention" took a bizarre twist, irrevocably dividing the different factions.

The outcome of this decisive spate of violence is difficult to interpret. What is clear, however – as stated in Chapter 3 – is that those who were on the losing end of the armed incidents (or appeared to be on the losing end), decided to split from Jebha in a bid for survival. Richard Sherman (1980, p. 44), one of the few close observers of the Eritrean insurgency at the time, makes a similar observation by noting that the splits following the Adhoba arrangements occurred because "by early 1970 it was clear to a number of those who had attempted to attain 'unity at any cost' that the agreement was fatal." Interestingly, those who would come to this conclusion included not only those who supported the move to oust the Supreme Council but also those who opposed it.

Fragmenting to Survive: Jebha's Dissidents, 1969–1971

One of the more significant groups to leave Jebha in the violence following Adhoba was the group of young highland Christians from the fifth zone who had been the reform movement's focal point. Under the command of Abraham Tewolde, this group was typical of Christian fighters who had joined Jebha in the mid- to late 1960s. Most had been university or secondary school students in Addis Ababa or Eritrea's towns, possessed Marxist leanings, and were committed to purging the organization of both its tribal/sectarian and pan-Arab sensibilities.

Yet they were deeply critical of the reform process that had culminated at Adhoba, and in particular, of their former allies in Kaida al-Amma. "Our Struggle and its Goals," a key document written by this group in 1971, noted that while Jebha's recent internal reform process "marked the beginning of a process of correction... since it was not built on the basis of revolutionary political principles, disguised opportunists managed to sabotage it."[11] Describing the efforts of these "disguised opportunists" as "The Second Phase of Oppression" (with the first phase being the treatment of Christians before the reform process began in 1967), the document went on to state that six Christian members of Kaida al-Amma had been placed under arrest in the days following Adhoba; that leading Christian cadres Kidane Kiflu and Woldai Gidey had been gruesomely killed in Kassala; and that there had been a concerted and coordinated effort to prevent Christian recruits from joining Jebha's ranks. On the latter point, the manifesto claimed that more than 200 Christian fighters had been killed at the hands of Jebha's leaders and their allies in Kaida al-Amma, a reference to the "Siyret Addis" incident in which several hundred new Christian recruits, mostly Eritrean workers from Addis Ababa, were purportedly executed.[12]

---

[11] This document is in the possession of the author. It was provided to the author by an Eritrean colleague.

[12] In the author's own view, Mohammed Abdu's main goal was to impose political order over the organization, and demonstrate that he was in fact in charge. He had the support

For Tewolde and his group, exit was the only option. Rhetorically asking, "What alternatives exist?" the authors of "Our Struggles and its Goals" mapped out the difficult choice:

> Conditions being such, should one opt to face butchery in the hands of "Jebha" simply because one was born Christian or should one surrender to the enemy, the Haileselassie government? Which option is better? Dying at the hands of religious fanatics or giving one's hand to the enemy? Both are abominable; both are poisonous pills to swallow; both mean death. Moreover to make neither choice is tantamount to sitting on the edge of a sharp blade. But rather than choose either of the two alternatives, it is better to sit on the edge of a sharp blade.

Fighting for their survival, but committed enough Eritrean nationalists to reject surrender to the government, the group fled to the Ala plains, which sit on the eastern escarpment of the highlands in the province of Akele Guzai. It was here that they came to be known as the "Ala group." Though the unit successfully made the long trek, Abraham Tewolde died from illness. Issais Afeworki, the former political commissar of the fifth zone and Kaida al-Amma member, became the de facto commander, and was supported by a five-man leadership committee.

The other group to split from Jebha was a faction led by Osman Saleh Sabbe. As mentioned in the previous chapter, tensions had always existed between Sabbe, Adem, and Glawedos over the distribution of power within the Supreme Council. Such tensions often had a sectarian tinge as each represented different tribal constituencies. In this context, the Anseba meeting in September 1968 had created an open rupture within the Cairo triumvirate, as the factional fight now spread to the leadership. Always keen to get ahead of events, Sabbe publicly endorsed the Tripartite Unity Force and the cause of reform, placing him at odds with Adem and Glawedos, who had been more circumspect about recent developments.[13] The question of how the Supreme Council should respond to the reformists spilled over into organizational matters, with fierce disagreements emerging over the need to

---

of a number of his Saho kinsmen in this respect. But it is important to note that his detractors accused him of realigning at Adhoba with those resistant to reform within the first and second zones. See interview with Osman Saleh Sabbe, conducted by Gunter Schroeder, December 29, 1980, Khartoum, Sudan; claims regarding Siryet Addis have been contested by Jebha. See, for instance, Woldeyesus Ammar's discussion at www.ehrea.org/syria.htm (October 29, 2017); also see "Siryet Addis: A Blatant Lie," Awate.com, March 24, 2012, which can be found at http://awate.com/srryet-addis-blatant-lie/ (Accessed June 12, 2015).

[13] In fact, as Markakis (1987, p. 110) notes, Sabbe had proposed the idea of a leadership selected by a popular congress upon joining Jebha's leadership in Cairo in 1960. However, Markakis viewed this as an effort by Sabbe to marginalize the executive body of Jebha, which Adem and Glawedos dominated at this time.

expand the leadership. One side of the debate argued that a renewal of the Supreme Council's legitimacy required broadening its ranks. Others suggested that this would only sharpen the differences within the Council.[14] These problems became worse in the months following Adhoba when Sabbe shifted gears, and attempted to prevent the usurpation of his authority by Kaida al-Amma through the unilateral "reorganization" of Jebha's external operations into a new body, the "General Secretariat." Since Sabbe had not consulted the Supreme Council about this move, which was announced at a press conference in Amman, Jordan, the gulf between Sabbe and his colleagues in the leadership widened. Finally, when Kaida al-Amma announced the suspension of the Supreme Council in December 1969, Sabbe declared it a "military coup" and openly broke with both Kaida al-Amma and the Supreme Council, formally moving into open competition with Jebha.[15] Having lost the power struggle within Jebha – a fact underscored by Kaida al-Amma's arrest of several of his key loyalists – Sabbe had little choice but to exit.[16]

There were other splinters in the days and weeks following Adhoba. They included Abu Tiyara and Omar Damer of the Marya tribe, who as commanders of Jebha's training and support units had joined the Tripartite Unity Force as members of its executive body. Following their fragmentation, these commanders and their followers went west into eastern Sudan. They were joined by another dissident element, consisting primarily of Muslims from the fourth zone and a sprinkling of Christians from the third and fourth zones who had supported the reform efforts. This group included Mohammed Ali Omaro, Ramadan

---

[14] Interview with Idris Glawedos, conducted by Gunter Schroeder, November 28, 1988, Khartoum, Sudan.
[15] Sabbe's claim, which was later endorsed by testimony given by Glawedos, was that the coup had been orchestrated with the assistance of a key ELF benefactor, the Iraqi government. The Iraqi view, according to Glawedos, was that they could better control the young and experienced cadres of the Kaida al-Amma. By contrast, the Supreme Council was too politically seasoned to be manipulated by the Iraqi Baathists. Interview with Idris Glawedos, conducted by Gunter Schroeder, November 28, 1988, Khartoum, Sudan.
[16] Sabbe's immediate entourage would include his close associate, Taha Mohammed Nur, one of the original Cairo exiles who first organized Jebha in 1960–61, and old nationalist leaders like Woldeab Woldemariam and Mahommed Said Nawud. Nur would go on to become a commissioner for the Constitutional Commission of Eritrea. He died in 2008 after being jailed by the Eritrean government for his antiregime activities. See a report from the *Sudan Tribune*, dated February 22, 2008, which can be found at http://www.sudantribune.com/spip.php?article26098 (Accessed October 29, 2017); much of Sabbe's entourage was outside of Eritrea when it fragmented, but it is clear that they had lost control of the military situation on the ground and would have faced serious sanctions if apprehended.

Mohammed Nur, al-Amin Mohammed Said, Mesfin Hagos, and Mehari Debassai.

Eager to build a new nationalist organization, Sabbe chartered a plane from Khartoum to Aden, and brought this contingent of Jebha dissidents in Sudan to Yemen for training. From there, this group traveled to southeastern Eritrea by sea, where with Sabbe's assistance, they rendezvoused with other splinter elements that had fled to the arid plains of the Danakil in southeastern Eritrea. This meeting, at a place called Sudoha Ela in late June 1970, was attended by 100 fighters, and selected a command of nine individuals headed by Omaro. It was at this time that this group collectively came to be known as the Popular Liberation Forces (PLF). Since Sabbe had been a member of the old-line leadership in the Supreme Council, the group sought to distance itself, refusing to name him to a leadership post within the nascent organization.

While the Ala group had argued in "Our Struggle and Its Goals" that they were "Freedom Fighters and not prophets of Christianity," the rhetoric of the manifesto was clearly rooted in Christian grievances. The PLF, by contrast, a more religiously and ethnically heterogeneous group, echoed the claims of its colleagues from the fifth zone, but avoided their Christian slant. They also reserved special venom for the chairman of Kaida al-Amma, Mohammed Abdu, accusing him of not only allying himself with the opponents of reform, Adem and Glawedos but also unlawfully extending his term.

A memo from the US Consul General in Asmara includes a copy of a 1971 article written by one of the only Western journalists to have spent time with the PLF at this stage. The article is based on a profile of one of the group's leaders, Mehari Debessai, and provides a clear statement of the reasons for the PLF's departure from Jebha. The article states:

Mohammed Abdu is one of the [Jebha] military leaders, and at the congress held at Adhoba in 1969 was given the responsibility of directing the Front's military operations only for one year, after which time he was to have passed on the "Marshall's Baton" to whoever was chosen by a new congress. Instead, Abdu ignored these recommendations; he didn't call a new congress.

The article continues, citing an instance of Abdu's purported violent excesses:

What has Mohammed Abdu done in order to remain chief of the Liberation Army beyond the year assigned to him by the 1969 congress? He associated himself with a political group (that of Cairo which is led by Idris Glawedos), which has pan-Arab tendencies, and he hunted down all those within the Front who were not in accord with his views. There have been incidents; there have been killings. Six Eritrean "adversaries" of Abdu were forced to flee abroad in order to avoid assassination. One of these, Ali Berhatu – an Asmara lawyer, a graduate in comparative law from the University of New York, and an ex-employee of the legal office of Ethiopian Airlines in Addis Ababa – attempted an effort at conciliation. He went to visit Mohammed Abdu one day when his band happened to be at Kassala and was surrounded by machine guns. Abdu took him away with him that same night to Eritrea. Abdu kept him prisoner for an entire year...[17]

This narrative illustrates the conundrum that many within the PLF encountered as events unfolded in 1968–69. Facing severe sanctions as their reform efforts began to falter, the heterogeneous PLF group was left with no other option but to exit Jebha.

The final group to part ways with Jebha was a faction that came to be known as Obel.[18] In contrast to Ala, PLF, and even Sabbe, this group was resolutely opposed to the Eslah, or reform movement, and was the last to be drawn into the cycle of contention that engulfed the organization. Composed of Beni Amer from the first zone, the faction was upset by the suspension of Idris Mohammed Adem, Jebha chairman and their coethnic, and what they viewed as the growing influence of Christian and Marxist radicals within the Kaida al-Amma. In addition, its leaders, Adam Saleh, Ahmed Adam Omer, Osman Ajib, and Mohammed Ahmed Idris, had come into open dispute with Saleh Hayouti – the head of the military committee within Kaida al-Amma and a Bilen from the second zone – about the distribution of supplies between the first and second zones. Indeed, the unrestrained chaos within the Jebha ranks provided Obel an opportunity to assert their claims on resources.

As a fragmented Kaida al-Amma, led by Mohammed Ahmed Abdu, sought to reassert control of Jebha's rapidly deteriorating internal situation, the recalcitrant Obel group became a clear target of violent reprisals. Facing sanctions for their disobedience, and too few in number to put up stout resistance, the group departed for the Obel River – from which they acquired their name – in their home province of Barka in early 1970, where they held a meeting and formally announced their opposition to Jebha.[19]

---

[17] Drawn from newspaper article attached to Airgram 11 from Asmara to State, April 15, 1971, RG 59, Central Files, "Recent Italian Magazine Articles on ELF [Jebha]." Article is from an Italian magazine called *Domenica del Corrier*.
[18] Obel was a river in the vicinity of where this group was organized.
[19] Author's interview, Shaebia commander, May 28, 2009.

Cooperation, Consolidation, and Organizational Emergence: Shaebia, 1972

In early 1972, the Ala group, Sabbe's General Secretariat, the PLF, and Obel merged into one rebel organization, Shaebia. On some level, the alliance made sense. As a schoolteacher in the Massawa area, Sabbe had built personal relationships with many of his coethnic Muslim fighters in the PLF, many of whom he taught and recruited into Jebha. Both the PLF and Ala group shared a common aspiration for reform that had fueled Jebha's fragmentation. Obel were comfortable with Sabbe, a conservative, Muslim member of the old-line leadership who shared the faction's distaste for Marxism, and had sought to firmly situate the Eritrean struggle within the broader pan-Arab nationalist movement.

But the organization remained a diverse collection of dissidents, many of whom possessed blatantly contradictory political views. Kibreab (2008, p. 212), for instance, argues that "with the exception of the few individuals in the PLF and Selfi-Natsanet [the Ala group], the organizations that met in Beirut had practically nothing that united them except the enmity of Ethiopia and the General Command [Kaida al-Amma]." In the eyes of the young Christian Marxists within the Ala group, Sabbe epitomized everything they had sought to change within Jebha – the pretentious nature of the conservative external leadership and its pro-Arab line. Predictably, the relationship between the Obel and Ala groups was awkward as well, as the two had been on opposite sides of the power struggle within Jebha, and were ethnically, religiously, and ideologically worlds apart.

So why did this collection of disparate splinter groups coalesce into a single rebel organization? The only trait that this patchwork of dissidents shared was that they were on the losing end of the factional violence that engulfed Jebha in late 1969, and decided to formally break with the organization in clear bids for survival.

While Jebha had been severely weakened by the defections after Adhoba, the organization managed to muddle along in the months after its fragmentation. At the Awate Military Conference in March 1971, 300 Jebha delegates met to formalize plans for a national congress that would transition power from Kaida al-Amma to an elected leadership. The preparatory committee for the upcoming congress formed at Adhoba was expanded and broadened, and the public statements that emerged from the meeting were largely conciliatory toward the splinter groups. Several efforts were made to negotiate with the dissidents, including a meeting between Jebha official Saleh Eyay and the PLF representatives in

Aden.[20] In an effort to heal sectarian divisions, Jebha nominated Herui Tedla Bairu, a Christian, as chairman of the upcoming congress.

Still, the splinter groups rejected Jebha's appeals. Those who had supported the cause of reform were particularly suspicious of Jebha's overtures. Their wariness was, in some respects, well founded. Jebha's old chairman of the Supreme Council, Idris Mohammed Adem, eventually regained his position via elections at Jebha's 1st National Congress of October 1971, despite his leadership failures and the initial usurpation of his authority by Kaida al-Amma. Ironically, the defection of so many reformists strengthened Adem's hand, and since he maintained the strong support of his Beni Amer kinsmen from the first zone – numerically the largest of all of the five zones – he garnered enough votes to win. Yet Adem went further in trying to reassert his authority at the congress, attempting to subvert newly introduced democratic procedures by vetoing the election of popular cadres Azien Yassin, Saleh Eyay, and Mohammed Omar Yahya, in favor of his own son, Ibrahim Idris.[21] In Eyay's case, Adem's efforts were unsuccessful, as Eyay's large margin of 100 votes more than Adem's heir apparent (out of a mere 600 voting delegates), was difficult for the chairman to overcome. Yet Yassin and Yahya were successfully defeated in an election that greatly tested the integrity of the new political order.[22]

For Sabbe and Obel, who had never really embraced the cause of reform but now sat outside the organization, reconciliation remained difficult. For somewhat different reasons, both groups worried about how they would fare in an organization that had dramatically changed its institutional structures and ideological orientations (Adem's election notwithstanding). Nor did they really believe that their defections would be forgotten and declared water under the bridge.

The unwillingness of the splinter groups to reconcile and return to the fold forced the hand of Jebha's newly elected leadership. Unwilling to tolerate the emergence of an alternative nationalist movement(s), Jebha's military command, led by Abdulla Idris, began to make preparations for operations against the splinter elements. This hardening of

---

[20] "The Near Liquidation of the (E)PLF," compiled in 1993 by Aida Kidane, which was found at www.eritrios.net/1970s.htm (Accessed May 16, 2009).

[21] Yassin, a staunch communist who got his start in the Sudanese Communist Party in the 1960s, served as Kaida al-Amma's chief information officer, and had been sharply critical of Adem's performance as Jebha chairman. This was likely the reason for Adem's hostility. The official rationale for Adem's opposition to Yahya was that the new Revolutionary Council already had too many Saho, and required more representation from the Marya ethnic group. Usman Ezaz eventually received this contested slot.

[22] Interview with Saleh Ahmed Eyay, conducted by Gunter Schroeder, October 1, 1988, Kassala, Sudan.

attitude toward those who had fragmented was reflected, as has been mentioned in the previous chapter, in the formal decisions of the 1st National Congress at Arr in October of 1971. A 1973 Jebha document emphatically summarized the hardening of Jebha's position, stating:

> It becomes crystal-clear that in societies similar to ours, only one democratic national front can be formed. The existence of more than one front under such conditions would either be a politically unconscious adventurist attempt underlying the dangerous strategic mistake of dividing the social forces of the democratic national liberation and hence, weakening it, or a conspiracy hatched by the colonialists to liquidate the revolution.
>
> In both cases those who stand behind such a political phenomenon betray the revolution... and acts of sabotage directed at the unity of such a front should be confronted with the most unwavering determination to secure/contain it.[23]

The dissidents were not impervious to the looming threat inherent in the declarations of the 1st Congress. At this juncture, Jebha retained more than 2,000 armed fighters, many of them well trained and reasonably equipped. By contrast, collectively, the splinters possessed no more than 500 fighters. The splinter units in the field possessed inadequate weapons, little ammunition, and an inconsistent supply of food. A member of the Ala group, for instance, recalls that "The early days were very difficult... they [Jebha] had superior manpower." Although the splinter groups understood that relations with their parent organization were tense, they naively assumed that a truce would be possible. The sharp change of tone and attitude was thus shocking to Ala, and would have far-reaching effects on its strategy in the weeks and months ahead. In the words of one fighter, "Nobody imagined they [Jebha] would attack us... it was like a dream."[24]

Like the Ala group, the Sabbe faction would come to understand that it faced a similarly dire situation. Sabbe's personal status and authority within the Eritrean nationalist camp had always hinged on his ability to attract military support from his Arab benefactors. Yet his break with Kaida al-Amma, which could not be offset by his tenuous links with the PLF group in the Danakil, was beginning to undermine his credibility. Without a strong presence on the ground within Eritrea, few Arab leaders were willing to offer Sabbe arms, or protection against Ethiopian agents and nationalist rivals. In early 1970, the Baathist governments

---

[23] Quote drawn from "The Near Liquidation of the (E)PLF," compiled in 1993 by Aida Kidane, which was found at www.eritrios.net/1970s.htm (Accessed May 16, 2009); and an ELF document titled "Liquidation of Counter Revolution," in *The Eritrean Struggle*, No. 3, 1973, p. 8.

[24] Author's interview, Shaebia commander, May 28, 2009.

of Syria and Iraq began to directly support Kaida al-Amma, effectively cutting Sabbe out of the loop.[25] While Sabbe was able to build a relationship with the newly installed Libyan government of Muammar Gaddafi around the same time, it was clear that he had to immediately consolidate his position within Eritrea, or risk becoming persona non grata. For the few hard-core loyalists he retained in the field, the consequences would be far worse.

The PLF was no better off. While a cordial relationship with Sabbe was maintained, the partnership did not yield the sort of material benefits that would enable the group to survive. The area in which they operated, the Danakil, was sparsely populated, with little vegetation, few sources of water, and summer climates higher than 50°C. As Pool (2001, p. 66) notes, early accounts of the group "present a picture of confusion, poor coordination, and vulnerability because of the spasmodic and unreliable supplies from South Yemen... As a consequence, there were high attrition rates..." Eventually, most of the group was forced to disperse, with small units moving to various parts of Eritrea in order to garner resources from more densely populated areas and avoid detection by the Ethiopian authorities.

Located in Barka, a western province that was Jebha's heartland, the Obel group faced the gloomiest prospects of all the dissident groups, since they would be the earliest and likeliest victim of Jebha attacks. Moreover, the group was clearly the smallest of the three in the field. With limited manpower, and lacking a steady source of arms and munitions, the group's position was deeply compromised. In order to survive, they would either have to flee across the border to Sudan or surrender to the Ethiopian authorities.

Thus, all of Jebha's four dissident groups were vulnerable and exposed. Spread around the country, they could not hope to survive the upcoming onslaught from their parent organization without coordinating their activities, however distasteful that might be. The complementarities between the different groups were clear. Sabbe offered the vulnerable units in the field arms and supplies. The units in the field, many of whom detested Sabbe, provided him the weight on the ground to continue attracting the support and protection of his foreign benefactors. Obel offered the reformists in Ala and PLF – with whom they were ideologically at loggerheads – access to the Sudanese border, since they hailed from the western province of Barka, while the larger PLF and Ala units provided the Obel group with much-needed manpower.

---

[25] Interview with Saleh Ahmed Eyay, conducted by Gunter Schroeder, October 1, 1988, Kassala, Sudan.

The paradoxical unity that drove the creation of Shaebia, then, was a function of the dire military situation that each splinter group faced. One of Shaebia's senior political leaders, Haile Woldense, confirmed this perspective in an interview with Dan Connell, one of the earliest chroniclers of Shaebia. In the interview, Woldense acknowledges that "what was the most unifying factor was the declaration of a civil war by the ELF [Jebha]. Then many secondary issues had to be overlooked." He further states that "because it was a question of survival," a "conducive climate" for cooperation between the dissident elements was possible (Connell, 2005, p. 52). Woldense continues with this line of thought: "When the ELF [Jebha] declared their intension to liquidate us [in 1972], this created an atmosphere to build some confidence, to concentrate on how much we needed each other. And this threat created the opportune moment to strengthen our unity" (Connell, 2005, p. 58). Clearly, the dynamics of security and survival weighed heavily on the convergence between the Jebha's dissidents. Shaebia would be the direct product of this prevailing threat environment.[26]

It was Sabbe who became the focal point for the emerging organization. The arms and external connections he provided rendered the venture viable in the eyes of the various splinter elements and helped to propel cooperation, as did the fact that the new organization had yet to be proven militarily inadequate. After gathering representatives of the various groups in Beirut, Lebanon, in February of 1972, Sabbe was able to broker a unity agreement, officially signed on February 12. Reflecting the fact that it represented the minimum that all parties could agree on, the agreement was vague, but did mandate the creation of a "united national front," and the operational unification of the dissident elements by the end of that year.[27] Resources would be distributed evenly to the three separate factions in the field, and Sabbe would be charged with sole responsibility of handling the external affairs of the nascent organization. Shaebia, as it was later to be known, was now officially up and running.[28]

---

[26] Kibreab (2008, p. 166), in his masterful history of the Eritrean struggle, echoes Haile Woldense's assessment, asserting that "while each group might have had different interests, none of these could be realized without their mutual cooperation, regardless of what they thought of each other."

[27] While the founding document was vague, there was a clear slant in favor of reform elements in general, and the Ala group in particular. For instance, one of the resolutions declared that in the sharing of resources, "the Christian element must be taken into consideration as for its excessive enumeration in order that it might effectively share in the revolution, and be able to direct blows against the enemies' interests in the Eritrean plateau."

[28] See *Journal of Eritrean Studies*, issue No. 1, Vol. V, Summer, 1991, "The Beirut Unity Agreement of 1972: Project of the United National Front." Those who signed the

However, as Markakis (1987, p. 131) notes, since the basis for unity was tenuous, Shaebia would unravel as the military picture changed:

> The coalition that went under this name until 1975 [Shaebia] embraced quite disparate elements whose only common feature was their opposition to the ELF [Jebha]. Representative of pastoralist traditionalism and Muslim sectarianism, the Obel group had little in common with the Christian radicals of the Ala group, who had been driven out of the ELF [Jebha] precisely by these traits. Sabbe's group was a mixed a bag. He himself was regarded as unprincipled and unreliable by the radicals, and as a Saho tribalist by those who applied the ethnic calculus. Predictably, the coalition was riven by mistrust and dogged by intrigue, even as it was fighting for survival against the ELF [Jebha]. When the struggle was over, the coalition disintegrated.

Markakis's observations, as the following sections will show, were precisely on point.

Early Survival, Expansion, the "Menka" Dispute, and the Obel Departure: Shaebia, 1973

A few weeks after the Beirut unity agreement, before the newly created Shaebia forces had an opportunity to concentrate their widely dispersed forces, Jebha units sprang into action. The Obel group in Barka was the first to be attacked, and was virtually wiped out, with one of its primary leaders, Adam Saleh, captured and imprisoned.[29] In March, a similar attack was launched against PLF forces that remained in the Danakil. Outnumbered, the group was forced to flee, making the long trek across Eritrea to the northern province of Sahel, where it was thought the geography would give them respite from Jebha attacks.

Keen to avoid exacerbating religious tensions, Jebha decided against attacking the Christians in the Ala group, at least for the moment. Despite this restraint, the Ala group was unnerved by the attacks on what were now members of its own organization, and quickly joined the PLF on the long journey to Sahel.

It was in Sahel that 250 PLF fighters, 150 Ala fighters, and the 20 to 30 Obel survivors began to regroup and develop a coherent strategy for collective defense.[30] Sahel offered natural advantages for the newly

---

agreement were Ramadan Mohammed Nur, Mesfin Hagos, Ali Said Abdella, Issais Afeworki, Osman Ajib, Saleh Osman Shater, Woldeab Woldemariam, Osman Saleh Sabbe, Taha Mohammed Nur, and Mohammed Said Nawud.

[29] Adam Saleh was not released until Jebha's 2nd National Congress in 1975.

[30] The figure for Obel is drawn from Aida Kidane's compilation of an interview with Haile Menkerios dated October 24, 2004, which can be found at www.ehrea.org/haile.htm (Accessed October 29, 2017). The figures for Ala and the PLF are drawn from Markakis (1987).

created Shaebia: its harsh, mountainous topography allowed the relatively small organization to conceal itself from the larger Jebha, and neutralized the advantages that normally accrued to mechanized and airborne units of the Ethiopian military. The area, though quite arid, had more rain and vegetation then the desolate plains of the Danakil, and sat along the Sudanese border and the Red Sea, providing access to both sea and land resupply routes (Markakis, 1987, p. 134).

Jebha responded by redeploying units to Sahel, in the hope of finally "liquidating" their wayward conationalists. Still not operationally unified, Shaebia sought to give more concrete form to the vague formulas articulated at the Beirut meeting. In October 1972, the organization created the Gehteb executive, a fifty-seven-member committee headed by a nine-person administrative body that handled the day-to-day affairs of the organization.[31] The fifty-seven-member committee comprised twenty-five Ala representatives, twenty-one PLF representatives, and eleven Obel representatives, a breakdown that was reflected in the nine-member executive committee whose chairmanship rotated among the three groups. It was at this moment that Shaebia resolved to retain a presence in Sahel, and pending the defeat of Jebha forces in the province, establish a base area (Pool, 2001, p. 74).

For the next few months, Jebha and Shaebia forces fought a series of running battles up and down the length of Sahel province. These battles culminated in a major engagement in the vicinity of Gereger, a set of twin villages on either side of Eritrean–Sudanese border, in mid-March 1973. The battle lasted over a week, and was a decisive moment. In the words of Markakis (1987, p. 134), "Both sides suffered losses, and neither could claim victory, yet it was a turning point because it proved that the ELF [Jebha] was unable to crush its opponents."

Shaebia sources tend to support the notion that Gereger marked a major shift in Shaebia's military trajectory. More than 100 Jebha fighters were wounded, including Jebha military commander Abdulla Idris, and another 130 were killed. Shaebia suffered only nineteen casualties. According to Shaebia fighter Tewdros Gebrezghier, "Experienced and veteran fighters of the ELF [Jebha] were killed in that [Gereger] battle. Although the ELF participated in many battles, this was the turning point of their decline as a formidable front."[32] Although there is some hyperbole in this statement, it does convey how the battlefield context was changing in Shaebia's favor.

---

[31] "Gehteb" is the name of the village in which the negotiations over the new structure were conducted.

[32] Quote drawn from "The Near Liquidation of the (E)PLF," compiled in 1993 by Aida Kidane, which was found at www.eritrios.net/1970s.htm (Accessed May 16, 2009).

Non-Shaebia sources also confirmed that a shift in power between the two rebel organizations had occurred. Scarcely two months after Gereger, US intelligence concluded:

> The two rival factions of the Eritrean Liberation Front [Jebha] – the General Command of Idris Mohammed Adem and the Popular Liberation Forces (PLF) of Osman Saleh Sabbe [Shaebia] – have resumed open warfare in earnest after a period of relative quiescence ... Although the split has existed for four years and may not be easily resolved, there are some indications that the PLF [Shaebia], which is the larger and stronger faction, is gaining the upper hand.[33]

Of course, the American view that Shaebia was the "larger and stronger" rebel organization was incorrect. Relative to Shaebia, Jebha was larger and stronger, both directly before, and after the battle at Gereger. Shaebia remained only a third the size of Jebha, and parity between the two organizations would be achieved only in later years. Yet the mistaken perceptions of American analysts suggested that in the eyes of many observers, Shaebia's military situation had improved by mid-1973.

It is worth asking how Shaebia managed to survive Jebha's early onslaught. Markakis credits the consolidation of the dissident elements into one organization for their ultimate survival. This view is of course consistent with a major claim of this book – that the creation of Shaebia was an intentional effort to manage imminent survival concerns. "To no small measure," Markakis confirms, "the survival of the dissidents was due to the fact that in the face of common danger, they were able to integrate organizationally and begin fashioning a political consensus that ultimately united the majority of them" (Markakis, 1987, p. 134).

Sabbe, whose ability to channel military and financial assistance to fighters in the field had been critical to incentivizing unity between the dissidents, proved to be an immediate military asset. As Shaebia fighter Tewdros Gebrezghier recalls, "Sabbe sent us much arms, food, medicine and materials like watches. When the ELF [Jebha] fought us with Guandi, a non-automatic gun, we used Kalashnikofs, Simanofs, and Greenofs etc. *We* had modern arms."[34] Badly outnumbered, these technological advantages ensured Shaebia's survival, and propelled the organization's military success in the coming years.

---

[33] INR Research Study, T. Murphy, May 10, 1973, RG 59, Central Files, "Ethiopia: Eritrean Liberation Front Persists Despite Weakness."

[34] Quote drawn from "The Near Liquidation of the (E)PLF," compiled in 1993 by Aida Kidane, which was found at www.eritrios.net/1970s.htm (Accessed May 16, 2009). The important point here is that Jebha forces were using single-shot rifles in battle, while Shaebia had the luxury of automatic weapons. Markakis (1987, p. 135) echoes this point, noting, "The Kalashnikov automatic rifle became the standard weapon of the ELF-PLF [Shaebia] long before the ELF [Jebha] managed to acquire it in quantities."

Fate also played a role in the decisive military engagement at Gereger. The battle spilled over to the Sudanese side of the border, prompting the Sudanese military to intervene and halt the bloody fighting. The intervention blunted Jebha's already costly offensive, producing an inconclusive outcome that was to Shaebia's advantage. Motivating the Sudanese was a desire to preserve order on the Sudanese–Eritrean frontier on the one hand, and retribution on the other. In 1972, a failed coup against Sudanese president Gaafar Nimeiry forced the perpetrators, many of whom belonged to the Sudanese Communist Party, to flee through Eritrea, where their connections with leftist members of Jebha's leadership guaranteed them safe passage to the People's Democratic Republic of Yemen.[35] In retaliation for Jebha's role in the affair, the Sudanese sought to alter the outcome at Gereger and prevent a conclusive Jebha victory. Moreover, when the fighting concluded, the Sudanese military escorted Shaebia units across the border to safe positions in Sahel, in an effort to deter a Jebha ambush.[36]

Whatever the cause of Shaebia military success at Gereger, the battle served to deter further attacks, and provided a platform for the consolidation of Shaebia's position in Sahel. The beginnings of a base area replete with centers for training and logistics were slowly constructed. Keen to balkanize the Eritrean nationalist camp, the Ethiopian government, for the time being, left Shaebia units in Sahel alone. In any case, at that point, the province was too remote to be of much concern to Ethiopian administrators.

The repulsion of Jebha's offensive, and consequent establishment of a base area, provided Shaebia an opportunity for territorial expansion. With its significant Christian membership, the organization was well suited to extend its operations into the strategically vital Christian plateau, an area that Jebha forces had failed to penetrate in any meaningful way. By May of 1973, Shaebia units numbering in the neighborhood of two companies had moved southward into the Christian

---

[35] Author's interview, OLF commander (with close links to Eritrean fronts at that time), April 2011.

[36] "The Near Liquidation of the (E)PLF," compiled in 1993 by Aida Kidane, which was found at www.eritrios.net/1970s.htm (Accessed May 16, 2009); also see interview with Ahmed Karar (chief of Sudanese security at the time), conducted by Gunter Schroeder, January 19, 1981, Khartoum, Sudan. Ahmed Karar argues that Shaebia's main concern, as expressed by Issais Afeworki, was that Jebha would pursue Shaebia units back into Eritrea if they left Sudanese territory. By this point, although bloodied, Jebha had a number of Shaebia units surrounded, and might have been able to deal the fledgling organization a critical blow. The Sudanese not only escorted Shaebia back into Eritrea but also warned Jebha forces on the Sudanese side of the border to refrain from reentering Eritrea for a further five days. This gave Shaebia the time it needed to escape and reestablish itself.

156   Rebellion in Ethiopia and Eritrea

Jebha areas of operation

Ethiopian areas of full control

Shaebia areas of operation

Joint Shaebia/Jebha areas of operation

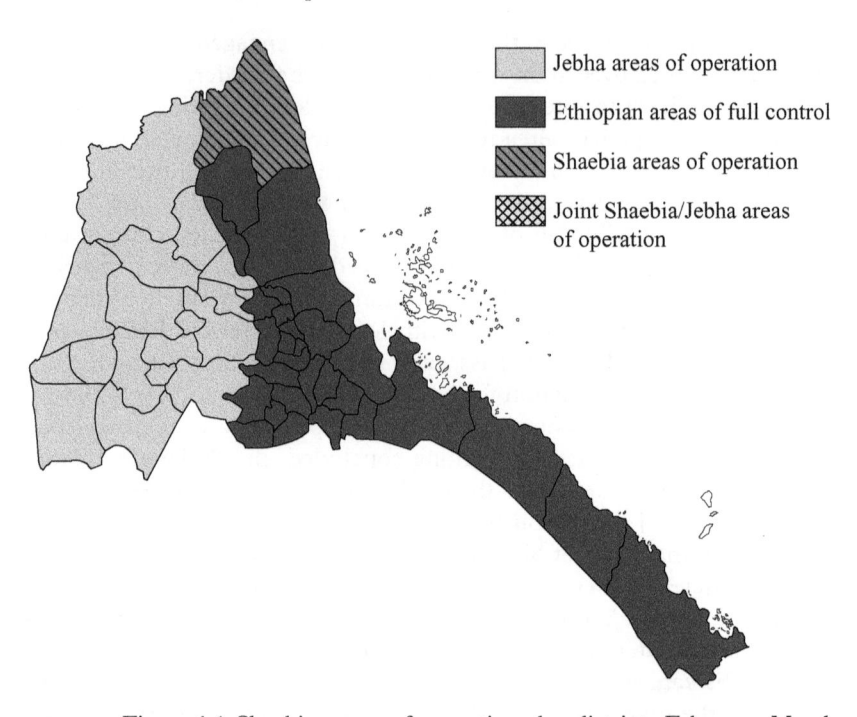

Figure 4.1 Shaebia areas of operation, by district, February–March 1973.

highlands, and were deftly probing the outskirts of major towns in an effort to politicize the communities and attract young recruits from the region's secondary schools and universities (Kibreab, 2008, p. 234). As a result, recruitment flows from the densely populated Christian highlands began to increase. This territorial expansion is visually demonstrated in Figures 4.1 and 4.2.[37]

The developments of the spring of 1973 served as a trigger that provoked a round of factional infighting that had seemed only a distant possibility in the difficult days of 1972. Military victory and territorial expansion reduced survival concerns, eroding the basis for cooperation and prompting the organization's constituent units to more forcefully advocate their own particularistic interests. "The consolidation of our position against the ELF [Jebha] was a big relief," recalls one fighter of this period, "but it created a new internal conflicts and contradictions

---

[37] Details on the units involved in Shaebia's expansion into the highlands, who were under the command of Wedi Fenkel, come from the interview with Abdurrahman Dolo, conducted by Gunter Schroeder, Autumn, 1989, Frankfurt, Germany.

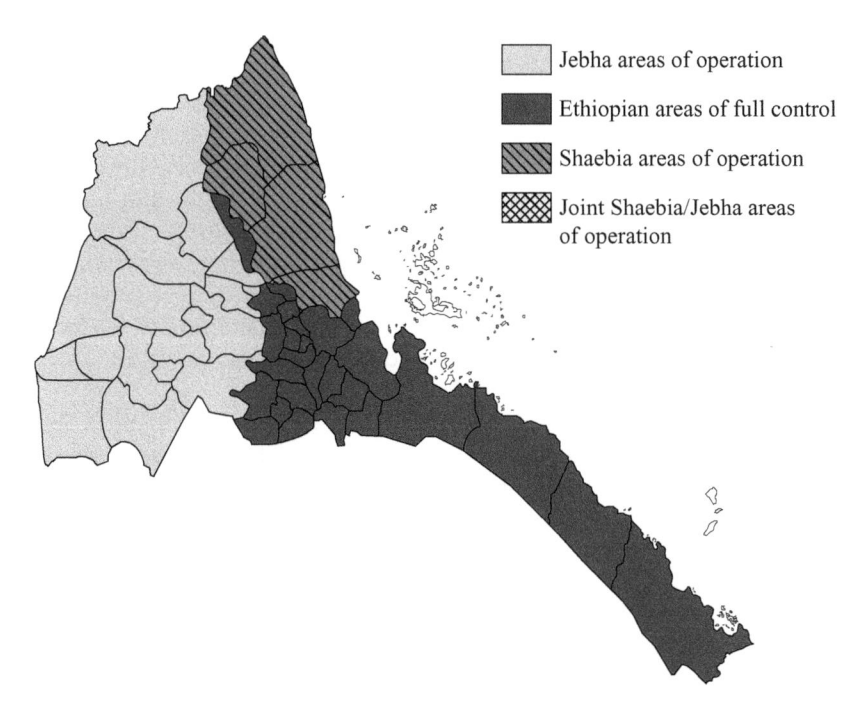

Figure 4.2 Shaebia areas of operation, by district, summer 1973.

we did not anticipate."[38] The opening rupture came from the most of unlikely of quarters, when the leaders of the five-man leadership committee of the Ala group began to fight among themselves. Rivalries between Solomon Woldemariam and several other members of the leadership – most cite Tewolde Eyob and Asmerom Gerezghier as his chief rivals – led to a public meeting in which a number of accusations were leveled at Solomon. The most explosive was the allegation that Solomon was a Hamasien regionalist, intent on protecting the interests of his province above all else. While religious and ethnic tensions had dominated the Eritrean nationalist scene from the early 1960s onward, the introduction of provincial or *awraja* politics among Christian highlanders was a bizarre twist.[39] More than likely, the charges were meant to marginalize Solomon, rather being a legitimate line of critique.

The public allegations against Solomon, which built on weeks of rumors and innuendo fostered by Solomon's rivals within the leadership,

[38] Author's interview, Shaebia commander, May 28, 2009.
[39] Awraja means "province." For Eritrea's nine provinces, see map of Eritrea in Chapter 3.

would trigger the involvement of a number of newer Christian recruits who had joined Shaebia in Sahel. The group was led by Mussie Tesfamichael and Yohannes Sebhatu, leftist radicals who had earned notoriety in nationalist circles for hijacking an Ethiopian Airlines flight departing Rome in 1970. Mussie was a gifted orator capable of mobilizing a significant number of cadres, and as a political commissar and head of political education, was well positioned to build a rapport with the newcomers. Yohannes Sebhatu also held a key position of power, serving as the director of publications and information. An important commonality that the leaders of this group possessed, beyond their affinities for Marx and Lenin, was that most of them had been students at Addis Ababa University in the 1960s.

As the meeting unfolded, the group led by Mussie and Yohannes Sebhatu sprang to Solomon's defense, as factional infighting began to spread to actors not involved in the original leadership dispute. Earlier that same year, a recruit named Meles Gebremariam had been accused of working for a foreign intelligence agency, and as a result, he was summarily executed by the leadership. Many of Meles's fellow newcomers were profoundly impacted by his death, as the seemingly arbitrary nature of the execution created a degree of uncertainty, fear, and disquiet within the ranks. "Nobody raised a finger for him. Fear and conformism reigned then. Everything was hushed up, except for dubious rumors," one fighter remembers in describing the unease created by Meles's execution.[40] Against this backdrop, the budding campaign against Solomon, which likely presaged a move to oust him from the leadership if not liquidate him entirely, sparked the anger of the newer recruits. The personal attacks against Solomon, these recruits came to believe, were emblematic of the whimsical manner in which the leadership sought to regulate the affairs of the rank-and-file.[41]

Several meetings were held in September–November, attended by the Ala leadership and representatives from Ala units in Sahel, in which the differences between the leadership were put into sharp focus.[42]

---

[40] "Dirty War in the Dejen," by Zekere Lebonna, February 2, 2004, which can be found at www.ehrea.org/nformatiDejen.htm (Accessed October 29, 2017); and author's interview, civilian encamped in Shaebia base area familiar with Meles's case, July 2009. Meles was accused of having CIA affiliations. His plight was made worse by the fact that his father was a senior security official within the imperial administration.

[41] Meles was not the only fighter summarily executed in this period.

[42] These meetings, of which there were two or three, became progressively larger as the divisions became an organization-wide concern. The earliest meeting involved ten to fifteen individuals, while the largest meeting involved around sixty to seventy. Precise numbers are difficult to come by. The best analysis of these meetings is Kibreab (2008, pp. 228–238).

Mussie Tesfamichael and his supporters saw the cracks within the Ala leadership body as an opportunity, and not only vigorously defended Solomon but also launched an all-encompassing attack on the entire leadership. Though Shaebia had managed to survive Jebha's onslaught, the Ala leadership was taken to task for the inevitable logistical and tactical problems that had manifested themselves during the fighting. More serious, however, were demands for political reform. The leadership lacked a proper Marxist political orientation, critics claimed. Too many fighters had been deprived of due process, and summarily punished without a fair hearing. Decision making was too centralized and lacked fighter and mass participation. More than a year after Shaebia's formation, no national congress had been held and the leadership remained an unelected and unaccountable cabal. Eventually, these critics demanded that an elected administrative committee provide immediate oversight of the leadership, a thinly veiled attempt to rob the five-man leadership committee of all executive authority. While territorial expansion and preference divergence had provoked a dispute within the Ala leadership and their loyal constituencies, the mobilization of Mussie Tesfamichael and Yohannes Sebhatu's group represented a clear diffusion of the factional fight as they sought to exploit the emerging cleavages.

What had simply been a tense and heated debate quickly descended into disorder when Tsegai Keshi, a close ally of members of the leadership who had been critical of Solomon, struck Mussie Tesfamichael in the head with the butt of his gun during one of the meetings in which leadership divisions were being discussed. Mussie, Yohannes Sebhatu, and their allies now moved into open opposition, holding meetings and penning pamphlets attacking the leadership and demanding political reform. Their detractors gave the group the pejorative title of *Menka*, which is the Tigrinya term for a bat, because Mussie and his colleagues preferred to hold their seminars in the late evenings.[43]

With contention having spread from the Ala leadership to the Ala rank-and-file now organized under the banner of Menka, it was only natural that other segments of Shaebia would be dragged into the dispute. At around the time that Menka was gathering steam the Ala and PLF groups – which were ideologically closely aligned – began to negotiate a more complete merger of Shaebia that would involve the full integration and mixing of units. Up to that point, the groups were integrated only at the leadership levels. Although there was consensus between Ala and

---

[43] The *Menka* label was coined by Naizghi Kiflu, a close associate of Issais Afeworki and early Shaebia member, who would later serve as independent Eritrea's minister of information. See recollections of Woldemariam Abraham, compiled by Aida Kidane, which can be found at www.ehrea.org/WeMenkae.pdf (Accessed October 29, 2017).

PLF on the necessity of merging their forces, members of Ala's leadership – particularly Ala's most significant personality, Issais Afeworki – sought unity with PLF forces in order to leverage their support against Menka. Issais was assisted in this regard by his close partnership his friend from his days in China, PLF leader Ramadan Mohammed Nur.

Obel, however, was taken aback by the factionalism within the Ala group. While they shuddered at the prospect of a Marxist takeover of what they perceived to be an already excessively leftist group, they saw the merger as a consolidation of Issais's power. As the smallest of the Shaebia's three founding factions, Obel was likely to fare poorly in a fully integrated organization, as its membership would be diluted and its political interests sidelined by their leftist coalition partners. As a consequence, they sought to block integration by refusing to merge with the other two groups, arguing, according to one fighter, that "they wanted to stay out until what they did not understand became clear to them."[44] Abu Tiyara, the Jebha commander who had defected from Jebha to join the PLF group, was similarly inclined and joined Obel in opposition.

At an impasse, the leadership of Ala and PLF made the decision to move forward with the full merger in September 1973. This forced Obel's hand, and it formally withdrew from Shaebia's leadership structures and redeployed to other areas, effectively fragmenting the organization. While the dispute between the groups did not involve violence, Obel's failure to win the power struggle over the integration of rank-and-file units had clear security and survival implications. Part of the issue here was that by failing to stop the merger, and at the same time not merging itself, Obel put itself in a position in which it was no longer able to access the armaments and logistical support provided by Sabbe, since the position of the majority was that access to supplies and weapons would be conditional on merging. Moreover, there was some fear that Obel could now expect to be attacked by its much stronger former colleagues (Kibreab, 2008, p. 272). Although Obel would not come into open conflict with Shaebia and did continue to coordinate its activities – largely because Sabbe continued to cultivate the Obel leadership – the groups experienced an awkward and uneasy coexistence for the next several years. In any case, Obel was much too small to be any more than a nuisance to a steadily growing Shaebia.[45]

---

[44] See "Menka Memory," which is recollections of Shaebia fighter Meharena Hadgu compiled by Aida Kidane, and can be found at www.ehrea.org/Memeharena.pdf (Accessed October 29, 2017).

[45] Not all of the Obel group exited Shaebia, and some who did later rejoined as individuals – for instance, Abdulla Moussa. Drawn from the author's interview, Shaebia commander, May 28, 2009.

Just as the dispute in the Ala group helped to propel the Obel split, the Obel split compounded in the crisis in the Ala group. Issais Afeworki – who had been a primary target of Menka criticism and a major critic of Solomon Woldemariam – sought to rally opposition to Menka in a bid to retain the leadership's authority. Asserting that the Menka were "opportunists" who wanted to break Shaebia's unity when "victory was at hand," Issais accused Menka of encouraging Obel to split from Shaebia until such a time that Menka had seized power within the Ala group.[46] Issais also portrayed the leftist radicals as anarchists naively unaware that the cold, hard realities of insurgent warfare demanded strict military discipline and centralized leadership. "Popular administration does not mean all people will administer," Issais Afeworki later declared in making this argument (Pool, 2001, p. 78).

Menka's insubordination virtually paralyzed the Ala group's leadership, and forced a change of tack. Recognizing that the dispute between Solomon and others within the Ala leadership had created a political opportunity for Menka, Issais sought to establish a compromise between Solomon and the rest of the leadership. Pointing out that Menka's demands were directed at the entire leadership, including Solomon, Issais was able to broker a truce. Solomon, in a Machiavellian twist, now turned against Menka, accusing its members of being Akele Guzai regionalists, even though they had come to his defense earlier on. "The reason for the conflict in the force was a power struggle," one fighter later said. "When they [the leadership] realized the situation was getting out of hand and that many fighters were hearing of it, the veterans concluded that they should come to agreement among themselves otherwise the educated ones [the newcomers] would overpower them."[47]

In order to guarantee reconciliation within the leadership, Solomon was appointed chief of internal security, a powerful post that would be responsible for taking punitive measures against Menka.

Solomon's defection was a decisive moment, creating momentum for Menka's opponents. Issais sought to further bolster the Ala leadership's position by bringing units that had been deployed to the highlands back to the base area in the Sahel, which was the epicenter of the factional fight between the Ala leadership and Menka. Since these units and their

---

[46] See "Menka Memory," which is recollections of Shaebia fighter Meharena Hadgu compiled by Aida Kidane, and can be found at www.ehrea.org/Memeharena.pdf (Accessed October 29, 2017). Also see Kibreab (2008, pp. 254–256); others also share the view that Menka's leaders were little more than political opportunists, since they had failed to legitimately raise their criticisms of the leadership in previous meetings or discussions – author's interview, Shaebia commander, May 28, 2009.

[47] See recollections of Woldemariam Abraham compiled by Aida Kidane, which can be found at www.ehrea.org/WeMenkae.pdf (Accessed October 29, 2017).

commanders had been operating in the highlands for several months, they were untainted by the propaganda of Menka's talented rhetoricians, and more likely to side with Issais and the existing leadership. Moreover, using his close personal relationship with key leaders of the PLF group, including Ramadan Mohammed Nur, Issais successfully consolidated the support of the largely Muslim PLF. To this key constituency, Issais Afeworki and Ramadan portrayed Menka not only as narrow Akele Guzai regionalists but also as Marxist ideologues who would bury their Korans.

Efforts by Issais to consolidate the Ala leadership's position by settling internal differences, and building a coalition with units deployed to the highlands and the PLF, proved to be effective. Committees were elected to resolve the dispute Menka had generated, adjudicate responsibility, and ascertain punishment. With the support of these key constituencies, the Ala leadership acquired the numbers within these committees to defeat the Menka's calls for regime change.

The Menka leadership was imprisoned and court-martialed. Eventually, a decision was made within a special committee, convened between June and August 1974, in a fashion that was not entirely clear, to execute the ringleaders of the movement. Eventually, fifteen to twenty members of the Menka leadership were killed, including Mussie and Yohannes Sebhatu. Those who were willing to reaffirm allegiance to the leadership were reincorporated into the organization, and some went on to occupy significant positions within the leadership.[48]

The decision to punish Menka with the most extreme of sanctions created further knock-on effects, as insecurity of other sectors of the organization increased. Tewolde Eyob, an Akele Guzai native who had been, along with Issais Afeworki, one of the chief critics of Solomon Woldemariam within the Ala leadership committee, argued that the committees should modify their harsh decisions regarding Menka's fate. He was joined in his opposition by a group led by Bitsay Goitom Berhe, a political commissar and law graduate from Addis Ababa University who served on the committees that determined Menka's sentences. Eyob was eventually arrested in mid-1974 and executed like the Menka leaders he belatedly sought to defend. One fighter describes Eyob's demise in this way: "A brave member of the leadership, Tewolde Eyob, did not even sign for the killing [of Menka]. He said, 'let us democratically solve the situation.' When it was said that this movement [Menka] is 'destructive,'

---

[48] For instance, Petros Solomon rose to become head of Shaebia's military intelligence unit, popularly known as "Brigade 51," and later foreign minister of independent Eritrea. Sebhat Ephrem rose to become head of Shaebia's department of public administration, and later served as independent Eritrea's minister of defense.

Tewolde said 'no...we can lead them the right way, it is not a criminal charge.' But it was said that he too was against Shaebia and he was eliminated."[49]

Bitsay Goitom and his followers turned to agitation, forming an underground entity within Shaebia called the Eritrean Revolutionary Party, which translated the works of Lenin, Marx, and Mao for popular consumption within Shaebia. Goitom's efforts were not viewed kindly by a leadership that sought to tightly control political education. The last straw occurred when Goitom published a manifesto suggestively titled "Who Is a Revolutionary?" in which he sharply criticized Shaebia's leadership. Goitom was eventually purged, and met the same fate as Eyob.

Goitom's death marked the conclusion of the factional disputes of 1973–74. Though the territorial shifts that triggered the dispute were relatively small, and did not signal a looming victory for Shaebia over either the Ethiopian government or Jebha, it did resolve the severe security concerns that had helped to drive cooperation between Shaebia's constituent in the first place. With survival guaranteed, the awkward relations within the Ala leadership broke down into a full-fledged factional fight. A group of newer recruits, later dubbed "Menka," were sucked into the dispute, and the widening cycle of conflict eventually compelled the Obel group to fragment and resulted in the purging and unsavory demise of the Ala leadership's opponents.

Had the outcome of the battle of Gereger been different, and Shaebia failed to expand its zone of operations onto the strategically vital Christian plateau, it is unlikely that the likes of Issais Afeworki and Tewolde Eyob would have sought to oust Solomon Woldemariam from the leadership with accusations of "regionalism." Once the dispute began, it acquired a momentum of its own, rocking the entire organization.

Territorial Gains and the Sabbe Split: Shaebia, 1974–1976

As was the case with Jebha, the collapse of the Haile Selassie regime and the ensuing chaos boosted Shaebia's fortunes. The inability of ruling elites in Addis Ababa to prosecute the war in Eritrea gave Shaebia a free hand in many parts of the country. The emergence of a truce with Jebha further consolidated Shaebia's position, as did the emergence of other rebel organizations in various parts of Ethiopia and the timely Somali invasion of Ogaden. In 1974, and again in 1975, Shaebia units

---

[49] See "Menka Memory," which is recollections of Shaebia fighter Meharena Hadgu compiled by Aida Kidane, and can be found at www.ehrea.org/Memeharena.pdf (Accessed October 29, 2017).

expanded the territory over which they operated, continuing the process of movement into the Christian highlands. The organization also began to operate in the vicinity of the city of Keren, as well as the arid plains of Semhar province where the strategic port of Massawa–Hirgigo was located.

The indiscriminate violence that disoriented Ethiopian units in Eritrea began to employ in 1975 dramatically increased Shaebia's ranks, as it had done for Jebha. One fighter who fled his home to join Shaebia during this period described the deep insecurity that drove recruitment:

> If I told you that I was politically conscious and understood the politics of Eritrea I would be lying. It wasn't that the fighters [Jebha and Shaebia] were capable to mobilize young people, but what the Ethiopians did helped to push people out of their villages and towns. I remember my uncle and cousins were killed, just killed. They were just ordinary people ... So, it was those kinds of things. It was a mixture of somebody pushing you, and the other person accepting you with open arms.[50]

Shaebia's growth in numbers, to about 10,000 by late 1975, served to reinforce territorial expansion. By mid-1975 the organization had shifted from guerrilla warfare to fighting positional warfare from fixed bases. The emphasis was now not only on expanding operational reach, but territorial control (see Figures 3.4 and 3.5 in Chapter 3).[51]

Rapid territorial expansion disrupted the uneasy cooperative equilibrium that emerged within Shaebia after the departure of Obel and the purging of Menka. As early as January of 1975, US intelligence sources noted "unconfirmed reports of fighting within PLF [Shaebia] in recent days. Some sources believe the PLF [Shaebia] is infiltrated by Ethiopian government agents to cause dissension."[52] Yet the American assessment was only partially correct, as the emerging internal conflict was entirely homegrown. Indeed, tensions between Sabbe and the leadership in the field, now dominated by Issais, Ramadan, and others, finally boiled over. In September 1975, negotiations between Sabbe and Jebha in Khartoum resulted in a unity agreement that built on the existing truce between the two rebel organizations, in which Sabbe committed Shaebia to a national

---

[50] Author's interview, Shaebia senior political cadre, June 12, 2009. Interviewee had twenty years of experience as a member of Shaebia.

[51] Dan Connell characterized the changing face of the war for Shaebia when he wrote "The EPLF [Shaebia] military strategy was like a perpetual game of cat and mouse. For years the Eritreans had played the mouse. Now they had transformed themselves into the cat" (Connell, 1993, p. 144).

[52] Airgram from Asmara to State, January 15, 1975, RG 59, Central Files, "Relationship between ELF and PLF."

democratic front based on Jebha's formula of a single rebel organization, with a unified command and a single coherent strategy.

Convinced that it remained the smaller of the two nationalist organizations, Shaebia's leadership in the field feared that full unification of command structures and forces would see them marginalized within the newly merged nationalist rebel organization. Issais's line, which was a delaying tactic, was that there should be a convergence in ideology between the two nationalist fronts before full organizational unification. The slogan at the time was "Unity of ideology before unity of the gun."[53] In the eyes of Shaebia's leadership, Sabbe was willing to accept any unification agreement that preserved his paramount position as the nationalist movement's chief spokesman abroad. They responded by arguing that Sabbe did not have the authority to make such an agreement, and had failed to consult the leadership in the field.[54] Sabbe was aghast, protesting that Issais and company were kept fully abreast of the negotiations, and had been invited to send a delegation. The dispute escalated, as Sabbe sought to coerce and cajole the leadership in the field by threatening to withhold supplies and funds from abroad. Events reached a point of no return in November 1975, when a public meeting of Shaebia cadres in Zager resulted in protracted debate, and a decision to reject the agreement wholesale.[55]

The public repudiation of the Khartoum agreement undermined Sabbe's standing within Shaebia. By early 1976, Sabbe and Shaebia's leadership in the field were no longer on speaking terms. Marginalized and without recourse, the situation was far too dangerous for Sabbe and his erstwhile supporters in the field to remain within the Shaebia fold. In their eyes, the rejection of an agreement Sabbe had signed in good faith was an abrogation of the cooperative status quo, and little more than a

---

[53] Interview with Osman Saleh Sabbe, conducted by Gunter Schroeder, December 29, 1980, Khartoum, Sudan.

[54] Eritreans for Liberation in North America, "EPLF [Shaebia] Memorandum," May 5, 1976, pp. 30–31, stated that "the Foreign Mission attempted to impose the Khartoum agreement – an agreement that serves its interests, enables it to perpetuate its claims of absolute dictation on the Eritrean revolution, and exercise political extortion against a people who have suffered the ugliest form of colonialism." Memorandum was posted by Aida Kidane in November 2010 at www.eritrios.net (Accessed June 1, 2011).

[55] This was also known as the *Semanawi Bahri* meeting. Interview with Osman Saleh Sabbe, conducted by Gunter Schroeder, December 29, 1980, Khartoum, Sudan. Sabbe also argues in this interview that Issais was not inclined to accept the Khartoum agreement because he planned to use the growing number of Christians within Jebha ranks to launch a coup within the organization. This would pave the way for a merger on Shaebia's terms; also see interview with Ahmed Karar, conducted by Gunter Schroeder, January 19, 1981, Khartoum, Sudan. Ahmed Karar is more critical of the way Sabbe handled the rupture over the Khartoum agreement, and claims that he tried to force a deal that would never be accepted by units in the field.

coup d'état. In March 25, 1976, Sabbe announced a formal break of the Foreign Mission from Shaebia, and his supporters in the field – which included members of the PLF and what remained of Obel – followed suit.[56] Underscoring the security and survival dynamics that prompted the exit, Sabbe's supporters abandoned Shaebia encampments clandestinely, under the cover of darkness. These elements were reorganized into a military force in Barka under the watchful eye of Jebha, but failed to gain any traction. Supplies that were intended for Shaebia were redirected to Sabbe's supporters, an action that turned Sabbe into the bête noire of the Shaebia camp.

Shaebia was quick to portray the rupture as the inevitable outcome of the deep ideological rift that existed between Sabbe – conservative and steeped in sectarianism – and the "progressive" elements in the field.[57] A public memorandum issued by Shaebia offices overseas stated the tensions in this way:

> The development of any national movement, like that of society itself, unfolds through the resolution of its internal contradictions. In a national democratic revolution, all patriotic forces unite and wage armed struggle against colonialism, imperialism and feudalism in order to solve the principal contradiction.
>
> At the same time, an internal struggle is waged within the patriotic front to resolve secondary contradictions. In any national movement, as the revolutionary vanguard gains strength and its correct line gains the upper-hand, the class struggle between the progressive and reactionary forces intensifies.
>
> As they see their power wane, their future interest threatened and their dreams coming to an end, the reactionary forces begin to move frantically to reassert their power and secure their position. If their efforts meet with failure, they actively work to obstruct and prevent the revolution from advancing forward. At this juncture, they are even prepared to ally themselves with the enemy in order to safeguard their selfish interest.

As such, Shaebia officially greeted Sabbe's departure with delight:

> Thus, the expulsion of such a reactionary group from the revolution is welcome. It not only saves the revolution from dangerous consequences but also helps it to make forward strides. It enables the revolutionary forces to strengthen and consolidate their unity and raise the class consciousness of the masses. It assures the revolution of its inevitable final victory. This is a truth borne out by world revolutionary experience.[58]

---

[56] This included important figures like Abu Tiyara, Abu Ajaj, and Abubakr Jima. Interview with Mohammed Said Nawud, conducted by Gunter Schroeder, July 6, 1986, Khartoum, Sudan.

[57] Most of my interviewees familiar with this incident framed the rupture in this way. For example, author's interview, Shaebia senior spokesman, March 29, 2009.

[58] Eritreans for Liberation in North America, "Reactionary Clique Forced Out of the EPLF [Shaebia]," May 5, 1976, pp. 11–16.

In some ways, Sabbe's reputation as conservative was well deserved. He was notoriously critical of the Marxist bent of his colleagues in the field. Unlike many other parts of Ethiopia, the Eritrean peasantry was not alienated from the land. Feudal landlords did not rule over toiling rural masses; instead, Eritrean communities had a relatively equitable land tenure system in which rights to cultivation rotated between families. Moreover, agrarian class analysis was largely irrelevant to Eritrea's large pastoralist population, nor did the territory possess a large urban proletariat. Under such social conditions, Sabbe argued, what did Marxist class analysis have to offer? Perceptions of Sabbe as a conservative "reactionary" were further reinforced by generational differences and age: at forty-three, Sabbe was significantly older than the leadership in the field.

In Shaebia's official rhetoric, Sabbe's pan-Arab/Islamic sympathies had also been a key source of tension. Here too, there was some evidence that this claim was valid. With his immaculate Arabic linguistic skills, light skin, and aquiline features, Sabbe was broadly perceived as the darling of pan-Arabist politicians across Middle Eastern and North African capitals who were interested in the Eritrean cause. His wife was the cousin of a Syrian prime minister and he was a close personal friend of the Syrian army chief of staff. As has been noted, he played up Eritrea's ties to the Arab world, and his own seemingly pro-Arab disposition, to great material effect.

But in many ways, the ideological/sectarian dispute was superfluous. Sabbe's private discussions with American and British officials, as reflected in classified American and British documents from the 1970s, paint a picture of a man who was deeply sensitive to the ideological and sectarian rifts that had plagued the Eritrean nationalist movement. As a result, Sabbe believed that Eritrea's nationalists required strictly homegrown solutions to the questions of the day, rather than imported ideologies from the West or the Arab world that might prove divisive. At the same time, ever the pragmatist, Sabbe's view was that Eritrea's nationalists needed to play whatever ideological or identity-based cards they could, in order to sustain the movement and draw support from abroad. Privately, Sabbe acknowledged that his pro-Arab orientation was necessary because in order to obtain material support, "one needed to tell the Arabs what they wanted to hear."[59] In one particularly revealing episode, from 1967, Sabbe actively courted the Chinese government in order to garner permission to send cadres to China for training. He promised to spread the teachings of Mao's Red Book throughout Eritrea, although,

---

[59] Author's interview, OLF commander, April 2011. Interviewee is paraphrasing what Sabbe said to him during a conversation.

given his perceived ideological predilections, it is hard to imagine he had the intention of actually doing so.

Sabbe's 1974 Arabic book, titled *The History of Eritrea* – written on the eve of his 1975 rupture with Shaebia – reflects just how superficial claims about Sabbe's ideological proclivities really were. While one of the major goals of Sabbe's text was to "fill the gap in the Arabic library about the past of a country which enjoys historical, geographical, and cultural ties with the Arab world," he was well aware of the "multiplicity of Eritrean history" (Sabbe, 1974, pp. 11–13). Indeed, the text took time to describe the Orthodox Church's contribution to the evolution of Eritrean society and institutions. Rather than a cartoonish Arab, pan-Islamic ideologue, the book demonstrated that Sabbe had a judicious view of Eritrean history, in which the territory and its peoples were an amalgamation and fusion of diverse ethnolinguistic heritages and religious traditions. The book seems to confirm that Sabbe was not a man deeply committed to any particular ideological or sectarian agenda.

Nor were Sabbe's opponents in the field particularly committed to any ideological position themselves. While Issais Afeworki and his colleagues, since their days as reformers in Jebha, had sought to portray themselves as Marxist radicals, the Menka dispute severely contested their leftist "revolutionary" credentials. After all, Menka leaders Mussie Tesfamichael and Yohannes Sebhatu had portrayed Issais and the Ala leadership as a reactionary, conservative, power-hungry grouping (albeit not of the Islamic variety), a claim strikingly reminiscent of the claims levied against Sabbe. Moreover, Bitsay Goitom Berhe's attempts to translate and distribute the Marxist classics among Shaebia cadres was one of the reasons the leadership in the field had him silenced, an odd response for a group of individuals who purported to be Marxists. Moreover, the outwardly Marxist orientation of many of the Shaebia cadres, both in the leadership and rank-and-file, was superficial. Many lacked the education and basic understanding of the Marxist–Leninist canon to be truly committed to its ideals; instead, leftist ideologies served as little more than fashion, a marker of one's purported "sophistication" rather than a practical guide that motivated action.

Taken from this perspective, the conflict between Sabbe and the leadership in the field was never about ideological or sectarian differences, as Shaebia claimed. Such differences may have been the idiom through which factional infighting was structured, but the dispute was fundamentally about personal rivalries and the balance of power between Sabbe, Shaebia's core external patron, and the leadership in the field led by Issais Afeworki and Ramadan. As one prominent Shaebia internal security official noted, "the Sabbe issue was an outright power struggle. Issais

[Afeworki] didn't like being under Sabbe's mercy."[60] The power struggle, in turn, was triggered by the simple fact that the leaders of the Ala and PLF groups no longer needed Sabbe, because of what this official termed "the new military facts on the ground."[61] Territorial expansion, primarily due to the disarray of the Ethiopian state and peace with Jebha, eliminated the raison d'être of Shaebia's original coalition – namely, guaranteeing the survival and security of its various constituent partners. This fact is acknowledged, somewhat unintentionally, by Shaebia's narrative of the split cited earlier, when it argued, "In any national movement, as the revolutionary vanguard gains strength and its correct line gains the upper-hand, the class struggle between the progressive and reactionary forces intensifies." Here, Shaebia was the vanguard that was gaining "strength," as it surged in the wake of Haile Selassie's ouster; the forces in the field were Shaebia's "progressive" elements; and Sabbe was the "reactionary" force embedded within the movement.

Once again, there were knock-on effects of Shaebia's split with Sabbe, as contention diffused to sectors of the organization not directly involved in the dispute. Emboldened and empowered by the exit of Sabbe, Issais and his colleagues in the leadership sought to sideline elements that had been closely linked to Sabbe, but remained within the Shaebia fold. At Shaebia's first congress in January 1977, Issais Afeworki and Ramadan successfully passed a resolution that barred those who had been senior commanders within Jebha from serving as members of the politburo and central committee of Shaebia. The new rule effectively eliminated Mohammed Ali Omaro, the old commander of Jebha's fourth zone, from the leadership ranks.

More importantly, the resolution undermined the position of Solomon Woldemariam, who had never been a close ally of Sabbe, but had served as Kaida al-Amma's head of internal security. Yet unlike Omaro, who was too severely weakened by Sabbe's departure to ever put up much of a fight, Solomon Woldemariam remained a significant pole of power. In his new position as head of Shaebia's internal security, Solomon Woldemariam and his supporters were feared. His leading role in the eradication of Menka had earned him a reputation for unbridled ruthlessness. Issais Afeworki and Ramadan were thus keen on sidelining Solomon by whatever extralegal means necessary.

In the weeks after Shaebia's January 1977 organizational congress, Solomon was accused of Hamasien regionalism and labeled *Yemin* by

---

[60] Author's interview, Shaebia internal security official (internal security department was called *Hawela Sewra*, or in Tigrinya, "Guardians of the Revolution"), August 16, 2009.
[61] Author's interview, Shaebia internal security official, August 16, 2009.

the leadership.[62] Though Issais Afeworki and others had been complicit in the killing of Menka, they now accused Solomon Woldemariam of the executions, in their attempt to mobilize those Menka supporters who had suffered at the hands of Solomon while in detention.[63] In yet another Machiavellian twist, Solomon had been sent to Sudan for medical treatment directly before the onslaught, and was unable to rally his supporters in the field. His most erstwhile supporters, including Haile Jebha, Shaebia's notorious interrogation chief, were imprisoned and summarily executed. By the time a bewildered and unsuspecting Solomon Woldemariam returned to Eritrea later that year, the purge had completely neutralized his power base. He was imprisoned and eventually executed.[64]

Soviet Intervention, "Strategic Withdrawal," and the EFLNA Split: Shaebia, 1977–1978

The massive Soviet-backed Eastern Bloc intervention in Ethiopia, described at length in the previous chapter on Jebha, had similarly deleterious effects on Shaebia. From Shaebia's perspective, the military turning point came during the Battle of Salina in December 1977, when Shaebia units, after seizing three-quarters of the port of Massawa, attempted to finish the job by seizing the city's strategic naval base. The attack on the base, located on a narrow peninsula that juts out into the Red Sea, was always going to be difficult, as it required that Shaebia troops make a full frontal assault through flooded salt plains. As the nationalist fighters waded through water that was chest high, a full barrage of Ethiopian fire rained down upon them. Skilled Soviet advisers had manned Ethiopian artillery positions, and Soviet naval vessels shelling Shaebia positions made the operation even more problematic.

This combination of factors led to a serious defeat – with hundreds of Shaebia casualties – that was followed by the comprehensive offensive against Jebha and Shaebia positions across Eritrea, or what became known as the "First Offensive." As noted before, since Shaebia's area of operation did not border Ethiopia proper, the organization had time to adjust to the surge of government forces heading northward from Tigray. In a clever maneuver, Shaebia forces withdrew to the northwest, and new front lines were established in the vicinity of Eritrea's second

---

[62] *Yemin* means "rightists." They were placed in explicit juxtaposition to Menka, who were perceived as extreme leftists.
[63] Author's interview, Shaebia senior spokesman, March 29, 2009.
[64] Interview with Ahmed Karar, conducted by Gunter Schroeder, January 19, 1981, Khartoum, Sudan. Other Yemin executed, most after 1978, include Dr. Eyob Gebreleul, Amanuel Filansa, and Fissahaye Kidane, among others.

largest city of Keren. But Ethiopian advances eastward from the port of Massawa rendered Shaebia's position in Keren vulnerable, and using the cover of a stunning victory at El Abared – where Shaebia forces annihilated Ethiopia's 10th division and captured thirty-one tanks – Shaebia withdrew from Keren on November 26, 1978. Further withdrawals were necessary to preserve Shaebia's fighting capacity. This process of withdrawal, redeployment, and retrenchment became known as the "Strategic Withdrawal" and was Shaebia's equivalent of the "Long March."[65] Figures 3.5 and 3.6 in Chapter 3 roughly depict Shaebia's changing military situation during this period, although because Figure 3.6 depicts the situation in 1981, these figures illustrate a more dramatic territorial swing than was apparent by 1978–79.

Whatever the military rationale for the strategic withdrawal, the maneuvers amounted to a stunning set of territorial losses visited upon Shaebia by its resurgent Ethiopian adversaries. In the context of these military defeats, journalist Dan Connell captured the mood within Shaebia ranks well, noting that the Shaebia leader, Issais Afeworki, was "distraught" and had declared, in reference to the war, that "It's finished" (Connell, 1993, p. 177).

Provoked by the stunning shift in the direction of the war, this general pessimism began to erode credible commitments between Shaebia's constituent units. The source of the rupture was the Eritreans for the Liberation of North America (EFLNA), an amalgamation of diaspora student and women's groups that were a crucial source of financial support. The group essentially functioned as Shaebia's external organ after the break with Sabbe in 1976, and by agreement, was a formal arm of Shaebia – or what was popularly known in Shaebia lingo as a "mass organization" (Hepner, 2011, pp. 76–96). While it was primarily a diaspora-based organization, many EFLNA members were in the field, and as such, it was as concerned with the politics of security and survival as Shaebia's other constituent units.

Many within the group were shocked by the territorial losses of 1978. Hepner (2011, p. 91), a leading scholar of Shaebia and its diaspora, describes the situation succinctly:

In the space of six months, the EPLF went from controlling large regions of Eritrea to regrouping at its base. To Eritreans abroad, it appeared a horrifying and sudden defeat... In the midst of these developments, EFLNA activists felt confused, disoriented, and desperate about the unfolding situation.

---

[65] This historical allusion to Chinese communist history was made by Shaebia Politburo member Haile Woldense (Connell, 1993, p. 172); for the best analysis of these military developments see Weldemichael (2009, 2013).

Led by its chairman, Mengisteab Isaak, the EFLNA sought a postmortem on the recent military reversals. The critique that emerged was that the recent losses were part and parcel of the leadership's unwillingness to more forthrightly confront the Soviets, whom Shaebia's leaders were reluctant to openly criticize due to their status as co-Marxists and a superpower. This sentiment was fueled by the fact that amidst the collapsing military situation, the EPLF had engaged the Derg in Soviet-sponsored talks in Berlin.

An August congress of the EFLNA resulted in a vote to break with Shaebia, since a takeover of Shaebia by those in the diaspora was never realistically in the cards. Additionally, EFLNA cadres knew well that if they remained within the organization they would be soundly punished for the criticisms of Shaebia's leadership in the field. Indeed, according to the EFLNA, several of their more erstwhile comrades had already been killed on returning to Eritrea.

By October 1978, the organization had published a stinging pamphlet about the war, in which Shaebia featured heavily (so did Jebha), suggestively titled "Eritrea: Revolution or Capitulation?" The authors of the text – Hepner asserts that it was primarily written Mengisteab – defended the EFLNA position to split in this way:

> The stand taken at our congresses is a culmination of a year and half of internal struggle with the EPLF leaders on major questions of strategy and tactics of the Eritrean revolution. The principal differences between us and the EPLF [Shaebia] leadership lie: whether to regard the Soviet-led revisionism as our enemy or friend, especially when it is directly confronting our revolution, on the question of peaceful solution and the characterized the Ethiopian military junta.

The EFLNA authors continued their sharp rebuke throughout the essay, noting that the performance failures of 1978 signaled that Shaebia and Jebha have "betrayed the national struggle" and "have proclaimed themselves as apologists of the Soviet-led revisionist's aggression." As such, the document concludes: "Under the guidance of Soviet revisionists, they [Shaebia] have renounced the banner of protracted people's war and are waving the white flag of 'peaceful solution.' Thus the leadership of the two fronts have become fifth columnists in the service of Soviet-led revisionism in Eritrea."[66]

The EFLNA's bold stand led to another cycle of contention that would split this faction/constituent unit of Shaebia in two. Several cadres

---

[66] These quotes were not taken directly from the ELFNA document "Eritrea: Revolution or Capitulation?" but from an article penned by Mehertab Mehari on July 26, 2007, and posted at http://theworkersdreadnought.wordpress.com/2011/03/01/historical-fragment-the-1978-split-within-the-eritreans-for-liberation-in-north-america-elfna/. The author has since acquired a copy of the original EFLNA essay.

did not accept Mengisteab Isaak's critique of Shaebia's leadership and thought rupture premature and poorly timed. A number of chapters, with the support of the Shaebia leadership, began to relentlessly criticize the leadership. The counterchage was led by Gebremichael Lilo, the secretary of the ELFNA, and Hagos "Kisha" Gebrehiwet, who today plays a major role in managing the economic affairs of independent Eritrea. The fragmentation of the EFLNA would lead to the creation of the Democratic Eritreans of North America (DEMA), and after Mengisteab Isaak's untimely suicide, effectively kill the EFLNA as functioning entity (Hepner, 2011, p. 94).

Yet again, as the war went, so went cooperation.

The Long Stalemate in Sahel, 1980–1987

As noted in the previous chapter, the resurgence of the Ethiopian state in the latter half of the 1970s led to the virtual encampment of Jebha and Shaebia forces in Shaebia's mountain redoubt of Sahel, located in Eritrea's extreme northwest. Eventually, tensions between the two nationalist organizations led to Jebha's expulsion from Sahel and its eventual demise in Sudan. Yet for Shaebia, the struggle against the Ethiopian state continued.

From 1979 until 1987, Shaebia fought the Ethiopian government to a virtual standstill. Repeated government offensives to take Sahel were repulsed, allowing Shaebia to maintain the territorial status quo. The biggest of these offensives, which came in 1982, was Ethiopia's sixth, and dubbed the "Red Star offensive." Much of the apparatus of the Ethiopian state, including President Mengistu Hailemariam, redeployed to Asmara to conduct the campaign. Eighty-four thousand government troops matched up against 22,000 Shaebia fighters, the latter of which were at a decided disadvantage in terms of weapons and logistics. Nearly half a billion dollars was spent on the offensive, which included mechanized armor, aerial support, and several amphibious assaults, supported by Soviet-manned command and control systems. Most outside observers believed that Red Star would be Shaebia's final curtain call. The offensive was anticipated for some time, with one analyst noting that the impending attack would be "Eritrea's Last Stand," and that even if the rebels survived, they would have to relinquish their Sahel base, disperse their forces, and fight a guerrilla war.[67]

---

[67] See the following newspaper articles: R. Lefort, "Eritrea's Last Stand," *The Observer*, November 25, 1979, and A. Matheson, "Ethiopia Stakes All on Final Offensive," *The Observer*, February 28, 1982.

Yet the primary Ethiopian strategy of employing frontal assaults against Shaebia's deftly constructed network of trenches and well-fortified mountain positions was a catastrophic failure. While Shaebia managed to maintain the territorial status quo by holding on to its narrow corner of northwest Eritrea, in the long term, it fundamentally changed the course of the war. In 1984–85, Shaebia forces did make some advances in western Eritrea, capturing the key strategic depots of Tessenei and Barentu, but were quickly pushed back by an Ethiopian counteroffensive, the *Bahr Negash*, which was Ethiopia's eighth offensive in Eritrea since 1978.

As my theory predicts, the long period of stalemate in Sahel mapped onto a sustained period of organizational cohesion within Shaebia ranks. This is remarkable, because the internal bloodletting of the 1970s had not cleansed the organization of its fissures and fault lines. The leadership was divided on many questions, and defectors from the period note marked political competition between Issais Afeworki and his supporters, on the one hand, and a group of senior leaders led by Mesfin Hagos and Ibrahim Afa, on the other. These leadership fissures, which objectively appear to be personality based, seeped down into the rank-and-file and were often played out in a variety of public forums. A basic theme of these fissures were efforts by Issais Afeworki – who was Shaebia's top man from the mid-1970s onward – to further consolidate and centralize his authority, through politicized anticorruption efforts like the "three privileges campaign," and resulting resistance by his rivals within Shaebia's politburo and central committee. Thus, the internal politics of Shaebia were definitely contentious in this era.[68]

Despite these objective facts, the internal tumult of the 1970s was not repeated. The 1980s were a "cohesive stalemate," and there was little evidence of factional infighting, much less full-fledged fragmentation. The reality was that the maintenance of the territorial status quo simultaneously affirmed perceptions of organizational viability while reinforcing the imminence of security threats. Cooperation and organizational

---

[68] Public interview given by Teklai Aden. Aden was the head of Shaebia's internal security department (known in Tigrinya as *Halewa Sewra*) before his defection to the Ethiopians in 1980. The interview was published in an Ethiopian newspaper, and republished by Jebha in *Eritrean Newsletter*, Special Issue, February, 1981, "EPLF: An Inside Story." The transcript is in possession of the author; also, author's interview, Shaebia fighter and finance department official, April 11, 2009. A 2014 Tigrinya-language memoir written by Colonel Tsegu Fesshaie, soon to be published in English, titled "The Hidden Party" also discusses internal squabbling within the EPLF in the mid-1980s See Chapter 3, in a section titled "The Life of Fighters in Sahel: Intra-Party Squabbles." As far as the author is aware, Dan Connell is really the only scholar to have discussed "the three privileges campaign" in any depth.

cohesion was the only possible result. In the words of one fighter, "We were in a struggle for our survival in those years. But morale remained high. We knew we had to persevere. The base area had to be defended at all costs. It created an unbreakable unity."[69]

The cohesive stalemate of the early and mid-1980s ultimately gave way to not only a conclusive Shaebia victory in Eritrea but, with the support of its TPLF allies in Ethiopia proper, the overthrow of the Derg. Shaebia's crushing defeat of Ethiopia's best divisions at the Battle of Afabet in March 1988 paved the way for this success. By 1990, the port of Massawa was seized in the daring Operation Fenkil, and in May 1991, Shaebia forces rolled into the Eritrea capital, Asmara, uncontested (Weldemichael, 2009, 2013, 2014).

Alternative Arguments

This section attempts to evaluate the plausibility of a number of alternative explanations for rebel fragmentation against the actual pattern of factional infighting and fragmentation within Shaebia described in this chapter. These alternative explanations have been introduced and motivated in Chapter 2.

State Repression and Counterinsurgency Strategies

Measures of numerical preponderance, as described in the previous discussion of Jebha, largely fail to explain the three cases of fragmentation cited in this chapter. The massive numerical increases in both the size of the Ethiopian armed forces and Ethiopian military expenditures, which occurred beginning in 1975–76 and would not be felt in the field until 1978, predates the fragmentation of Obel and the Menka uprising, as well as the onset of the Sabbe dispute.

Improvements in military technology employed by the Ethiopian government, and therefore improvements in the quality and quantity of state repression, are also an inadequate predictor of rebel fragmentation. The surge in Soviet equipment and military technology to Ethiopia formally began only at the end of 1976, and again, did not begin to improve the Ethiopian military's performance in Eritrea in a meaningful way until 1978. The departures of Obel in 1973 and Sabbe in 1976 predate these developments.

---

[69] Author's interview, Shaebia fighter and finance department official, April 11, 2009.

When state repression is framed in terms of large government offensives, it remains a poor predictor of rebel fragmentation. With the exception of the 1967 offensive, when Shaebia did not exist, Shaebia was also targeted by the government offensives launched against Jebha. Of these, only the partially successful offensives of 1978–79 correlated with Shaebia's fragmentation – in this case, the EFLNA split. Other offensives that were launched solely against Shaebia, after Jebha's demise in 1982 – including the Red Star offensive of 1982, the Stealth offensive of March–August 1983, and the Bahr Negash offensive in October–December 1985 – did not result in Shaebia's fragmentation.[70]

Nor were efforts to drive a wedge between Shaebia's various constituent units through negotiations and concessions responsible for Shaebia's fragmentation. Again, Minorities at Risk data demonstrates that political discrimination against Eritreans remained constant during the duration of Shaebia's operational life. Like Jebha, the Ethiopian government of Haile Selassie largely refused to engage or even recognize Shaebia. During secret 1978 negotiations with Haile Selassie's successor, the Derg, Shaebia secretary-general Issais Afeworki made exactly this point, wryly noting that despite the seventeen-year insurgency in Eritrea, "not one meeting took place between Eritreans and Ethiopians."[71] Even the 1978 negotiations – which were brokered by Eastern Bloc countries and included the separate talks with Jebha mentioned earlier – were characterized by the Derg's unwillingness to make any concessions, for many of the same reasons outlined in the previous chapter.[72]

External Support and Control

Variation in levels of external support – and thus variation in the leadership's ability to control disaffected elites – is also an inadequate explanation for rebel fragmentation. As has been made clear from the preceding narrative, Osman Saleh Sabbe was the chief source of arms for Shaebia. Sabbe's key benefactor, in turn, was Libya's strongman Muammar Gaddafi, who supplied hard currency and weapons. In staking his claim to the mantle of Arab leadership, Gaddafi was keen to support Jebha's

---

[70] For a meticulous chronicle of Ethiopian offensives of the 1980s, see Fantahun Ayele (2014). Tareke's (2009) book focuses more narrowly on Red Star and the defeat at Afabet in 1988.

[71] "Memorandum of a Conversation between East German leader Erich Honecker and Siassi Aforki, General Secretary of the Revolutionary Party of Eritrea," in Berlin, January 31, 1978, which can be found at Cold War International History Project Virtual Archives.

[72] "SED official Hermann Axen to E. Honecker, enclosing Draft Letter from Honecker to Brezhnev on Ethiopian-Eritrean Talks," April 19, 1978, which can be found at Cold War International History Project Virtual Archives.

rivals, since the Iraqis and Syrians were already deeply embedded within Jebha. From the earliest days, the majority of Libyan support was filtered by sea through the People's Democratic Republic of Yemen, and then dropped on the arid coast for pick-up by Shaebia fighters. Tewdros Gebrezghier, a Shaebia fighter who had participated in the decisive battle at Gereger in Sahel, describes the transport of arms and munitions in this way:

> Arms collected by Sabbe were sent from Yemen to an island depot between us. A boat brings them to the shore and we carried them inland by camels. The way we went to get the weapons was through "no man's" land desert called "Fits-fitso," where only insects are seen. Walking through the area with Congo shoes, one's hot feet got peeled like tomatoes. I have made the trip only once starting from Gereger. One has to carry enough food and water to take that trip and always with camels to carry the loads.[73]

Onerous though it seemed, these supplies were crucial to Shaebia's early successes – as has been pointed out. Yet the Ethiopian revolution and rise of the Derg changed Gaddafi's attitude toward Shaebia, as the Derg was regarded as an "anti-imperialist" force, in contrast to their predecessors, the feudal empire of Haile Selassie. The final Libyan shipment to Sabbe and Shaebia was made at the end of 1974 and both the Libyans and Yemenis became openly hostile toward Shaebia by 1976–77.

On its face, the rupture with the Libyans coincides nicely with the Sabbe split from Shaebia, which began in 1975 and reached its logical conclusion in 1976. Yet the loss of external support does nothing to explain the Menka uprising and the Obel split, which began in the summer of 1973. Moreover, Sabbe proved to be resilient in his ability to funnel arms to the fighters in the field. As was the case for Jebha, the loss of support from radical Arab states created an opening for attracting support from more conservative Arab states such as Saudi Arabia and Kuwait. In fact, it is only when Sabbe departed Shaebia ranks in 1976 that Shaebia fighters in the field noticed that "we were in a crisis economically."[74] In other words, it was the Sabbe split that led to a real loss of material support, rather than the other way around.

In any case, there were no real significant losses of external support after the Libyan betrayal and Sabbe's departure, in part because Shaebia's system of external support consisted of a varied patchwork of different relationships. On some level, connections with the Arab world were

---

[73] Recollections of Tewdros Gebrezghier, in "The Near Liquidation of the (E)PLF," which was compiled in 1993 by Aida Kidane, and found at www.eritrios.net/1970s.htm (Accessed May 16, 2017).
[74] Author's interview, Shaebia internal security official, August 16, 2009.

rebuilt. Shaebia politburo member Mohammed Siad Barre was sent to the Middle East to set up Shaebia's new foreign mission (since Sabbe was gone) and canvas regional leaders for support, an effort that was partially successful. For instance, by the 1980s, Shaebia was able to purchase fuel from the Iraqi regime of Saddam Hussein.[75] The loss of support from Sabbe also necessitated the cultivation of the Eritrean diaspora, an effort that began with the incorporation of the EFLNA into Shaebia in the mid-1970s. By the mid-1980s, most Eritreans who resided abroad were devoting about 10 percent of their income to Shaebia coffers, not to mention other important goods like clothing and canned foods. The money was collected by Shaebia representatives, in what were essentially underground banks located in cities that possessed large Eritrean diasporas: Washington, DC, Milan, Beirut, Khartoum, and Jeddah. Europe and the Middle East were the single largest sources of cash, and donations were reported in three currencies: Ethiopian birr, Sudanese pounds, and US dollars. Foreign governments such as the United States and Italy, although not directly supporting Shaebia's secessionist aims, provided "tacit support," one Shaebia official remembered. "They knew we were sending back money to support the struggle."[76]

There were other resources as well. Shaebia set up a network of underground banks set up in territories occupied by the Ethiopians, which involved incredibly dangerous collection missions by members of Shaebia's economic department. These efforts were further complemented by the sale of contraband, like cigarettes, in Sudan, and small-scale farming and livestock production. By the early 1980s, Shaebia had also established a relief wing called the Eritrean Relief Association, to deal with devastation wrought by recurring droughts in the region. Humanitarian aid not used for civilians was used to feed Shaebia troops. By the late 1980s, a Shaebia finance official who "used to do the books," recalled that "we were not poor... our revenue never shrank, it just got bigger and bigger."[77] By 1987–88, Shaebia had an annual budget of a whopping USD 50 million.

Actual military hardware, particularly heavy artillery and tanks, was seized directly from Ethiopian troops in battle. Shaebia's official slogan of "self-reliance" was a product of necessity, as direct military support from other countries was limited by the 1980s. "We would say 'fight the

---

[75] Author's interview, Shaebia fighter and finance department official, April 11, 2009. Hussein had increasingly tenuous relations with the Soviets, and had long been reluctant to withdraw support for the Eritrean nationalist fronts.
[76] Author's interview, Shaebia senior spokesman, March 29, 2009.
[77] Author's interview, Shaebia fighter and finance department official, April 11, 2009.

enemy with their own weapons,'" a Shaebia official recalled.[78] Further military assistance, though limited, came through Sudan. Though successive regimes in Khartoum were periodically cool toward Shaebia – much as they had been toward Jebha – Sudan's inability to control its borders and the cooperation of local officials in the east of the country ensured that this supply route remained open. Significant amounts of ammunition were also provided by the Chinese, whose open hostility toward the Soviets facilitated a sustained effort to undermine Soviet client states like Ethiopia.

For the purposes of the analysis here, the important point to remember is that after the Sabbe split in 1976, there was no real significant loss of external support. Thus while the absence of factionalism during the 1980s can be explained by the stability of Shaebia's multifaceted network of external support, it cannot explain the EFLNA split of August 1978.

Organizational Structure, Centralization, and Control

Shifts in Shaebia's organizational structure, from a decentralized to a more hierarchical, centralized model, cannot explain the pattern of factional infighting and fragmentation within Shaebia. While Shaebia was run by an administrative committee called the *Gheteb executive* in its early days, Shaebia's three founding groups – Ala, the PLF, and Obel – essentially functioned independently of one another. While the administrative committee was designed to coordinate the operations of the different groups, and develop a uniformity of practice among the various units, this failed to occur. The three groups did not mix their fighters, and the commanders of the three groups handled their external and internal affairs with significant autonomy. Indeed, coordination was so poor, and functional autonomy so great, that in February 1973 Shaebia forces accidently attacked the Marya forces of Abu Tiyara, who had joined Shaebia as a member of the PLF (Pool, 2001, p. 134). This was four months after the Gheteb executive had been established.

It was in this context that Obel fragmented and the Menka uprising occurred. But shortly thereafter, Ala and PLF units merged into a cohesive military force based on the following standard structure: the lowest level of military organization was the squad, three of which composed a platoon, three of which formed a company, and three of which then made up a battalion consisting of around 400 fighters. It was not until the massive troop increases of 1976–77 that Shaebia established brigades, which consisted of three battalions (Pool, 2001, p. 151). This

---

[78] Author's interview, Shaebia senior spokesman, March 29, 2009.

command structure was under the direct control of military committee within the Gheteb executive, which reported directly to Issais Afeworki and Ramadan Mohammed Nur, who were the top-ranking officials within Shaebia by this point. Fighters from all social backgrounds were mixed in the new organizational structure, and a common military and political training program was established.

Two other organizational developments that occurred after the factional cataclysms of 1973 were also important. First, Shaebia constructed different functional departments: finance, public administration, foreign relations, training and education, etc. Key among these was a robust internal security apparatus called *Hawela Sewra*, or "Guardians of the Revolution." The department, which was first headed by Solomon Woldemariam, was replete with an interrogation division and a secret network of prisons. Much of the department's time was devoted to screening new recruits and purging internal dissidents, as the case of Menka illustrates. Its role, in the words of a senior Shaebia official was "enforcing law, order, and discipline," and its emergence at the service of the leadership's aims can largely be viewed as a major step in the increasing centralization of the organization.[79]

The second important development was the emergence of the Eritrean People's Revolutionary Party (EPRP). The EPRP was a secret party within Shaebia led by Issais Afeworki and several of his close associates within the leadership. While the size of the secret party varied, its membership reached about 1,000 members in the war's twilight in the late 1980s. The party essentially created parallel structures within the EPLF, with its own departments and committees. Members were sworn to secrecy, and largely policed the broader organization by monitoring nonmembers in various units whose intentions (and ambitions) were difficult to establish a priori.

All of these organizational innovations were in place by the time that the Sabbe split began. Thus an argument about organization centralization versus decentralization cannot seem to explain the Sabbe split. Moreover, at Shaebia's first organizational congress in 1977, these new structures were formally legitimized by the election of a central committee of forty-five, by delegates from Shaebia's various units and branches. These forty-five, in turn, elected a politburo of thirteen from among themselves, who were tasked with the day-to-day management of Shaebia. Ramadan Mohammed Nur became Shaebia's secretary-general, while Issais Afeworki became his deputy. However, Issais was considered by most to be the center of power within the leadership – as had

---

[79] Author's interview, Shaebia senior spokesman, March 29, 2009.

likely always been the case – while Ramadan Mohammed Nur was, in the words of one fighter, was little more than a "Queen Elizabeth."[80] In fact, it is a widely accepted fact that Issais Afeworki and his associates carefully handpicked the list of candidates that contested elections at the 1977 congress. Crucially, the 1977 congress – which marked the formalization and legitimization of centralized leadership structures along with Issais Afeworki's growing personal dominance – occurred over a year and half before the EFLNA split. Thus, the fragmentation of Shaebia in 1978 could not have been because of some shift to decentralized organizational structures.

Organizational Size and Complexity

Neither aggregate size nor a rapid increase in membership can explain Shaebia's fragmentation.

Like Jebha, Shaebia fragmented both when it was very small (as in 1973 when it numbered only roughly 450 fighters) and when it was relatively large (as in 1978 when it could rely on 18,000–20,000 troops).

On the other hand, while sharp increases in membership were certainly part of the eruption of factionalism and eventual fragmentation of Shaebia in 1973 and 1975–76, the variable provides no leverage in understanding the EFLNA split. In fact, evidence suggests that Shaebia's previously astronomical recruitment rates began to erode directly following Ethiopia's Soviet-backed counteroffensive in mid-1978, although the number of fighters within Shaebia ranks largely remained stable. Recruitment would eventually become such a big problem that Shaebia forces began to forcibly conscript young Eritrean refugees who fled west across the Sudanese border in anticipation of Ethiopian violence following its reoccupation of Eritrea's urban areas.[81] Thus, it does not seem that a surge in troop levels could have triggered the EFLNA split in August 1978, since the organization's membership was either constant or slowly declining in the period directly prior to the eruption of factional infighting.

The other important variable to consider is organizational heterogeneity. Could increases in the level of ethnic or religious diversity within Shaebia undermine the causal story I have identified? Although the precise social composition of Shaebia's membership is difficult to precisely

---

[80] Author's interview, Shaebia fighter and finance department official, April 11, 2009.
[81] Author's interview, Eritrean refugee who fled Keren in 1978, June 1, 2009. While official policy of Shaebia throughout the 1970s was the maintenance of an all-volunteer army, this changed after the Ethiopia's Red Star offensive of 1982, when Shaebia lost a massive number of fighters.

ascertain, a few things are clear. Shaebia was fairly diverse from the outset, a fact that did not change for the duration of the organization's existence. The only aspect of Shaebia's demographics that fundamentally changed was the proportion of the organization that came from the Christian highlands. While Christians were a minority within Shaebia's founding coalition – about one-third of the total membership – this proportion shifted with the massive expansion of membership in the mid-1970s. By the time Shaebia defeated the regime of Mengistu Hailemariam in 1991, about two-thirds of the organization consisted of highland Christians. The rest were Muslim fighters of various tribal and ethnic backgrounds. Since there was little variation in the organizational heterogeneity, due to the fact that Shaebia was always fairly heterogeneous, the variable could not be driving Shaebia's fragmentation.

Absolute Position, Victory, and Defeat

The final issue to consider is to what extent factional infighting and fragmentation is affected by where a rebel organization sits in absolute terms, rather than shifts or shocks to the territorial status quo. Is it possible that each case of fragmentation outlined in this chapter is caused by the passing of some threshold toward absolute victory or failure, rather than the simple occurrence of gains and losses? As pointed out in the previous chapter, if this were the case, we would expect fragmentation to take place when a rebel organization controls or operates only a small sliver of territory, or when it controls or operates over the vast majority of territory. Using the logic of the exercise in the previous chapter, this would be categories 1 and 5.

However, fragmentation occurs only in categories 1 and 2. Moreover, it seems unlikely that the gains of 1973, which resulted in Shaebia operating in more than 20 percent of Eritrea and the organization's fragmentation, could have pushed the organization over a threshold toward "victory." As pointed out earlier, in a larger strategic sense, these territorial gains were marginal, signaling Shaebia's survival, but not a final military victory.

Conclusion

This chapter initially demonstrated that the factions that fragmented from Jebha did so because they had lost a power struggle triggered by the military failures of 1967–68. The factional fight that gave rise to fragmentation diffused to broad sectors of the organization not involved

Table 4.1 *Shaebia – gains, losses, and the onset of fragmentation over time*

Year	Gain/Loss/Stalemate	Onset of Fragmentation
1972	Stalemate	No
1973	Gain	Yes*
1974	Gain	No
1975	Gain	Yes*
1976	Gain	No
1977	Gain	No
1978	Loss	Yes*
1979	Stalemate	No
1980	Stalemate	No
1981	Stalemate	No
1982	Stalemate	No
1983	Stalemate	No
1984	Gain	No
1985	Loss	No
1986	Stalemate	No
1987	Stalemate	No
1988	Gain	No
1989	Gain	No
1990	Gain	No
1991	Gain	No

* Denotes the number of groups that split.

in the initial dispute. The chapter then went on to describe how serious security threats from Jebha leaders drove these different factions to consolidate themselves into a new rebel organization called Shaebia. Later sections showed how territorial gains triggered the Menka dispute, the Obel departure, and the Sabbe split, while the territorial losses of 1978 laid the foundations of the EFLNA split. The 1980s, characterized by Shaebia's long stalemate in Sahel, was a period of relative internal cohesion. The relationship between gains, losses, stalemate, and fragmentation is depicted in Table 4.1.

The evidence presented provides conclusive evidence that rebel organizations are, at their core, institutions designed to mitigate risk and guarantee survival in war. Territorial gains tend to promote preference divergence in rebel organizations, while territorial losses drive commitment problems. Both mechanisms lead to fragmentation. Territorial stalemate produces the opposite outcome.

My two corollary arguments also receive some support. First, fragmentation is usually an option of last resort, and second, factional fights have a diffusive quality, starting narrowly but spreading to encompass broad sectors of the organization. The chapter concludes with a careful consideration of alternative causal variables.

The next chapter turns to several other rebel organizations in an effort to further test my theory of gains, losses, and territorial stalemate.

5 The Second Wave of Rebellion
Tigrayans, Oromos, Afars, and Somalis, 1973–2008

This chapter evaluates the theory of gains and losses against a broader set of strategically selected cases from the Ethiopian civil war. These case studies are designed as "shadow cases" and as such, do not possess the level of detail of the Jebha and Shaebia narratives, but they do allow for a careful consideration of causal processes and mechanisms outlined in preceding chapters. This chapter, like the one that follows, does not provide an evaluation of alternative causal explanations.

Tigray People's Liberation Front: 1975–1991

The province of Tigray was, until the incorporation of Eritrea in 1961, Ethiopia's northernmost territory. It was bounded by Eritrea to the north, the province of Gondar to the southwest, and Wollo to the south. The province consists of more than 90 percent ethnic Tigrinyas – the same ethnolinguistic group as Eritrea's highland Christians. Italian colonialism, beginning in the 1860s, split the Tigrinya ethnic group in half, creating modest differentiation in the social, cultural, and economic practices of the Tigrinya in Italian Eritrea, and those within Tigray who remained in Ethiopia proper. The rest of Tigray's population consisted of smaller minorities like the Afar, Oromo, Kunama, and Tigre.

Unlike parts of Eritrea, or other areas of Ethiopia that saw armed insurgent groups emerge in the mid-1970s, Tigray was the historic core of successive Ethiopian empires. In this sense, rather than a battle between center and periphery, the insurgency that emerged in Tigray in the 1970s was a battle at Ethiopia's political center. In fact, the emergence and consolidation of modern Ethiopia in the latter half of the nineteenth century was, at least in part, led by a Tigrayan – Emperor Yohannes of Tigray. However, Yohannes's death in 1876 at the hands of Mahdist forces from Sudan led to a shift in royal power southward, to the province of Shoa. From then on, two successive Shoan Amhara rulers – Emperors Menelik and Haile Selassie – would expand the modern Ethiopian state to its current borders, and assert Amhara hegemony over the state apparatus.

Given their historic claims to the Ethiopian throne, Tigrayans often bristled at being ruled by Amhara leaders. But beyond the Shoan Amhara elite's dominance of key institutions – the military, the civil service, and the commercial sector – it was the imposition of the Amharic language that truly provoked Tigrayan ire, much as had been the case in Eritrea. By the 1970s, fewer than 10 percent of Tigrayans actually spoke Amharic, and a failure to learn the language could seriously undermine one's ability to matriculate at Ethiopian universities or join the state bureaucracy – a common gateway for those hoping to move up the socioeconomic ladder.

The province had also fallen on hard times economically. Part of the problem was the fragility of the agricultural sector on which the overwhelming majority of the province's mostly rural population depended. This fragility, in turn, was a consequence of unstable rains and severe land degradation, due to overpopulation and Tigray's fragmentary system of land-holding. Government policy, which tended to focus on the development of Shoa and Addis Ababa, only compounded these problems. A round of famines in 1972–73 devastated the province, killing thousands and stoking a fresh wave of Tigrayan nationalist sentiment.

In fact, Tigrayan displeasure with the Amhara-dominated Ethiopian monarchy was apparent as early as 1943, when a peasant uprising against Emperor Haile Selassie shook the foundations of the regime.[1] The troubles were precipitated by Italy's successful, albeit short-lived, invasion of Ethiopia, which broke down existing patronage networks and turned many Tigrayan elites against the emperor. In what came to be known as the *Woyane* rebellion, Tigrayan rebels seized the provincial capital of Mekele, forcing Haile Selassie to call on British air support to brutally put down the insurrection. While Haile Selassie tried to reduce Tigrayan dissatisfaction with Amhara elites in Addis Ababa by appointing a hereditary Tigrayan governor, Ras Mengesha Seyoum, Tigrayan anger persisted.

As my theory would suggest, what became known as the Tigray People's Liberation Front (TPLF) emerged as a coalition of differentiated interests. Although these interests were united by their violent opposition to Haile Selassie and broad commitment to Tigrayan nationalism, they held divergent preferences on a number of core issues. The organization's emergence was presaged by the activities of two overlapping

---

[1] For the best treatment of what became known as the Woyane rebellion, see Tareke (1991).

nonviolent student movements, the Tigrayan United Student Association (TUSA) and the much smaller Tigray Nationalist Organization (TNO), whose activities were centered primarily at Haile Selassie University in Addis Ababa. The young Marxist student radicals from these organizations were firmly divided on the issue of what the TPLF's core objective should be: Tigray's secession or some form of broad-based autonomy within the Ethiopian state.[2] The young student radicals, who constituted the core of the TPLF's leadership up until its final victory in 1991, were joined by popular Tigrayan politician and former rebel Gesessew Ayele – better known as "Sihul" – who was older than his student partners and able to mobilize peasant communities who would have otherwise found the largely urban and untrained student fighters to be unreliable, not to mention politically obscure.[3] A final element were a few Shaebia fighters of Tigryan descent, led by Mehari Tekle (also known as Mussie), who were sent by Shaebia to provide operational expertise to the nascent movement in Tigray, and ensure that the TPLF served as a buffer between the Eritrean front and the Ethiopian heartland.[4] On February 18, 1975, this motley crowd, no more than thirty strong, redeployed from Sihul's home in the town of Endaselessaie to a place in central Tigray called Dedebit, marking the beginning of the armed struggle. From here, the TPLF's numbers began to steadily increase.

Cooperation in this period was underpinned, as I have suggested in my earlier theoretical exposition, by serious collective threats. The Ethiopian revolution, and the emergence of the Derg, had unleashed an orgy of violence against Tigrayan student radicals and old-line Tigrayan political figures like Sihul. These elements had been hit hard, as most had initially been based in Ethiopia's urban centers, and were left exposed to the government's security apparatus. In order for these Tigrayan nationalist forces to survive militarily, they had to build a durable organization that could enhance unity and more efficiently produce violence. The emergence of other potential competitor rebel organizations in Tigray,

[2] Author's interview, TPLF Central Committee member, May 6, 2015. For a contemporaneous expression of the TPLF's ambitions for an independent state (a still controversial idea in the context of Ethiopia's current politics), see "Manifesto of the Tigray People's Liberation Front: Volume 1," February 1976, p. 4. The manifesto states, "Hence, the first task of this national struggle, which will be the establishment of an independent democratic republic of Tigray free from reformist feudal, imperialist and other forms of oppression and exploitation that prevail today."
[3] Sihul was in his late fifties at the time, and a sitting member of parliament. He had become famous for his armed resistance to Italian invaders in the late 1930s.
[4] For a full discussion of the contentious relationship between Shaebia and the TPLF see Young (1996), Trivelli (1998), Negash & Tronvoll (2001), Reid (2003), Woldemariam (2015), and Woldemariam & Young (2016).

including Teranafit/Ethiopian Democratic Union (EDU) and the Ethiopian People's Revolutionary Party (EPRP) – both of which received a modicum of support from Jebha in Eritrea – rendered the TPLF's position even more precarious. At the same time, the fact that the organization was militarily untested (and thus had yet to experience failure) provided a semblance of hope that reinforced the impression that the nascent TPLF could be a viable organization.[5]

After TPLF units established a base area in Dedebit they were joined by a small contingent of TPLF recruits who had trained with Shaebia in its Sahel base area. At this point, the TPLF's founding leadership of eight (mostly former students) selected an official leadership, with Sihul as chairman. The TPLF was then organized into three companies of about fifteen men each for the conduct of military operations. As my theory would predict, it was a decision to expand the TPLF's operations to the northeast of their base area in Dedebit (as well as move the organization's base area altogether) that signaled a reduction of collective security risks and increasing preference divergence, which in turn triggered widespread dissension among many peasant fighters.

The expansion was rendered possible by the general collapse of government military operations across Ethiopia, particularly in rural areas, and propelled by the TPLF's desire to establish themselves in zones closer to the Eritrean border populated by other Tigrayan rebel organizations.[6] Since Dedebit was an area of operation that the peasant fighters knew relatively well, they viewed the redeployment with alarm, perceiving it as an underhanded attempt to undermine their leverage within the nascent organization.

These developments exacerbated existing tensions between peasant fighters, who felt themselves marginalized within the leadership despite their relative military competence, and the Marxist-oriented students who tended to dominate the leadership. According to Aregawi Berhe, a member of the TPLF leadership and a senior military commander:

The peasant fighters were not content with the student leaders. In their first encounter with them [the students], they felt they were clumsy school boys "who could only play with paper," and not shoulder the heavy burden of armed struggle. The peasants thought the struggle was just a military campaign, and that they were in a better position to handle it. For them, a leader meant somebody who could lead them in battle. They believed themselves to be battle-tested

---

[5] Background on Tigray and the early orgins of the TPLF is drawn from Berhe (2004, 2009) and Young (1997).
[6] The objective was to more easily link with Shaebia forces operating in Eritrea, and open a dialogue with the other Tigrayan fronts.

heroes considering the number of shots they fired in their villages or in the bush." (Berhe, 2009, p. 74)

Moreover, many peasant fighters believed that the TPLF's leadership organs were needlessly deliberative, since the existing system involved a high degree of consultation between Sihul, as chairman, and student leaders like Gidey Zerastion, Abay Tsehaye, and Aregawi Berhe. In the interests of efficiency, the peasant fighters believed, more discretion should be delegated to Sihul. The dissident group of peasants was led by Sihul's younger brother, Alemayehu Gesessew (also known as Dirar), although Sihul was unaware of his brother's machinations.

The dispute became more serious as the peasant group began to plot in private meetings. While the student faction was aware of the peasants' grievances, they did not anticipate what was to come. Dirar and his colleagues hatched a plan to kill the student contingent while Sihul was away on a mission. The attack was to occur at lunch, when all the fighters gathered at the Dedebit encampment to take their meals. As the students began to assemble, peasant fighters occupied strategic vantage points from which they would possess the maximum firing range on the lunch area. But fate would intervene. The TPLF's cook for the day, Tsegay Tesfay, noticed what was occurring, and quickly dispersed the student fighters. As a result, the peasant coup collapsed in disarray.[7]

Confused and bewildered by the failure of their plan, Dirar and the peasant faction he led were forced to flee, taking with them the few weapons the TPLF had assembled. It was the student radicals who had forged links with the TPLF's key external backer, Shaebia, and in a protracted factional fight, they would likely leverage these connections and prevail. As my theory would predict, the failed attempt to alter the cooperative status quo and seize power within the organization left Dirar's faction with no other option but to exit. Eventually, these elements dispersed, with the majority fleeing to exile in Sudan.[8]

War with the EDU and EPRP, Territorial Losses, and Fragmentation: TPLF, 1976–1978

The departure of the faction led by Sihul's brother did little to slow the TPLF's momentum throughout late 1976 and 1977. Another rival

---

[7] My description of the peasant coup is drawn from Berhe (2009, pp. 73–76).
[8] In the dataset introduced in Chapter 2, this case is not coded as fragmentation since this group largely decided to leave the political sphere and go into exile. However, this moment of factionalism is consistent with the theory of territorial gains and losses, even though it did not evolve into "fragmentation" as I have defined it.

front, called the Tigray Liberation Front (TLF), was forcibly absorbed into the TPLF, further increasing the organization's numbers. Headline-grabbing attacks, including raids on security and banking installations in large towns like Shire and Aksum buoyed the organization and raised morale. The Ethiopian military's nationwide collapse as an effective fighting force further drove the TPLF's expansion.

Yet the TPLF's circumstances rapidly changed. In Sudan, conservative monarchist forces tied to Tigray's hereditary governor (I refer here to the EDU), Ras Mengesha Seyoum, planned a full-scale invasion of Tigray designed to expel not only the Derg but also the Marxist TPLF. The war was formally triggered when the TPLF's chairman, Sihul, was assassinated by EDU forces while trying to prevent the EDU's hijacking of a civilian bus.

The first phase of the EDU's invasion went well for the TPLF, as the TPLF successfully defended their positions in Tigray, and forced the EDU to redeploy back to Sudan in September 1976 after taking substantial losses. However, one major casualty of this phase of fighting was former Shaebia fighter Mussie, who had become TPLF's senior military commander after Sihul's death.

The second phase of the war with the EDU began in March 1977. The EDU had managed to attract support from anticommunist regimes in Sudan and Saudi Arabia, as well as the American CIA, and successfully recruited thousands of commercial farm workers from large plantations along the Sudanese borders. This support complemented ongoing support from Jebha. More than 10,000 well-equipped EDU fighters crossed from Sudan into Gondar en route to Tigray, facing no more than a few hundred poorly equipped TPLF fighters. On the way to Tigray, the EDU crushed government forces at Metema and Humera (in the province of Gondar), signaling the dire situation that TPLF forces would face once the EDU wave hit their zone of operation. Indeed, the TPLF was badly mauled in the first major engagement between the two sides at Sheraro. A few days later, at Adi Nebrid, they lost another engagement, and were forced to vacate the town. From here on out, the TPLF was compelled to avoid direct military engagements with the stronger EDU, and operate through guerrilla warfare.

By 1978, the EDU challenge was compounded by a resurgent Soviet-backed Ethiopian military, and war with another rival rebel organization, the EPRP. With base areas to the south and east of TPLF positions, the conflict with EPRP left the TPLF encircled, as the EDU was attacking from the west. It was only meager support from the TPLF's northern allies, Shaebia, that provided the TPLF reprieve. By the middle of 1977 the TPLF had lost more than a third of its membership in battle, as well as three-quarters of its weaponry, which further reduced the territory over which the organization could effectively operate.[9] In the TPLF's own reading of history some years later, these "were very hard years" as the organization "had to face political and military assaults from very many enemies."[10]

Military hardship and territorial loss provoked major commitment problems within the TPLF, as various segments of the organization began to question the leadership's capacity to keep the organization afloat and ensure the membership's survival. This is confirmed by TPLF senior leader Aregawi Berhe, who has noted, "As the [military] situation appeared to become unbearable, many fighters began raising questions about the calibre of the TPLF leadership to guide the struggle" (Berhe, 2009, p. 113). Some accused the leadership of sending units into battle without proper equipment, and even more seriously, of demonstrating cowardice in the midst of military operations.

The factional fight, which was triggered by military failure and the erosion of credible commitments, eventually morphed into a much broader dispute with sectarian overtones. Critics, many of whom hailed from the recently absorbed TLF, began to assert that the TPLF's leadership was dominated by individuals from western Tigray at the expense of easterners who were marginal to the entire struggle. They demanded that power be reallocated within the organization, and that democratic decision making be more firmly enshrined within TPLF's structures. The leadership, for its part, largely failed to heed these calls for reform, forcing its critics into open insubordination. Under the threat of sanctions, large sections of the organization defected to Sudan, the Ethiopian government, and rival militias. Since they failed to alter the organizational status quo in the manner they would have preferred, fragmentation was the only option for reformist elements.

Yet the episode of factional infighting and fragmentation did not end with these defections, and developed into a broader cycle of contention that encompassed segments of the organization not involved in the original dispute. The defection of many fighters had left the mostly Marxist-oriented student leadership besieged and insecure. With an organizational congress scheduled for 1979, the TPLF leadership decided to clean house. An ad hoc investigative committee led by TPLF central

---

[9] Some of the best information on the TPLF's battles against the EDU and the EPRP actually comes from EPRP sources. See Kifu Tadesse's (1998) "The Generation: Part II" and a new book by EPRP insider Solomon Gebreselassie (2014, pp. 11–21). Author's interview, Senior EPRP cadre, March 22, 2009.

[10] "Some Stands of the Marxist-Leninist Core in the Tigray People's Liberation Front, T.P.L.F.," May 1984, p. 13.

committee member Sebhat Nega rooted out all opponents to the TPLF's founding leadership, both real and perceived. Many were arrested and summarily executed.

The generalized climate of fear that this program of cleansing produced created yet more fissures within the organization, even among the leadership itself. In 1979, Dr. Haile Atsbaha split from the TPLF, citing its "terroristic tendencies," and created the Tigray People's Democratic Movement (TPDM), in what was likely a clear bid for survival.[11]

Though seriously weakened by the fragmentation of 1977–79, the TPLF, to quote one its own memoranda, "went on to write some of its most glorious pages."[12] It would survive militarily and eventually defeat both the EDU and EPRP. The TPLF's superior discipline and tactics proved decisive, as did the EDU and EPRP's virtual annihilation by resurgent government forces in the late 1970s. Support from Shaebia was also probably an important factor at this critical juncture. In the TPLF rendition of events, the ideological positioning of the movements was central: the EDU promised a return to the old feudal political order, while the EPRP did not fully embrace the cause of Ethiopia's marginalized nationalities. Both positions were untenable among the Tigrayan peasantry that was to provide the backbone of any sustainable insurgency in Tigray.[13]

From 1979 onward, the TPLF remained in virtual territorial stalemate. Although it was able to operate across much of Tigray, Gondar, and Wollo, as a guerrilla army, Soviet intervention and severe famine in 1984–85 constrained the organization's further expansion and transition to more fixed positional warfare that could hold and defend territory. At the same time, since the Derg's strategic approach treated the Eritrean theatre as the main front in its counterinsurgency effort, the TPLF was spared from the full force of Derg operations and associated territorial losses – with a few exceptions. The TPLF, of course, recognized how important Shaebia's survival was to its own strategic aims, and

---

[11] "Tigrai People's Democratic Movement: Statement of Background and Aims," (publication date unclear). Document was accessed by author at the archives of Institute of Ethiopian Studies, Addis Ababa, in March 2009. Document provides a trenchant critique of TPLF's pitfalls, although the precise ideological program of the TPDM is unclear. Interestingly, the document draws a direct connection between the TPDM's decision to fragment and the TPLF's "erroneous fighting tactics" in the battles of 1977. Most of the information regarding the war with the EDU and EPRP, and the second internal crisis, which was called the second *Hinfishfish*, is drawn from Berhe (2009, pp. 103–124) and Young (1997, pp. 134–135).

[12] "Some Stands of the Marxist-Leninist Core in the Tigray People's Liberation Front, T.P.L.F.," May 1984, p. 14.

[13] Some Stands of the Marxist-Leninist Core in the Tigray People's Liberation Front, T.P.L.F.," May 1984, p. 14.

committed significant resources to the war in Eritrea: during the Red Star offensive of 1982, over 2000 TPLF troops were deployed to Eritrea to serve with Shaebia in a last-ditch defense of its Sahel base area. But the war in Eritrea was never a central preoccupation of the TPLF's struggle.

The stalemated military picture was reflected in classified US government documents from the period. A CIA military assessment, dated 1983, referred to a "continuing military stalemate" in Tigray, and predicted that "the military confrontation is likely to continue indefinitely with little or no prospect for a major breakthrough by either side."[14] While the Derg lacked the ability to defeat the TPLF or attenuate its operations, the assessment conceded, the TPLF simply did not have the capabilities necessary to decisively break the balance.

Consistent with my theory, this was a period devoid of any discernible factional infighting or fragmentation within the TPLF. In 1988, with the support of their Eritrean allies (Shaebia), the territorial stalemate was to be broken for the final time, as the Derg collapsed under the weight of rebel offensives. In May 1991, the TPLF assumed power within Ethiopia, and TPLF chairman Meles Zenawi became Ethiopia's transitional president.

The Oromo Liberation Front: 1973–2008

The Oromo Liberation Front is the longest-running insurgency in modern Ethiopian history. The organization made self-determination claims on behalf of the Oromo ethnic group, which at 35 percent of the Ethiopian population was the country's largest. The Oromo, who arrived in modern-day Ethiopia in the sixteenth century as part of what could be single largest migratory movement in African history, were among Ethiopia's most marginalized people. In contrast to the Tigrayans and Eritreans, the growth and expansion of the Amhara-dominated Ethiopian state saw the Oromo dispossessed from their lands, largely because it was Ethiopia's most fertile, capable of producing cash crops such as coffee and qaat. Many Oromo became serfs, and some outright slaves, after a series of brutal military campaigns led by Emperor Menelik throughout the 1880s and 1890s.[15]

The chaos that followed Haile Selassie's fall in 1974 provided the opportunity for the Oromo to organize armed resistance, although the

---

[14] Directorate of Intelligance, Central Intelligance Agency, General CIA Records, November 4, 1983, "Ethiopia: The Tigrean Insurgency."
[15] For good histories of the Oromo see Hassen (1990), Melbaa (1999), and Jalata (2005). Donald Levine (2000) also presents some useful information on the Oromo in his landmark study.

prospect of land reform encouraged by the Marxist regime initially took the wind out of the sails of Oromo nationalists. Like all of the other organizations examined in this book, the OLF was a motley crowd united by a commitment to armed struggle and a generalized Oromo nationalism. Indeed, one finds some disagreement among the early founders of OLF about its precise goal: self-determination up to, and including, secession, or political autonomy within the Ethiopian state. The OLF's founding meeting in December 1973, which was followed by a founding congress in June 1976 that formalized the organization's structures, brought together members of an embryonic militant organization called the Ethiopian National Liberation Front (ENLF) – which was led by old-line Oromo notables affiliated with Haile Selassie's government and a number of well-connected Oromo merchants – and several Marxist-leaning Oromo student organizations.[16]

Although members of both groups had some involvement in an Oromo collective called the Machu Tuulama association – a nonviolent organization effectively crushed by Haile Selassie in the late 1960s – the differences between the students and the more senior Oromo figures in the ENLF were stark. Yet the emergence of competitor organizations like the WSLF, which made claims to huge portions of Oromo land on behalf of Somali irredentists, drove cooperation. Moreover, the ENLF had fallen on hard times, as the death of three leaders, Elemo Qiltu, General Tadesse Birru, and Colonel Hailu Ragassa, and the jailing of a core contingent of ENLF fighters traveling from Aden en route to Ethiopia by the Somali government, severely undermined the organization's military capacity (Markakis, 2011, p. 195). For their part, those who hailed from the Oromo student organizations lacked any real military expertise, and could not sustain the armed struggle on their own.[17]

By September 1977 the OLF had forged a new institutional structure, consisting of a central committee of forty-one and an executive command of five. The student intellectual, Dima Nego, would serve as the OLF's first chairman, and was supported by the chief military commander, Sheikh Jaraa Abugaada, who had been part of the ENLF

---

[16] Eventually, sectarian differences – between mostly protestant Oromo from the east, and Muslim Oromo from Bale and Hararghe – as well as ideological cleavages, would play a larger role in the internal politics of the organization. For more on the early evolution of the OLF, see a chronology on the organization's website at www.gadaa.com/OromoLiberationFront.html (Accessed October 27, 2017).

[17] For a quick primer on OLF see International Crisis Group Report, "Ethiopia: Ethnic Federalism and its Discontents," September 4, 2009, which was found at www.crisisgroup.org/~/media/Files/africa/horn-of-africa/ethiopia-eritrea/Ethiopia%20Ethnic%20Federalism%20and%20Its%20Discontents.ashx. The report can now be found at https://d2071andvip0wj.cloudfront.net/153-ethiopia-ethnic-federalism-and-its-discontents.pdf (Accessed October 30, 2017).

contingent from Aden arrested by the Somali government. Just as the fledgling organization began to establish itself, the Somali invasion of Ethiopia in 1977 would throw it into complete disarray. Sandwiched between the two competing hostile states, and Somali proxy organizations like the WSLF and Somali Abo Liberation Front (SALF) – the latter a largely ineffectual Muslim Oromo group centered in Bale, Sidamo, and Arsi, but at that time still problematic – the OLF found that their area of operation was significantly reduced. The OLF's base of operations in the province of Hararghe became ground zero of the Ethiopian–Somali war, and pushed the OLF southwest. The Somali forces in particular, were quite brutal, inflicting serious damage on OLF units and economically devastating the Oromo populations in Bale and Hararghe on which the OLF depended for supplies.[18] The OLF's military position only became worse when the Ethiopians reasserted control of eastern Ethiopia in the spring of 1978.

Somalia's scorched-earth campaign in eastern Ethiopia, and the territorial losses it caused, precipitated an outbreak of factional infighting and fragmentation within OLF ranks in 1978. Abdel Karim Ibrahim – the birth name of the aforementioned Sheikh Jaraa Abugaada – was an Oromo notable and candidate for Haile Selassie's parliament who had joined the OLF and become its principal military commander, and would soon find himself at odds with other members of the OLF's central committee that hailed from a student background. While it is hard to discern exactly what happened, it is clear that credible commitments within the OLF had broken down, as Jaraa's confidence in other members of the leadership waned, and vice versa. A critical juncture was reached in September 1977, when the OLF elected a new chairman, Magarsa Bari, and in April 1978, when significant alterations were made to the executive committee at an OLF congress in the Chercher Mountains.

These changes did not sit well with Jaraa. In addition to ridiculing the student intellectuals within the ranks of the leadership and challenging their military acumen, he began to mobilize supporters, some would say along religious and regional lines (he was a Muslim from the eastern part of Oromia). His critics responded by accusing him of "conspiring with Somalia to spread Islam."[19] At a leadership meeting later that year, a fire-fight broke out in which a senior military commander, Barut Hamse,

---

[18] Author's interview, Oromo civilian and activist, September 17, 2009, and OLF member, March 13, 2009. Also OLF senior spokesman, October 8, 2009, and senior OLF commander and politburo member, April 2011.

[19] "Failure to Deliver: The Journey of the Oromo Liberation Front in the Last Two Decades," written by Jawar Siraj Mohammed, July 28, 2009, and posted on his blog. Many of Sheikh Jaraa's critics were Protestants from the western province of Welega.

was killed. Although Jaraa did not take responsibility for the killing, and evidence later emerged that he was not responsible, it was interpreted by many within the OLF as a power grab (Markakis, 2011, p. 196). Without enough support to seize control of the organization, Jaraa fragmented with roughly twenty followers. With the support of several backers from the Middle East, particularly from Saudi Arabia, he would reemerge a few years later as head of a new organization, the Islamic Federation for the Liberation of Oromia (IFLO).[20]

As my theory predicts, there were knock-on effects of the initial rupture between Jaraa and the student leaders within the OLF. Many OLF fighters left after the crisis, reducing the OLF strength from several thousand to several hundred. A senior military commander and Jaraa's replacement named Bobassa Mohammed, displeased with the OLF's misfortune and his own inability to correct the organization's problems, split from the organization in early 1979, only to be persuaded to rejoin the OLF later on.[21]

Between 1980 and 1991, the OLF went through a long period of stalemate that evolved into a moment of rapid territorial change. Both periods were devoid of any factional infighting and fragmentation. After allying with Shaebia and the TPLF to overthrow the Derg, the OLF joined the TPLF in a transitional government that would rule Ethiopia (minus Eritrea) until national elections were conducted. The union between the two organizations only lasted until 1992, when disputes over power sharing resulted in a TPLF attack on OLF forces. The OLF, for its part, made a strategic blunder by agreeing to encamp its forces during the transitional phase, and the TPLF-led government (with Shaebia support) made quick work of the poorly deployed OLF, capturing 18,000 fighters. While many of the organization's leaders – including some of its most well-respected founding members – were held personally responsible for the military failures, these recriminations remained part and parcel of the organization's normal political processes and did not create an open rupture.

This all changed in 1999, when an OLF force of several hundred, trained and equipped in Eritrea – which now backed the OLF after its border dispute with Ethiopia – was deployed back into Ethiopia. En route, the group spent a significant amount of time in the war-torn Somali capital of Mogadishu, a fatal mistake, since Ethiopian intelligence was soon tipped off about the large unit's presence. Despite the dangers, the OLF failed to move their forces quickly enough. Left

---

[20] For details of the Jaraa split, see also Markakis (1987, pp. 258–264).
[21] Author's interview, senior OLF commander and politburo member, April 2011.

vulnerable and exposed in urban Mogadishu, OLF units were quickly routed by Ethiopian forces and virtually expelled from southern Somalia.

The defeat sent shock waves throughout the OLF, yet again breaking down credible commitments within the organization. This breakdown was most clearly reflected in a collapse of confidence in OLF secretary-general Galassa Dilbo, who had been chairman of the organization since the murder of Magarsa Bari and a contingent of senior OLF personalities by the WSLF in 1980. The deputy chairman of the OLF, Dawud Ibsa, called an impromptu congress in Eritrea, and with Eritrean support was able to replace Galassa as secretary-general. This was followed by a purge of members of the leadership who were Galassa affiliates. Galassa refused to acquiesce to his loss of status within the organization, and began a countercampaign in which he accused his political opponents of participating in an effort to compromise on the issue of Oromo independence. Since Galassa had been a fervent advocate of this position as leader of the OLF, and Dawud Ibsa and his allies had been cool toward the idea of Oromo independence (instead preferring autonomy within a united and democratic Ethiopia), Galassa obtained some support, particularly among OLF supporters in the diaspora. The reality, however, is that these ideological differences were not particularly sharp, and probably served as cover for a more fundamental power struggle between the two OLF leaders.[22]

In the end, Galassa's perceived mismanagement of the Mogadishu operation permanently undermined his credibility, and along with the weight of Eritrean support for Ibsa, it was too much to overcome. Having decisively lost the power struggle within the OLF, Galassa and his supporters fragmented in what was a clear bid for survival, retreating to the diaspora to create another organization, the OLF–Transitional Authority in 2001.[23]

From 2001 to 2007, the OLF faced territorial stalemate. This situation was largely underpinned by the conclusion of the Ethiopian–Eritrean border war, after which the Eritrean government – formerly Shaebia – made efforts to restrict the scale and scope of OLF operations. The goal, from the Eritrean perspective, was to preserve the peace agreement with Ethiopia that had ended the border war (the Algiers Agreement of December 2000), as Ethiopia had come to view the OLF as little

---

[22] Author's interview, senior OLF commander and politburo member, April 2011.
[23] For more on the acrimony between the OLF and OLF–Transitional Authority see an OLF memorandum titled "Malicious Misinformation Cannot Alter the Truth," April 6, 2011, which can be found at http://www.oromoliberationfront.org/News/2011/OLF%20Statement%2004-06-2011.pdf (Accessed October 30, 2017).

more than an Eritrean proxy. At the same time, the Eritrean government kept the OLF operational, in the event they would need to employ them as auxiliary forces in renewed hostilities with Ethiopia. As my theory predicts, this was also a relatively tranquil period within OLF ranks.

By 2006, Ethiopia's refusal to honor the peace agreement prompted Eritrea to directly support an expansion of OLF operations. This led to a small, though perceptible expansion of OLF activities in Wellega and areas along the Kenyan border in the following years. This territorial expansion was also associated with a sharp increase in OLF engagements with the Ethiopian military in 2007–08, as can be seen from data collated by Armed Conflict Location and Events Data (ACLED). Indeed, in 2007, the pace of OLF activity seemed to have bottomed out, as there wasn't a single OLF military engagement recorded in that year. However, by 2008, that number had spiked to twenty-four.[24]

The shift in the military balance was also propelled by some high-level defections to the OLF, including the commander of the Ethiopian Army's 18th division, Brigadier General Kemal Gelchu and some 150 of his troops in August 2006. Sometime later, this defecting contingent was joined by a few other high-profile officers, such as General Haile Gonfa and Colonel Gemechu Ayana. Writing around this time, one longtime Ethiopia analyst, Martin Plaut, argued that these developments and others suggested that "the Oromo are exhibiting more confidence than they have for many years."[25]

Consistent with the theoretical predictions of my model of rebel fragmentation, these battlefield successes served to guarantee the immediate security of the OLF's various internal constituencies, and drive preference divergence within the organization. OLF chairman Dawud Ibsa found himself at odds with newly arrived General Kemal Gelchu, who had now been given responsibility over the OLF's military forces. In alliance with several older members of the organization that had been purged by Galassa in the 1990s, Dima Nego and Leencho Latta, an effective coup against the chairman was announced. The effort, which garnered some support amongst Kemal Gelchu's Arsi Oromo kinsman, largely failed to mobilize the critical mass of support necessary to take over the organization, as Ibsa retained the loyalty of many of the Eritrea-based OLF units (and possibly benefited from Eritrean support himself). The dissident faction was forced to split, and established another independent entity called the OLF-Change. This organization

---

[24] ACLED data can be accessed at www.acleddata.com/index.php/data (Accessed October 30, 2017). For a visual depiction of the OLF ACLED data, see Woldemariam (2011, p. 243).
[25] Quote drawn from Plaut (2006, p. 589).

would garner some support in the western-based Oromo diaspora, and retained an operational presence in the Oromia region of Ethiopia. Many of its fighters would surrender en masse to the Ethiopian government in early 2010, contributing to a growing narrative that Gelchu sought to strike a modus vivendi with the Ethiopian government. He remains in Asmara, Eritrea, where he seems to have fallen out of favor with his Eritrean hosts and his movements are closely monitored.[26]

West Somali Liberation Front: 1973–1988

The West Somali Liberation Front (WSLF), which officially came into existence in January 1976, purported to represent the aspiration for the self-determination of Ethiopia's several million ethnic Somalis. Ethiopia's Somalis lived in a territory that was popularly known as the "Ogaden," which made up much of the Ethiopian provinces of Hararghe and Bale. The Ogaden is vast, and occupies roughly a third of Ethiopia's current landmass, although it is sparsely populated with few natural resources.[27]

The origins of the conflict in the Ogaden were tied to Britain's decision to cede the territory – which in 1896 became a British protectorate – to Emperor Haile Selassie at the end of the World War II. The Ogaden had never been ruled by the Orthodox Christian rulers of highland Ethiopia, and the British decision was taken without the consultation of the Ogaden's overwhelmingly Somali population. In fact, popular sentiment at the time dictated that the region become either independent or part of a Somali Republic including the former Italian colony of Somalia, the British protectorate of Somaliland, the French protectorate of Djibouti, and the Northern Frontier District of British Kenya.

Efforts in the 1960s to wrest the Ogaden from Ethiopia by the newly independent Somali Republic largely failed. Yet the chaos and disorder surrounding the collapse of the Ethiopian monarchy in 1974 created

---

[26] For an OLF perspective on the split, see OLF memorandum "Statement of OLF Executive Committee on Unconstitutional Activities and Conspiracies Against the OLF," July 31, 2008, which can be found at www.oromoliberationfront.org/News/2008/Statementonconspiracy.pdf (Accessed October 30, 2017). Much of my narrative of the 2001 and 2008 splits is drawn from the author's interview, senior OLF commander and politburo member, April 2011. Although there is some overlap, there is a noticeable difference between my narrative of these splits and that provided by Markakis (2011, pp. 284–285). Additional information on Gelchu can be found from the following source, which, it should be said, is highly critical: "Kemal Gelchu & Co.: 'OLF' Trojan Horse," January 7, 2012, which can be found at http://oromoaffairs.blogspot.com/2012/01/kemal-gelchu-co-olf-trojan-horse-part-i.html (Accessed January 17, 2017).

[27] The area is thought to have significant oil reserves, but these have yet to be exploited fully.

an opportunity for Somali strongman Siad Barre. Wary of leaping into direct confrontation with Ethiopia at that early date, but anticipating direct hostilities in the near future, Barre decided to create what he hoped would amount to an auxiliary force of the Somali military, the WSLF. The inaugural meeting took place in a village close to the Somali capital of Mogadishu called Yaq Badhiwayn. Barre, who was born in the Ogaden and whose mother comes from the region's largest clan bearing the same name, attended the meeting and aimed (quite successfully) to dominate its proceedings.[28]

The organization, though numerically dominated by the Ogaden clan, was an amalgamation of various clan constituencies, and represented a clear coalition of disparate interests. While in theory organizational decision making was centralized under a secretary-general – Abdullahi Hassan Mohammed – and a twenty-five-person central committee, the structure of military operations in the field corresponded to clan divisions. Tareke (2009, p. 224) makes this point clearly when he writes:

> The WSLF was as fractured as the Somali community itself, although it had a single leadership headed by a secretary general. Its nine divisions represented clans, which quarreled, competed for water and pasture, and jealously protected their respective zones not only against government forces but also against one another. When attacked, they were not quick enough and were often reluctant to aid one another. Clanism posed such a serious threat to unity of action that the WSLF had made its advocacy punishable by death.

The other important cleavage within the WSLF was on the basic issue of broad political objectives. While some within the organization were irredentists, and sought to bring the Ogaden into a "Greater Somalia," others sought an independent state. Barre was particularly dismissive of the latter, and from the organization's earliest days, actively sought to repress factions that espoused this line of thinking.

What brought these various clan and ideological constituencies into the WSLF fold was the insecurity wrought by the Ethiopian revolution. The emergence of new organizations, like the OLF and the Somali Abo Liberation Front (an amalgamation of Somalis and Oromo from the provinces of Bale, Sidamo, and Arsi who perceived themselves as culturally distinct from both the Oromo and Somali), who laid claim to territories that the WSLF's various clans regarded as their own, created a very real threat that reinforced cooperation. Moreover, the increasing prospect of a full-scale Somali invasion of the Ogaden required that various clan and ideological constituencies quickly develop a common

---

[28] Some sources argue that as early as 1973 Siad Barre had already begun clandestinely supporting a network run by Yusuf Dheere that would become the nucleus of WSLF.

platform through which they could cooperate with Barre, lest they be marginalized in the event of an increasingly likely Somali victory.

With Somali military officers running command and control, and operating out of rear bases near Mogadishu and Hargeisa, the WSLF made rapid territorial gains in eastern Ethiopia. In the first half of 1977 the organization destroyed portions of the Addis Ababa–Djibouti railway line, severing one of Ethiopia's most vital commercial arteries in the eastern part of the country. By late summer 1977, Somali regulars supported by mechanized units had come to the WSLF's aid, and seized virtually the entire Ogaden and the key strategic depot of Jigjiga, while laying siege to the vital urban arteries of Dire Dawa and Harar.[29]

It is no surprise that exactly at this moment tensions within the WSLF erupted, although this episode of factional infighting did not evolve into fragmentation because the losers of the dispute were successfully imprisoned. With WSLF and Somali regular forces surging, Siad Barre was eager to reaffirm control over the WSLF, lest elements within the organization seek to undermine the writ of the Mogadishu-based Somali government in the Ogaden in a bid for independence or autonomy. Using his allies within the WSLF central committee, Barre managed to move the entire WSLF leadership to the Somali capital, Mogadishu, in what was a clear case of growing preference divergence within the organization. Frustrated by their removal from the war zone, Markakis writes, members of the WSLF were "chafing under the tight grip of the Somali regime" (Markakis, 1987, p. 227). Indeed, in a later research, Markakis (2011, p. 211) notes the centrality of battlefield gains to preference divergence and the erosion of the WSLF's cooperative equilibrium in this period, arguing, "For many WSLF members, the joy of victory was marred by a dawning awareness that their aspirations were not shared by their patrons in Mogadishu; in fact, they were an anathema to them." With the threat of insubordination looming, Barre's allies purged several central committee members from the leadership, including the WSLF deputy secretary-general Mohammed Diriye Urdoh, who was soon arrested (Markakis, 2011, p. 211).

The purging of these elements had knock-on effects, spreading contention to other sectors of the organization. WSLF commanders in the field, angered by the interference of Barre in WSLF affairs, began to set up robust governance structures in the conquered territories, asserting the autonomy of the WSLF and the Ogaden more generally. Barre's colleagues in the WSLF leadership did not look kindly on this behavior, and recalled the recalcitrant commanders to Mogadishu, where they were

---

[29] These military successes are chronicled in Tareke (2009, pp. 182–217).

promptly arrested. WSLF units, particularly those that hailed from the Ogaden, were redeployed to other parts of the war zone lest they challenge the Somali army in the newly conquered territory. Local WSLF administrative structures were completely disbanded and replaced by administrative structures consisting of Somali government officials.[30]

While this episode of factional infighting came at the apex of the WSLF's military success in the Ogaden, the next internal eruption was due to unprecedented military failure. The resurgence of the Ethiopian military in 1978 forced the WSLF and the Somali state to relinquish full control over most of the Ogaden. However, WSLF units retained a residual presence, operating as guerrilla forces in a manner that effectively made it impossible for Ethiopia to govern the territory.

Yet this changed in September 1980, when Derg deployed 60,000 troops to eradicate WSLF bases and clear the Ogaden of WSLF activity. In the face of what came to be known as the Derg's "Operation Lash," the WSLF stood little chance, and by December 1980 it was effectively no longer able to operate in the Ogaden (Tareke, 2009, pp. 220–225).

The defeat was made worse by the precarious position of the WSLF in Somalia. As part of its strategy to clear the Ogaden and undermine Siad Barre, Ethiopia had helped to establish several Somali rebel organizations, most prominently the Somali National Movement (SNM) and the Somali Salvation Democratic Front (SSDF). By 1980, in what had become a nightmare scenario, the SSDF was attacking WSLF rear bases in northern Somalia. The security situation in Somalia had deteriorated to such an extent that Siad Barre declared a state of emergency in the northwest of the country.[31]

Territorial loss and military failure served to undermine credible commitments within the WSLF, triggering events that would eventually lead to the organization's fragmentation. While many within the WSLF who favored some form of autonomy if not outright independence for the Ogaden demanded that the organization replenish itself and resume war with Ethiopia, others – supported by Barre – believed that the WSLF stand down for the time being, lest a rejuvenated Ethiopia respond harshly. Omar Nur, the WSLF's military chief, was dismissed for crossing Barre and his supporters on this issue.

But the dismissal was only the beginning, as factional conflict spread. At the WSLF congress in February 1981, opponents of the Barre faction managed to successfully pass an organizational platform that proclaimed

---

[30] Information drawn from Markakis (1987, pp. 222–234).
[31] Author's interviews with Somali National Movement commanders, Hargeisa, Somaliland, October 2010.

that the goal of the WSLF was self-determination (read independence) for the Ogaden. Urdoh, who had since been released from prison, was once again elected secretary-general.

Predictably, Barre supporters were incredulous. Since the WSLF was based in Somalia, these elements used the coercive capacity of the Somali state to purge Urdoh from the leadership, and replace him with Abdi Nassir Sheikh Aden, who was more amenable to Barre's political position. Having clearly lost the power struggle, and facing another series of purges, Barre's opponents fragmented, and by 1984, had set up a new rebel organization committed to the Ogaden's independence, the Ogaden National Liberation Front (ONLF).[32]

Between 1981 and 1988, the WSLF faced virtual stalemate, as it was unable to expand its base of operations within Ethiopia, largely due to the effectiveness and growth of organizations like the SNM and SSDF. Many of its units were incorporated into the Somali defense forces. This was also a period of relatively little internal rancor, as my theory predicts. After a peace deal between Barre and Ethiopia's Derg in 1988, the WSLF ceased to be operational.

Ogaden National Liberation Front: 1984–2008

Throughout the 1980s the WSLF's offspring, the ONLF, maintained a low profile. Like every other organization discussed in this project, the ONLF was complex and internally differentiated. Cooperation in the organization's earliest years was driven by threats from the Ethiopian military and its Somali allies, the SNM and SSDF, as well as the clear hostility of Barre's regime and the WSLF. While consisting mostly of the Ogaden clan, subclan cleavages played an important role in the internal politics of the organization.

As was the case for most of Ethiopia's rebel organizations, the collapse of the Derg in the late 1980s provided the opportunity for territorial expansion. Like the OLF, the ONLF decided to join the TPLF in the coalition government that replaced the Derg and was designed to be a transitional bridge to democratic elections. But tensions persisted between the ONLF and the TPLF, partly because the TPLF was committed to maintaining control of the central state, and partly because the ONLF insisted on self-determination for the Ogaden.[33] In 1994, the TPLF launched an attack on the ONLF, much as it had done against the

---

[32] See Markakis (1987, pp. 222–234) and ONLF website at www.onlf.org/viewpage.php?page_id=5 (Accessed October 30, 2017).

[33] In February 1994, regional parliamentarians, affiliated with the ONLF, demanded a referendum on independence.

OLF, after the ONLF's January 1994 declaration that it would pursue self-determination for the Ogaden. Several of the organization's political leaders were arrested, a number were killed, and ONLF bases in Ogaden were overrun, severely curtailing the organization's operations and its ability to operate throughout the Ogaden. The EPRDF was assisted in this effort by a number of non-Ogaden clans, who perceived the ONLF as a political vehicle of the Ogaden clan. Many ONLF units were forced into the chaos of neighboring Somalia, and its leaders compelled to go underground or overseas.

Once again, the territorial loss engendered commitment problems within ONLF ranks, as a dispute emerged between factions over the need to enter into a lasting peace agreement with the TPLF-led EPRDF government. After failing to mobilize the support necessary to bring the entire organization back into the coalition with the EPRDF, a faction led by Abidrizak Tibba and Bashar Abdi Hussein fragmented, first creating a "legal wing" of the ONLF and then joining the EPRDF's local satellite party, the Ethiopian Somali Democratic League (ESDL) in 1998. More hard-line members of the ONLF, led by Chairman Sheikh Ibrahim Abdalla, continued the armed struggle.[34]

From the late 1990s until 2005, the ONLF went through a period of territorial stasis, as the emergence of a relatively coherent and hostile government in Somaliland prevented the ONLF from expanding its area of operation, particularly on the Ogaden's northern frontier. As such, the ONLF's operations were restricted to border areas in the south, where units could easily retreat into the chaotic morass of clan warfare in southern Somalia. It also didn't help that much of the organization's leadership had been displaced overseas. While the infrastructure of the organization was intact – a new chairman and a central and executive committee were elected at an ONLF Congress in 1998 – only one of the ONLF's primary leaders remained in the Ogaden.

In 2005–06, things quickly began to change as the collapse of the Eritrean–Ethiopian border agreement created an opportunity for real external support. Units were deployed for training to Eritrean camps, while weapons, supplies, and troop reinforcements were funneled to ONLF units in the field through southern Somalia. Several bold attempts were also made to forge supply routes through Ethiopian-allied administrations in Somaliland and Puntland.[35]

---

[34] See "The TPLF's Hidden Agenda: Mediation as a Tactic," by Saafi Labafidhin, November 20, 2007, which was found at www.garoweonline.com/artman2/publish/Opinion_20/Ethiopia_TPLF_s_Hidden_Agenda_Mediation_as_a_Tactic.shtml.
[35] Author's interview with Somaliland Minister of Defense, Yusuf Haj Adami, Somaliland, Hargeisa, October 2010.

The transformation in ONLF capabilities led to a sizeable expansion of its area of operation, and an increase in the raw number of ONLF military engagements with Ethiopian government forces. Data gleaned from the Armed Conflict Location Event Dataset illustrate this latter point well. In 2006, the ONLF was involved in sixteen combat events within Ethiopia. By 2007, that number was at thirty-four, and in 2008, it would reach forty-three. April 2007 was a particularly important turning point, when ONLF fighters made headlines with a raid on a Chinese-managed oil exploration site that killed sixty-five Ethiopian soldiers and nine Chinese oil workers.

Yet these territorial gains also drove preference divergence, unleashing a spiral of factional infighting that eventually led to the organization's fragmentation.[36] The dispute began with an effort by Chairman Mohammed Omar Osman – a former admiral who had been the head of Siad Barre's navy – to remove Mohammed Abdi Yasin from his post as liaison with the Ogadeni diaspora, in addition to several central committee members. The effort drew a sharp rebuke from the head of the ONLF's planning and research department, Dr. Mohammed Sirad Dolal. The incident triggered a protracted power struggle between the chairman and Dolal, and the Ogaden subclans they represented – the Rer Abdilleh and the Rer Issak, respectively.

These differences could have been resolved at a leadership meeting that was called in Eritrea in 2005, but it was here that the dispute turned into an open rupture. While Osman's term was extended for another year, a preparatory committee was established to help convene the organization's next general congress. But some argue that Osman, intent on ensuring himself another two-year term, tampered with the structure of the committee a few months after its creation.

Dolal and his colleagues moved into open opposition, and as a result, units loyal to Osman made several attempts to assassinate Dolal during his travels to the region throughout 2008. These events culminated in Dolal's murder in January 2009. While Osman officially denied any role in Osman's death – blaming it on Ethiopian security forces – the event reverberated throughout the organization, diffusing contention to other sectors of the organization. An investigative committee, stacked with ONLF cadres and members of the public sympathetic to Dolal, was established to evaluate the circumstances behind his death. The committee's report fingered Osman and his colleagues in the leadership as the sole perpetrators.[37]

---

[36] Hagmann (2014, p. 43), who is an excellent scholar of the Ogaden/ONLF, argues that "ONLF's military strength peaked in 2007–08."

[37] See "The Committee for the Investigation of Dr. Mohamed Sirad Dolal's Murder," which was found at http://xaajo.com/upload/files/committee%20report.pdf.

Emboldened by the report, a senior ONLF leader affiliated with Dolal named Abdiwali Hussein Gaas unilaterally declared another ONLF leader, Salahudin Maow, the new chairman of the ONLF. However, the cycle of conflict did not end there, as the two factions continued to compete for control of the organization. With Eritrean backing, Osman was able to reassert control of the ONLF's primary leadership organs, diaspora networks, and units in the field. At an impasse, Maow entered into negotiations with the Ethiopian government, and on June 15, 2010, signed an agreement with the Ethiopian government, effectively fragmenting the ONLF. Twenty-one former members of the ONLF's central committee joined him, as well a large chunk of Rer Abdilleh units in the field. In return, the Ethiopian government released a number of high-profile ONLF detainees.[38]

Afar Revolutionary Democratic Unity Front: 1993–2004

The Afar Revolutionary Democratic Unity Front (ARDUF) – better known as *Ugogomo*[39] – was an amalgamation of three separate Afar political organizations with different bases of clan support within Ethiopia's Afar region. The organization, led by former Derg-era regional leader Mahmouda Ahmed Gaas, mobilized in opposition to the division of Afar-inhabited areas between Eritrea and Ethiopia following Eritrean independence in 1993. There is, however, some evidence that the organization had its roots in the early 1980s, as a kind of self-defense militia designed to block TPLF encroachment on Afar areas and ward off threats from the Afar's age-old copastoralist competitor for resources, the Issa-Somali (Yasin, 2010, p. 127).

Eritrean statehood was effectively the second partition of Afar territory – the first being the emergence of an independent Djiboutian state in 1977 that was dominated by the Issa-Somali – leaving the Afar distributed across three states. This created real fear amongst the Afar, since the division "tilted the balance of power in favor of the Issa/Somali by weakening the Afars politically, militarily, and economically (Yasin, 2010, p. 126). In this context, while the ARDUF's precise goals were

---

[38] Other material used in this section on the ONLF includes Hagmann (2005, 2014), Abdullahi (2007), Markakis (2011, pp. 321–322), and "Admiral of the Desert – Muhammaed Omar Osman and the Ogadeni Rebellion," which can be found at www.biyokulule.com/view_content.php?articleid=2804 (Accessed October 30, 2017). Also see N49 Country Update, "The Somali Regional State of Ethiopia and the Ogaden," which was found at www.n49intelligence.com/N49-Somali-Region-Update-July-2010.pdf.

[39] *Ugogomo* means "revolution" in Afar language.

somewhat murky, it would seem that a united Afar homeland was a central ambition. Such a "homeland" would be either an independent state or an autonomous state within a united Ethiopia. Like many Afar groups that have arisen in the context of the region's civil wars, the ARDUF was maligned as harboring an expansionist agenda built on the notion of a "Greater Afar," designed, in the view of its detractors, to encroach on the historic territories of neighboring ethnic groups.

Although the evidence on this specific organization is somewhat thin, it appears that early cooperation within the ARDUF was underpinned by multiple threats. Both the Eritrean and Ethiopian governments launched small offensives against the ARDUF in the mid-1990s, while neighboring Djibouti was hostile and unwilling to allow ARDUF forces to operate out of their territory.

Largely because the dry, sparsely populated Afar regions of Ethiopia and Eritrea were so marginal, the ARDUF was able to maintain a territorial stalemate, though their level of activity was low. Where the ARDUF attracted attention were the few instances in which it captured foreigners – often tourists visiting the area's unique geology – passing through the region. Yet the situation dramatically changed in 1998, with the Ethiopian–Eritrean border war. The TPLF-led Ethiopian government decided to give the ARDUF a free hand in the Afar region, as long as it augmented Ethiopia's military campaign against Eritrea. As a result, the ARDUF's area of operation expanded, particularly in territories along the Eritrean border.

With security guaranteed and survival concerns minimized, tensions arose within ARDUF ranks over the precise nature of the ARDUF's alliance with the Ethiopian government. The issue became particularly acute at the conclusion of the Ethiopian–Eritrean border war. After a protracted fight that he could not win, Mahmouda Ahmed Gaas took a faction of the ARDUF into the Ethiopian government, eventually becoming a regional minister. Gaas was accused of treason by his former colleagues, who effectively continued the fight by aligning themselves on the side of the Eritrean government. Yet by 2004–05, the organization seems to have run out of steam, although there were occasional reports of kidnappings in the Afar region perpetrated by ARDUF forces that drew some occasional Ethiopian retaliation.[40] While the Eritrean government

---

[40] In 2007 there was a serious incident in which several tourists were kidnapped, as were a number of British embassy staff. Beyond Yasin (2010), this section draws from "Afar: The Impact of Local Conflict on Regional Stability," May 2007, by Tadesse Berhe and Yonas Adaye, which was found at www.iss.co.za/uploads/CPRDPAPERAFAR.PDF. Another copy of this document can be found at https://www.files.ethz.ch/isn/123909/ 2007_05_01_Afar.pdf (Accessed October 30, 2017). Also see BBC report, "Q&A:

continued to provide the ARDUF training, equipment, and logistical support, it would seem that the organization's effectiveness waned with the fortunes of its Eritrean benefactors, who seemed unable to compete militarily with their much larger Ethiopian neighbor by the latter half of the 2000s.[41]

Conclusions

Although the cases elucidated in this chapter are designed as mere shadow cases, they do provide support for this study's primary claims about the relationship between gains, losses, stalemate, and fragmentation. Corollary arguments advanced in Chapter 2 were also supported by five case studies presented in this chapter. The next chapter turns to issues of external validity.

Ethiopia's Afar Community," at http://news.bbc.co.uk/2/hi/africa/6419791.stm, and Yasin (2008).

[41] Yasin (2010, p. 127) mentions a military facility at Wede near Assab as the site where Eritrean forces trained and equipped the ARDUF.

Part III

Rebel Fragmentation in the Broader Horn

6 The Long War in Somalia
The Somali National Movement, Islamic Courts Union, and Al-Shabaab, 1981–2013

The preceding chapters have provided a compelling picture of the sources of rebel factionalism and fragmentation during Ethiopia's long civil war. The evidence, marshaled from a wide array of sources, suggests a clear picture. At their inception, organized rebellions are often diverse collections of politically disparate constituencies, bound together by common security concerns. Territorial gains and losses can disrupt this cooperative equilibrium, triggering a bevy of factional infighting and fragmentation that carries deep consequences for rebels and the civil wars in which they fight. The argument's main corollaries are generally supported in the preceding chapters as well: fragmentation tends to be the optimal strategy for the losers of factional fights, while infighting and fragmentation can sometimes lead to a process of diffusion that incorporates broader swathes of the organization.

This chapter deals with critical issue of external validity. Since this book has analyzed temporal variation in factional infighting and fragmentation across the full sample of rebel organizations that participated in the Ethiopian civil war, there are obvious questions about how far the book's arguments travel. On this point, it should be said that while every civil war has its unique features, there is nothing about the Ethiopian civil war that suggests that the underlying relationship between rebel fragmentation and battlefield outcomes would somehow operate distinctly in this context, beyond the already mentioned fact that Ethiopia is a resource-poor environment where rebels have incentives to territorially expand their operations. In any case, resource-poor civil war contexts tend to be more common than civil wars where lootable natural resources are in abundance, so this issue is more a boundary condition of the book's main arguments rather than a serious problem of external validity.

Nonetheless, it is important to take the issue of external validity seriously. Toward this end, this chapter provides an analysis of three rebel organizations that were participants in the Somali civil war, a multisided conflict that began in 1978 and has persisted until the present. The style and structure of these three case studies is in keeping with previous

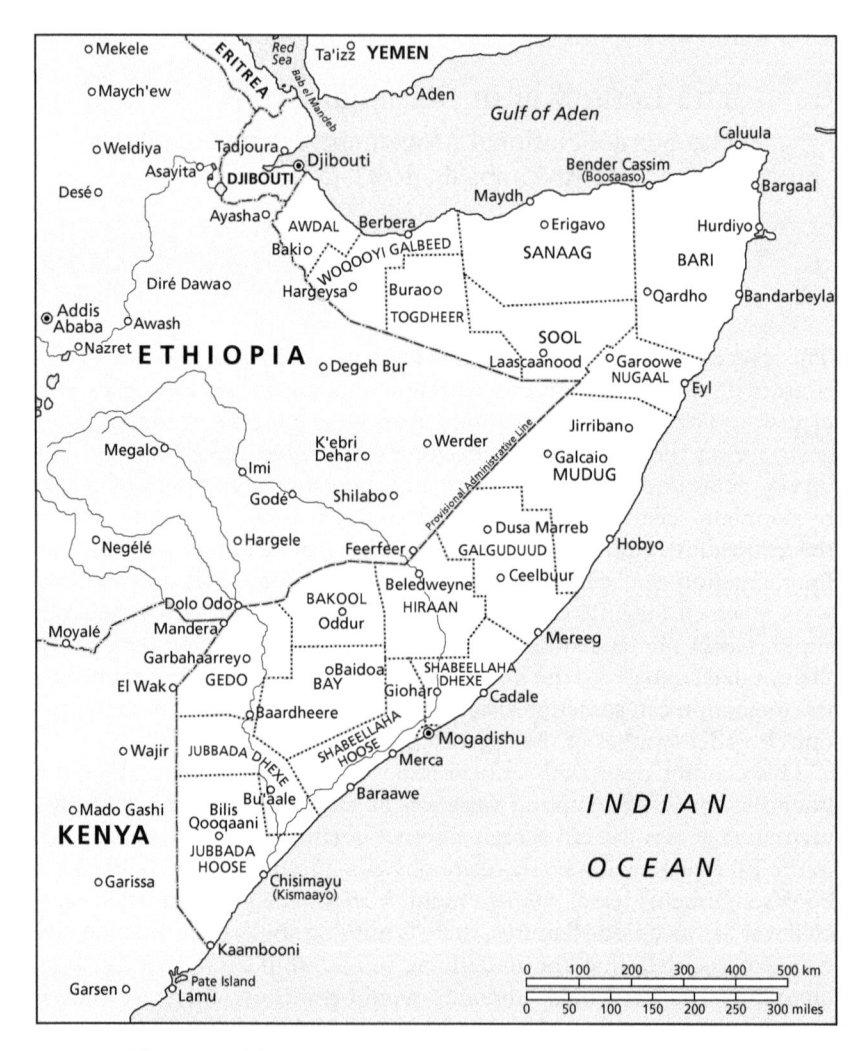

Figure 6.1 Map of Somali regions.

chapters, although the analysis runs through 2013 instead of concluding in 2008. Like the Ethiopian case, I look for evidence of gains and losses at the district level (there are ninety districts in Somalia) annually over time, although data limitations prevent me from measuring these shifts with the level of precision that I do in the Ethiopian context (see Figure 6.1 for a map of Somalia). I then look for causal linkages between these territorial shifts and rebel fragmentation. Since most battlefield shifts in the Somali civil war were fairly decisive, I am fairly confident that I have captured most of the critical battlefield turning points for each of the rebel organizations under consideration.

The Somali civil war provides a useful window into the issue of rebel fragmentation for many of the same reasons as the Ethiopian civil war. The Somali civil war was a long conflict even by African standards, and thus provides the possibility of tracking rebel organizations over a period of time long enough to capture meaningful variation in both rebel fragmentation and battlefield outcomes. Somalia, like Ethiopia, is also a resource-poor civil war context, where the logic of territorial expansion and control applies, thus rendering Somalia an appropriate setting to test an argument about the effects of territorial gains and losses on the cohesion of organized rebellion.

There were a total of sixteen rebel organizations that participated in the Somali civil war, and I have selected the three that provide analytic leverage in exploring this book's underlying argument. Two of the three organizations that are the subject of this chapter – the Somali National Movement (SNM) and Al-Shabaab – had relatively long lives with substantial variation on the dependent and independent variables of interest. The third, the Islamic Courts Union (ICU), had a shorter lifespan, but is appealing for an additional reason that also makes the Al-Shabaab case attractive: the ICU was not an armed nationalist movement making political claims on behalf of a subnational ethnoreligious community, but a pan-Somali Islamist group that was, at least officially, driven by purely ideological concerns. Up until now, this book has largely focused on armed nationalist organizations – that is, rebel organizations based on subnational identities and grievances – on the grounds that these were "hard cases" for the book's theory. But this research strategy raises questions about the book's scope conditions, and whether its argument applies to rebel organizations that are not nationalist in orientation. As such, the analysis of Al-Shabaab and the ICU allows us to investigate in a preliminary fashion whether the book's theory can be applied to organized rebellions premised on a diverse array of mobilizing logics.

Background to Rebellion

In its origins, the Somali civil war shares some important commonalities with the Ethiopian civil war. The Ethiopian civil war, as we have learned, had its early origins in Italy's colonial acquisition of Eritrea in the late nineteenth century, and the contentious disposal of the Red Sea territory in the 1950s. The same is true of Somalia, which the European powers parceled into colonies in the 1890s and disposed of in the 1950s – both critical historical turning points that incited a long chain of events that would eventually result in the Somali civil war.

The history of the Somali-speaking peoples of the Horn prior to the colonial partition of the late nineteenth century is complex and somewhat fragmented. Like much of precolonial Africa, the geography of statehood and governance in the Somali-speaking territories was fluid, as Somali states expanded, contracted, and disappeared, in an environment in which violent political competition waxed and waned. At the basis of this political competition were distinctions of clan – segmented kinship groupings based on lines of patrilineal descent – which, with notable exceptions, have functioned as the main categories of social mobilization in Somali political life throughout modern history.[1]

On the Somali coast, Arab states had established their own zones of political authority, through which they extended their social and political influence into the Somali communities of the interior. One of the best-known precolonial Somali states, Adal, was the fusion of Arab and Somali political institutions, bound of course by the Islamic traditions that the Arabs had introduced into the region.

Perhaps the most important aspect of the precolonial period to understand, for the purposes of this chapter, was the massive territorial expansion of the Somali from the tenth century onward. From what is now the gulf coast of Somaliland and Puntland, the Somali gradually moved south, into the fertile plains of riverine Somalia and down into what is now Kenya, where they warred with the Bantu communities of these regions and began to transition to more agropastoral modes of production. They also moved west and southwest into the Haud and Ogaden territories of modern-day Ethiopia. These population movements, likely triggered by drought, Arab immigration, and natural population growth, brought the Somali clans and their Islamic faith into a series of long conflicts with the neighboring Oromo and Abyssinians, the other large civilizations in the Horn, creating historic rivalries that have left a lasting imprint on the region.[2] By the seventeenth century, when the Oromo and Abyssinians halted the long Somali advance, the major Somali clan families – the Darood, Isaaq, Hawiye, and Digil Rahanweyn – had reached their present-day boundaries. The territory the Somali now inhabited was vast, a reality that would have serious implications for the colonial partition that was to occur.

---

[1] For a good descriptive primer on Somali clans, see Lewis (1994) and Abbink (1999).
[2] "Abyssinians" is the historical term referring to highland Orthodox Christians. The term "Habesha" is a common synonym.

The Anglo-Ethiopian treaty of 1897 marked the culmination of what had been an extended process of colonial partition in the Horn, in which the allocation of Eritrea played a crucial part. The extended nature of the partition was largely due to geopolitical dilemmas, owing both to the strategic stakes in the Horn – given that it sat adjacent to a major global trade route – and the existence of an indigenous power (Ethiopia) that complicated European efforts. For the Somalis, the partition's most significant implication was that it divided the Somali-speaking territories into five distinct states. These were French Somaliland (Djibouti), British Somaliland, Italian Somaliland, Britain's colonial holdings in Kenya, and Ethiopia. Though there would be some adjustment, the states created by the colonial partition would be the basis of the Horn's postcolonial political map.

The Somalis were not uniquely affected by the colonial partition of the Horn, in that many other ethnic groups in Africa found themselves separated by the boundaries of independent African states. This is because an organizing principle of Africa's postcolonial international relations, as enshrined in the Organization of African Unity's founding charter of 1963, was that colonial borders would be sacrosanct, and could not be reengineered to meet ethnic demographic realities (Clapham, 1996; Herbst, 2000). However, what was different about the Somali case was that the colonial treaties that divided the Somali were more ambiguous and contradictory than most. The Anglo-Egyptian treaty of 1897, which the British felt compelled to sign after Emperor Menelik's earth-shattering victory over the Italians at Adwa in 1896, gave the Ethiopian monarchy legal title over the Somali-populated territory of the Haud and Ogaden. The problem was that the treaty was at odds with older agreements the British had signed with Somali clans in these areas, which committed the British Crown to their protection. At the very least, these treaties called for the affected Somali population to be consulted in the event that the British transferred legal title of their land to another sovereign power.

These historical realities meant that when Somalia became an independent state in 1960 through the union of British and Italian Somaliland – as a largely ethnically homogeneous polity premised on pan-Somali identity – its core foreign policy commitment was to be the "reunification" of all Somali-populated territories in the Horn. This would put the new state at loggerheads with its neighbors – most consequentially Ethiopia.

Even before Somalia's independence in 1960, Somali political forces had mobilized behind the reunification of the Somali-speaking territories of the Horn. This effort was given impetus by Italy's defeat during

World War II, which left all the Somali-speaking territories under British rule. In effect, this was the first (and only) time in modern history that the Somalis had been unified under a single administration, a new reality that strengthened aspirations for a Somali state that encompassed all Somali-speaking territories. Mistakenly, the British raised Somali expectations in the late 1940s when they openly considered unifying the Somali-speaking territories under something called the Bevin Plan. Yet Ethiopian and French resistance torpedoed the proposal, and in 1948, the Haud and Ogaden were formally handed back to the Ethiopian monarchy. In 1958, European and Afar votes defeated a plebiscite that would have attached French Somaliland to an independent Somali state. Britain further antagonized Somali nationalists in March 1963, when, after commissioning an independent body to investigate the status of Kenya's Somali–populated Northern Frontier District, it decided that independent Kenya would retain the province.

The newly independent Somali state responded to these realities with a territorially revisionist foreign policy, in which it extended military support to irredentist Somali militants in Ethiopia and Kenya. This led Somalia into low-intensity conflict with Ethiopia and Kenya from 1964 to 1967. Yet the sponsorship of these Somali insurgencies failed to wrest the Somali-speaking territories from Somalia's two neighbors. In 1967, the government of Prime Minister Mohammed Ibrahim Egal was able to come to a modus vivendi with the Kenyan government, while cooling tensions with Ethiopia.

These initiatives, however, were only of short-term significance, particularly as they related to Ethiopian-Somali affairs. The emergence of military junta in Mogadishu in 1969, under the leadership of General Siad Barre, decisively shifted relations between Somalia and its neighbors. As outlined in Chapter 3, the chaos triggered by the Ethiopian revolution created an opportunity for Barre to realize Somalia's territorial claims against Ethiopia. Somalia's foray into the Ogaden was a creeping invasion, launched first through armed auxiliaries like the West Somali Liberation Front (WSLF) and later with uniformed Somali troops, which publicly entered the war in 1977. As noted earlier, the effort initially met with great success. In the end, however, the war was a military disaster for the Somali state and led to a tsunami of political problems for the Barre regime. The Somali civil war, in which the SNM was an early participant, has its roots in the aftermath of this failed war against Ethiopia.[3]

---

[3] This fairly straightforward review of Somali history is drawn from a range of classic sources (Laitin & Samatar, 1987; Lewis, 2003).

The Somali National Movement: Origins

The rise of the SNM was fueled by the grievances of Somalia's Isaaq clan family, who occupy much of what is now the de facto republic of Somaliland. The failure of the war in the Ogaden led to a rapid collapse in public support for the Barre regime. The first serious sign of discontent occurred in April 1978, when military officers from the Majarteen clan attempted a coup. Although the effort failed, and many of its most important participants were summarily executed, key figures managed to escape and establish the Somali Salvation Democratic Front (SSDF) – the first real organized armed resistance to the Barre regime. While the Isaaq would not join the SSDF in large numbers, the fallout from the 1978 coup attempt helped pave the way for more organized Isaaq resistance.[4]

Isaaq grievances were rooted in a number of factors. To be sure, the Isaaq had been governed as part of British Somaliland, and there was a strand of popular sentiment that believed that the union of British and Italian Somaliland had been undertaken through surreptitious means. Yet Isaaq resistance was not, in the first instance, about reclaiming lost autonomy. The Isaaq, much like the Hawiye, had a somewhat tense relationship with Barre's government, as the regime was informally based on the "MOD" alliance, which united Somalia's three major Darood clans – the Marehan, the Ogaden, and the Dhulbahante – at the apex of state power.[5] Thus, the very structure of the ruling clique was such that the Isaaq sat at the very margins of the political system.

It was also the case that the fallout of the war in the Ogaden had very specific consequences for the Isaaq. As many as 1.5 million refugees from the Ogaden fled into Isaaq-populated regions of northwest Somalia, putting a stress on local resources. Barre's regime tended to favor the large cohort of Ogadeni refugees in local disputes over land and water. The volatile situation was compounded by the fact that Hargeisa, a largely Isaaq city, was damaged by Ethiopian bombing during the war, and basic public services had ground to a halt. The flood of international relief aid that followed the influx of the refugees could have

---

[4] As will be clear, the SNM and SSDF would be political and military competitors. But there were a number of Isaaq fighters that would join the SSDF before later moving to the SNM. In this sense, the SSDF did help – perhaps unintentionally – to mobilize the Isaaq. Author's interview, Bobe Yusuf, SNM Central Committee member, SNM Secretary of Information, and later Minister of Information for Republic of Somaliland, October 19, 2010, Hargeisa, Somaliland.

[5] As any Somali expert will know, Barre's own clan connections were key to the alliance. The Marehan was his lineage; the Ogadeni clan that of his mother; and the Dhulbahante the clan of his son-in-law, who was also head of the feared National Security Services.

alleviated the difficult situation, but was monopolized by Barre and his supporters.

As the specter of resistance to the Barre regime began to emerge, the ruling clique became increasingly repressive, particularly in areas populated by Somali clans perceived as disloyal. In 1980, Barre placed northeastern Somalia under military administration. A tipping point was reached in early 1982, when the government arrested a group of Isaaq professionals called the Hargeisa Group, who were guilty of little more than organizing philanthropic activities in Hargeisa to fill the void left by the collapse in public services. The arrests generated public outrage, and deadly riots in which protesters clashed with government forces soon followed. Barre's regime, in typical authoritarian fashion, meted out hefty sentences to the Hargeisa Group, although the small number that had been given the death penalty would have their sentences commuted. Most would receive sentences between twenty-five and thirty-five years in prison. In the end, the entire cohort would serve in one of Barre's most notorious jails until their release in 1989.[6]

Amidst steadily deteriorating conditions in the northeast, a network of Isaaq émigrés in Saudi Arabia began to organize an anti-Barre resistance. It was this group, along with a network of activists in London, and defecting Isaaq militiamen in Ethiopia, who would form the foundation of the SNM. Following a congress in Jeddah, Saudi Arabia, the Saudi émigrés created what was the early forerunner of the SNM. After the appointment of full-time staff of three, cadres were sent to London and a few other diaspora communities to generate support. For the Saudi group, inroads into the London community were particularly critical. Since Saudi Arabia and Somalia retained amicable relations, and open political organizing was generally frowned on by the Saudi monarchy, the Saudi group needed to move the center of their operations to a more open political setting. Given its large Somali diaspora, the United Kingdom was an obvious choice. The Saudi group also needed to broaden its clan base, and in particular, attract support from the Isaaq subclans like the Habar Jaalo and Arab that were not represented within its ranks.

In London, the SNM's earliest organizers found a warm reception. By this time, there was already sizeable resistance to the Somali government in London, in the form of a steadily evolving mix of political parties and community associations. For the most committed anti-Barre activists within this milieu, most of them Isaaq, the overtures of the Saudi

---

[6] See Renders (2012, pp. 60–64). Also see the author's interview, Yusuf Adan Abokor, Hargeisa Group member and well-known Somaliland intellectual, Hargeisa, Somaliland, October 2010.

group were of keen interest. First, the London group's initial efforts in organizing a movement with a strong anti-Barre stand had run into difficulty. Many of the London activists were students, and lacked the social standing within the community necessary to generate public support. The diaspora in Britain was also composed of a large number of retired seamen who had served in the British merchant navy and now depended on the Somali government for passports and other documents to work and travel. As such, they were lukewarm toward the idea of public resistance to the regime. In this context, the Saudi group was an attractive ally, as they counted a number of well-known Isaaq community members among their numbers. More importantly, the Saudi group tended to be a wealthier constituency, with a number of businessmen and educated professionals within its network. Thus, at this early stage, the SNM was a coalition in struggle, whose diverse preferences and backgrounds were bound together in what was perceived as a viable cause against a formidable external threat (Lewis, 1994, pp. 85–205; Renders, 2012, pp. 64–67).[7]

In April 1981 the organization went public, issuing a communiqué committing itself to the violent overthrow of the Barre regime. In October, the SNM had a founding congress in London, where it elected a chairman, Ahmed Jimaale, from the Saudi group, and an executive committee. Predictably, the SNM's key challenge was that it lacked boots on the ground. Although it did possess some clandestine supporters that distributed its literature and passed on relevant intelligence, it did not have a proper military wing operating in the region. This meant that from 1981 until mid-1982, the SNM was little more than a band of diaspora activists.

The SNM's transition to a rebel organization occurred in the midst of the tumult surrounding the arrest of the Hargeisa Group. Although the Hargeisa Group was not directly linked to the SNM, the arrests provided the impetus for the shift to military operations.[8] The SNM made the key decision to move to Ethiopia, which would become a central base of operations. Meanwhile, another crucial development was unfolding in Somalia. The Barre regime had used Isaaq fighters in the war against Ethiopia, folding many of them into the WSLF. This group came to be known as the Fourth Brigade, or the *Afraad*. Given the overarching

---

[7] In discussions with historian IM Lewis (1994, p. 195), SNM founder Abd al-Rahman Abd al-Qadir Farah acknowledged the dynamics of necessity that brought the two groups together, noting that "the Saudi Somalis wanted to contact their London counterparts at the same time as the latter wanted or needed their brothers from the Middle East."
[8] Author's interview, Yusuf Adan Abokor, Hargeisa Group member and well-known Somaliland intellectual, Hargeisa, Somaliland, October 2010.

tension between the Isaaq and Barre, the brigade had an increasingly acrimonious relationship with the government. As one member of the brigade recalls,

> The people [the Fourth Brigade] were not fighting for the liberation of the Ogaden. They wanted a way to raise arms indirectly so that they can fight against Siad Barre later. That was a way of getting ammunition and guns... We were not allowed to get – you know you cannot a gun or ammunition. So you have to pretend that you are fighting against the Ethiopians.[9]

In 1980, the brigade was involved in clashes with the WSLF's Ogaden clan militias who were encroaching on Isaaq territory in the northwest. With their loyalty to Barre now an open question, the Isaaq militias were transferred to another part of Somalia, and eventually incorporated into the defense architecture of Barre's regime as a government militia. In the context of steadily increasing repression against the Isaaq, the clandestine resistance of Isaaq military units within Somalia became increasingly untenable.[10] Beginning in February 1982, a steady stream of fighters from the Fourth Brigade began to trickle into Ethiopia, where they linked up with their Isaaq brethren from the diaspora. This flow, in the words of noted Somaliland expert Marleen Renders (2012, p. 72), "was a concerted operation, led by Isaaq army officers and Isaaq senior government officials in Mogadishu." Indeed, four Isaaq colonels would join the SNM during this period, and they would be followed by important civilian political figures later. It was these fighters who would be the "first nucleus of SNM forces."[11]

Taken from a broad perspective, it is once again clear how survival and security considerations were central to the incorporation of what was a critical component of the SNM's founding coalition. The Barre defectors provided the diaspora contingent a presence on the ground; meanwhile, the diaspora activists, now in Ethiopia, provided the Barre defectors a safe setting to transition from clandestine to more direct forms of resistance. In effect, this was an alliance that was structured by both the seeming viability of early rebellion and immediate threats to survival created by their opposition to Barre's despotic rule.

This all meant that the SNM was a motley crowd of dissidents who agreed on the bare minimum: the need to oust the Barre regime. This was reflected in a political program that was somewhat ambiguous about

---

[9] Author's interview, Bobe Yusuf, SNM Central Committee member and later Minister of Information for Republic of Somaliland, October 19, 2010, Hargeisa, Somaliland. Interviewee was also a member of the Fourth Brigade and a WSLF central committee member.
[10] Ibid.   [11] Ibid.

what the post-Barre order ought to look like. Deep cleavages existed between civilian and military wings, between Islamists (the Saudi group) and Marxists, and between Isaaq and pan-Somali nationalists. Later, issues of clan would become central. Bobe Yusuf, former SNM Central Committee member and part of the early cohort that joined from the Fourth Brigade, summarized it best, arguing:

> Number one, the SNM was not a political party. It was called the Somali National Movement and when you talk about a movement you are talking about a front where everybody comes in. You have got all tracks. You have everybody who hates Siad Barre and wants to take the gun to fight against him. You have got the clerics, you have got the military officers, you have got the intellectuals, you have got the socialist-oriented people, you have the capitalist-oriented people. You have every Dick and Harry united against Siad Barre. We had to accommodate that.
>
> At certain times there was the discussion that this may lead to a feud between the SNM rank and file, but we were saying Siad Barre will not be sparing anyone, any one of us. No matter what difference we have. He will kill you and he will kill me.[12]

From Stalemate to the "Hawiye Split": 1982–1987

Throughout its eleven-year history, the SNM went through a multitude of organizational changes. The most obvious were the repeated leadership transitions: between 1981 and 1992, there were six organizational congresses and five different chairmen, although over time, there was a trend toward longer terms for leadership.[13] Many SNM stalwarts argue that this was because of the organization's "democratic" character, and the fear of replicating internally the tyranny of Barre's regime.[14] The reality, however, was that leadership changes were more an expression of the rough-and-tumble internal politics of the SNM, and the fractious competition between its constituent units. For instance, the SNM's third congress in Harar, Ethiopia, saw secular military officers led by Colonel Abd al-Qadir Kosar replace the Saudi group led by incumbent chairman Yusuf Sheikh Madar. The fourth congress in 1984 witnessed the

---

[12] Author's interview, Bobe Yusuf, SNM Central Committee Member and later Minister of Information for Republic of Somaliland, October 25, 2010, Hargeisa, Somaliland; also quoted in Bennet & Woldemariam (2011).
[13] Ahmed Mohamed Gulaid Jimaleh, Yusuf Sheikh Ali Sheikh Madar, Abd al-Qadir Kosar Abdi, Ahmed Mahmoud Silanyo, and Abdirahman Tuur. The last three had all been defectors from Barre's government.
[14] Author's interview, Abdiwali Dirawal, SNM commander, October 2010, Hargeisa, Somaliland; Author's interview, Bobe Yusuf, October 19, 2010.

election of Ahmed Mahmoud Silanyo – the longest-serving SNM chairman – and signaled a shift in political power toward civilian politicians and the Habar Jaalo clan, and away from military officers and the Habar Yunis.

Somewhat remarkably, these fissures were resolved amicably, although tensions were severe. In one critical moment, Habar Yunis fighters threatened to defect to the Barre regime amidst the back and forth of the 1984 congress. It seems the cooperative equilibrium within the SNM was often preserved by avoiding contentious electoral processes. Instead, through protracted debate and politicking, different factions of the SNM would come to public consensus outside the official congress hall, endorse a single candidate, and then approve it by acclamation through the formal proceedings.[15]

As this book argues, the overarching military context was important to the maintenance of the cooperative status quo and organizational cohesion. Like all groups discussed in this book, territory was central to the SNM strategy. Reflecting on the SNM's withdrawal from its base area in Somalia in 1990 (to be discussed), SNM vice-chairman Hassan Isse Jama acknowledged that such developments undermined confidence in the movement among the broader public, leading to a situation where the SNM would be a "fish out of water," deprived of critical recruits and logistics.[16] Moreover, as time passed, and the SNM became a movement more narrowly reflecting Isaaq aspirations for autonomy and self-government, it began to resemble the subnational movements in Ethiopia, which retained a strong commitment to territoriality. In these ways, the acquisition and loss of territory was thus central to understanding the SNM's military position, and thus the incentives that structured its cohesion and fragmentation.

Between 1983 and early 1986, the SNM was largely in a holding pattern, launching the occasional high-profile attack but achieving no discernible shift in the geographic scope of its operations. The attack on the Mandera prison, orchestrated with the assistance of Isaaq military officers in Barre's government, was particularly significant, but as Renders (2012, p. 73) notes, "... despite the occasional spectacular military victory, SNM was not in a position to enforce a major military or political breakthrough."

The SNM's military constraints were serious. There was the incessant feuding amongst its different factions. The SNM was also not the favored

---

[15] Author's interview, Bobe Yusuf, October 19, 2010, Hargeisa, Somaliland.
[16] Hassan Isse Jama, SNM founder and vice-chairman, October 27, 2010, Hargeisa, Somaliland.

partner of the Ethiopian government, a distinction that went to the older SSDF, who saw the SNM as a competitor and sought to marginalize it.[17] Finally, Isaaq nomads, whose support was vital to the expansion of operations in northeast Somalia, were initially lukewarm toward the revolutionary ideas being peddled by what seemed to them to be a distant diaspora group.

The year 1986 marked a decisive shift in the military operations of the SNM, inaugurating a period of dramatic battlefield swings that would have serious implications for the internal cohesion of the organization. Fearing reports of a rapprochement between Barre and Mengistu, the SNM launched a campaign of urban raids that resulted in the deaths of hundreds of government troops. In addition, the regional chief of Barre's National Security Service was killed, and several areas along the Ethiopian Somali border were occupied temporarily (Gilkes, 1989, p. 55). A key element of the 1986 campaign was the SNM effort to establish a toehold in portions of southern Somalia – in other words, non-Isaaq areas – a strategic move enabled by the support of Dir militiamen and the inclusion of a sizeable contingent of Hawiye politicians within the SNM leadership (Lewis, 1994, pp. 212–214).

As battlefield circumstance seemed to turn in the SNM's favor, the fragile internal consensus within the organization began to unravel. While in an earlier period the diverse preferences of its various constituent units had been reconciled, a new military surge led to preference divergence. At its 1984 congress, the SNM had brought into the leadership the sizeable contingent of Hawiye figures mentioned earlier. This included the appointment of a Hawiye vice-chairman, Ali Mohammed Ossobleh, in what was a watershed moment for an organization so thoroughly dominated by the Isaaq. The congress, however, would put Ossobleh – charismatic and ambitious – on a collision course with newly installed chairman Silanyo. Silanyo was a big fish within SNM circles, in part because he had served as Barre's minister of commerce before defecting to the rebels. Using the weight of his own reputation, Silanyo pushed through a number of changes that helped him consolidate his power. Key among them was that the term of chairman be extended to three years, and that regulations that cast a pall over SNM members that had been senior Barre officials be removed.

Differences between Ossobleh's Hawiye faction and a leadership increasingly dominated by Silanyo seemed to crystallize over the SNM's military strategy, which to the Hawiye appeared far too focused on

---

[17] Author's interview, Hassan Isse Jama, SNM founder and vice-chairman, October 27, 2010, Hargeisa, Somaliland.

operations in the Isaaq heartland in the northeast. Things took a dangerous turn when Barre's forces orchestrated the killing of former SNM chairman Colonel Kosar by Hawiye gunmen. In the Somali context, where claims and debts are often ascribed not to the individual but their clan, this must have cast a serious shadow over the Hawiye members of the SNM.[18] Ossobleh and the Hawiye contingent would fragment from the SNM shortly thereafter, congealing into a new Hawiye force called the United Somali Congress (USC) (Lewis, 1994, p. 213; Kapteijns, 2012, p. 115).

Although many SNM sources assert that Ossobleh's departure was voluntary, the cycle of contention that it seemed to trigger suggests otherwise.[19] Beginning in May 1987, there was a spate of more serious factional infighting within SNM ranks, this time pitting some of the main Isaaq subclans against one other. Several dozen SNM fighters were executed, and in June–July, three senior officials were killed (Renders, 2012, pp. 77–78). While fears of infiltration played a key role in these tensions, the purge seemed to play into Silanyo's hands. At the 1987 congress Silanyo was reelected to an unprecedented three-year term. Ossobleh's position of vice-chairman was abolished, and the newly reelected chairman was given the right to nominate ten of the fifty-five-member Central Committee (Lewis, 1994, p. 213), effectively cementing his control. As the war went, so went the cooperative status quo.

State Collapse and the SNM's Implosion

The offensives of 1986 inaugurated a new phase of conflict in northwest Somalia. Under the guidance of General Mohammed Said Hirsi Morgan, the commander of the northwest region and Barre's son-in-law, the government responded with massive and indiscriminate violence against the Isaaq. A key pillar of this approach was the arming of Darood and Dir progovernment militias in the region. The SNM did not back down militarily, even as it suffered from its internal crisis, and the intensity and geographic scope of fighting remained consistent.

---

[18] Many of the Isaaq rank-and-file suspected non-Isaaq as Barre infiltrators, which contributed to a contentious climate. Author's interview, Bobe Yusuf, October 25, 2010, Hargeisa, Somaliland.

[19] Author's interview, Mohammed Hashi Elmi, SNM founder and Central Committee member, later Somaliland's Minister of Finance, October 2010, Hargeisa, Somaliland. The notion that Ossobleh's move was part of a strategic effort to build a Hawiye front fits nicely with contemporary SNM narratives, since the SNM would later support Somaliland's secession, and the Hawiye are not a clan that resides in Somaliland. But to be clear, the SNM was not a secessionist group in 1986–87, so it is hard to view Ossobleh's departure as being part of the SNM master plan for an independent state.

A major transformation, however, occurred in March 1988, when Ethiopia and Somalia signed a peace agreement and agreed to stop supporting each other's internal opponents. The agreement was born of desperation, as both regimes were now seriously threatened by internal resistance. In Somalia, Barre's opposition in the south was rapidly growing, with the emergence of militias among the Hawiye. Moreover, the changing winds of the Cold War threatened to deprive both Addis and Mogadishu of the superpower largesse that had sustained their military machines.

Whatever the cause of the agreement, it shocked the SNM. With its rear bases now in jeopardy, it struck out into the northwest once again, launching a major offensive designed to capture territory. Large swathes of territory were acquired, including major urban centers like Burao and parts of Hargeisa. This success, however, was short-lived, as Barre responded with massive aerial bombing that made the occupation of these territories untenable. The SNM was forced to move back into Ethiopia in the face of the government's onslaught.

This moment in the war had massive implications for the nature of internal cleavages within the SNM. The bombing campaign, indiscriminate and brutal, led to massive exodus of Isaaq into refugee camps in Ethiopia, where for the time being, they cohabitated with SNM forces. With external support on the wane, the SNM realized it needed to better tap the resources of the thousands of refugees that were now in Ethiopia, as well as those Isaaq that remained in northwest Somalia. Moreover, as a practical matter, the SNM was overwhelmed by the needs of this population, and now subject to many of its demands and political preferences. To resolve these issues, and gain proper control of the masses, the SNM decided to rely on Isaaq elders, who quite obviously possessed significant currency within the Isaaq community. There were a number of implications that followed from this. First, the SNM incorporated a council of Isaaq elders – called a *Guurti* – into its leadership structures. This council was advisory, but as a practical matter it was very influential, since it had the capacity to raise resources from the Isaaq population. Second, the SNM grew dramatically – it was a mere 3,000 strong in 1988, but would grow to 50,000 by 1991. This was made possible by the massive absorption of non-SNM Isaaq militia, an arrangement brokered through the efforts of the elders. Finally, and most importantly, the SNM was effectively reorganized along clan lines – in part at the elders' behest – so that the membership of many military units corresponded to specific Isaaq subclans.

Cumulatively, this meant that clan rivalries would weigh more heavily on the internal dynamics of the SNM. To be sure, clan had always mattered in the SNM's politics, and clan elders were not new actors within the organization. Yet there was a perceptible shift.

By late 1990 the SNM had wrested control of most of what is now Somaliland from the Barre regime. There were minor setbacks in early 1990 when the base area the SNM had established in Somaliland was raided by Barre's forces, forcing the SNM to flee once again into Ethiopia. But the growth of allied opposition in the south had allowed the SNM to expand its territorial control. The critical juncture was a decisive offensive in mid-1990 that saw the SNM occupy most parts of the northwest. The war continued until January 1991, when Barre was ousted from Mogadishu by the SNM's allies the USC. Yet in many ways, Barre's ouster opened up a new phase of struggle for the SNM, which frankly, had not really anticipated the rapidity with which the regime would collapse. A number of non-Isaaq clans to the east and west of Isaaq territory – the Gadabursi and Harti respectively – had fought on Barre's side, and remained unreconciled with the SNM. In January 1991, the alliance between the SNM and USC fell apart, when USC chairman Ali Mahdi declared himself the head of an interim government. The SNM and the other main USC faction, led by Mohammed Farah Aideed, rejected the new administration. As the situation in the south descended into protracted and bloody conflict between an assortment of Hawiye and Darood clans, the SNM bowed to popular pressure and declared Somaliland an independent republic. The popular consensus on the logic of this declaration is that the indiscriminate violence of the late 1980s had turned Isaaq public opinion decisively against continued union with the south.

The declaration of independence occurred at the Burao conference in May 1991, a meeting critical to forging a new political structure for the SNM and the fledgling territory of Somaliland. It was agreed that the SNM would transition into an interim administration, with a term of two years. Representatives from rival non-Isaaq clans were incorporated into the SNM's executive committee, and the SNM's central committee, expanded to ninety-nine would function as a legislative body. SNM chairman Abdirahman Tuur and his deputy, Hassan Isse Jama, would become Somaliland's president and vice-president.

Although a general consensus on the transition had been reached between the SNM's different factions during the April 1990 SNM congress, the battlefield gains seemed to drive preference divergence over the distribution of power within the newly ascendant movement. The looming factional conflict brought some of the old SNM personal and ideological dichotomies to the fore. But the conflagration that was to come was more complicated, as these elite rivalries tapped into, and were reinforced by, the clan cleavages that had been inscribed within the SNM since the crisis of 1988.

Major problems emerged in response to efforts by Tuur to centralize the SNM administration. The events of 1988 onward had turned the SNM into a vast and unwieldy organization, with an array of affiliated Isaaq clan militia operating nominally under the SNM banner. After their election in 1990, Tuur and Hassan Isse Jama had sought to exert greater levels of control over these militias, because of concerns that they were creating problems in a number of localities with their indiscipline.[20] Attempts by the SNM senior leadership to establish a military police command were thwarted by the heavy fighting of 1990–91, as the SNM decided to focus its resources on a final assault on Barre's positions. After the Burao conference, Tuur sought once again to create an integrated police force comprising SNM fighters from a variety of clans. Almost automatically, this triggered a tug-of-war between Tuur and the defense chief, Mohammed Kahin, over who would control the force: the SNM executive or the defense chief.

While Kahin was tasked with creating the force, the pace was slow. Tuur was of the belief that Kahin was deliberately stalling. Kahin was eventually ousted as defense chief, amidst difficult-to-verify claims that he planned a coup, and his portfolio was handed to the vice-president, Hassan Isse Jama. Others were soon fired, including the powerful minister of interior, Mohammed Suleiman Aden Gaal. This situation split the SNM leadership down the middle, between the Tuur group and a faction of senior SNM personalities called the Red Berets – a band of socialists and military men in which Kahin and the heavyweight former chairman, Silanyo, featured prominently (Renders, 2012, pp. 93–95).

Some SNM sources claim that there was a deliberate effort to undermine Tuur's administration. In this narrative, the former leadership, led by Silanyo, worried that the battlefield successes during Tuur's tenure might grant him a degree of popular legitimacy that he could leverage to win another term. In any case, the split at the top of the organization diffused, and soon took on a clan tinge, as SNM elites appealed to the SNM's clan units, clan militia, and their respective clan elders. These elites seemed to believe that in the Somali context, clan appeals were the only effective way to mobilize support. In the end, the elite rupture between the Tuur and the Red Berets pitted the Habar Yunis against the Habar Jaalo, since Kahin, Aden Gaal, and Silanyo were all from the Habar Jaalo. A range of deep intra-Isaaq clan animosities helped to fuel

---

[20] Author's interview, Hassan Isse Jama, SNM founder and vice-chairman, October 27, 2010, Hargeisa, Somaliland.

the morphing of the SNM dispute into broader clan conflict. The Habar Yunis are among Somaliland's largest clans, and since the days of the British protectorate, the broad perception had been that they occupied a privileged political status among the Isaaq clans. Much of this was related to Britain's own policy of favoritism, which led to the Habar Yunis's incorporation into the imperial bureaucracy in large numbers. Once Tuur, a Habar Yunis, appeared at the helm of the newly ascendant SNM, the sentiment of "Let us avoid another hundred years of Habar Yunis rule" found broad appeal among the other Isaaq subclans.[21] As this book has argued, territorial gains had now placed the question of clan power front and center.

The breakdown of the SNM's cooperative equilibrium was formalized when Tuur sent loyal forces across the country to disarm the clan militias, under the banner of consolidating the authority of the SNM-run state and putting an end to militia banditry. This led to clashes between Habar Yunis and Habar Jaalo militia in Burao in January 1992, and began a round of devastating SNM infighting that became known as the Sheep Wars. As the violence escalated, efforts to convene the SNM Central Committee and resolve the crisis were thwarted when opposition forces denied the meetings a quorum by refusing to attend. Hundreds were killed and thousands displaced (Bradbury, 2008, pp. 87–90; Renders, 2012, pp. 93–95).

At this point, the conflict diffused yet again, as the battle between Tuur and the dissidents swept into the strategic port of Berbera. Here, clan dynamics played a key role in the broadening of the cycle of contention. Tuur's group recognized that port revenues were key to the reestablishment of political order. The problem was that the port was dominated by the SNM's Habar Awal militias who nursed serious grievances over their seeming underrepresentation in the SNM administration created at the Burao conference. Fighting soon erupted between Habar Yunis militia in the city and the Habar Awal commander of Berbera, Ibrahim Dagaweyn, as the Habar Awal bandwagoned with the dissidents (Bradbury, 2008, pp. 87–90; Renders, 2012, pp. 93–95).

The infighting would soon place Tuur in an impossible situation. Given the breadth of opposition, the SNM chairman faced a stark choice: either a fight to the death that he could not win or the pursuit of an exit option. In his treatment of this period, Bradbury (2008, p. 90) largely concurs with this assessment: Dagaweyn had control of Berbera by August 1992, and was a mere thirty miles from the Habar

---

[21] Author's interview, SNM Central Committee member, October 2010, Hargeisa, Somaliland. Interviewee asked to not have his name revealed.

Yunis heartland in Hargeisa. The Saad Muse clan – Habar Awal but living in Hargeisa – had initially supported Tuur, but now pulled out of his coalition.[22]

For Tuur, now "facing military defeat and public opposition," fate would intervene to give him an exit option. When a proposed UN mission to the territory was not forthcoming (Bradbury, 2008, p. 90), Gadabursi clan elders intervened to reconcile the warring Isaaq clans, an effort that culminated in a clan conference between February and May 1993 at Borama. The conference would include elders and civil society from all the major clans, Isaaq and non-Isaaq. Tuur, responding to the opportunity, announced that he was relinquishing executive authority and vesting it in the Isaaq Guurti. Once convened at Boroma, the Isaaq Guurti, along with the elders of other clans, would be responsible for mapping out a political transition. In this bold stroke, Tuur was effectively exiting the SNM by abolishing it as an organized force. In any case, the SNM Central Committee had not met for two years. The elders stepped into the political void at Boroma, sidelined the SNM remnants, and installed a new non-SNM president, Mohammed Ibrahim Egal. Tuur's dissidents were swallowed up in the new administration of Egal, which, given Guurti pressure, was their only real alternative to Tuur's reinstatement (Bennet & Woldemariam, 2011; Lewis, 2012, pp. 96–102).[23]

The paradox of this situation, of course, was that clan elders had stoked the violence only to play peacemakers once the situation had escalated beyond what was acceptable. Meanwhile, Tuur's action, a clear act of fragmentation born of survival concerns, would result in him fleeing the northwest for Mogadishu, where he would reinvent himself as a unionist politician associated with USC warlord Mohammed Farah Aideed.

As can be seen, SNM's 1992 implosion is entirely consistent with this book's central argument and its corollary claims. The territorial gains of 1990–91 laid the stage for the subsequent bout of factional infighting and fragmentation. The initial rupture between Tuur and the Red Berets diffused, incorporating a range of clan militias and aggrieved Tuur opponents in Berbera. Facing outright military defeat, Tuur dissolved the

---

[22] To be clear, the Sheep Wars were not a simple fight between the Habar Yunis on one side and the Habar Jaalo and Habar Awal on the other. The Idagalle clan fought with the Habar Yunis – collectively, the two clans that make up this lineage line are known as the Garhajis. The Habar Awal were initially divided, with the Issa Musse of Berbera resisting Tuur, and the Saad Musse initially supporting him.

[23] Author's interview, Mohammed Fadal, civil society participant at Boroma conference, and later Somaliland's Minister of Planning, October 25, 2010, Hargeisa, Somaliland.

SNM, and eventually defected to the south. As the war went, so went cooperation.

Islamic Courts Union: 2004–2006

The ascendance of the Islamic Courts Union (ICU) represented the apogee of Somalia's modern Islamist movement. By 2006, the ICU had consolidated its rule over much of south-central Somalia, including key urban centers like Mogadishu and Kismayo, establishing the most coherent administration these regions had seen since the fall of Siad Barre. As will be clear, the ICU was in the truest sense a broad coalition of militant Islamists forged in the midst of existential security threats. But when the organization no longer appeared capable of serving the ends for which it was created – guaranteeing the security of its constituent units – the ICU collapsed into a disastrous episode of factional infighting and fragmentation that would seal its demise.

Political Islam has been a potent force throughout Somali history. During the colonial period, Islam served as a mechanism through which Somali nationalists sought to mobilize anticolonial sentiment. The Dervish rebellion of Sheikh Mohammed Abdullah Hassan, a man inspired by the Sahiliya teachings of his Sudanese mentor, Mohammed Salih, is perhaps the most powerful illustration of Islam's mobilizational capacity in the colonial era. The "Mad Mullah," as he has come to be known, quickly built support among the Darood clans of Northern Somalia, and sustained rebel activity against the British, Italians, and Ethiopians for nearly twenty years.[24]

Decades later, in the years spanning the late colonial period and the early independence era, Somalia became home to a vibrant and politically conscious field of Islamic associations. Organizations like the Somali Islamic League, Al-Nahda, Jamiyat huma al-Diin, and Jamiyat Ihya al-Sunna, sought to promote Islam in public life and the broader use

---

[24] The Islamic orientation of the Dervish rebellion can be seen in a letter the Mullah wrote to British administrators in 1899, in which he declared: "You have oppressed our ancient religion without cause... Now choose for yourselves. If you want war, we accept it. But if you want peace, pay the fine" (Jardine, 1923, p. 43; Hess, 1964, p. 419). Hess (1964, p. 420) also underscores the religious underpinnings of Mohammed Abdullah's *jihad*, arguing that the jihad was moved not simply by anticolonial sentiment but by a desire to assert the hegemony of Mohammed Abdullah's Sahiliya teachings over its main Sufi competitor, the Qadiriyah order: "With all the fervor of a man certain of the exclusive truth of his religion, he declared a holy war on all infidels. The jihad, it seems, was at first aimed at Somalis of the Qadiriyah sect, but it was only a matter of time before the term was applied to the Ethiopians and the British as well. The proclamation of jihad led to an increase in the strength of the Mullist dervishes, who in their religious enthusiasm soon turned to excesses of fanaticism and forced conversions."

of Arabic languages.[25] Yet political Islam would go through an important transformation with the military coup of 1969, and Siad Barre's declaration of scientific socialism as the official ideology of the state the following year. Initially, Barre's socialism – known by its Somali name, *Hantiwadaag* – sought to ideologically embrace religion in a way that most socialist regimes of the era did not. Instead, the regime focused its revolutionary ire on clannism within Somali society, which was seen as the far more destructive vestige of traditionalism. But the Family Law of 1975, established by presidential decree in January of that year, created a more adversarial relationship between the state and Somalia's religious elite. The law sought to equalize inheritance rights between women and men, restrict polygamy, and provide women firmer rights to seek divorce from their husbands. The country's religious elites publicly opposed these measures, not least because they reduced their authority, since family matters were were traditionally regulated by customary and religious jurisprudence (Mohamed, 2015, p. 1). In the furor that followed, Barre's security establishment would respond with typical brutality, executing ten dissenting sheikhs, sentencing another twenty-three to terms between twenty and thirty years, and arresting hundreds of others (Mohamed, 2015, p. 6).[26]

The effect of this crackdown on Somalia's Islamists was twofold. First, the episode rendered political Islam (yet again) an ideology of resistance in the Somali context. From this moment on, Somalia's Islamists sought to overtly and covertly undermine Barre's socialist regime. Second, much of the Somali Islamist community was forced abroad, where it came under the influence of some of the broader Islamic ideological currents in the Middle East at the time – in particular, Salafist trends that emphasized takfiri practice and jihad.

The ICU Coalition: Clan Courts, Professional Jihadists, and Mogadishu's Business Community

In the years following the collapse of the Somali state in 1991, a diverse array of Islamists sought to fill the political void and compete militarily with the panoply of clan-based insurgent groups and warlords who had succeeded in ousting the Barre regime. It was out of this milieu that four distinct elements would emerge, and eventually forge the common

---

[25] See unpublished 2008 paper by Abdurahman Moallim Abdullahi titled "The Islah Movement: Islamic Moderation in War-Torn Somalia," pp. 5–8.
[26] For an excellent history of Islamism in Somalia, told through the experience of Al-Islah (Somalia's Muslim Brotherhood), see the full dissertation of Abdurahman Moallim Abdullahi (2011), which builds on the unpublished 2008 paper cited earlier.

organizational front that was to be the ICU. These elements included Mogadishu's Hawiye Islamic courts, remnants of a Somali militant organization known as Al-Ittihad, and the foreign fighters of Al-Qaeda. Mogadishu's business community, which lacked a particularly fervent Islamist orientation, would be the fourth network crucial to the ICU's emergence. In trying to understand the ICU founding coalition that would congeal in 2004, and the security concerns that bound this diverse array of groups together, we must examine the checkered performance of Somalia's Islamists in the years following Barre's collapse. The simple reality was that Islamists repeatedly failed to provide an alternative to the clan-based political fiefdoms that emerged following Barre's ouster. That history of failure, in combination with the specific security exigencies Islamists faced in south-central Somalia in 2004–05, largely explains what bound the ICU coalition together.

The first significant Islamist organization to emerge during the upheavals of 1991 was Al-Ittihad al-Islamiya, which was originally founded in 1982. The remnants of this organization were to be a key constituent unit of the ICU coalition. Up until Barre's removal, the Salafist organization, which was committed to the creation of an Islamic state in Somalia, remained nonviolent. Yet, propelled by the opportunities Barre's collapse presented, funds from wealthy Saudis and the transnational Somali business community, and the influx of trained Somali veterans of the Soviet–Afghan War, Al-Ittihad sought to militarily assert its claims.[27] In January 1991, it seized the strategic seaport of Kismayo.[28] This success, however, would be fleeting. In a matter of months, the Hawiye clan militias of warlord General Mohammed Farah Aideed succeeded in pushing Al-Ittihad out of the port, despite the Islamist

---

[27] It is difficult to know how many veterans of the Afghan War joined Al-Ittihad. A. Duale Sii'arag claims that nearly 1,000 Somalis fought with the Afghan mujahidin. But whatever their numbers, it is clear that these veterans played an important role in Al-Ittihad and its militant Islamist successors. See A. Duale Sii'arag, "The Birth and Rise of Al-Ittihad Al-Islami in the Somali Inhabited Region of the Horn of Africa," May 15, 2006, which can be found at www.maanhadal.com/maanhada/Al-Ittihad%20_maanhadal.html (Accessed November 1, 2015).

[28] The chairman of Al-Ittihad was Sheikh Ali Warsame, a founder of the Muslim Youth Union, also known as Wahdada. He had also been a former member of Al-Islah. His deputy, who was largely concerned with military affairs, was a colonel in the Somali army and a veteran of the Ogaden War named Sheikh Hassan Dahir Aweys. The latter would play a critical role within the ICU. As a Habr Gedr-Hawiye, Aweys initially joined the USC militias of Gen. Mohammed Farah Aideed after Barre's ouster, and was deployed by Aideed to negotiate Al-Ittihad's peaceful handover of Kismayo. At that moment, Aweys defected to Al-Ittihad. See Markus Hoehne, "Counter-Terrorism in Somalia: How External Interference helped produce militant Islam," *SSRC: Crisis in the Horn of Africa*, p. 4, which can be found at http://webarchive.ssrc.org/Somalia_Hoehne_v10.pdf (Accessed February 8, 2016).

organization's best efforts to build common cause with the Somali National Front–Somali Patriotic Front alliance – a constellation of forces ironically composed of former Barre loyalists in addition to other Darood militias in the city (Shay, 2008, pp. 43–44).

The defeat forced Al-Ittihad to move north and regroup in what is now Puntland. Just as it had in Kismayo, Al-Ittihad forces soon asserted themselves, taking control of the port of Bosasso and other key areas. And yet again, the experiment was short-lived, as the organization was ousted from Puntland in June 1992 by a more capable SSDF that was seeking to implant itself as the uncontested political authority in the region. The defeat eventually forced Al-Ittihad to move to its secondary bases in Gedo region, where for a time they emerged as a viable force. In October 1993, Al-Ittihad fighters joined the fight against the Americans at the infamous Battle of Mogadishu, and subsequently sought to harass UN troops that had been deployed in support of the ongoing humanitarian relief effort in south-central Somalia (Bryden, 2003, p. 30).[29]

It would be in neighboring Ethiopia that the most consequential effects of Al-Ittihad's Gedo operations were to be felt. Although Al-Ittihad did not share the truly transnational political aspirations of organizations like Al-Qaeda, it did seek to unite ethnic Somali communities in neighboring countries under a single Islamic regime. Gedo, the only Somali region to border both Ethiopia and Kenya, was a logical place from which to pursue this ambition. A string of Al-Ittihad attacks in Ethiopia and against Ethiopian targets in Somalia soon followed, with the violence reaching its apex in the summer of 1996 (Bryden, 2003, pp. 31–32).[30]

Al-Ittihad's Ethiopia campaign would prove to be overreach. It provoked the Ethiopians, who had already crossed into Somalia on several prior occasions and struck Al-Ittihad targets, into a concerted

---

[29] It is generally recognized that it was Hawiye clan militias, not Al-Ittihad, that played a key role in the October 1993 fighting in Mogadishu. What is fascinating about Al-Ittihad's participation in the battle is that the organization's commercial arm was heavily involved with UNISOM I and UN-affiliated assistance programs, providing them with contracting services in a wide variety of sectors, including security. See A. Duale Sii'arag, "The Birth and Rise of Al-Ittihad Al-Islami in the Somali Inhabited Region of the Horn of Africa."

[30] There was no parallel campaign in Kenya, probably because Al-Ittihad did not want to jeopardize the significant revenues it was raising there. See A. Dualie Sii'arag, "The Birth and Rise of Al-Ittihad Al-Islami in the Somali Inhabited Region of Ethiopia." The spate of attacks in Ethiopia was likely executed with the support of the ONLF, which found common cause with Al-Ittihad because it required a rear base in Somalia and shared a common enemy with the Islamists. Clan allegiances were also important, as senior Al-Ittihad leader, Sheikh Hassan Turki, hailed from the Rer Abdilleh subclan of the Ogadeni, which is a significant political constituency of the ONLF.

counterinsurgency effort. In August 1996, Ethiopia would deliver a serious blow, marching on Al-Ittihad bases in Luuq and Bulo Hawo, and engaging Al-Ittihad fighters at the Battle of Dolow City (Hansen, 2013, pp. 21–22). Al-Ittihad prospects were greatly diminished when Marehan militias of the SNF cooled on Al-Ittihad's presence in the region and withdrew their support (Shay, 2008, p. 44). In 1997, Ethiopia undertook further mop-up operations that dispersed the organization and largely ended its reign as a capable fighting force.

In the wake of the defeat, Al-Ittihad would split.[31] Clan dynamics had played a role in its Kismayo, Puntland, and Gedo defeats, and they again became a key line of internal cleavage.[32] Ideological differences were also important, with major disputes emerging between those who sought to continue armed struggle and more moderate members who believed armed struggle was no longer possible. In the end, the organization morphed into a nonviolent network of activists who sought to promote an Islamist agenda through proselytization and the provision of social services.[33] Remnants of the organization would eventually filter into Mogadishu, where, as noted earlier, they would eventually form an important constituent unit of the ICU.

Al-Ittihad's disappointing experience as a militant Islamist organization was echoed by Al-Qaeda's efforts in Somalia. Osama Bin Laden, with the support of Hassan Turabi and Sudan's National Islamic Front (NIF), sought to establish a presence in Somalia in the early 1990s. In 1993, two key Al-Qaeda operatives, Mohammed Atef and Ali Mohammed, visited Somalia in order to more firmly establish Al-Qaeda's operational presence in the country.[34] Although Al-Qaeda has probably exaggerated the nature and scale of its efforts in Somalia, it did provide military support to Al-Ittihad and other clan militia, and Al-Qaeda fighters probably played a role in the Battles of Mogadishu

---

[31] Al-Ittihad is not a case study in this book, but its fragmentation is obviously quite consistent with my primary claims.

[32] As a general rule, all of Somalia's Islamist organizations officially spurn clan politics. But the reality is that clan issues have been at the center of their internal fragmentation.

[33] Hansen (2013, pp. 21–22) suggests that the organization broke into two components – a more moderate faction called Al-Itisaam, and a more hardline faction that retained the name Al-Ittihad. This may have mapped onto a cleavage between Al-Ittihad's Ethiopian and Somali wings. Roland Marchal (2011, p. 13) says that the more hardline faction, which was "vibrantly Salafi," took the name Al-Itisaam. Perhaps the discrepancy reflects the military irrelevance of Al-Ittihad after its defeat in Gedo.

[34] The former was Bin Laden's deputy, and the latter Al-Qaeda's chief military trainer (Bryden, 2003, p. 27). Also see "Al-Qaida's (Mis)Adventures In The Horn of Africa," *Harmony Project, Combatting Terrorism Center at West Point*, 2006, p. 79, which can be found at www.ctc.usma.edu/wp-content/uploads/2010/06/Al-Qaidas-MisAdventures-in-the-Horn-of-Africa.pdf (Accessed October 2, 2016).

and Dolow City (Bryden, 2003, pp. 27–28). Yet Al-Qaeda's East Africa network would not last long in the Somali theatre, in part because the country's stateless environment was an unforgiving setting for foreign jihadists. The proliferation of clan-based militia and unscrupulous criminal networks made the cost of military operations in Somalia quite high for foreign fighters, as Al-Qaeda found it difficult to carve out safe space between these competing interests. The collapse of the Somali state also meant that regional and international powers could readily cross Somali borders to pursue Al-Qaeda targets (Bryden, 2003, p. 28).

By the late 1990s, as Al-Qaeda central moved from Sudan into Afghanistan, its East African network would be forced to reorganize and consolidate most of its assets into northeastern and coastal Kenya. The 1998 Nairobi and Dar es Salaam attacks, 9/11, and the 2002 Mombasa attacks would compel key parts of this network to move back into Somalia in the early 2000s, where its history of difficulty would inform its strategic decision to join the ICU coalition.[35]

The phenomenon of the Islamic courts emerged not long after Al-Ittihad and Al-Qaeda had begun to make their presence felt in Somalia, and its record was equally disappointing. The courts were an extension of the system of Hawiye clan politics in Mogadishu, and emerged as an organic solution to address the problem of lawlessness that afflicted the city in the years after Barre's ouster. Since the court's jurisdictions corresponded to the geographic distribution of Mogadishu's major Hawiye subclans – in other words, many of the Hawiye subclans had their own courts – its legal decisions were enforced by clan militias. The courts thus sat in an awkward and often fatal embrace with Mogadishu's main clan warlords. Importantly, the courts were staffed by religious figures well versed in Islamic law, but it was an ideologically diverse experiment by no means dominated by the Salafism of Al-Ittihad and Al-Qaeda.

The first Islamic court emerged in 1994 in north Mogadishu, led by Islamic clerics of the Abgaal subclan of the Hawiye. The experiment was short-lived, however, because Abgaal strongman Ali Mahdi – whose premature self-appointment as Barre's successor in 1991 plunged Mogadishu into chaos – found the courts to be a threat to his authority. He decided to demote the court's chairman, Sheikh Ali Dheere, and issue a decree dismantling the courts. This combination of actions proved to be fatal for the fledgling court system.

---

[35] The key Al-Qaeda members that were to play a role in the ICU (and later Al-Shabaab) were all foreigners, hailing from other countries in East Africa. They include Fazul Abdullah Mohammed (Tanzania), Tahla al-Sudani (Sudan), and Saleh Ali Saleh Nabhan (Kenya).

In the late 1990s, led by the Ifka Halane Court of the Ayr subclan of the Habr Gedir-Hawiye, Hawiye subclans in south Mogadishu forged an alliance called the Joint Islamic Council. Again, this promising Islamist effort was thwarted, this time by an internationally sponsored agreement brokered in Arta, Djibouti, that created the Transitional National Government (TNG) of Abdiqasim Salad Hassan.[36] The TNG cleverly incorporated these courts into TNG structures, a move no doubt enabled by the fact that Abdiqasim Hassan himself hailed from the Ayr clan. The governing council of the courts was then disbanded, effectively neutralizing it as a political force, although the courts did continue to exist in Mogadishu as a more marginal actor (Barnes & Hassan, 2007, p. 153; Hansen, 2013, p. 33). The surviving courts would be the nucleus of the ICU in 2004.

The disappointing experience of the Al-Ittihad remnants, Al-Qaeda's East African network, and Mogadishu's Islamic courts no doubt illustrated to them the importance of collaboration between the diverse array of Islamists in the Somali theatre. While they had substantive ideological disagreements and very different social bases, the rough-and-tumble environment of politics in south-central Somalia required that they cooperate on an institutionalized basis, lest they fall victim to the mistakes of the past. The ICU, which came into being in late 2004 after the consolidation of the clan courts in north and south Mogadishu under its first and only chairman, Sheikh Sharif Ahmed, was a recognition of this reality.[37] At its core, the constituent units of the ICU were united under a minimalist political program of creating an Islamic state, although they had fundamental disagreements about exactly what this meant.

It is important to note that this vexing record of political failure was not the only factor that drove Al-Ittihad, Al-Qaeda, and the Mogadishu courts into the warm embrace that was the ICU. Indeed, this history of political failure cannot explain why 2004 was the moment in which these groups came together to forge a new Islamist front.

---

[36] Abdiqasim was a former senior official in Barre's government, serving as Minister of Finance.

[37] Mukhtar Robow, an Al-Ittihad member who would go on to become a senior leader of the ICU and later Al-Shabaab, supports this view: "Some officials of the Islamic movements who were in the country at the time held a meeting having felt their groups were not that active as far as jihad was concerned. There were various Islamic movements that in the past that tried to carry out jihad but they were faced with many obstacles and dropped their operations all together. The men who were previously in these groups held a meeting and decided to form a movement and take part in jihad and spread the religion. They decided to spread the religion alongside jihad" (Hansen, 2013, p. 26).

The years 2002–06 were an important period in Mogadishu, as new threats emerged that imperiled the survival of Somalia's militant political Islamists. The 9/11 attacks turned Somalia into an important, if secondary battleground in the War on Terror. Al-Qaeda's East African network, now based in Mogadishu, became the target of concerted counterterrorism efforts orchestrated by the United States and its Western partners. Local warlords and their clan militias, who saw Islamists as real political rivals, were critical allies in this effort.[38] Soon, Al-Ittihad remnants found themselves to be a target as well, in large part because of the belief in Western counterterrorism circles that they were Al-Qaeda collaborators.[39] In fact, a mere two weeks after 9/11, Al-Ittihad finances were the target of sanctions by the US government. Later on, Al-Barakaat – the Somali money transfer company believed to help finance Al-Ittihad – would have its operations curtailed by US regulators. Al-Ittihad leaders Hassan Dahir Aweys and Hassan Turki were the target of executive orders signed by President George Bush as well as UN sanctions, actions that placed them at a heightened risk of apprehension and prosecution in Western courts.

The Western counterterrorism campaign in Somalia culminated in what was called the "Shadow War" of Mogadishu, in which Western-backed warlords were pitted against Al-Qaeda and Al-Ittihad remnants – particularly those who had served in Afghanistan – in a war for supremacy that descended into a string of assassinations and kidnappings (Hansen, 2013, p. 26).[40] ICU sources indicate that the covert war was a major

---

[38] Many of the warlords and associated criminal networks received money for their collaboration. While the warlords were likely to be suspicious of any political organization that they could not control, the very idea of Islamism was anathema because in the Somali context it posed a direct challenge to the clan politics that sustained the warlords – if not in practice at least in theory. As noted before, Islamists were generally opposed to clan as a political instrument. For the warlords, this was a problem, since they derived their power from the political mobilization of clan, and were empowered by clan elders during the civil war to defend the clan's economic and political interests. These "warlords" (and perhaps the term "warlord" is a misnomer) were selected because they had the expertise or the means to militarily defend their clan. Indeed, many warlords were former officials within Barre's administration or wealthy businessmen. See author's interview with Somali State Minister who hails from Lower Shabelle, Mogadishu, January 2014.

[39] There were also financial incentives that drove warlord collaboration with the Western counterterrorism program. In many cases, unscrupulous militia leaders often captured innocent individuals, accused them of being jihadists, and then offered them up to Western counterterrorism agencies for a fee.

[40] See the kidnapping of alleged Al-Qaeda member Salim Hemed-Issa 'Tanzania' (Hansen, 2013, p. 27), and the Somali jihadi, Mohammed Abdi "Isse Yusuf." The former was captured by militiamen loyal to Mogadishu warlord Mohammed Deere and then turned over to American officials.

impetus for Al-Qaeda and the Afghan veterans from Al-Ittihad to consolidate their efforts into a single organization (Hansen, 2013, p. 26).[41]

Meanwhile, the relationship between Al-Ittihad and Al Qaeda fighters, on the one hand, and the Hawiye courts on the other, was absolutely essential to the former, since Al-Qaeda operatives and many Al-Ittihad fighters were "guests" in Mogadishu: Al Qaeda operatives were often non-Somalis, hailing mostly from other parts of East Africa, while many of Al-Ittihad fighters hailed from clans that had no real influence in Mogadishu.[42] This reality meant that joining the ICU provided these militants with the clan protection of Mogadishu's dominant clan, the Hawiye. Jihad in Mogadishu without clan protection from one of the major Hawiye clans would have been suicide for the Al-Qaeda and Al-Ittihad network, leaving the Islamist militants exposed to other clan militia, criminal networks, and counterterrorism collaborators.[43]

For its part, the immediate interests of the Hawiye Courts in forging the founding coalition of the ICU were fairly clear-cut. Since the Courts had a historically tense relationship with the Mogadishu warlords, they were naturally threatened by the manner in which the warlords had been empowered by Western intelligence agencies. The Court's vulnerability, to reiterate a point made earlier, was greatly accentuated by the reality that they often depended on clan militias and the warlords to enforce their legal decisions. In effect, the warlords functioned as the Court's military muscle while at the same time holding a vested interest in the Court's demise. Seen from this view, the experienced jihadists of Al-Ittihad and Al-Qaeda provided the Courts a motivated, well-trained network of militants who could operate as an alternative to the warlords. Embracing these militants was thus a strategy of autonomy, without which the Courts would be unable to survive and expand their writ.

---

[41] For a compelling account of the "dirty war" in Mogadishu during these years, see the International Crisis Group's (2005) report, titled "Counter-Terrorism in Somalia: Losing Hearts and Minds?" Also see Jeremy, Scahill, "Blowback in Somalia," *The Nation*, September 7, 2011; and Jeremy Scahill, *Dirty Wars: The World Is a Battlefield* (New York: Nation Books, 2013), Chapters 10, 19, 22, 31.

[42] Unlike the clan militias, Al-Ittihad was a cosmopolitan group with members that came from a variety of clans. Many of the Al-Ittihad remnants in Mogadishu hailed from the Isaaq clans of Somaliland, including two men who would play crucial roles in the ICU and later Al-Shabaab: Ahmed Abdi Godane and Ibrahim al-Afghani. Such individuals were thus in desperate need of clan protection. The influence of Somalilanders in Al-Ittihad may have something to do with the fact that former Al-Ittihad chairman Sheikh Warsame was Isaaq.

[43] It is important to understand that lines between the Hawiye courts and the ICU remnants were not always clear. Hassan Dahir Aweys and Aden Hashi Ayro, the latter who had been a more junior member of Al-Ittihad, were both Ayr-Habr Gedir and would become key members of the Ifka Halane court. Their presence was critical in forging the new ICU alliance and protecting Al-Ittihad and Al-Qaeda operatives.

The diverse coalition of Islamists that was at the heart of the ICU was joined by a final, but no less critical grouping – Mogadishu's business class. The value of the business community to the ICU coalition doesn't deserve much explanation: businessmen had the capacity to offer significant finance to fund ICU operations, and as the ICU developed, the business community would readily provide much-needed cash.[44]

Yet what incentive did the business community have to join the militant Islamist camp? To be sure, this community did have some natural affinities for the ICU's Islamist experiment, as levels of religiosity had increased within the business community over the preceding decade. In the late 1990s, as the violence in Mogadishu began to temporarily subside, many Somali businessmen returned to the city from the Gulf, and brought with them a certain affinity for Islamist rule, and in some cases, even Salafism. Moreover, as the civil war wore on, the collapse of law and order caused many Somali consumers to patronize religiously pious (and presumably more trustworthy) businessmen. This trend greatly increased the ranks of the religiously inclined within Mogadishu's business community.[45]

However, there were other immediate security concerns that drove Mogadishu's business community to join the ICU. First, like many of the other groups that would be part of the ICU's founding coalition, the business community was on a serious collision course with the warlords. The major issue was that by the late 1990s, the power of the warlords was beginning to wane, as clan militias and their diaspora support base fragmented and multiplied along subclan lines.[46] A consequence of such developments was that individual warlords were no longer able to guarantee economic activity over any significant territorial expanse, a fact that increased the costs of commercial transactions and made the warlords less useful to Mogadishu's business community. In response, Mogadishu's commercial class began to create their own militias, the largest being the 2,000-man force of Abgaal Hawiye businessman Abukar Omar Adane. This pushed Mogadishu's business community into increasing conflict with the warlords, who were keen to maintain their monopoly on violence in the city.[47] The tension would eventually

---

[44] As will soon be explained, many businessmen also had their own militia. This is also what made them attractive partners to the other elements of the ICU coalition.
[45] Interviews, electoral official and FGS diplomat, Mogadishu, Somalia, January 2014; interviews with FGS minister and former Central Bank official, Mogadishu, Somalia, January 2014.
[46] Interviews, electoral official and FGS diplomat, Mogadishu, Somalia, January 2014.
[47] It is also the case, as Aisha Ahmad (2015) demonstrates with some impressive survey data, that Mogadishu's business community preferred the Islamic courts to the

boil over in 2006, and culminate in an armed dispute between Adane and warlord Bashir Rage over control of Mogadishu's El Maan port. Since Adane was already within the ICU structure by this time, the various constituent units of the ICU would come to his defense, dealing the first blow to the warlords in a conflict that would eventually see the warlords expelled from Mogadishu. It was exactly this sort of confrontation that the business community had anticipated when they joined the ICU. In a real sense, the El Maan incident illustrates exactly why security threats and survival concerns were of paramount concern to Mogadishu's enterprising business community in 2005–06.

The issue of clan interests was the final piece that bound the business community to the ICU's founding coalition. This is an important, if sometimes underappreciated point. Given Hawiye political dominance of Mogadishu, it is no surprise that Hawiye businessmen dominated the economic affairs of the capital. Their continued success as political and military actors thus depended on Hawiye hegemony in Mogadishu. Yet by 2003, Hawiye influence in the capital was perceived – rightly or wrongly – as an increasingly tenuous proposition, in large part because of changes in the nature of the externally backed government that was emerging, dissolving, and reconstituting itself abroad. This was a serious concern for Hawiye businessmen.

By 2002, a coalition of warlords led by Hussein Farah Aideed had emerged to challenge Abdiqasim Hassan's TNG.[48] This group, which was called the Somalia Reconciliation and Restoration Council (SRRC), had the strong backing of the Ethiopians, who were suspicious of what they believed were the Islamist leanings of the TNG government. In an effort to bring these sides together and reduce escalating violence, yet another internationally sponsored conference was convened in El Doret, Kenya. This led to the creation of the Transitional Federal Government (TFG) in Kenya led by Puntland's president, Abdullahi Yusuf. The TFG was established in April 2004, and it is telling that its formal establishment predates the creation of the ICU by just a few months.

For Hawiye businessmen in Mogadishu, this new government was a problem for two reasons. First, the replacement of Abdiqasim Hassan, a Hawiye, with Abdullahi Yusuf, a Majarteen-Darood, created real fears that this new government would dispossess the Hawiye if and when it

---

warlords because Islamists were more capable of guaranteeing economic activity across clan lines, thus reducing transaction costs for businessmen. This is in large part because the Islamic courts were evolving into an entity that involved multiple Hawiye clans.

[48] The son of former USC leader and Habir Gedr warlord Mohammed Farah Aideed. After his father's death in 1996, Hussein would take over the organization his father led just prior to his death, the Somali National Alliance.

came to Mogadishu.[49] Historic rivalries between the Hawiye and Darood in Mogadishu played into this fear. When Hawiye militias of the USC ousted Barre in 1991, Mogadishu's Darood were targeted as collaborators (Kapteijns, 2012).[50] This led to massive population transfers and a redistribution of wealth that enabled the emergence of the Hawiye as the ascendant clan in the Somali capital. For the Hawiye, then, there was real concern that Abdullahi Yusuf's TFG would be a vehicle of Darood revenge.[51]

The second reason the TFG was of concern to Hawiye businessmen was its backing by the Ethiopian government, the most influential external player in Somalia. Addis Ababa's support meant that, unlike previous internationally backed governments created after Barre's ouster, the TFG stood a reasonable prospect of escaping purgatory in Kenya, since it would have the military support to establish itself in Somalia. This reality came to pass in June of 2005, when the TFG returned to Somalia and established itself in the Somali town of Baidoa under the protection of Ethiopian forces. In fact, the increasingly formidable TFG–Ethiopia alliance was a real threat to the other constituent units of the ICU as well, since Ethiopia was doggedly opposed to Islamism in Somalia and would use the TFG to battle these elements. As is widely known, the Ethiopian link to the TFG was largely due to the fact that Puntland's Abdullahi Yusuf, who was avowedly anti-Islamist, had been a longtime Ethiopian ally dating back to his time as chairman of the SSDF.

It should be noted that the TFG was also designed to presage the creation of a more permanent "federal" administration, which the Ethiopians preferred to a more centralized Somali state on ideological and strategic grounds.[52] It is on this point that the TFG–Ethiopia link created further concern for Hawiye elites, chief among them its

---

[49] It should be noted that the TFG had an Abgaal-Hawiye as its prime minister – Ali Mohammed Gedi.

[50] As has already been stated, Barre was an Marehan Darood whose regime was perceived by detractors as an alliance among three major Darood clans – the Marehan, Ogaden, and Dhulbahante.

[51] The scale of Darood displacement from Mogadishu was severe, and can be illustrated by the growth of cities like Garowe (a Majarteen Darood city), which went from a small village of fewer than 10,000 in the early 1990s to more than 60,000 today. Interviews attribute this growth to displaced Majarteen Darood who fled Mogadishu in the years following the collapse of the central government. Many Darood have outstanding grievances related to very specific claims of land and property that were taken from them in the early 1990s (as do members of many other Somali clans). See author's interviews, January 2014, Garowe, Puntland, Somalia.

[52] Ethiopia is an ethnic federal state, and thus supports the export of its political model to other countries in the region. Eritrea is a case in point, where the Ethiopian government has provided military support to ethnic minority insurgent groups that seek to turn Eritrea into a federal state. On the strategic side, many believe Ethiopia sought to use

businessmen. While the Somali have historically been suspicious of Ethiopian interference in their affairs, the Hawiye were particularly hostile toward Ethiopia's "federal strategy," and for very specific reasons. Many critics of federalism believed it would render Somalia a permanently weak and fragmented state, and this was of great concern to the Hawiye, who generally preferred a more centralized government. This was because the Hawiye dominated the Somali capital and were a large clan family whose clans were distributed across many parts of central and southern Somalia. As a consequence, many Hawiye elites in Mogadishu were at the intellectual and political forefront of opposition to "Ethiopian-backed" federalism, a position that was framed in terms of a Somali nationalism and a large dose of anti-Ethiopian animus.

In the final analysis, the TFG–Ethiopian threat was central to propelling many of Mogadishu's Hawiye elite – including its business community – into the arms of the Islamist militants in the ICU. The need to guarantee this community's survival as an economic, political, and military actor in the context of Somalia's long civil war was the critical issue. Summarizing the stark choice that Ethiopian intervention posed for Hawiye nationalists (and Somali nationalists more generally), a Mogadishu resident argued the following:

From Ethiopia's perspective it will be a war between Ethiopia and the Islamists [Ikhwaan]. But for Somalis, it is not so simple. I have to fight side by side with anyone that is fighting Ethiopia... People do not want to join the Islamists, but if it comes to that, how can you refuse a coalition with them? It won't matter who chews qaat and who doesn't when the enemy is just over the horizon.[53]

In sum, the ICU was a security-based coalition designed to guarantee the survival of its constituent units in the context of south-central Somalia's complex civil war. The Hawiye business community, Al-Ittihad remnants, Al-Qaeda militants, and Hawiye courts each had their own

---

federalism to weaken and fragment a reconstituted Somali state. Author's interviews, Mogadishu, January 2014.

[53] "Somalia's Islamists," *International Crisis Group Report*, December 12, 2005, p. 21, which can be found at https://d2071andvip0wj.cloudfront.net/somalia-s-islamists.pdf (Accessed August 5, 2016). Quote can also be found in "Counter-Terrorism in Somalia: Losing Hearts and Minds?" *International Crisis Group Report*, July 11, 2005, which can be found at https://d2071andvip0wj.cloudfront.net/95-counter-terrorism-in-somalia-losing-hearts-and-minds.pdf (Accessed August 5, 2016). Qaat is a popular stimulant among the Somali. It is grown and imported from Kenya and Ethiopia. Islamists generally do not look favorably on the drug, and in November 2006 the ICU instituted a consumption and transportation ban over significant public protest and internal dissent. Some argue that the ICU ban was designed as retaliation for a Kenyan decision to cease all flights to and from Mogadishu. See "Qat Ban in Somalia Exposes Cracks in ICU Leadership," December 27, 2006, which can be found at www.jamestown.org/single/?tx_ttnews%5Btt_news%5D=982&no_cache=1#.VqZjZktN1uY (Accessed January 4, 2016).

distinct and powerful security-related incentives to forge a common front. This was an alliance of convenience built in the crucible of early rebellion. As Sheikh Ahmed Mohammed Islam "Madobe," a senior ICU official who would later defect from the Islamist cause, later admitted: "Those of us within the ICU were people with different views; moderates, midlevel and extremists... there was no commonly shared political agenda."[54] This heterogeneity would have serious implications down the road.

The Cohesive Stalemate: Mogadishu and the Era of Awkward Cohabitation

From the ICU's creation in late 2004 until the fateful dispute between Adane and Bashir Rage in January 2006, the ICU was not an aggressive military power. It remained in Mogadishu, alongside the Hawiye warlords, dispensing justice throughout the city. Yet behind the scenes, elements of the ICU engaged the warlords in a covert war of assassination and kidnapping, as discussed in the previous section. The TFG, though officially recognized as the government of Somalia, had no real presence in the country outside of Baidoa. Mogadishu's warlords, however, were formally aligned with the TFG, and functioned as the face of the TFG in the city. As the ICU's influence and power grew, it became increasingly obvious that the ICU and the warlords were on a collision course.

In this era of awkward cohabitation, the ICU went through a slow but imperfect process of internal consolidation. The eleven courts of north and south Mogadishu were incrementally forged into a more unified structure. By mid-2006, it would be led by a fifteen-member executive council and ninety-one-member legislative Shura. Sheikh Sharif Ahmed, from the powerful Sisi Court, remained the ICU chairman throughout this process, while Hassan Dahir Aweys would head the Shura Council.[55] In July 2005, Aden Hashi Ayro emerged as the ICU's de facto military commander, and would play a vital role in the establishment of a training facility for ICU fighters, as well as the coordination and integration of the ICU's various militia.[56]

---

[54] This is a modified quote taken from Jeremy Scahill, "Blowback in Somalia," *The Nation*, September 27, 2011.
[55] According to Markus Hoehne, "Counter-Terrorism in Somalia: How External Interference Helped Produce Militant Islam," p. 28, the appointments of Sharif and Aweys to the ICU's two most critical posts was powerful recognition of the ICU's coalitional dynamic and an explicit effort to balance between the two major Hawiye clans that had effectively subdivided Mogadishu: Sharif (Abgaal) and Aweys (Habr Gedr).
[56] Ayro was a member of the Ifka Halane court and a protégé of Aweys. He had served as a junior member of the Al-Ittihad. The training facility, controversially built on the site of

Politically, the ICU sought to make its presence felt among Mogadishu's population, quickly establishing a reputation for administrative efficiency in the neighborhoods it ran. But it also courted controversy. In December 2004, it issued a *fatwa* that designated New Year's celebrations punishable by death. Another edict declared that terrorism suspects found on Somali soil – including those whose alleged crimes were committed overseas – should be tried in Somali courts. In November 2005, it shut down a number of Mogadishu cinemas under the premise that they were spreading corruption and immorality (Shay, 2014).

For the purposes of the argument in this book, it is important to note that the geography of ICU operations remained static in this period. From its creation in late 2004 to early 2006, the ICU made no attempt to extend its political administration outside of Banaadir district, as it was seemingly content to consolidate its influence within the city of Mogadishu. As the argument of this book predicts, there was no evidence of factional infighting or fragmentation within the ICU at this time. The fault lines that did exist within the organization would become toxic only when the battlefield circumstances, and the basis for cooperation, began to shift. It is to this issue that we now turn.

To the Brink of Victory: The Second Battle of Mogadishu, the Advance on Baidoa, and the Bur Hakaba Defections

Although a showdown between the ICU and Mogadishu's warlords was inevitable, it was two specific incidents that were to drive them into direct conflict. The first was the rupture between Abukar Omar Adane and Bashir Rage. The two had initially been business partners, dividing lucrative profits from El Maan and El Adde harbors, as well as Mogadishu's makeshift Eisly airport. A clash over ownership of several vehicles in mid-January triggered a fight for control over these key installations. Adane, by now a key financier of the ICU, called on the ICU to defend his interests, and it obliged. For the ICU, it was not common ideological concerns that were at stake in the defense of Adane, but rather the underlying security logic that had made the business community an attractive partner of the ICU in the first place – i.e., the business community possessed the much-needed finance for ICU operations. Stig Hansen (2013, p. 34), author of the most comprehensive book on

---

an Italian cemetery, was called *Muasker Mahkamad* (Troops of the Islamic Courts), and was a project of both Ayro and Khalif Adale. The facility also included a madrassah. The training camp is regarded as instrumental in the early emergence of the shadowy network of jihadists that would morph into Al-Shabaab (Marchal, 2011, p. 15).

Somalia's Islamists, drives this point home well, noting that "from February onward the Sharia Courts Union supported Adane; strategically it could not afford to see him lose, it would most likely have ended his financial support for the Union."

The other incident that was to drive the ICU and the warlords into direct conflict largely followed from the Adane–Bashir Rage dispute. In February, sensing that Adane and the ICU might gain the upper hand, the warlords sought to formalize the loose alliance that had been forged as a bulwark of Western counterterrorism concerns. The organization that emerged was suggestively titled the Alliance for the Restoration of Peace and Counter-Terrorism (ARPCT), and was deliberately designed to garner resources from the United States and its allies that the warlords could parlay into a more aggressive strategy against the courts.[57] The CIA, which had cultivated the warlords during Mogadishu's "Shadow War," provided encouragement to the alliance through greater levels of covert assistance, as it became increasingly concerned that the ICU was providing sanctuary to Al-Qaeda elements.[58]

The Second Battle of Mogadishu, as the fight between the ICU and the ARPCT came to be known, ended decisively in favor of the ICU. By June 2006, the warlords had been cleared out of the city, and chased along the main artery road that flowed north out of Mogadishu. It was the first time since the end of Barre's ouster that the city had been unified under a single administration. Days later, the courts extended their control over ninety kilometers northward, capturing the strategic towns of Balad and Jowhar, and effectively ending the ARPCT's resistance as an organized force.[59]

The ICU's Mogadishu victory came as a shock to most outside observers, although a close analysis of conditions on the ground suggested that the new Islamist organization would prevail. Early in the confrontation between the two sides, Adane and the ICU successfully seized the contested ports and Mogadishu's airport, establishing control over much-needed sources of revenue that they could convert into

---

[57] The ARPCT included some of Mogadishu's most powerful Hawiye warlords: Bashir Rage, Mohammed Dheere, Mohammed Qanyare, Abdi Nur Siyad, and Abdi Hassan Awale Qeybdid, Omar Mahmoud Finnish, Botan Ise Alin, and Musa Sudi Yalahow. For more background on these figures, see "In CIC's Wake, Warlords Seek to Reassert Their Influence in Somalia," Wikileaks, which can be found at https://wikileaks.org/plusd/cables/07NAIROBI5408_a.html (Accessed January 8, 2015).

[58] See "Efforts by C.I.A. Fail in Somalia, Officials Charge," *New York Times*, June 8, 2006, which can be found at www.nytimes.com/2006/06/08/world/africa/08intel.html?pagewanted=2&_r=2 (Accessed January 27, 2016).

[59] The warlords were dispersed. Some fled into areas of Somalia not occupied by the ICU, while others went to Ethiopia. A number would return when Ethiopia ousted the ICU in December 2006.

military power. Of course, these early military successes raise more questions than they answer: namely, why was the ICU able to gain the strategic initiative so early? The answer hinges on a point made earlier in this chapter regarding the growing weakness of the warlords. The fragmentation of the clan militias the warlords commanded, as well as their diaspora support bases, and growing rifts with the business community, placed the warlords under serious financial duress. As a result, they became increasingly unable to pay their militia, which led to the predictable outcome of clan militia gunmen refusing to fight or defecting to the ICU in the heat of battle.[60]

These problems were compounded by the reality that the ARPCT's conflict with the ICU placed it at loggerheads with Abdullahi Yusuf and the TFG. Although the TFG remained an insignificant player in Mogadishu, its political support was important to the warlord's position in the city. Since the TFG was the closest thing Somalia had to an internationally recognized central government, it could provide a veneer of legitimacy to the warlord's anti-ICU campaign. Yet the TFG balked at the ARCPT's militaristic approach to the ICU, insisting that it preferred negotiations to the use of force. The reality of the government's position was probably more complicated, as it took issue with the support that Western intelligence agencies were providing the warlords, fearing that it threatened the TFG's claim to be the sovereign representative of the Somali people.[61] In any case, the TFG greatly undermined the ARCPT in June 2006 – conveniently, just as it appeared that the warlords had lost the upper hand in Mogadishu – when it unceremoniously fired the four ARCPT members who also held ministerial appointments within the TFG.

With Mogadishu and its northern corridor now under its control, the ICU turned to the remainder of the country. By August, the expansionist project was in full swing, as the ICU moved northwest and began to occupy portions of Hiran, Galgudug, and Mudug. Eventually, the key city of Galkayo was threatened by ICU forces, which at 465 miles from Mogadishu now demonstrated the enormous reach of the ICU. This push brought the ICU into conflict with the local and regional entities in these territories, including Puntland and powerful Hawiye pirate enclaves in Harardhere and Hobyo. The ICU, as would be its modus operandi (and the modus operandi of Al-Shabaab as well), exploited clan

---

[60] The fact that the ICU–warlord dispute pitted Hawiye clans against one another made this sort of side switching more readily possible.

[61] See "Efforts by C.I.A. Fail in Somalia, Officials Charge," *New York Times*, June 8, 2006, which can be found at www.nytimes.com/2006/06/08/world/africa/08intel.html?pagewanted=2&_r=2 (Accessed January 27, 2016).

divisions well, causing some clans – and the militias they supported – to bandwagon with the ICU in an effort to gain advantage in their prevailing local rivalries. Eventually, the ICU's northern march was slowed, when the Sacad subclan of the Hawiye decided to establish a regional government that could both prevent the ICU from swallowing them whole and block an increasingly jittery Puntland regional administration from encroaching on their territory. This region, which came to be known as Galmudug, created a thin buffer between ICU forces and the powerful militia of Puntland.[62] Yet by November 2006, through a combination of political manipulation and military force, it appeared the ICU might puncture this stalemate (Shay, 2014).[63] Had it not been for events that unfolded in other parts of Somalia, the ICU may well have done so.[64]

So what were these developments? Southwest of Mogadishu, the dominoes began to fall into place for a rapid ICU advance. When Ayr-Hawiye warlord Yusuf Mohammed Siad "Inda'adde" joined the ICU it created a corridor through Lower Shabelle that allowed Islamist forces to sweep down the coast and conquer the strategic port of Kismayo and much of the Middle and Lower Juba regions.[65] These advances now placed the ICU in direct confrontation with the TFG and its Ethiopian backers in Baidoa. The TFG had initially been keen to establish a modus vivendi with the ICU when it emerged as the dominant authority in Mogadishu. On June 22, 2006, it met with the ICU negotiators in Khartoum under the auspices of the Arab League, and recognized the ICU as a political reality in Somalia that had to be acknowledged. The ICU, in turn, confirmed the TFG as the legitimate government of Somalia. But ICU advances in central Somalia, and now the south, revealed that the ICU was intent, in the words of Seifulaziz Milas, "to

---

[62] Although some elements of the Sacad supported the ICU, the clan's resistance was linked to the ICU's tense relationship with Abdi Hassan Awale Qeybdid, one of the ARCPT warlords who had fled Mogadishu to the protection of his Sacad clansmen. See "Special Report: What Is Galgmudug?" August 4, 2012, which can be found at www.somaliareport.com/index.php/post/3120 (Accessed January 27, 2016). Also see Seifulaziz Milas, "Failed Sheikhs and Flawed Strategies: Lessons of the Jihadist Debacle in Somalia," *SSRC: Crisis in the Horn of Africa*, February 20, 2007, which can be found at http://hornofafrica.ssrc.org/Milas/index1.html (Accessed November 4, 2015).

[63] It appears that the emergence of local Islamic courts in Galmudug and Puntland, presumably sympathetic to the ICU, had the potential to put the regional administration on the defensive yet again. The ICU also captured Hobyo. See Moshe Terdman, "Somalia at War – Between Radical Islam and Tribal Politics," 2008, p. 52, which can be found at www.tau.ac.il/humanities/abraham/publications/somalia.pdf (Accessed January 5, 2016).

[64] See "Puntland, Somalia Clash South of Galkayo; Iran's Hand," *The Long War Journal*, November 12, 2006, which can be found at www.longwarjournal.org/archives/2006/11/puntland_somalia_cla.php (Accessed January 5, 2016).

[65] In return, Inda'adde was made the defense chief of the ICU.

talk peace while conquering new territory."[66] The ICU was seeking to simply buy time, establishing a fait accompli that would lead its total dominance across Somalia.

The seizure of Kismayo was particularly alarming to the TFG because it came at the expense of the Juba Valley Alliance (JVA), which was spearheaded by Colonel Barre Hirale and his Marehan–Darood militia. The JVA was a key ally of the TFG, so much so that Hirale was the TFG's sitting defense minister. The swiftness of the ICU approach had taken the JVA by surprise, and the ill-timed defection of key non-Marehan clan militias to the ICU side would force Hirale to vacate the city with little resistance. A month later, in October 2006, Hirale attempted to retake Kismayo but was defeated, fleeing to join the corpus of TFG forces in Baidoa.[67] The ICU now pressed its advantage, approaching Baidoa from the south, and making real gains in Gedo and Bakool designed to encircle the TFG and put pressure on its northern supply lines.

Facing an increasingly bleak military situation, and beset by its own internal problems, the TFG leaned on external support to ward off the ICU threat. Given his close relations with the Ethiopians, TFG president Abdullahi Yusuf encouraged Addis to scale up its presence in Baidoa, which the Ethiopians did. With key border towns like Beledweyne having fallen into ICU hands, Ethiopia was increasingly coming to the view that it would need to deal militarily with the ICU. Indeed, in a leaked November 2006 conversation with US officials, Ethiopian prime minister Meles Zenawi insisted that "Ethiopia would defend Baidoa to the end."[68] An emerging link between the ICU and external backers in the Gulf, and more seriously, Ethiopian rivals like Eritrea (and to a lesser extent Egypt), seemed to fuel an Ethiopian narrative of threat.[69] The

[66] Also see Seifulaziz Milas, "Failed Sheikhs and Flawed Strategies: Lessons of the Jihadist Debacle in Somalia," *SSRC: Crisis in the Horn of Africa*, February 20, 2007, which can be found at http://hornofafrica.ssrc.org/Milas/index1.html (Accessed November 4, 2015).
[67] Hansen (2013, pp. 39–40) discusses the ICU's capture of Kismayo at length. Again, the exploitation of clan politics was key. The JVA was actually an alliance between Hirale's Marehan militias and the Ayr subclan of the Habr Gedr-Hawiye. Since Aweys and Inda'adde hailed from this clan, and could make credible promises about protecting their interests in Kismayo, the Ayr units of the JVA defected. Although Hansen doesn't make the link, the fact that the initial thrust of the ICU offensive was led by Sheikh Hassan Turki and his Ras Kamboni militia was also important, as Turki was from the Ogaden clan – a key constituency in Kismayo that was marginalized within the JVA's local administration and would support the new ICU administration.
[68] "An American/Ethiopian Partnership so Critical and so Criticized," Wikileaks, November 15, 2006, which can be found at https://wikileaks.org/plusd/cables/06ADDISABABA3048_a.html (Accessed June 15, 2015). Memo nicely describes the strategic concerns informing Ethiopian policy toward the ICU's rise.
[69] There was also the reality that the ICU had links with Ethiopian rebel groups like the OLF and ONLF.

prominent presence of Aweys within the ICU leadership – Ethiopia's old Al-Ittihad nemesis –added to Ethiopian insecurity about the gains of militant Islamists in neighboring Somalia.

The TFG also encouraged the efforts of the Horn of Africa's regional organization, IGAD, in an effort to cope with the ICU's surge. In September 2006, IGAD sought to protect the TFG by creating an intervention force called IGASOM. Yet the mission ran into a serious obstacle because the only member states capable of contributing the required forces were Somalia's Ethiopian and Kenyan neighbors – a reality that the international community found unpalatable, since it was a widely held view at the time that the participation of frontline states in Somalia would worsen the security situation. By February 2007 the mission would be handed over the African Union, which was able to mobilize troops from Uganda and Burundi and eventually deploy into Mogadishu that same year.

In the meantime, the specter of foreign intervention seemed to radicalize the ICU, instead of serving as deterrent for further territorial expansion. Hardliners became increasingly influential within ICU decision-making processes. While the ICU insisted it was not interested in war with the TFG, it declared jihad to liberate Somalia from what it framed as a creeping foreign occupation, and began to more consistently attack TFG and Ethiopian positions. In November 2006, Aweys even suggested that the ICU would rehabilitate the "Greater Somalia" project.[70] If Ethiopia had any red lines, an increasingly confident ICU – which now dominated the map of south-central Somalia – seemed intent on crossing every one of them.

It is at this point, as the ICU surged to the apex of its power in Somalia, that it experienced fragmentation. On December 1, 2006, one of the ICU's local clan-based militia hailing from Bur Hakaba – a small town that was on the ICU's southern approach to Baidoa – decided to defect to the TFG. Although the ICU would dispute the numbers, evidence suggests that 350 ICU militia joined the TFG camp in Baidoa during this episode.[71] The factional infighting appears to have been triggered by differences of ideology, which played out in a dispute over the consumption of the widely used stimulant called qaat. Many ICU-affiliated clan militias were motivated by their own parochial local interests, and sought

---

[70] Bill Rogio, "Ethiopian Convoy Ambushed in Aweys' 'Greater Somalia,'" *Long War Journal*, November 20, 2006, which can be found at www.longwarjournal.org/archives/2006/11/ethiopian_convoy_amb.php (Accessed June 5, 2015).
[71] It seems the militia were led by three officers: Abdi Madey Ibrahim, Abdi Gaas Hussein, and Barow Mohamed Hassan.

to preserve the consumption of qaat and other social practices inconsistent with the puritanical doctrines of the ICU's Salafi ideologues. This put it at loggerheads with the ICU leadership, which had difficulty tolerating what it perceived as a moral corruption within its own ranks. As the ICU surged, and the incentives to cooperate shifted, these tensions no doubt got worse. Eventually, the ICU sought to enforce its prohibition of qaat on the concerned units, which naturally led to an attempt to seize the Bur Hakaba militia's battlewagons.[72] On the precipice of being disarmed, and fearing for their safety, this militia fled to a place called Karkor village, roughly twenty kilometers from Baidoa. From here, they were quickly picked up by TFG trucks and delivered to the safe confines of Baidoa, in what could only be termed a rescue mission.[73]

The Bur Hakaba episode again underscores the salience of my overarching argument about battlefield gains and losses. Rapid territorial gains, best reflected in the quick advance on the last bastion of TFG strength in Baidoa between February and December 2006, drove preference divergence within the ICU camp, creating a context in which ICU ideologues and the ICU's clan militias came into increasingly open conflict. Fragmentation was the result. There is support for a key corollary as well: the attempt to disarm the Bur Hakaba militia exposed them to ICU punishment, such that fragmentation and defection to the TFG was the only credible strategy for survival.

Ethiopian Intervention and the ICU's Implosion: Clan Revolts and the Fragmentation of the Vanguard

The fragmentation of the Bur Hakaba militia did not bode well for the unity of ICU forces going forward. In a few short weeks, a much different military context would trigger a more serious internal rupture that the organization could not recover from. On December 12, 2006, the ICU gave the Ethiopians a one-week ultimatum to leave Somali territory. Predictably, the government in Addis Ababa was in no mood to heed this warning. Last-minute efforts by the Italians and EU to halt the inevitable showdown over Baidoa yielded little. On December 20, 2006, escalating

---

[72] "Battlewagon" is another term for "technical," which are pick-up trucks loaded with heavy machine guns. This technology was a staple of the Somali civil war.

[73] The claim that the debate about qaat – which was really a proxy for the issue of religious purity – was central to the Bur Hakaba episode, was made by the ICU itself. See Mohamed Abdi Farow, "350 Militia Went to the TFG – ICU Official Confirmed," December 1, 2006, which can be found at www.somaliaonline.com/community/topic/bur-hakaba-again-in-the-news-350-militia-went-to-tfg-icu-official-confirmed/ (Accessed June 5, 2015).

hostilities around the town precipitated a full-fledged Ethiopian counteroffensive. Classified cables from the US mission in Addis Ababa suggest that the offensive involved careful planning and the prepositioning of significant military assets, including 10,000 Ethiopian troops, 36 artillery pieces, and 40 to 50 T-54/55 tanks, which were supported by helicopters and Ethiopian fighter jets. Joining Ethiopian forces were 8,000–10,000 TFG militia and 3,000–4,000 troops from the Puntland Defense Forces. Covert support from the United States, which would use the Ethiopian offensive as an opportunity to strike what it viewed as terrorist targets, would also be brought to bear. Arrayed against Ethiopia were about 5,000 ICU troops and hundreds of technicals.[74]

The Ethiopian-led counteroffensive had three main prongs. The first was a southwest advance out of Baidoa toward Mogadishu. The second was inaugurated by the Ethiopian seizure of the border town of Beledweyene, and saw Ethiopia and its allies move down the Shabelle River Valley, through Jowhar, and approach Mogadishu from the north. Once Mogadishu fell without a fight on December 29, attacking forces moved further down the Shabelle River Valley, until they met and defeated ICU forces at Jilib. A third prong moved south down the Juba River and approached Jilib from the north. When Jilib fell, Ethiopia and its allies converged on Kismayo, which was also captured with little resistance. What remained of organized ICU resistance retreated to Ras Kamboni, in the extreme southern corner of the country, where they were pinned between advancing Ethiopian forces, the Indian Ocean, and a sealed border with Kenya. On January 12, 2007, after five days of heavy fighting, Ras Kamboni fell amidst the disintegration of remaining ICU forces.

At this point, the defeat of the ICU was complete. The Ethiopian-led offensive had turned into a rout. The ICU's spectacular rise seemed pedestrian compared to the manner in which it had folded. Even before Ras Kamboni had fallen, classified US government assessments of the situation judged Ethiopia's intervention a sweeping military success for its ruling elites. One cable, dated January 4, 2007, stated the following:

The GOE's [Government of Ethiopia] decisive military victory in Somalia sends a strong message for those, both inside and outside Ethiopia, who believed that confronting the CIC [another acronym for the ICU] might reveal to be a fatal

[74] "Ethiopia Girds for High Risk in Somalia," Wikileaks, December 6, 2006, which can be found at https://wikileaks.org/plusd/cables/06ADDISABABA3211_a.html (Accessed on November 4, 2015).

mistake for the EPRDF [Ethiopia's ruling party]... the ruling party was able to direct a successful military campaign against a determined adversary.[75]

Consistent with the theory of this book, Ethiopia's intervention provoked a serious bout of factionalism and fragmentation within ICU ranks that split the organization in fundamental ways. Ken Menkhaus, a prominent expert of contemporary Somali politics, makes the link between territorial losses and the ICU's fragmentation clear, writing: "Lurking beneath the genuine support for the Courts was a bundle of anxieties, mistrust, latent rivalries, clan divisions and alliances of expediency, which quickly resurfaced the moment the Courts began to lose ground to the Ethiopians."[76]

Although these fissures were complex, the December losses exacerbated the rough line of internal difference between "hardline" and "moderate" factions of the ICU. These distinctions were not just about long-running disputes over the proper role of Salafist ideology within the ICU, but the ICU's posture toward Ethiopia. Moderates, whose power had been waning, were of the opinion that the hardliners were actively stoking conflict with Somalia's western neighbor, using the Ethiopian threat to solidify their position within the ICU while risking the broader gains the organization had achieved in recent months. The hardliners included much of the old Al-Ittihad network, including Aweys and Turki, as well as a younger batch of Al-Ittihad protégés who had been consolidated into the shadowy militia known as Al-Shabaab.[77] These hardline elements were joined by the ICU's Al-Qaeda operatives and a growing cohort of foreign jihadis. The moderates included Sharif Sheikh Ahmed, foreign affairs chief Ibrahim Hassan Adow, the business community, and many of the clan militia who had joined the Courts in various parts of the country.[78]

The fragmentation of the ICU took shape midway through the Ethiopian offensive, as Ethiopian forces converged on Mogadishu.

---

[75] "Ethiopia: PM Reports to Parliament on Successful Military Operation," Wikileaks, January 4, 2007, which can be found at https://wikileaks.org/plusd/cables/07ADDISABABA18_a.html (Accessed on November 4, 2015).

[76] Menkhaus, "There and Back Again in Somalia," *MERIP Online*, February 11, 2007, which can be found at www.merip.org/mero/mero021107?ip_login_no_cache=6ec769eb26f4f9276a192a04f263b04f (Accessed April 14, 2016).

[77] At this stage, Al-Shabaab included key personalities like Aden Hashi Ayro and Ahmed Abdi Godane.

[78] For a deeper analysis of these rifts, see "Analysis: Splits Emerging in Somali Islamist Movement," *BBC Monitoring Africa*, July 6, 2006. Like is so often the case in Somali political rivalries, clan competition was never far from the surface. Aweys's increasing prominence, at the expense of Sharif Sheikh Ahmed, was believed to signal the expanding influence of the Ayr-Habr Gedir at the expense of the Abgaal.

Stunned by Ethiopia's rapid advance on the city, Mogadishu's business elites and many of its Hawiye clan elders balked at the suggestion – proffered by a number of ICU hardliners – that the ICU wage a protracted urban insurgency against Ethiopian forces. Although it was possible that this strategy could have stymied advancing Ethiopian troops, early losses had so damaged credible commitments between the ICU's constituent units that many now doubted that resistance in the city was possible. Amidst recriminations about the ICU's strategic hubris at Baidoa, those who had been erstwhile components of the organization turned on many of the hardliners and much of the leadership, and sought to forcibly expel them from the city. With their support base dwindling, ICU loyalists soon recognized their predicament, and grudgingly exited Mogadishu in what was a clear bid for survival. This led to the effective fragmentation of the ICU.

Menkhaus describes the dissolution of the ICU coalition in Mogadishu in exactly this way:

> The sudden dissolution of the Courts was the result of deep, unresolved divisions within the Islamist alliance in Mogadishu. The battlefield losses to Ethiopia took the lid off simmering tensions within the movement. Hardline leaders faced recriminations from clan elders, businesspeople and even fellow Islamists, who accused them of dragging the movement into a costly and reckless war with Ethiopia. The Courts were compelled to return most weapons and fighters to clan authorities and businesspeople. The most significant turn of events was the insistence of Mogadishu constituencies that the Courts not attempt to launch an urban insurgency in the capital, forcing the residual militia and leadership of the Courts to flee southward to the port city of Kismayo.
>
> While there is only fragmentary information about these internal divisions, it appears that the Courts' hardliners had taken both their policies and their rhetoric too far. Business leaders were unwilling to permit the Courts to engage in an urban insurgency that risked heavy damage to property; clan leaders feared the loss of lives and power within their lineages in a long war with Ethiopia; and moderate Islamists refused to back what they saw as an irresponsible policy of confrontation with a powerful neighbor.[79]

Jeffrey Gettleman, a *New York Times* journalist with years of experience in the region, largely echoes Menkhaus's interpretation of events in Mogadishu. He makes clear that recent territorial losses had shaken the cooperative equilibrium that had been at the core of the ICU from its very foundation. Reporting amidst the ICU's collapse in the city on December 27, 2006 Gettleman wrote:

---

[79] Ken Menkhaus, "There and Back Again in Somalia," *MERIP*, February 11, 2007, which can found at www.merip.org/mero/mero021107 (Accessed on October 5, 2015).

Gunfire rattled from neighborhood to neighborhood as the disparate clan-based militias that had joined forces to form the Islamist movement began to fragment and turn on one another.

With the war going badly for them, clan elders had been rapidly losing faith in the Islamist leaders, residents said. The quick defeat the Islamists suffered earlier on Wednesday at Jowhar, the last major town on the road to Mogadishu, seemed to be the final straw.

The Islamists started out as a grass-roots movement of clan elders and religious leaders who banded together earlier this year to rid Mogadishu of its notorious warlords, earning them a lot of public support.

But much of that good will seems to have been sapped by their decision to go to war against the transitional government and the Ethiopian forces protecting it.[80]

It is worth noting that the spate of losses even rattled some of the ICU hardliners in Mogadishu, with a number of young Al-Shabaab fighters, in Gettleman's words, "deserting in droves." He cites one young Al-Shabaab fighter describing his defection as part and parcel of a hopeless military situation: "We can't resist," the young fighter said, "We thought this fighting would be like the others. It's not."[81]

As has been illustrated in other parts of this book, there was a strong element of diffusion to the factional infighting and fragmentation that hit the ICU in Mogadishu. The evidence suggests that the initial crack within the ICU coalition in the city was triggered when "leaders of several major clans – and some business people who had been financing the Islamists – demanded that the Islamist leaders return the armed pick-up trucks that had been lent to the movement." Yet this act soon provoked similar behavior on the part of other clan militia that had initially remained loyal. "Faced with the loss of support from their counterparts," Gettleman writes, "other clan leaders saw the coalition begin to crumble and withdrew their trucks as well, leaving little of the organized force that once lent the Islamists their power."[82]

The pattern of events witnessed in Mogadishu was echoed in other critical battlegrounds in south-central Somalia. No doubt, the cycle of contention triggered by the actions of Mogadishu's clan militias could not be contained within the confines of Somalia's largest city. In a seeming reprise of what occurred in the Somali capital, the ICU's clan militias in Kismayo turned against the organization's leadership, initiating a chain of events that led the remaining fighters aligned with the ICU

---

[80] Jeffrey Gettleman, "Islamist Forces in Somali City Vanish," *New York Times*, December 27, 2006, which can be found at www.nytimes.com/2006/12/28/world/africa/28somalia.html?fta=y&_r=0(Accessed December 5, 2015).
[81] Ibid.   [82] Ibid.

to flee ahead of the Ethiopian advance. Like in Mogadishu, the key issue that provoked the rupture was the question of whether an urban insurgency should be waged in the city. As the Ethiopians approached Kismayo, thirty-six Kismayo clan elders met with ICU leaders "to persuade them that resisting the huge Ethiopian-backed force would be futile." In the words of one clan elder, "We told them we were going to lose... and our city would get destroyed."[83] With their confidence in the ICU crumbling, and no doubt swayed by events in Mogadishu, Kismayo's clans had decided it was time to act against their allies in the ICU leadership.

As had been the case in the Somali capital, ICU stalwarts did not leave Kismayo voluntarily. There was real internal strife within the city and key surrounding towns that pitted the ICU's constituent units against one another. As losers of the factional fight, the ICU units that remained loyal to the leadership were compelled to flee through force. In fact, the initial entreaties of clan elders were rejected by ICU hardliners: one Ogaden clan elder in Kismayo, no doubt frustrated by the situation, declared after failed consultations that "these guys are bent on war."[84] At the eleventh hour, with the Ethiopians at the key junction at Jilib, the clan militias moved against the ICU. Gettleman describes what transpired next in the following way:

Around 5 p.m., the fighting started, with the Ethiopian-backed forces unleashing an artillery barrage against Islamist troops dug in near Jilib, a town about 30 miles north of Kismayo. As the shells began to rain down, residents said, clan militias within Kismayo turned on the Islamists. That set off running gun battles across the city, with several people reportedly killed.[85]

Gettleman's Kismayo account is largely confirmed by the memoirs of Omar Hammami, a prominent American jihadi who joined the ICU just months before the Ethiopian intervention. As part of a band of loyal ICU fighters on the move near Jilib, he recounts the tensions between his unit and the large number of ICU clan militia in the area. Inconclusive armed clashes and unsuccessful attempts to disarm the clan militia, combined with the overwhelming superiority of clan forces, made clear that loyal ICU contingents would be unable to subdue the increasingly recalcitrant clan militants. Hammami summarized the impossible situation of his

---

[83] Jeffrey Gettleman, "Islamists, Cornered in Somalia, Lose Local Support," *New York Times*, December 31, 2006, which can be found at www.nytimes.com/2006/12/31/world/africa/31cnd-somalia.html?_r=3&hp&ex=1167627600&en=0f985fc2206a870b&ei=5094&partner=homepage&oref=slogin& (Accessed December 5, 2015).
[84] Ibid. [85] Ibid.

unit in the following way: "Once again we were surrounded by Mooryaan [his term for clan militia]. A lot of them. At times, I was more concerned about protecting myself from them than the Ethiopians."[86] When it was all said and done, and Hammami and his band had broken with their former comrades, he admitted that he felt "relieved and vulnerable all at once."[87] Later, after the American jihadi's unit had commandeered vehicles to make their retreat through the main thoroughfare of Kismayo, clan militia began firing on their vehicles, even disabling one of them.[88] The point here is that the fragmentation of the ICU in Kismayo did not involve an element of choice; it was the byproduct of a factional fight that ICU loyalists had lost.

Up until this point, the territorial losses wrought by the Ethiopian intervention had not pushed the different ideological poles of the ICU leadership into open conflict. The clan militias and business elites who had risen up against ICU hardliners were no doubt critical constituent units of the ICU, but they sat on the periphery of its leadership structure. Moderate elements within the executive and Shura councils were sympathetic to these dissenting voices, but had remained loyal to the organization. This was probably because a key moderate, Sharif Sheikh Ahmed, occupied the chairmanship of the ICU, even though his faction had lost substantial influence to the hardliners. Yet the defections in Kismayo further unsettled the situation, diffusing contention within ICU ranks by prompting moderates in the leadership to act. On January 8, 2007 foreign affairs chief Ibrahim Adow – a key moderate – announced that the ICU was prepared to enter into talks with the TFG without the precondition of an Ethiopian withdrawal.[89] A few days later, in a turn of events that was likely not coincidental, Sharif Sheikh Ahmed appeared in the custody of the Kenyan government, through which he entered into discussions with US officials. After these discussions concluded, US diplomats dubbed Sharif a "moderate Islamist, who can play a great role in soothing the tense situation and rebellion in the country."[90] It seemed a deal had been struck, and once he was released, the United States would facilitate Sharif's travel to Yemen, where he

---

[86] Abu Mansuur al-Amriki, "The Story of An American Jihadi: Part One," p. 61, May 16, 2012, which can be found at https://azelin.files.wordpress.com/2012/05/omar-hammami-abc5ab-mane1b9a3c5abr-al-amrc4abkc4ab-22the-story-of-an-american-jihc481dc4ab-part-122.pdf (Accessed December 6, 2015).
[87] Ibid.   [88] Ibid., p. 64.
[89] "Somali Islamist leaders say ready for talks with government," *BBC Monitoring Africa* (excerpt taken from Shabelle Media Network), January 8, 2007.
[90] Bill Roggio, "Somalia's Islamist Courts regroup," *The Long War Journal*, February 3, 2007, which can be found at www.longwarjournal.org/archives/2007/02/somalias_islamist_co.php (Accessed December 5, 2015).

joined Ibrahim Adow and other moderate leaders who had reassembled there.

Sharif's consultations with the Americans represented the logical conclusion of the process of factional infighting and fragmentation between moderate and hardline wings of the ICU leadership. In embracing the Americans, who had been the hardliners' bête noir, Sharif crossed a red line that could not be walked back. This was, in effect, an act of fragmentation. Important for the argument of this book is that even before Sharif made his move, it had become apparent that his faction had lost the struggle for authority within the ICU, and as such, faced real threats to their safety. A key indication of this reality is that Sharif's agreement to be taken into Kenyan custody and open dialogue with the Americans was conditional on Kenyan and American guarantees that he would not be returned to Somalia.[91] This request was based on the belief that if returned, Sharif could be assassinated by the hardline Al-Shabaab and Al-Qaeda operatives that had remained in Somalia.[92] Such fears were well placed. By January 2007, the International Crisis Group reported a "campaign by the hardliners to portray Sharif as an Islamist fraud" and even designate him an "apostate."[93] Tellingly, when ICU moderates began to trickle back into Mogadishu in 2008–09, having made peace with the newly installed government in Mogadishu, they were ruthlessly targeted by hardline elements such as the Al-Shabaab militia. Ibrahim Adow, for instance, would be killed by an Al-Shabaab bomb attack at a university commencement ceremony at Hotel Shamo in Mogadishu. Sharif himself would survive multiple attempts on his life when he returned to Somalia in 2009.[94]

---

[91] A fellow clansman and close ally of Sharif, the businessman Abukar Adane, was also taken into custody by Kenyan authorities and later released to coordinate activities with Sharif and others.

[92] Jeffrey Gettleman, Mohammed Ibrahim, and Yusuf Mohamed, "Somali Islamists' No. 2 Leader Surrenders in Kenyan Capital," *New York Times*, January 23, 2007. In my view, it is fairly clear that Sharif feared his own comrades, and not the TFG or Ethiopians. TFG officials had made clear that as long as they renounced violence, moderates like Sharif were welcome to return to Mogadishu.

[93] "Somalia's Divided Islamists," *International Crisis Group Report*, May 18, 2010, which can be found at www.crisisgroup.org/~/media/Files/africa/horn-of-africa/somalia/B74%20Somalias%20Divided%20Islamists.pdf (Accessed March 5, 2016).

[94] "Blast kills 19 at graduation ceremony in Somalia," *CNN*, December 4, 2009, which can be found at http://edition.cnn.com/2009/WORLD/africa/12/03/somalia.attacks/index.html?eref=onion (Accessed December 7, 2015). Of course, by the time of this attack Sharif and Adow had joined the TFG, and were thus diametrically opposed to Al-Shabaab. Seen from this view, the targeting of these two men is not direct evidence of the dynamic that existed in January 2007 as the ICU was collapsing. However, it is clear that Adow's assassination was meant to eliminate moderates who had once been in the ICU, and was a reflection of Al-Shabaab's extreme antipathy toward their former

Over time, the diffusion of factional infighting across the ICU opened up a final cleavage within the organization that defied some of the clean distinctions between "moderates" and "hardliners" that had characterized initial fissures. This cleavage was essentially within the hardline camp, and pitted veteran Islamists like Aweys against their younger protégés in the shadowy Al-Shabaab militia and many of the most radical of the ICU's foreign jihadis. In the face of the crushing Ethiopian offensive, and key defections, many of these young radicals began to question the strategic acumen of senior leaders such as Aweys. According to Omar Hammami, who was part of the group of foreign jihadis, the key indictment was that the ICU's military leadership had been unprepared for the Ethiopian incursion, and failed to quickly pivot to a strategy of guerrilla warfare that could have slowed the Ethiopian advance and bloodied the nose of invading troops. In his memoirs, Hammami summarizes these failings:

> In hindsight I decided the entire strategy of "conquering" Baidoa was a complete failure on behalf of the entire leadership of the Courts... The folly of this strategy is found in the fact that the Ethiopians essentially allowed the Courts, the supposed home team, to extend their supply lines and take on the role of the offensive; while they, in turn, remained comfortably on the defensive in a built up city close to their own borders. Even if the war was to be fought conventionally, the Courts should have used their strategic depth to their advantage by drawing the Ethiopians all the way to Mogadishu. If the conventional battle failed, the capital city would be within reach for the fighters to fade into the populace for urban guerilla warfare. Instead of such a strategy the Courts ended up simply running away after a short conventional fight (which sapped them of most of their manpower, weapons, and equipment) far from refuge; without laying ambushes for the oncoming Ethiopians and without allowing for urban warfare in Mogadishu."[95]

Of course, it is easy to see how Hammami's criticism of the ICU leadership was misplaced. While he asserts that the Courts had sought to "salvage" Mogadishu by fleeing, the reality, as we have learned, was that the ICU's fragmentation left the leadership with no other choice but to flee. Yet whatever the facts on the ground might have been, perceptions became reality in ways that politically undermined some of the ICU's most senior hardliners.

moderate comrades. This is because the Hotel Shamo attack, which killed many new university graduates, came at the cost of tremendous popular anger that seriously hurt the Al-Shabaab's brand. See "Three Ministers Killed in Mogadishu Suicide Bombing," Wikileaks, December 3, 2009, which can be found at http://cables.mrkva.eu/cable.php?id=237894 (Accessed October 5, 2015).

[95] Abu Mansuur al-Amriki, "The Story of An American Jihadi: Part One," p. 59.

These performance-based criticisms were compounded by accusations of absenteeism directed at much of the ICU's leadership core. Many ICU leaders were abroad during the Ethiopian intervention, including Aweys and political allies such as fellow clansman and ICU defense chief, Yusuf Inda'adde. Although the same was true of Al-Shabaab members who were part of the ICU leadership, such as Mukhtar Robow and Fuad Shongole, the accusation was particularly damning for Aweys, who effectively sat atop the ICU's hierarchy and shouldered much of the blame for the organization's failings.[96] Although open hostility between Aweys and younger hardliners would not be apparent at this stage, the fact that he would not return to Somalia until April 2009 is perhaps an indication of the frayed relationship with many of his younger protégés within Al-Shabaab, most prominently Aden Hashi Ayro and Ahmed Abdi Godane.[97]

The final chapter in this episode of fragmentation became apparent in June 2008, when Sharif Sheikh Ahmed and his allies signed a peace agreement in Djibouti with the TFG. The agreement paved the way for Sharif's emergence as the president of the TFG, his return to Somalia under the protection of an African Union force, and the withdrawal of Ethiopian troops from Somalia in early 2009. Aweys, who up until the Djibouti agreement had been in a loose Asmara-based coalition with Sharif called the Alliance for the Reliberation of Somalia (ARS), vehemently rejected the Djibouti agreement. Aweys's group, which would morph into an organization called Hizbul-Islam, was grudgingly joined by what would prove to be the most potent successor of the ICU, Al-Shabaab, in forging an allied resistance to the newly reconfigured TFG.

---

[96] Aweys was in Egypt receiving medical treatment. The others traveled to Mecca for Hajj. See Abdulkadir Khalif, "West Backing the Wrong Horse in Mogadishu Peace Initiatives," February 5, 2006, *The East African*, which can be found at http://web.archive.org/web/20070202014246/http://www.nationmedia.com/eastafrican/current/News/news2901200710.htm (Accessed on December 5, 2015).

[97] There is good evidence that the relationship between Aweys and his fellow clansman and protégé, Ayro, had become frayed as early as 2005, although Ayro clearly continued to benefit from Aweys's patronage. In January of that year, Al-Shabaab asserted itself by making the unilateral decision to seize Mogadishu's colonial-era Italian cemetery, desecrate the remains found there, and establish an Al-Shabaab–ICU facility on its grounds. This facility was referred to as *Muasker Mahkamad* (Troops of the Islamic Courts). This triggered outrage locally and internationally. When confronted by Ayr leaders about this incendiary act, Aweys denied involvement, and insisted that "Ayro was beyond his control." In fact, it appears the cemetery had been occupied by the very Ifka Halane militia commanded by Aweys. The International Crisis Group, writing in July 2005, noted that many analysts believed Ayro "has split with Aweys and is now directly affiliated to the Al-Qaeda network through its operatives in Somalia." See "Counter-Terrorism in Somalia: Losing Hearts and Minds?" *International Crisis Group Report*, July 11, 2005, p. 6.

Al-Shabaab: 2007–2013

Since its emergence as an independent rebel organization in 2007, Al-Shabaab has succumbed to several episodes of factional infighting and fragmentation. As will be seen, the causal pattern exhibited in the Al-Shabaab case neatly reflects the patterns seen throughout this book. In 2009, Al-Shabaab ruptured after a slew of territorial acquisitions made possible by Ethiopia's departure from the Somali theatre. In 2012, the organization went through another internal crisis, this time following an offensive by African Union troops that expelled Al-Shabaab from Mogadishu and its immediate environs. Importantly, the intervening periods of military stalemate saw Al-Shabaab reconcile its most serious internal cleavages and cohere.

Al-Shabaab as a Coalition within a Coalition

Al-Shabaab emerged organically under the ICU umbrella – in what Hansen (2013, p. 31) refers to as "in the shadow of the Courts" – as a loose network of militants that, over time, developed a more coherent sense of its own corporate identity. This network would seamlessly repackage itself into an independent rebel organization when the ICU collapsed. Generally speaking, Al-Shabaab members were the most hardline Salafists within ICU ranks, although many of its most significant players lacked proper theological training. It was also the case, perhaps owing to its hardline, militant Salafist ethos, that Al-Shabaab was the most cosmopolitan of the ICU's constituent units, in that its members came from a diverse array of Somali clans and regions. In its rhetoric, but less so in its practice, Al-Shabaab was unreservedly anti-clan.

The most important thread linking many of the main personalities within the Al-Shabaab network was that many were veterans of the Afghan Jihad or members of the old Al-Ittihad network. Some, like Ibrahim al-Afghani and Abdullah Sudi Arale, had cut their teeth in the struggle against the Soviets. Others, like Ahmed Abdi Godane, Mukhtur Robow, and Aden Hashi Ayro, attended Al-Ittihad schools in Somalia before joining up with the Taliban in the 1990s and early 2000s. As was highlighted earlier, Al-Shabaab's core tended to consist of the younger protégés within the Al-Ittihad network.

As was the case with other rebel organizations discussed in this book, there were real differences that divided Al-Shabaab's cohort of leaders. Omar Hammami, in capturing these differences, aptly referred to the Al-Shabaab as a "coalition within a coalition" – the latter coalition of course referring to Shabaab's parent organization, the ICU. Some of these differences within Al-Shabaab oddly reflected fissures within its patron organization, the ICU, but they were relatively less pronounced, particularly in the early stages of Al-Shabaab's evolution. As had been the case within the ICU, cleavages between hardliners and moderates were important, but meant something different in the context of Al-Shabaab's internal debates. For example, the constituent units of Al-Shabaab appeared united in their radical posture toward the Ethiopians and foreign intervention in Somalia more generally, whereas this seemed to be a more contentious question within the broader ICU.

The real point of difference within Al-Shabaab was about the use of tactics that would lead to mass civilian casualties, as well as the question of whether Al-Shabaab ought to formally align itself with Al-Qaeda. Behind these differences of strategy and tactics were deeper fissures about clan and political power. The hardliners tended to hail from clans in northern Somalia. Godane and Afghani, for instance, were members of Somaliland's Isaaq clan, and had been part of a network of militants responsible for a spate of attacks against foreigners in Somaliland.[98] Meanwhile, many of the moderates came from clans that populated Al-Shabaab's primary operational zone in south-central Somalia. This meant that relative to the hardliners, the moderates politically benefited from the formal or informal invocation of clan in internal Al-Shabaab debates. As such, the moderates were wary of indiscriminate violence in Al-Shabaab's operational areas, and the transnational jihadist project it was often associated with, because such behavior held the potential of alienating them from their local clan constituencies.

The other line of internal difference that existed was that between Al-Shabaab's Somali militants and its foreign fighters, or what were popularly known within Al-Shabaab ranks as the *Muhajarin*. Many of these individuals were of course the hard-core members of Al-Qaeda referred to earlier in this chapter. Yet Al-Shabaab's cohort of foreign fighters was a fairly diverse group, and most probably lacked direct links to Al-Qaeda central. At its largest point, the foreign fighter population probably numbered somewhere around 1,000 fighters. This included many fighters from neighboring East African states such as Kenya and Tanzania, Arab countries, and Somali diaspora from North America and Europe.

---

[98] "Somalia: Al-Shabaab – It Will Be a Long War," *International Crisis Group Report*, June 26, 2014, p. 5, which can be found at https://d2071andvip0wj.cloudfront.net/somalia-al-shabaab-it-will-be-a-long-war.pdf (Accessed August 5, 2015).

The dynamics that brought the founding constituent units of Al-Shabaab together were not much different than the forces that propelled the consolidation of the ICU. Al-Shabaab's constituent units were probably the most vulnerable within the broader Islamist alliance, given that they were key counterterrorism targets in Mogadishu's Shadow Wars. Individuals like Ayro, who hailed from the Ayr-Habr Gedir, were well positioned to provide clan protection to the large number of Al-Shabaab fighters who did not hail from south-central Somalia. At the same time, these fighters did much to strengthen the position of Al-Shabaab leaders hailing from clans in Al-Shabaab's operational heartland. Ayro obviously appeared to be the focal point in the early consolidation of the Al-Shabaab network, and perhaps the bridge in bringing the different camps together, as he was by all accounts a hardline Salafist, but local to south-central Somalia and thus subject to its political realities.

Forged in the violent cauldron of Mogadishu's Shadow Wars, the early network that was to become Al-Shabaab was responsible for a number of attacks on the CIA-backed warlord alliance, as well as assassinations of a broader range of political opponents. Saleh Ali Saleh Nabhan, the Kenyan Al-Qaeda member, seems to have been the architect of many of these early operations (Hansen, 2013, p. 27). The most notorious of these, and that which was responsible for putting the network on the political map, was the assassination of peace activist Abdulkadir Yahya Ali in July 2005. Well regarded across Mogadishu's fractious political divides, Abdulkadir Yahya Ali's murder shocked the Somali public and the international community, and even provoked UN Secretary General Kofi Annan to issue a public statement specifically condemning the act.[99]

Another critical event in the early consolidation of the Al-Shabaab network – and perhaps something that granted it even greater notoriety in its incipient stages – was the creation of a training facility on the grounds of Mogadishu's Italian cemetery. The facility, known as *Muasker Mahkamad* (Troops of the Islamic Courts), also included a mosque, and was the project of Ayro and his Al-Shabaab colleague and fellow clansman Khalif Adale. To be clear, the entire venture was a coercive project, made

---

[99] Author's interview, parliamentarian and friend of Abdulkadir Yahya Ali, Mogadishu, January 2014; Hansen (2013, pp. 27–28), says that Abdulkadir's killing was revenge against the Hawiye–Murosade clan for the military action of their clan members – the warlords Mohammed Qanyare and Abdi Waal. Others suggest that Abdulkadir's connections with the international community and the ICG are what led to his assassination. See "Somali death 'undermines peace,'" *BBC News*, July 12, 2005, which can be found at http://news.bbc.co.uk/2/hi/africa/4671813.stm (Accessed November 1, 2015).

possible by the forceful seizure of the cemetery. The act was controversial because Al-Shabaab's forceful seizure came at the expense of the allied Ifka Halane court militia that had previously controlled the cemetery, and because Al-Shabaab decided to desecrate the remains of the Italians who had been buried there. In the end, the Italian government had to offer the Al-Shabaab network a large cash reward to return the remains.[100] These funds and the new facility enabled the Al-Shabaab group to emerge as a real corporate interest within the ICU, and provided a platform for its expansion (Marchal, 2011, p. 15). Although still deeply reliant on the broader ICU structure, and numbering no more than a core group of thirty-three, from this point onward Al-Shabaab operated with some ability to execute unilateral military operations and occupy territory (Hansen, 2013, p. 28).

As Al-Shabaab acquired a more defined sense of its own status within the ICU, it also began to formalize its political structure. Key figures in the early days were the Al-Ittihad veteran Omar Dheere and Hawiye businessman Abdullahi Maalim Mukhtar, but neither would remain particularly influential as the organization evolved. Not long after the controversy at Mogadishu's Italian cemetery, the group would appoint Ahmed Abdi Godane as its *Emir*. Ahmed Madobe, who was a member of an allied militia called Ras Kamboni, was selected as his deputy. In addition, a Shura Council was appointed.

Al-Shabaab's structure sat parallel to the broader ICU organizational apparatus, but it was not entirely distinct. When the ICU established its new Shura and executive councils after its capture of Mogadishu, Al-Shabaab's leaders were handsomely rewarded for their support. Godane was made secretary-general of the ICU's executive council, although he did resign his post in Al-Shabaab and made way for a new Emir, Ismail Arale. Other key Al-Shabaab personalities were given key portfolios within the ICU executive committee – Mukhtar Robow (deputy head of defense), Aryo (overall military commander), Abu Ubaidah (head of security), and Sheikh Omar (health).[101] From this relatively well-positioned perch, Al-Shabaab acted as the radical wing of the ICU, pushing its parent organization into the fateful confrontation with the TFG and its Ethiopian backers.

---

[100] The Italian government denied payment. The ICG reports that the payment was a whopping 1.5 million euros. See "Somalia: Al-Shabaab – It Will Be a Long War," *International Crisis Group Report*, June 26, 2014, p. 6.

[101] "Somalia: Al-Shabaab – It Will Be a Long War," *International Crisis Group Report*, June 26, 2014, p. 7.

Al-Shabaab Strikes Out on Its Own

Ethiopia's intervention led to the dispersal of Al-Shabaab fighters throughout south-central Somalia, much as had been the case with the broader ICU membership that had managed to stay within the country. Over time, and after a number of intermediate stops, small groups of Al-Shabaab fighters would converge on the coastal region of Lower Shabelle, in the areas around Barawe and Buulo Mareer, the former of which would serve as the operational focal point of the group going forward. At this early stage, Al-Shabaab was one of several anti-Ethiopia/TFG groups operating in south-central Somalia, and as such, it chose to cultivate tactical alliances with like-minded militants. As a consequence, the exact boundaries of Al-Shabaab were somewhat amorphous, until the group eventually asserted its control over the anti-TFG camp some years later.

The first half of 2007 was a period of survival, retrenchment, and consolidation for Al-Shabaab. Following the ICU's unceremonious departure, there was a two-month lull in major fighting in the capital. Yet major resistance to the TFG in Mogadishu reemerged in late March 2007. This was triggered by Ethiopia's decision to enter Mogadishu neighborhoods populated by clans that had heavily supported the ICU. In disarming and demilitarizing these neighborhoods, the Ethiopians sought to reduce the sporadic attacks on their positions. The Ethiopians were backed by a fresh deployment of 1,500 African Union (Ugandan) peacekeepers, Abgaal and Saad clan militias mobilized by the TFG, and of course, the Darood militias of Abdullahi Yusuf. Ayr, Suleiman, and Murosade clans fought the Ethiopians tooth and nail, as did the militia of the Abgaal businessman Adane. Ethiopia would bring overwhelming firepower to bear on the recalcitrant clans, forcing their clan elders to sue for peace by April 2007. During this time, when many anti-TFG/Ethiopian forces suffered heavy losses, Al-Shabaab fighters largely sat on the sidelines and conserved their strength (Hansen, 2013, pp. 51–53).[102]

This is not to say, of course, that the group was dormant. In Mogadishu, Al-Shabaab maintained a loose network of loyalists under the direction of Mahad Karate, an individual who would go on to serve as the head of Al-Shabaab's intelligence wing – the *Amniyat* – and the

---

[102] Also see Moshe Terdman, "Somalia at War – Between Radical Islam and Tribal Politics," 2008, pp. 59–62, which can be found at www.tau.ac.il/humanities/abraham/publications/somalia.pdf (Accessed on January 5, 2016).

organization's deputy Emir (Hansen, 2013, p. 53).[103] This network allowed the organization to wage a campaign of targeted assassination and intimidation during the first half of 2007, while avoiding much direct confrontation with the much better equipped Ethiopian military. It is here that Al-Shabaab began to develop the repertoire of violence that would become its hallmark: the use of remote control explosive devices and IEDs, and, more unprecedented on the Somali scene, suicide attacks. A major exception to this somewhat timid strategic posture was Al-Shabaab's participation in the successful offensive on Beledweyne in May 2007 (Hansen, 2013, p. 56).

Although the rupture between Al-Shabaab and the more senior members of the ICU had already taken shape by early 2007, it was reaffirmed by ongoing negotiations in Eritrea that would bring Sharif Sheikh Ahmed, Aweys, and other anti-TFG discontents into an opposition umbrella. Al-Shabaab ideologues already had their misgivings about ICU leaders, and the organization of the resistance under the tutelage of the secular regime in Asmara was icing on the cake. From that point onward, Al-Shabaab steered a mostly independent and decidedly more radical course, although tactical alliances with other anti-TFG/Ethiopian groups would remain common.

Al-Shabaab's break with more senior Islamists in the ICU who were organizing themselves in Asmara was on some level made possible by the increasing prominence of Godane, Robow, and others in Al-Shabaab leadership circles. Many senior Al-Shabaab leaders had been captured in the chaos of the Ethiopian invasion. Arale, Al-Shabaab's sitting Emir, had been arrested in Djibouti and delivered to the Americans, who promptly placed him in detention in Guantanamo Bay, Cuba. Ahmed Madobe, Arale's deputy, had been captured by the American operatives in southern Somalia and placed in an Ethiopian jail. Even the charismatic military commander Aden Hashi Ayro would be killed by an American missile in May 2008. The decapitation of much of Al-Shabaab's leadership allowed Godane to emerge as the new Emir and, with his allies, assert himself as the dominant force within Al-Shabaab leadership circles.

Under Godane, Al-Shabaab's institutional structures developed at a rapid pace. An initial Shura of eight would eventually expand to around fifty. Administrative departments (defense, internal security, religious

---

[103] "Al Shabaab intelligence chief killed: Kenyan army," *Al Jazeera*, February 18, 2016, which can be found at www.aljazeera.com/news/2016/02/al-shabab-intelligence-chief-killed-kenyan-army-160218092749014.html (Accessed March 6, 2016).

affairs, etc.) were responsible for executing Shura decisions. *Wilayahs* would serve as regional administrations – which of course became critical when the organization moved toward occupation of major towns – and were headed by a governor who was a senior Al-Shabaab member. *Wilayahs* would be supported by local Shuras, which consisted of personalities from the local community, and would ensure local support (Marchal, 2011, pp. 20–22). It was through this reinvigorated platform that Al-Shabaab emerged as the premier militant organization in south-central Somalia.

Steady Expansion and the Madobe Split

The latter half of 2007 saw a significant shift in Al-Shabaab operations, marked by a decided uptick in the intensity of Al-Shabaab's asymmetric attacks. By the winter of 2007, Al-Shabaab was responsible for more than 50 percent of all attacks in Somalia, an increasing share of which explicitly focused on military targets. The organization's deft use of new media attracted a growing range of foreign fighters, many who hailed from the Somali diaspora. In the Somali hub of Minneapolis, Minnesota, alone, twenty-seven Somali-Americans were recruited into Al-Shabaab between 2007 and 2011.[104] A number of these individuals would be involved in high-profile suicide attacks of the type that became Al-Shabaab's trademark. Several hundred non-Somali foreign fighters from East Africa, the Arab world, and South Asia joined the fray as well.[105]

The pace of Al-Shabaab operations, and its broader notoriety, went hand in hand with an expansion in its territorial reach and control. Mukhtar Robow was sent to establish a presence in the Bay region, where his Rahanweyn clan was a political force. Further south, in Lower Shabelle, Al-Shabaab was able to establish control over Merka and Barawe by mid-2008. In August 2008, Kismayo fell to Al-Shabaab and its Islamist allies, in what made for a triumphant return for Islamist forces just eighteen months after their ouster. In January 2009, the move to

---

[104] Laura Yuen and Sasha Aslanian, "Minnesota Pipeline to Al-Shabaab" *MPR News*, which can be found at http://minnesota.publicradio.org/projects/ongoing/somali_timeline/ (Accessed April 5, 2016); Deena Templeton Raston, "For Somalis in Minnesota, Jihadi Recruiting Is Recurring Nightmare," *NPR*, February 18, 2015, which can be found at www.npr.org/2015/02/18/387302748/minneapolis-st-paul-remains-a-focus-of-jihadi-recruiting (Accessed April 5, 2016).

[105] Isabelle Duyvesteyn and Bram Peters, "Fickle Foreign Fighters? A Cross-Case Analysis of Seven Muslim Foreign Fighter Mobilisations (1980–2015)," *ICCT – The Hague Research Paper*, October 2015, p. 11, which can be found at www.icct.nl/wp-content/uploads/2015/10/ICCT-Duyvesteyn-Peeters-Fickle-Foreign-Fighters-October2015.pdf (Accessed April 5, 2016).

establish a beachhead in the Bay region paid off, when Robow captured Baidoa after a protracted siege. As Hansen (2013) notes, the territorial expansions of 2009 were the most significant in Al-Shabaab's short history; along with other opponents of the TFG, it quickly came to occupy most of south-central Somalia, outside of portions of south Mogadishu and a few remaining towns.

Beyond the clever use of new media, and the utilization of the increasing flow of foreign fighters, Ethiopia's withdrawal from Somalia in January 2009 was the most decisive factor behind Al-Shabaab's territorial surge. Ethiopia had always envisioned a short operation in Somalia, lasting no more than a few weeks. Yet the TFG was a weak and fragmented military actor, and it would be some time before AMISOM deployments were to reach their mandated level. Even then, AMISOM forces would be undermanned for some time. This meant that Ethiopia was forced to stay on in Somalia in order to prevent the TFG's collapse. Yet Ethiopia had steadily scaled back its presence in the country throughout 2008, limiting its patrols and military footprint. The Ethiopian National Defense Forces (ENDF) clearly had no interest in paying the cost of a robust counterinsurgency campaign, and was thus increasingly content with remaining within its well-fortified garrisons. This enabled Al-Shabaab successes in 2008. By early 2009, AMISOM's marginal growth gave Ethiopia the full exit option it wanted. At this point, there were about 3,450 AMISOM troops in Somalia, with another Ugandan deployment on the way, out of an authorized contingent of 8,000.[106] This was almost double the number of AMISOM troops in Mogadishu at the end of 2007. This fact, along with the political bargain struck through the Djibouti Accords in late 2008 that brought Sharif Sheikh Ahmed to Mogadishu as the TFG's new president, paved the way for Ethiopia's withdrawal. Still, the TFG and AMISOM were ill prepared for the vacuum Ethiopia's departure created. A number of Ethiopian bases in Mogadishu were occupied by Al-Shabaab and its allies just hours after Ethiopia's withdrawal.[107]

The territorial gains of 2009 created a bout of serious factionalism and fragmentation within Al-Shabaab. Major cleavages within the group came to the fore just as security threats to the organization seemed to recede. Nearly all those who would defect from Shabaab in this period

---

[106] See "Somalia: April 2009 Monthly Forecast," *Security Council Report*, March 30, 2009, which can be found at www.securitycouncilreport.org/monthly-forecast/2009-04/lookup_c_glKWLeMTIsG_b_5053255.php (Accessed April 10, 2016).

[107] "Ethiopian Troops Begin Somali Withdrawal," *CNN*, January 13, 2009, which can be found at http://edition.cnn.com/2009/WORLD/africa/01/13/ethiopia.somalia/index.html (Accessed April 10, 2016).

would explain their actions as a rejection of the increasingly radical and indiscriminate tactics of Al-Shabaab Emir Godane.[108] Yet as mentioned earlier, the issue of clan was really never far from the surface.

As had been the modus operandi of its predecessor the ICU, Al-Shabaab sought to manipulate local clan rivalries in a way that allowed it to capture territory with minimal sacrifice. This strategy existed, once again, even though as Islamists Al-Shabaab generally frowned on clan politics. This tension would soon create problems. The first signs of trouble occurred in Baidoa, where the opening of Robow's Bay front had proved enormously successful. From Godane's perspective, Robow must have appeared to be a serious rival: unlike the Emir, Robow hailed from south-central Somalia and could count on a growing number of Rahanweyn clansmen within Al-Shabaab ranks for support. Throughout 2008, the rivalry between the two had played out along lines identified earlier: between Godane, the radical hardliner with no local constituency, and Robow, the tactically more moderate leader, who came from a clan that was an important political constituency within south-central Somalia. In this context, the fall of Baidoa created a serious problem. The town's capture had been enabled by the collapse of TFG forces in Baidoa, as there was a split between the militias of the major Rahanweyn subclans. Key members of the TFG in the town, who hailed from Robow's Laysan subclan, decided against putting up protracted resistance to advancing Al-Shabaab forces. In return, TFG figures like Mohammed Ibrahim Hapsade and Ibrahim Yarow, who were Robow's Laysan clansmen, were given protection and safe passage out of the town by Robow. This move seemed to incense Godane and his allies within the Shura, who used these events as evidence of Robow's own purportedly clannist inclinations. Although this did not lead to a full break within Al Shabaab – Robow would fragment only later in 2013 – he was publicly criticized by Shura member Fuad Shongole, demoted from his post as spokesman, and replaced as commander of Al-Shabaab forces in Baidoa (Hansen, 2013, pp. 77–79).

Over the next few months, events in Baidoa would reverberate in the ever-contentious port of Kismayo, although in this case, it remains hard to find a direct link of diffusion between Robow's troubles and the much more concrete break that was to occur in the southern port. There can be no doubt, however, that those who would fragment in Kismayo were intimately aware of the Baidoa crisis.

---

[108] For example, see "Senior Al Shabaab Officer Defects to the Government," *The Somaliland Times*, December 5, 2009, which can be found at www.somalilandtimes.net/sl/2009/410/26.shtml (Accessed April 11, 2016).

Al-Shabaab's capture of Kismayo – which by now had changed hands nearly thirty times since Siad Barre's ouster in 1991 – was an allied effort made possible by a partnership with the Ras Kamboni group, a vehicle of Ogaden clan interests in Kismayo that was dressed in Islamist garb. Ras Kamboni was a member of a larger coalition of Islamist groups, the aforementioned Hizbul Islam, a four-member alliance that would be headed by Hassan Dahir Aweys on his return to Somalia. At the time, Hizbul Islam was often referred to as the ICU, although it is generally recognized that the ICU was a defunct organization by this juncture. In taking Kismayo, Al-Shabaab and Ras Kamboni had allied to expel the mostly Marehan militias of the warlord Barre Hirale, an effort that was aided by the estrangement between the Marehan-dominated authorities in the city and the TFG. Yet the boundaries between Ras Kamboni, whose Ogaden militias had also been part of the ICU, and Al-Shabaab were fuzzy. In part, this is because Hassan Turki, a close ally of Al-Shabaab who remained a mentor to many Al-Shabaab leaders, was the head of Ras Kamboni. His de facto deputy, who also happened to be his son-in-law, was fellow clansman Ahmed Madobe – the former deputy Emir of Al-Shabaab until his unceremonious capture by US Special Forces. This meant that rather than being a distinct organization, Ras Kamboni and Al-Shabaab were overlapping networks. This is an important point, because in the midst of Al-Shabaab's rapid territorial successes, the fusion of the two camps would become a central problem, raising issues over the distribution of political power in Kismayo that had not been particularly important in an earlier phase of more pressing security threats.[109]

In September 2008, just a few weeks after the capture of Kismayo, Al-Shabaab and Ras Kamboni established a joint administration in the city. Al-Shabaab, with the support of Turki, formed a ruling council of seven, in which it reserved three seats for itself, another three for Ras Kamboni and allied Islamist/former ICU militia, and one for a local clan elder. Yet Al-Shabaab kept the most critical posts, including that of provincial commissioner and his deputy, as well as the city's security chief and deputy head of security. What made the situation more contentious was that while Ras Kamboni was by and large an Ogaden clan militia and the Ogaden clan had been instrumental to the Islamist takeover of Kismayo, Turki had failed to secure adequate representation of the Ogaden clan in the council. Immediately following the creation of the administration Sheikh Ibrahim Shukri, an ICU veteran and

---

[109] The fusion of Al-Shabaab and Ras Kamboni is also important because I am coding Ras Kamboni's eventual case as an instance of organizational fragmentation.

powerful Ras Kamboni commander who hailed from the Ogaden clan, let his displeasure with the new dispensation be known, arguing, "Shabaab appointed its people to top posts without inviting local people and the ICU that played a military role in taking over Kismayo" and that the process was "hijacked by elements who met in a small room."[110]

It was in this tense context that Madobe returned to Lower Juba in March 2009.[111] As a the governor of the region during the days of the ICU, he was a known quantity among Ogaden clan elders in Kismayo, who by now were incensed by Turki's failure to secure their clan's interests. Clan elders hoped to replace Turki with Madobe, since they believed the latter would more firmly resist Al-Shabaab hegemony. Al-Shabaab, for its part, recognized the danger that Madobe's return posed, even though he was a former deputy Emir of the organization and part of the early Al-Shabaab network. Since the Turki-led Ras Kamboni already functioned as an arm of Al-Shabaab, Godane had little to gain from Madobe's assertion of influence. Moreover, by 2009, Madobe was increasingly regarded as a subversive force within the Al-Shabaab camp, as the Sharif-led TFG had intervened on Madobe's behalf in securing his release from an Ethiopian jail. As part of the deal, Madobe was appointed to the TFG parliament, although he quickly resigned the parliamentary post in recognition of the fact that it made his position vis-à-vis Turki and Al-Shabaab in Kismayo untenable. Despite Al-Shabaab's protests, familial links between Turki and Madobe, Turki's declining popularity among his own clansmen, and Turki's own deteriorating personal health prevented him from taking a strong stand against Madobe's full incorporation into the Ras Kamboni fold.

The situation in Kismayo worsened when Al-Shabaab decided to redeploy Ras Kamboni fighters to Mogadishu to participate in a May 2009 offensive against the TFG. To Ogaden clan elders, the deployment of Ogaden clan fighters outside Lower Juba was perceived as a deliberate effort to weaken their hand in Kismayo. To Ras Kamboni fighters themselves, this move left them exposed far from their traditional heartland. There were also major problems over an agreement about the distribution of rents from Kismayo port, as Ras Kamboni was receiving far less

---

[110] Nick Grace, "Islamic Emirate of Somalia Imminent as Shabaab Races to Consolidate Power," *The Long War Journal*, September 8, 2008, which can be found at http://www.longwarjournal.org/archives/2008/09/islamic_emirate_of_s.php (Accessed on April 10, 2016).

[111] For a profile of Madobe, see "Kismayo Sheikh Ahmed Mohamed Islam Madobe," *The Africa Report*, December 3, 2012, which can be found at www.theafricareport.com/East-Horn-Africa/kismayos-sheikh-ahmed-mohamed-islam-madobe.html (Accessed April 11, 2016).

than its allotted share. At this point, Madobe swung into action, going to Mogadishu to rally Ras Kamboni fighters and gather clandestine support from the TFG. This effort was largely successful, at least in the short term. A meeting of Ras Kamboni in Afmadow led to the selection of Madobe as the new commander of the group, and Sheikh Ibrahim Shukri as the head of internal affairs. Madobe's secret goal was to assert control over Kismayo and Lower Juba, bring Al-Shabaab to heel, and create a de facto state in the Juba regions that would permanently guarantee Ogaden clan interests.[112]

An uneasy standoff in Kismayo between Madobe loyalists and those who remained committed to Al-Shabaab's core leadership persisted until October 2009. By this time, Madobe's forces were in control of Afmadow, portions of Jilib, and a few other towns, imperiling Al-Shabaab's supply lines into Kismayo and separating the Kismayo forces from the key front in Mogadishu. Seeking to avoid what looked like a slow-moving coup against its administration, Al-Shabaab moved against Madobe. In the fighting that ensued, Madobe was abandoned by his allies in Hizbul Islam, Turki, and the TFG, the latter of which had doubts about Madobe's state-making project in Juba and had promised support that was beyond its capacity to deliver. By November, Madobe was largely a spent force, and was forced to formally defect to Kenya. In 2011, Kenya would be the platform from which he would launch a new, much more successful military operation against his former Al-Shabaab colleagues.

In any case, Madobe's defection did produce a cycle of contention that, although not serious, led to the departure of key cadres. Three mid-level Al Shabaab commanders fragmented with their troops between November and December 2009, directly following Madobe's failed putsch. This included Sheikh Muhammed Abdullahi "Pakistani," Ali Hassan Ghedi, and Abdurahman Abdi Adow.[113] Although the evidence is somewhat circumstantial, it is clear that Abdurahman Abdi Adow's defection was directly triggered by the death of Ras Kamboni fighters at the hands of Al-Shabaab troops.[114] The others, who were not based in

---

[112] The Madobe split was extensively monitored by US intelligence, which gathered information from key Madobe confidants like Abdi Ali Rage (also Turki's son-in-law). See Wikileaks cable from August 2009, which can be found at https://wikileaks.org/plusd/cables/09NAIROBI1732_a.html (Accessed April 11, 2015); also see Hansen (2013, pp. 80–81).

[113] Al-Shabaab would deny that Pakistani was a member of their organization. Ghedi was the deputy commander of Al-Shabaab forces in Lower Shabelle.

[114] "Al Shabaab Fighters Tell Why They Abandoned Jihad," *AFP*, November 24, 2009.

Lower Juba, likely found the infighting the appropriate opportunity to escape Al-Shabaab's grasp.

In the end, the cooperative equilibrium within Al-Shabaab was ruptured by the significant gains of 2008–09. A former TFG minister, in reflecting on this period, makes exactly this point, arguing that "Shabaab was not ready for the problems that came with occupying all those new areas. Especially the towns. They only thought about the military side of the issue, not the politics, not the divisions that would come. They almost paid a heavy price for this in Kismayo."[115]

While Al-Shabaab was far from achieving total victory, owing in part to the ever-increasing deployment of AMISOM troops and the remaining array of Islamist and non-Islamist rivals, battlefield success eroded the security concerns that had preoccupied its constituent units in 2007 and early 2008. It was only at that point that tensions in Baidoa, and more significantly in Kismayo, over the distribution of power, came to the fore and triggered a serious round of factional infighting and fragmentation.

From the Mogadishu Stalemate to the Godane "Coup"

According to Hansen (2013, p. 81), by the summer of 2009, Al-Shabaab "was facing the limits of its capacities." Like an octopus, the organization, at the vanguard of broader array of Islamist militias, had spread its tentacles across south-central Somalia as Ethiopian forces withdrew. But in Mogadishu it met fierce resistance, from an expanding, but still undermanned AMISOM contingent that protected the port, Villa Somalia, and a few other key installations in the city's southern districts. At this point, AMISOM numbered around 6,000 Ugandan and Burundian troops, supported by fairly inept TFG militia.[116] Al-Shabaab sat at around 5,000 troops, supported by Hizbul Islam, and any other clan militia that had temporarily decided to throw in their lot with the Islamists. Sitting in a defensive crouch with its back to the sea, AMISOM troops weathered repeated Al-Shabaab offensives by using its superior armor and heavy weapons. Foot by foot, block by block, the two sides fought, with AMISOM occasionally launching a small counterattack to relieve its position. This was dense urban warfare, with the frontlines in

---

[115] Author's interview, TFG Minister, and later a parliamentarian, January 29, 2016, Mogadishu, Somalia.
[116] The assassination in June 2009 of Omar Hashi Aden, the TFG's head of security, greatly compounded the TFG's command problems (Hansen, 2013, p. 81).

some cases cutting through actual homes.[117] The stalemate in the city would persist until about February 2011, when the pendulum would again swing against Al-Shabaab. Hansen describes the military situation in this way:

> From 2009 onwards, the military situation in Mogadishu was turned into a bloody stalemate, not unlike World War I trench battles. Al Shabaab simply did not have the forces to dislodge the Ugandan and Burundian AMISOM forces, while the latter lacked the mandate to expand their areas. (Hansen, 2013, p. 82)[118]

What is germane about this period of stalemate was that it is consistent with the argument of this book: it was a "cohesive stalemate," and one of the few periods in which Al-Shabaab was not riven by serious factional infighting. This "cohesive stalemate" existed despite serious internal problems. Consider two major issues.

By early 2010, Al-Shabaab's capabilities far exceeded those of its Islamist allies. As a result, Godane and Al-Shabaab's hardline wing sought to absorb the constituent militias of Aweys's Hizbul Islam, by force if necessary. In fact, from the very beginning of Hizbul Islam's emergence in 2009 – a coalition between Ras Kamboni, Aweys's ARS, Anole (mostly Islamists from the Harti clan), and Jabhat Islamiya (mostly Hawiye Islamists) – the organization was clandestinely undermined by Al-Shabaab. For example, after Madobe fragmentation, Al-Shabaab swallowed the remaining Ras Kamboni forces loyal to Turki, in an act that directly undermined the Hizbul Islam coalition and Hassan Dahir Aweys. When a leading commander who had remained loyal to Turki resisted the merger, he was publicly executed by Al-Shabaab in Mogadishu's Bakara market. Soon after, Al-Shabaab slowly began to occupy Hizbul Islam's territory, and assassinated many of its key operational commanders. Key defections from Hizbul Islam to Al-Shabaab followed as the fortunes of Aweys's outfit looked increasingly bleak. Finally, by December 2010, Aweys was forced to concede to the incorporation of his forces into Al-Shabaab. It was clearly not a matter of choice.

---

[117] This description is drawn from author's interview, foreign private security consultant based in Mogadishu, Mogadishu, January 2014.
[118] A report from *Geopolitical Monitor* from August 2010 concurs with this view, stating that "the military balance between the sides remains a stalemate," and cites a Somali source who notes, "As long as these [AU] forces are in Mogadishu, I think it will be unlikely for Al Shabaab to take over [the city]." See Zachary Fillingham, "Analysis: Al Shabaab Offensive," *Geopolitical Monitor*, August 24, 2010, which can be found at www.geopoliticalmonitor.com/analysis-al-shabab-offensive-4128/ (Accessed April 11, 2016).

Al-Shabaab's moderate wing, again represented by Robow and his allies, was highly critical of the tactics deployed by Godane against Hizbul Islam, believing that it sowed needless discord with allied Islamist groups. Even Fuad Shongole, a part-time ally, part-time critic of Godane, publicly chastised the Emir at a public speech in Bakara market, by insisting that "fighting everyone is not the solution." There were even rumors that Robow and Aweys would join forces to create their own organization. The situation was eventually defused when Robow and Shongole met with Aweys and negotiated an agreement on the merger. The very fact that these two men negotiated the final agreement, and not Godane – who had previously signed the merger agreement with Turki's Ras Kamboni remnant – is suggestive of the tense political dynamic within Al-Shabaab that existed at the time.[119]

The other point of contention was the so-called Ramadan Offensive of August–September 2010. Announced with much public fanfare, Al-Shabaab spokesman Ali Mohamud Rage promised that it would be the "final offensive" against AMISOM. Key assets were deployed to Mogadishu in an effort to overrun AMISOM-TFG positions in the city. Yet the operation was a disaster, as Al-Shabaab was badly mauled by AMISOM troops, who took the opportunity to execute a number of highly effective counteroffensives. While the state of play shifted little territorially (a key point I will come back to), and largely remained a stalemate, hundreds of Al-Shabaab fighters were killed, as were a number of experienced commanders.

The failure largely fell in Godane's lap, as he had been the architect of the offensive and ignored the arguments of many of his colleagues who objected to the timing of what was a large-scale offensive against AMISOM's well-fortified positions. Writing just after the offensive, Ethiopian sources describe how these events again widened the rupture between Godane and moderates like Robow:

Al Shabaab has also begun to be affected by internal disagreements. There was a dispute about the timing of the offensive. Once Al Shabaab forces failed to advance towards the State House, disputes over tactics and strategy began to surface. Other divisions have become more apparent. According to sources inside Al Shabaab, one main cause of the conflict arose over financial matters. As a result, Sheikh Muktar Robow Abu Mansur has withdrawn the Al Shabaab fighters from the Digil and Mirifle clans [which include Robow's Rahanwey clan]. He has also demanded that the Amir of Al-Shabaab, Ahmed Abdi Aw-Mohamed

---

[119] "Somali Jihadist Groups Merge," *Stratfor*, December 22, 2010, which can be found at www.stratfor.com/analysis/somali-jihadist-groups-merge (Accessed April 12, 2016).

"Godane" and Fu'ad Mohamed Khalaf Shangole, who commanded the offensive in Mogadishu, should resign.[120]

For Robow, the Ramadan Offensive was particularly problematic because fighters from his Rahanweyn clan, who formed the backbone of Al-Shabaab forces at that time, had perished in large numbers. The carnage again seemed to highlight the fissures between Al-Shabaab leaders with political bases in south-central Somalia and those not indigenous to the region.

Yet what was extraordinary about this crisis is that it did not morph into factional infighting and fragmentation. A series of meetings, in which the mediation of foreign fighters within Al-Shabaab ranks played a key role, helped defuse the situation. A key part of the bargain was that Godane retained his role as Emir, but would be forced to relinquish control of the *Amniyat* – Al-Shabaab's internal security branch and a key tool that Godane had used to project his influence throughout the organization (Hansen, 2013, pp. 105–106). This deescalation is entirely consistent with the main claims of this book. Given the battlefield context, in which Al-Shabaab had sought to revise the territorial status quo in Mogadishu and failed, there was little impetus for a broader split. Since territory had not changed hands, Al-Shabaab remained a viable organization that faced a real security threat in the minds of its critical cadres and the constituent units they led. As such, nothing had decisively changed the twin pillars that sustained the cooperative equilibrium within Al-Shabaab. Robow, for his part, had little incentive to fragment or revise the organizational status quo, and Godane had little incentive punish his recalcitrant subordinate. One source, in describing the situation, argued that "though the group's various power brokers are in constant competition over power, resources, and the direction of the group, they also understand they need one another to maximize their strength." Yet maximizing strength was only a logical proposition if external threats were significant, and Al-Shabaab actually remained a viable military entity capable of protecting the interests of its various constituent units. And again, nothing that happened during the Ramadan Offensive changed this reality.[121]

---

[120] "A Week in the Horn," *Ethiopian Ministry of Foreign Affairs*, which can be found at www.aigaforum.com/news/A_Week_in_the_Horn_100810.htm (Accessed April 12, 2016). It is worth noting that Hansen's (2013, p. 103) landmark study of Al-Shabaab concurs with the Ethiopian view, noting, "The Ramadan offensive led to the most serious internal crisis in the history of the organization."

[121] "Somali Jihadist Groups Merge," *Stratfor*, December 22, 2010, which can be found at www.stratfor.com/analysis/somali-jihadist-groups-merge (Accessed April 12, 2016). This source continued, "Abu Mansur's (Robow) main problem is finances; Abu

What did decisively shift the cooperative equilibrium between Al-Shabaab's main factions were battlefield losses that, unlike the Ramadan Offensive, were also territorial in nature. In the summer of 2011, enabled by yet another increase in AMISOM troop levels, AMISOM and the TFG began to apply pressure to Al-Shabaab's position in Mogadishu. Beginning in February–March 2011, AMISOM troops, taking some of their worst casualties of the war, slowly occupied one neighborhood after the next, taking key junctions and compounds as they advanced. In May–June they began to strike Bakara Market, a key source of tax revenue for Al-Shabaab. By August 2011, Al-Shabaab announced its withdrawal from the Somali capital, and by October, AMISOM had occupied the suburb of Daynile, the militants' last remaining toehold in Mogadishu.

Al-Shabaab's collapse in the all-important Somali capital was just the beginning of its troubles. In October 2011, the Kenyan Defense Forces decided to intervene in the fight against Al-Shabaab, citing repeated cross-border provocations. Ahmed Madobe's militia was at the forefront of the Kenyan effort, with the unstated ambition of the Kenya–Madobe alliance being the establishment of an Ogaden clan buffer state centered in Kismayo that might guarantee Kenyan security.[122] By 2012, Ethiopia had formally joined the anti-Shabaab effort, and eventually, both the Kenyan and Ethiopian deployments would be rehatted as AMISOM forces. The results of the intervention by neighboring states were to be decisive, and in the first half of 2012, Badhaade, Afmadow, and Afgoye would fall to the anti-Shabaab alliance. The reality was that Al-Shabaab was now fighting a war on three distinct fronts: in the south, in the east along the Ethiopian border, and along the major corridors outside Mogadishu. According to a senior minister within the newly inaugurated Federal Government of Somalia (FGS) – the TFG's successor – the new military effort had placed Al-Shabaab on life support.[123]

Zubayr (Godane), in turn, has an interest in tapping [in]to Abu Mansur's manpower." That was the nature of the bargain between these two specific factions, but the existence of a real external threat, and organizational viability, is what made this partnership logical.

[122] For more on the Kenyan intervention and its implications, see Daniel Branch, "Why Kenya Invaded Somalia: The Opening of an Aggressive New Chapter," *Foreign Affairs*, November 15, 2011, which can be found at www.foreignaffairs.com/articles/africa/2011-11-15/why-kenya-invaded-somalia; and Anderson & McKnight (2014, 2015). There has been a lengthy debate on the rationale for Kenya's 2011 intervention. Kenya's desire to create an Ogaden clan buffer state run by Madobe was in large part driven by the fact that many of the most senior Somali officials within the Kenyan government at the time hailed from the Ogaden clan – for example, the defense minister Mohamed Yusuf Haji and the deputy speaker of the Kenyan Parliament, Farah Maalim. Author's interview, Somali community leader/elder from Wajir, Nairobi, Kenya, July 2012.

[123] Author's interview, senior FGS Minister and close confidant of Somali president Hassan Sheikh, January 2014, Mogadishu, Somalia. Interviewee said that because of these

But for the purposes of empirical clarity, it needs to be said that Al-Shabaab did not hang on the precipice of total defeat. Despite the prognostications of senior government ministers, Al-Shabaab's battlefield losses were not fatal, and as time wore on, it would prove its resilience. Moreover, although Al-Shabaab was losing territory, it retained the capacity to infiltrate behind enemy lines, and through asymmetric attacks, including on Villa Somalia and other key government installations in Mogadishu, wreak havoc.[124] The Kenyan offensive, for its part, was soon weighed down by poor weather, the heavy Al-Shabaab infiltration of allied Somali columns advancing alongside the Kenyan forces, and heavy contention over how power would be distributed between clans once Kismayo was retaken.[125]

This reality helps underscore the weakness of a key alternative argument: that factional infighting and fragmentation were about Al-Shabaab's absolute military position. Al-Shabaab's losses in Mogadishu were real, but it was far from defeated. But as would soon be clear, these battlefield shifts were enough to create the impression among the organization's constituent units that the insurgency was in serious jeopardy. It was for this reason that the cooperative equilibrium began to collapse.

The power struggle that ensued was played out over a number of issues. The withdrawal from Mogadishu occurred only after a serious attempt to preserve Al-Shabaab's position in the city, a fact that generated criticism from Aweys, Robow, and other moderates who thought the withdrawal had been needlessly delayed. A more pressing controversy was an emerging famine in many of the key food-producing regions that Al-Shabaab controlled. In the end, 260,000 people would perish in the crisis.[126] Godane's approach to the famine was much maligned, as he resisted providing NGOs full humanitarian access to affected communities. In November 2011, Al-Shabaab's Office for Supervising

---

recent dynamics, "I do not expect Al Shabaab to be around next year." To be clear, there was a transition process that led to the establishment of a new federal government, the FGS, that would replace the TFG.

[124] Mohammed Ibrahim and Nicholas Kulish, "Militants Attack Presidential Palace in Somalia," *New York Times*, February 21, 2014, which can be found at www.nytimes.com/2014/02/22/world/africa/somalia.html?_r=0 (Accessed April 25, 2016).

[125] Author's interview, AMISOM commander, January 2014, Mogadishu, Somalia. Commander acknowledged that the infiltration problem was so severe that in the latter stages of the push toward Kismayo, the Kenyans had to turn off communication radios, to prevent allied Somali soldiers passing on intelligence to Al-Shabaab that allowed the group to lay ambushes. Ken Menkhaus, "After the Kenyan Intervention in Somalia," *The Enough Project*, January 2012, which can be found at www.enoughproject.org/files/MenkhausKenyaninterventionSomalia.pdf (Accessed April 19, 2016).

[126] "Somalia famine 'killed 260,000 people,'" *BBC*, May 2, 2013, which can be found at www.bbc.com/news/world-africa-22380352 (Accessed April 19, 2016).

the Affairs of Foreign Agencies banned sixteen aid organizations operating in its territory.[127] Earlier bans and informal barriers to access had already made humanitarian access quite difficult. Tension no doubt increased when many moderate commanders hailing from affected areas ignored the edict, and chose to collaborate with NGOs in areas they controlled. For Godane and his supporters, this was a dangerous behavior, not least because the main concern regarding aid organizations was that they allowed for the infiltration of spies into Al-Shabaab-controlled zones and thus increased the vulnerability of the organization to aerial strikes.[128] In any case, it was exactly this kind of issue – famine and relief assistance – that could throw the locally rooted moderate factions into conflict with the hardliners that did not hail from south-central Somalia.

Godane's detractors called for a meeting of the Shura, which was the legal body through which grievances against the leadership could be aired. Yet the Emir avoided this, convening other, impromptu gatherings of the senior leadership to revise strategy and rally support. In February 2012, the split between Godane and the moderates widened further, when he declared that Al-Shabaab had formally joined Al-Qaeda. Although there had been a de facto partnership between the two organizations, many worried that a formal alliance would draw far more counterterrorism attention from the international community than Al-Shabaab could afford. The move angered Aweys, who was already targeted by US and UN counterterrorism sanctions, and had long been resistant to a close formal linkage with Al-Qaeda central. In March 2012 Aweys delivered a highly contentious sermon at the Ealash Biyaha mosque during which he criticized the decision to ally with Al-Qaeda, and questioned the notion that Al-Shabaab could be considered the sole spokesman of Somalia's Muslims.[129] These were charges that Aweys would repeat.

By 2013, the moderate's critique of Godane's centralizing authority had found broad appeal. As the rising tide of discontent diffused to other sections of the organization, it found expression among many actors who had not identified with moderates early on. Abdullahi Sheikh Ahmed, a former ICU official, confirms this view, and argues that while initial "back-to-back losses" had triggered factional infighting between hardliners and moderates, "As time passed, allegiances and interests

---

[127] "Somali group bans aid organizations," *Al Jazeera*, November 28, 2011, which can be found at www.aljazeera.com/news/africa/2011/11/20111128203817843905.html (Accessed April 20, 2016).
[128] Author's interview, ICRC Somalia official, July 2013, Nairobi, Kenya.
[129] "Somalia: Al-Shabaab – It Will Be a Long War," *International Crisis Group Report*, June 26, 2014, p. 10.

The Long War in Somalia 279

changed until Godane's more radical wing... considered the most solid group within Al Shabaab based on its connection with its parent organization, Al Qaeda, and its control over sources of funding and power, disintegrated."[130] A group led by Ibrahim al-Afghani, the Afghan veteran and a Godane mentor, who also hailed from the same clan as the Emir, was surprisingly sympathetic to the moderates and joined the growing anti-Godane coalition.

Foreign fighters, led by the particularly vocal Omar Hammami, also made calls for a meeting of the Shura that would likely challenge Godane's grip on the organization. Foreign fighters had a history of mediating between competing Somali factions within Al-Shabaab, and in part, this might explain why Hammami was sucked into the vortex of factional infighting. Yet there were other issues as well. Foreign fighters tended to be a dissatisfied population, as the romantic notions of jihad that had moved them to come to Somalia quickly ran up against the austere realities of insurgent life. The death of Fazul Mohammed – Al-Qaeda's top man in Al-Shabaab – in mysterious circumstances during fighting in Mogadishu in the summer of 2011 seemed to underscore Godane's widely held concerns over Godane increasing authoritarianism. Hammami would eventually go on an extended social media campaign criticizing Godane's leadership.

Events finally reached a head in April 2013, when the disparate group of dissidents issued an open letter to Al-Qaeda leader Ayman al-Zawahiri. Presumably authored by Afghani, the letter underscored the nature of the battlefield crisis Al-Shabaab faced: "Now, this is no time to wait or an occasion to be patient... We are walking in a dark tunnel and we do not know what is hiding for us in it, except for Allah the sovereign and wise."[131] To Afghani and company, recent territorial reversals were the sine qua non of the current battlefield trouble – much as this book has argued. On this point, they noted the following: "We have witnessed an obvious drawback in the achievements of the muhajideen. Ten states were under the rule of the movement four years ago, which came with the possession of huge human resources and the sympathy of our Muslim people."[132]

In response to the dissidents, Godane swung into action, armed with a fatwa from supporting religious scholars who declared that his opponents submit to the will of the leadership. Although this legal opinion

---

[130] "Somalia: Open Letter to Al-Qaeda Leader, Al-Zawahiri, Rocks Foundations of Al-Shabaab," *Somaliland Sun*, April 13, 2013, which can be found at www.somalilandsun.com/news-feeds/somalia/2660-somalia-open-letter-to-al-qaeda-leader-al-zawahiri-rocks-foundations-of-al-shabaab (Accessed April 22, 2016).
[131] Ibid.   [132] Ibid.

was highly contested, since a number of Al-Shabaab-aligned clerics had already sided with the dissidents, it was enough to rationalize what was to come. After regaining control of the Amniyat through a purge of its ranks, Godane used this branch to incredible effect. On June 22, 2013, in the Al-Shabaab base area in Barawe, Godane sent hit squads to kill Ibrahim al-Afghani and another senior leader, Maalim Burhan. Aweys and Robow, under threat of being murdered, hastily fled the port city by sea with their supporters, and eventually ended up in the hands of their fellow clansmen where they were afforded protection. Through an agreement brokered by Habr Gedir elders, Aweys would surrender to FGS authorities in Mogadishu, where he would be placed under house arrest. Hammami, who was already on the run after surviving an assassination attempt in April 2013, was eventually killed alongside fellow foreign fighter Osama al-Brittani Towfiq by Godane's operatives. Other key members of Hammami's supporting network, like the Egyptian commander Khattab al-Masri, were spared.

There was little doubt that most of those who defected from Al-Shabaab during the "Godane Coup" did so under threat of violence. Zakariya Ahmed Ismail Hersi, Al-Shabaab's head of military intelligence, and someone who had sided with the dissidents, made clear that his eventual fragmentation was a bid for survival, admitting that "when we failed to get an agreement with Godane and his inner circle, they started to silence all opposition" and that he had "abandoned Al Shabaab to save his own life."[133] Again, this is entirely consistent with this book's argument that fragmentation is a second-order effect of a serious military shock. Having been unable to prevail in their effort to challenge Godane and alter the cooperative status quo, Aweys, Robow, and their allies had little choice but to abandon ship.

In the end, Al-Shabaab would stabilize its internal situation under Godane's leadership. It was given significant reprieve by the failure of the newly inaugurated FGS under President Hassan Sheikh to reconcile Somalia's disparate clans and rebuild the Somali state. Things seemed to turn somewhat in the fall of 2014, when Godane was killed by an American airstrike and Al-Shabaab relinquished its base area in Barawe. Yet Al-Shabaab would move to the rural hinterland, from which it has continued to strike isolated AMISOM garrisons in different parts of south-central Somalia and wreak havoc in the country's urban areas. It remains a potent insurgent organization.

[133] Andrew Harding, "Somali defector: Why I Left al-Shabaab," *BBC News*, May 20, 2015, which can be found at www.bbc.com/news/world-africa-32791713 (Accessed April 23, 2016).

Conclusion

This chapter has provided compelling confirmation of the main claims developed in previous chapters. Across time, it is clear that the fragmentation of the SNM, ICU, and Al-Shabaab was precipitated by battlefield gains and losses, measured in terms of territory. These facts are clear from an analysis of the SNM's splits in 1987 and 1991–92, the ICU's fragmentation in the summer and winter of 2006, and Al-Shabaab's Madobe split and Godane coup. Moreover, key corollary arguments find support. Processes of diffusion were often critical to the manner in which factionalism and fragmentation unfolded, and fragmentation was the by-product of factional struggles in which the losers exited in a bid for survival. The next chapter summarizes the book's main findings and points to the way forward in terms of future research.

7 Concluding Thoughts

This project began with the goal of understanding why, and under what circumstances, rebel organizations fragment. Data I collected on patterns of fragmentation across postcolonial African rebel organizations found that rebel fragmentation was common, and had occurred at least once within nearly one-third of all organizations. The sheer prevalence of the phenomenon, in addition to the theoretical and practical importance of the question – as outlined in Chapter 1 – helped motivate and frame this study.

Chapter 2 made a set of theoretical arguments, which began with the assumption that in civil wars, survival concerns are paramount. Cooperation within rebel organizations is tied to acute perceptions of external threats, and a belief in organizational viability. But territorial gains erode cooperation by driving preference divergence within rebel organizations. Similarly, territorial loss undermines the credible commitments that underpin organization cohesion and solidarity. Both scenarios produce factional infighting, and on many occasions, fragmentation. Somewhat counterintuitively, territorial stalemates promote organizational cohesion, a phenomenon I call "cohesive stalemates." The chapter then introduces an empirical testing strategy, and employs original data from Ethiopia's civil wars to draw broad statistical relationships between the variables of interest.

The chapter also introduces two important corollary arguments that are more clearly supported in the following historical analysis. First, rebel fragmentation is the result of factional struggles in which the losers of these struggles are forced to "exit," in a bid for survival. Second, factional struggles are often characterized by a process of diffusion, in which actors not party to the original dispute are mobilized. This often means that fragmentation involves several of a rebel organization's constituent units exiting in close sequence.

Chapters 3, 4, and 5 seek to evaluate the plausibility of my core argument against histories of several rebel organizations. Chapters 3 and 4 go into particular depth, and involve a careful analysis of alternative arguments. The cases employed in Chapter 5 are designed as "shadow cases."

Chapter 6 seeks to probe the external validity of the core argument about territorial gains and losses, by analyzing the evolution of three of the most prominent insurgent participants in the Somali civil war: the SNM, the ICU, and Al-Shabaab. This chapter, like those that preceded it, is based on substantial original research.

Linking Theory and Practice: A Counterinsurgent's Perspective

Yet what is the real contribution of the argument, in practical terms? Even if the theory advanced in this study is true, what are the policy implications? I would argue that the policy implications depend, in part, on a proper recognition of the intellectual stakes of my argument. To be clear, this book has argued that battlefield gains, losses, and stalemate – conceived of in terms of territory – shape the dynamics of factionalism and fragmentation within rebel organizations. But this book's claim about territorial gains and losses is that they are a necessary, but not sufficient, condition for rebel fragmentation. This is best depicted by the two-by-two matrix displayed in Chapter 2, where I find that across the Ethiopian civil war (between the years 1960 and 2008), there were seventy-six cases of territorial gains and losses that did not result in fragmentation (indeed, as noted before, rebel victory would be virtually impossible if every battlefield success led to fragmentation). These cases of fragmentation that "did not happen," despite seemingly fortuitous circumstances, underscore that rebel fragmentation is jointly produced. This fact is likely clear from the preceding case studies, where it is obvious that a range of factors intersected with, and reinforced, the fragmentary effects of a shifting battlefield context.

On one level, the contingent nature of the causal relationship at the heart of this book can spark an important research program that links battlefield shifts and a range of organizational and environmental variables, to rebel fragmentation. In this way, the argument of this book complements, rather than refutes, existing theories of rebel infighting and organizational fragmentation. For instance, work by Staniland (2014) and Weinstein (2007), in combination with this book, might suggest how the founding social and resource bases of rebel organizations can make some organizations more or less susceptible to the fragmentary effects of battlefield shocks. It might be possible that the rapid incorporation of new recruits similarly structures the effects of territorial gains and losses. Older or more organizationally centralized rebel groups might have a comparative advantage in managing the political fallout of territorial gains and losses.

For policymakers, this means that it is important not to interpret the findings of this book in a linear way. For counterinsurgents who seek to divide rebel organizations in order to gain military and political advantages, it might be tempting to view my argument as a simple endorsement of applying military pressure or a strategy of temporary withdrawal. For instance, while much of the extant policy discourse on US counterinsurgency operations in Afghanistan implies that the primary way to separate the "reconcilable" or "persuadable" members of the Afghan Taliban from more hardline Al-Qaeda-affiliated members is by applying military pressure, it would seem an equally effective strategy to allow insurgents a modicum of success. Indeed, the counterintuitive result that battlefield success can sow the seeds of discord within rebel organizations seems to provide the outlines of a relatively cheap way for counterinsurgents to divide their opponents.

Moreover, since my theory is about "gains" and "losses," rather than where a rebel organization sits in absolute terms, one could argue that it need not be the case that counterinsurgents concede so much on the battlefield that should their opponent fail to fragment, counterinsurgents consign themselves to defeat. Since fragmentation can occur anywhere along a continuum from complete victory to complete failure, counterinsurgents can yield what are in a strategic sense relatively modest territorial victories, in recognition that these victories may fragment their opponents, but not yield a decisive and unfavorable shift in the balance of power.

For instance, coalition forces in Afghanistan could cede portions of southeastern Afghanistan to Taliban forces in order to incite internal unrest within what is an admittedly diverse organization. Coalition forces could retain territorial control over the rest of the country, and the capacity for counterattack. Once preference divergence begins to drive a breakdown of cooperation within the Taliban, coalition forces can exploit these fissures militarily or politically. If cooperation breakdown and factional infighting does not occur, coalition forces can swiftly recover.

Yet this would be too simplistic a reading of what this book has argued. What this book instead suggests is that tactics of military pressure of strategic withdrawal can be a starting point for counterinsurgents, but not the totality of a strategy of rebel fragmentation. Rebel fragmentation depends on a number of forces, among which the battlefield context is key. As such, strategies of military pressure and withdrawal must be complemented by other efforts to encourage fragmentation. Here, the range of possible complementing strategies is vast – amnesties, patronage offers, political concessions, decapitation efforts, etc.

Lessons for Mediators and Peace Negotiators: Holding Rebels Together

The link between territorial stalemate and organizational solidarity – what I have called "cohesive stalemates" – also provides some useful policy guidance for those who are involved in mediating or negotiating the end of civil wars. In such settings, as pointed out by the literature on spoilers (Stedman, 1997) and civil war duration/veto players (D. Cunningham, 2006), the fragmentation of rebel organizations can be an obstacle to comprehensive and sustainable peace agreements.

My theory suggests that those who seek to ensure that a rebel organization does not fragment in the context of peace negotiations should take careful stock of the conditions that give way to the peace talks. Where peace talks emerge out of territorial stalemate, we can expect those talks to be characterized by unity within the rebel camp. When talks follow serious gains and losses, they will witness the fragmentation of rebel participants. This is not because of incentives produced by the talks themselves, I would argue, but because the talks are directly preceded by events that have triggered factional infighting and fragmentation.

Moreover, my theory suggests that during peace talks, well-maintained cease-fires should be actively pursued, lest territorial shifts rupture the internal coherence of participating rebel organizations. Without stability and stalemate on the battlefield, success at the negotiating table is a difficult proposition.

This research also suggests some interesting modifications to I. William Zartman's famous theory about "hurting stalemates." In Zartman's view, the success of peace negotiations largely hinges on seizing a moment in which the existing conflict is "ripe" for resolution. "Ripeness" tends to occur, Zartman argues, when a "mutually hurting stalemate" obtains. Such stalemates signal to participants in war that unilateral means of achieving their objectives are unlikely to yield results, and that a continuation of conflict will produce painful costs. Peace negotiations work, Zartman claims, when the dynamics of war provide unique incentives for contending parties to resolve their differences (Zartman, 1989).

While this study agrees with Zartman's view that military stalemates may be the most auspicious circumstances under which to hold peace negotiations, it disagrees on the mechanisms. Stalemate increases the success rate of peace negotiations not because competing sides believe they can no longer win and the costs of continued conflict are prohibitively high, but because stalemates reduce the likelihood that negotiations will yield spoilers that will sink the process. Stalemates ensure that rebel organizations remain coherent and united while at the bargaining table – and that simple fact is crucial to understanding the outcomes of peace processes.

It should be also said that for those interested more generally in maintaining the internal coherence of rebel organizations outside the context of peace processes – whether it be external patrons or rebels themselves – this book suggests that addressing potentially divisive internal disputes are best left for periods of territorial stalemate. Divisive party congresses, negotiations on the internal distribution of power, and the selection of new leaders could lead to full-fledged factional infighting and fragmentation if they occur in the context of serious battlefield gains or losses. This means that those that seek to hold rebel organizations together must carefully think about the issue of timing when navigating contentious internal fissures.

The Primacy of Territory

This study is also important in that it highlights the importance of territory in the calculation of rebels in resource-poor environments. If the objective is to trigger factional infighting and fragmentation within rebel organizations, it is vital that counterinsurgents focus on the dynamics of territorial control, rather than other aspects of military power. While men and material no doubt affect the likelihood of losing or gaining territory, this project finds that their independent effects on rebel fragmentation is quite limited. Cutting off external military aid to a rebel organization or limiting recruitment flows, counterinsurgents must recognize, will not sow the seeds of internal discord within rebel organization. Rather, such shocks must be translated into battlefield outcomes like territorial exchange.

In making such claims, this book has the potential to open up new debates about how we should conceive of military power and success and failure in contemporary civil wars. Ultimately, I have argued that we must think about these concepts in context-specific terms. I leave it to other research programs to help clarify relevant contextual distinctions across civil wars, and theorize the markers of military success and failure in these diverse settings.

Avenues for Further Research

The study suggests a number of interesting avenues for future research, many of which stem from this book's limitations.

First, by employing a more nuanced measure of territorial gains and losses, the argument can be further refined. As currently conceptualized, any shift in the total number of districts a rebel organization operates over constitutes a gain or loss. But this is a blunt measure, and it is likely that differentiating between the sizes of gains and losses may produce more interesting insights. For instance, prospect theory suggests that individual decision makers weigh losses more than gains of equal size. Thus, more fine-grained data would allow us to evaluate whether losses, all things equal, are more likely to produce fragmentation than gains – a fact that could have important, and very different policy lessons than those advanced in this conclusion.

Second, as suggested earlier, because territorial gains and losses are argued to be necessary, but not sufficient, conditions for rebel fragmentation, much work is needed to identify other factors that interact with the variables I have identified in producing the outcome of interest. In particular, this study ignores more static organizational characteristics while privileging the dynamics of war. Yet intuitively, organization matters, and the neglect of organizational characteristics should be rectified. Moreover, a focus on the different characteristics and tendencies of rebel organizations may help to explain cross-sectional differences in fragmentation that this study cannot.

Third, a more thorough evaluation of causal mechanisms is required. While there is a clear link between territorial exchange and fragmentation, the mechanisms remain hard to pin down and test directly. While the balance of evidence suggests that credible commitments and preference divergence are the avenues through which rebel fragmentation occurs, future research should more directly evaluate alternative causal processes that link the variables I have identified to rebel factionalism and fragmentation.

Fourth, it would be interesting to examine the extent to which the arguments I have proposed in this study have broader applicability in the study of political organizations. What can the theory of gains and losses tell us about factionalism and fragmentation in political parties, social movement organizations, unions, corporations, and formal militaries? In what ways could the findings of this study modify existing analyses of this diverse array of organizations? Can the argument travel to contexts not characterized by a deep amount of physical insecurity?

Finally, the book's major corollary arguments suggest that while factional infighting is a phenomenon we can predict with some certainty, its translation into full-fledged organizational fragmentation, and the breadth of that fragmentation, remains a more muddled picture. Readers will recall that factionalism *often* results in fragmentation, but only when certain factions fail in their bid to alter the cooperative status quo within their organizations, survive that failed bid, and exit the organization in an attempt to survive the inevitable repercussions. Moreover, the diffusive nature of factional infighting within rebel organizations can *often* draw in factions and networks that had little to do with the initial factional cataclysm, and eventually lead to the fragmentation of the organization along multiple dimensions.

Future work needs to more effectively explain the circumstances under which failed challengers to the cooperative status quo survive their failed bid and are able to fragment. Invariably, some will be eliminated or neutralized long before they have been able to fragment. In addition, we need a firmer understanding of when factional infighting diffuses within rebel ranks, since, as several cases studies have illustrated, diffusion is not an intrinsic property of all factional moments.

These avenues and gaps suggest that the potential for expanding the scope of my argument is vast.

Appendix: Narrative of Fieldwork and Description of Data Sources

Interviews

Beyond its use of rich secondary sources, this book relied on a range of primary sources. The interview sources include the following:

Data drawn from roughly 125 structured and unstructured interviews and conversations conducted in the following locations: Ethiopia, Somaliland, Puntland, south-central Somalia (Mogadishu), Kenya, Sudan, North America, and Europe, between 2009 and 2016. The majority of these interviewees were interviewed individually, and on a single occasion. Roughly one-fourth of the interviews were audio recorded with the interviewee's agreement and remain in the author's possession. Interviews were conducted in English, Tigrinya, Amharic, and Somali. Translators assisted in the conduct of interviews conducted in Somali and some of those conducted in Amharic. The interviewees came from a variety of backgrounds: rebels (both at the leadership and rank-and-file level), government officials from the civilian and military sector, aid workers, journalists, academic experts, informed citizens, and foreign diplomats. Most were selected because they could shed some light on particular moments of rebel fragmentation and/or the evolving battlefield situation. In a number of cases, interviewees were selected to provide input on entirely different research questions, but would prove to be of value to this book's subject matter. A few interviews/conversations were impromptu and occurred by chance encounter. Like all research with human subjects, interviewees varied in their ability to provide useful and credible information.

Owing to Internal Review Board (IRB) restrictions and a good deal of common sense, the identities of interviewees are treated as confidential. Both Eritrea and Ethiopia remain authoritarian political contexts, and many of the organizations, personalities, and events discussed in this book are of continuing political relevance. South-central Somalia, for its part, remains mired in violent conflict, and thus much of the "history" recounted about this conflict in this book is quite central to the contemporary political milieu. For these reasons, disclosing the identities of interviewees might expose them to retaliation and other adverse consequences. Indeed, at the time of this writing, one of my informants had been assassinated in south-central Somalia, albeit for reasons that had nothing to do with this book. It is doubtful I could have secured many candid interviews had I been unable to guarantee the anonymity of interviewees.

Thus, in citing interviews, I provide a short description of the interviewee to signal why they are relevant to the topic at hand, the date of the interview, and the location. In the interviews relevant to Eritrea and Ethiopia, I exclude the location of the interview, since in a number of instances that might make the interviewee readily identifiable.

The exceptions to the protocols described previously are many of the interviewees relevant to the SNM. Much of that research (although not all) was conducted in my capacity as a PhD affiliate for Innovations for Successful Societies (ISS) in October–November 2010, with the support of my colleague Richard Bennet. Since participants in ISS research are usually not anonymous, I can be more flexible in identifying these interviewees. In any case, Somaliland is a functioning democracy at peace, and as such, it is unlikely that any of the material cited in this book could adversely affect the safety and security of any particular interviewee. The relevant interviewees from Somaliland are the following:

(Positions are not current in many cases, but are meant to convey some of the significance of the interviewee to project)

Abdillahi Darawal – Senior SNM commander

Abdillahi Sheikh Hassan – Member of Somaliland's House of Elders (Guurti), chairman of International Relations Subcommittee

Abdulqadir Jirde – Deputy Speaker of House of Representatives

Abdulrahman Yusuf Artan – Member of Somaliland's Parliament; officer at Somaliland's Academy for Peace and Development

Dr. Adan Yusuf Abakor – Hargeisa Group member; Somaliland Representative – Progressio; noted scholar of Somaliland

Ahmed Haji Adami – Somaliland's Minister of Defense; first chairman of National Election Commission

Bobe Yusuf – SNM Central Committee member; Somaliland's Minister of Information

Haroon Ahmed Yusuf – Officer with Action Aid in Somaliland, working on peacebuilding issues

Hassan Isse Jama – SNM vice-chairman

> Hussein Bulhan – President, Hargeisa University; cofounder and executive director, Somaliland's Academy for Peace and Development; noted scholar of Somaliland; led Peace Committee designed to mediate between Somaliland's major armed factions in the 1990s
> Mohamed Hashi Elmi – SNM founder and Central Committee member; Somaliland Minister of Finance; mayor of Hargeisa
> Wife of Mohamed Hashi Elmi – SNM member; prominent civil society figure
> Shukri Ismail – Civil society leader; served on Somaliland's first National Election Commission
> Suad Ibrahim Abdi – Civil society activist; researcher with Somalin
> Ulf Terlinden – Noted scholar of Somaliland; worked for a number of international NGOs operating in Somaliland; EU representative in Somaliland
> Mohamed Fadal – Somaliland's Minister of Planning; director of Social Development Institute in Somaliland and coordinator for the Independent Scholars Group; lead researcher at Somaliland's Academy for Peace and Development; noted scholar of Somaliland
> Sultan Umar – Traditional elder and *Sultan* from Arab-Isaaq clan; father was one of the more prominent sultans to join SNM in its early days
> Edna Adan Ismail – Somaliland's Minister of Foreign Affairs; Somaliland's Minister of Family Welfare and Social Development; First Lady of Somalia; First Lady of Somaliland

Archives

This book used three main archives:
>The UK National Archives – London, England
>The US National Archives – College Park, MD, United States
>Institute of Ethiopian Studies, Addis Ababa, Ethiopia

In addition, I used 122 interviews with senior leaders of Jebha, Shaebia, and several Ethiopian rebel organizations, conducted by Gunter Schroeder in the 1970s, 1980s, and 1990s. Schroeder is a German journalist/analyst who traveled to the Horn beginning in the 1970s, and established a rapport with the Eritrean insurgents. He remains a balanced and astute observer of Eritrean history and current affairs. These interviews were provided to the author directly by Schroeder himself, although it is the author's understanding that transcripts of these interviews are also available at the Research and Documentation Centre in Asmara, Eritrea.

Aside from these sources, an array of primary documents were secured from Eritrea-related websites, and several private sources.

Sampling of Archival Material Used in Assessing Territorial Shifts in Ethiopia and Eritrea (From US National Archives)

US National Archives

Airgram 174, Asmara to State, October 9, 1968, RG 59, Central Files, "The ELF and Kagnew: An Assessment."

In physical terms, the IEG was menaced with sabotage and ambushes in mid-1967, in the key population center, the Christian Highlands around Asmara, and losing control over the countryside of the Western Moslem Lowlands. Today, both key areas are secure from all but the most sporadic and unorganized ELF [Jebha] activity. Most ELF strength seems to have been pushed back into the unpopulated Northwest corner bounded by the Red Sea and Sudan. Terrain gives the ELF effective camouflage, however, and small pockets of rebels can hide out in a number of parts of the province without discovery.

Telegram, Asmara to State, March 20, 1970, RG 59, Central Files, "Large Scale Confrontation between IEG forces and ELF North of Keren."

After a 52 week lull in ELF [Jebha] activity around Keren, IEG launched full scale joint Army/Commando police offensive in area north of Keren. ELF forces which apparently run out of Danakil by defection of major part of Danakil tribes to IEG, now locked in combat 32 kilometers north of Keren with Second Division and Commando polict units. Second engagement 60 kilometers northwest of Keren beyond Hal Hal also in progress. There are reported to be about 300 government troops involved in first engagement which measure size of campaign. Government forces suffered 3 killed, 15 injured. ELF reported to have suffered 'many' casualties. Normal pattern followed by government troops of returning corpses of slain ELF to Kere for public display not being followed in this instance because of new tactics being employed by IEG forces. Whereas government forces previously travelled by truck to and from battle area, they now leave army and policy vehicles 10 kilometers north of Keren under guard and then proceed into battle area on foot in order to avoid ELF ambushes of truck convoys. Therefore, not practicable to transport slain ELF back to Keren...

After a year of relative quiet, Keren reportedly has now returned to its "normal state of instability." Wednesday night March 18, trigger happy Second Division troops in Keren opened fire on small ELF infiltrator group which drew return fire from Commando policy patrol, setting off 30 minute-long battle between Second Division and Commando police during which Second Division unlimbered their 50 calibtre machine guns. Meanwhile, ELF infiltrators slipped away.

List of Eritrea's Districts (City of Asmara Counted as One District Instead of Four)

Adi Keih
Adi Qwala
Adi Teklezan
Adobha
Af'abet
Akurdet City
Are'eta
Areza
Asmara
Asmat
Assab City
Barentu City
Berikh
Central Southern Red Sea
Dahlak
Dbarwa
Dekemhare
Dghe
Elabered
Emni Haili
Foro
Forto
Ghala NefhGhela'elo
Gheleb
Ghinda'e
Gogne
Goluj
Habero
Hagaz
Halhal
Hamelmalo
Haykota
Karora
Keren City
Kerkebet
Logo Anseba
Mai-Aini
Mai-Mne
Massawa

Mendefera
Mogolo
Molqi
Nakfa
Segeneiti
Sel'a
Sen'afe
Serejaka
Shambuko
She'eb
South Southern Red Sea
Tesseney
Tserona
Upper Gash

References

Abbink, J. (1999). The Total Somali Clan Genealogy: A Preliminary Sketch. Leiden-ASC Working Paper, 1–23.

Abdullahi, A. M. (2007). The Ogaden National Liberation Front: The Dilemma of Its Struggle in Ethiopia. *Review of African Political Economy*, 34(113), 556–562.

Abdullahi, A. M. (2011). *The Islamic Movement in Somalia: A Historical Evolution with a Case Study of the Islah Movement*. Montreal: PhD Thesis, McGill University.

Ahmad, A. (2015). The Security Bazaar: Business Interests and Islamist Power in Civil War Somalia. *International Security*, 39(3), 89–117.

Anderson, D., & McKnight, J. (2014). Kenya at War: Al-Shabaab and Its Enemies in the Horn of Africa. *African Affairs*, 114(454), 1–27.

Anderson, D., & McKnight, J. (2015). Understanding Al-Shabaab: Clan, Islam, and Insurgency in Kenya. *Journal of Eastern African Studies*, 9(3), 536–557.

Asrat, G. (2007). Towards a Sustainable Peace between Eritrea and Ethiopa. In L. Lata, *The Search for Peace: The Conflict between Eritrea and Ethiopia* (pp. 53–60). Oslo: Allkopi As.

Ayele, F. (2014). *The Ethiopian Army: From Victory to Collapse, 1977–1991*. Evanston, IL: Northwestern University Press.

Balcells, L., & Justino, P. (2014). Bridging Micro and Macro Approaches on Civil Wars and Political Violence: Issues, Challenges, and the Way Forward. *Journal of Conflict Resolution*, 58(8), 1343–1359.

Balthasar, D. (2013). Somaliland's Best-Kept Secret: Shrewd Politics and War Projects as a Means of State Making. *Journal of East African Studies*, 7(2), 218–238.

Barnes, C., & Hassan, H. (2007). The Rise and Fall of Mogadishu's Islamic Courts. *Journal of Eastern African Studies*, 1(2), 151–160.

Barrera, G. (2003). The Construction of Racial Hierarchies in Eritrea. In Patrizia Palumbo (ed.), *A Place in the Sun: Africa in Italian Colonial Culture from Post-Unification to the Present*. Berkeley, CA: University of California Press.

Baumgartner, F., & Jones, B. (1993). *Agendas and Instability in American Politics*. Chicago, IL: University of Chicago Press.

Bayart, J. F. (1993). *The State in Africa: The Politics of the Belly*. New York, NY: Longman.

Bennet, R., & Woldemariam, M. (2011). Navigating a Broken Transition to Civilian Rule: Somaliland, 1991–2001. Princeton ISS Case Studies, 1–11.

Berhe, A. (2004). The Origins of the Tigray People's Liberation Front. *African Affairs*, 103(413), 569–592.

Berhe, A. (2009). *A Political History of the Tigray People's Liberation Front: Revolt, Ideology, and Mobilization in Ethiopia.* Los Angeles, CA: Tsehaye Publishers.

Bernal, V. (2014). *Nation as Network: Diaspora, Cyberspace, and Citizenship.* Chicago, IL: University of Chicago Press.

Biddle, S. (2004). *Military Power: Explaining Victory and Defeat in Modern Battle.* Princeton, NJ: Princeton University Press.

Blattman, C., & Miguel, E. (2010). Civil War. *Journal of Economic Literature*, 48(1), 3–57.

Bradbury, M. (2008). *Becoming Somaliland*. Bloomington, IN: Indiana University Press.

Bryden. M. (2003). No Quick Fixes: Coming to Terms with Terrorism, Islam, and Statelessness in Somalia. *The Journal of Conflict Studies*, XXIII(2), 24–56.

Christia, F. (2008). *Closest of Enemies: Alliance Formation in the Afghan and Bosnian Civil Wars.* Cambridge, MA: PhD thesis, Harvard University.

Christia, F. (2012). *Alliance Formation in Civil Wars.* Cambridge: Cambridge University Press.

Christman, H., ed. (1987). *Essential Works of Lenin: "What Is to Be Done" and Other Writings.* New York, NY: Dover Publications.

Clapham, C. (1990). *Transformation and Continuity in Revolutionary Ethiopia.* Cambridge: Cambridge University Press.

Clapham, C. (1996). *Africa and the International System: The Politics of State Survival.* Cambridge: Cambridge University Press.

Clapham, C. (1998). *African Guerrillas.* Oxford: James Currey.

Clauswitz, K. V. (1968). *On War.* London: Penguin Books.

Cohen, N. & Arieli, T. (2011). Field Research in Conflict Environments: Methodological Challenges and Snowball Sampling. *Journal of Peace Research*, 48(4), 423–435.

Collier, P., & Hoeffler, A. (2004). Greed and Grievance in Civil War. *Oxford Economic Papers*, 563–595.

Connell, D. (1993). *Against All Odds: A Chronicle of the Eritrean Revolution.* Trenton, NJ: Red Sea Press.

Connell, D. (2005). *Conversations with Eritrean Political Prisoners.* Trenton, NJ: Red Sea Press.

Crenshaw, M. (1981). The Causes of Terrorism. *Comparative Politics*, 13(4), 379–399.

Cronin, A. K. (2009). *How Terrorism Ends: Understanding the Decline and Demise of Terrorist Campaigns.* Princeton, NJ: Princeton University Press.

Cunningham, D. (2006). Veto Players and Civil War Duration. *American Journal of Political Science*, 50(4), 875–892.

Cunningham, D. (2011). *Barriers to Peace in Civil War.* Cambridge: Cambridge University Press.

Cunningham, K. G. (2011). Divide and Conquer or Divide and Concede: How Do States Respond to Internally Divided Separatists? *American Political Science Review*, 105(2), 275–297.

Cunningham, K. G. (2013). Actor Fragmentation and Civil War Bargaining: How Internal Divisions Generate Civil Conflict. *American Journal of Political Science*, 57(3), 659–672.

Cunningham, K. G. (2014). *Inside the Politics of Self-Determination*. Oxford: Oxford University Press.

Cunningham, K. G., Bakke, K. & Seymour, L. (2012). A Plague of Initials: Fragmentation, Cohesion and Infighting in Civil Wars. *Perspective on Politics*, 10(2), 265–283.

Cunningham, K. G., Bakke, K. & Seymour, L. (2016). E pluribus unum, exo uno plures: Competition, Violence, and Fragmentation in Ethnopolitical Movements. *Journal of Peace Research*, 53(1), 3–18.

Cunningham, K. G., & Pearlman, W. (2012). Nonstate Actors, Fragmentation, and Conflict Processes: Introducing the Special Issue. *Journal of Conflict Resolution*, 56(1), 3–15.

Cyert, R., & March, J. (1963). *A Behavioral Theory of the Firm*. Englewood Cliffs, NJ: Prentice-Hall.

Daly, S. Z. (2016). *Organized Violence after Civil War: The Geography of Recruitment in Latin America*. Cambridge: Cambridge University Press.

David, S. R. (1991). Explaining Third World Alignment. *World Politics*, 43(2), 233–256.

de Waal, A. (1991). Evil Days: Thirty Years of War and Famine in Ethiopia. New York, NY: Human Rights Watch.

de Waal, A. (Ed.) (2007). *War in Darfur and the Search for Peace*. Cambridge: Global Equity Initiative, Harvard University.

Dirar, U. C. (2007). Colonialism and the Construction of National Identities: The Case of Eritrea. *Journal of Eastern African Studies*, 1(2), 256–276.

Dorman, S. R. (2006). Post-Liberation Politics in Africa: Examining the Political Legacy of Struggle. *Third World Quarterly*, 27(6), 1085–1101.

Eckstein, H. (1975). Case Study and Theory in Political Science. In F. Greenstein & N. Polsby (eds.), *Handbook of Political Science* (pp. 79–137). Reading, MA: Addison-Wesley.

Erlich, H. (1983). *The Struggle over Eritrea, 1962–1978*. Stanford, CA: Hoover Press.

Findley, M., & Young, J. (2012). More Combatant Groups, More Terror? Empirical Tests of an Outbidding Logic. *Terrorism and Political Violence*, 24(5), 706–721.

Flint, J. & de Waal, A. (2008). *A New History of a Long War*. London: Zed Books.

Galula, D. (1964). *Counter-Insurgency Warfare: Theory and Practice*. New York, NY: Fredrick Praeger.

Gates, S. (2002). Recruitment and Allegiance: The Microfoundations of Rebellion. *Journal of Conflict Resolution*, 46(1), 111–130.

Gebremedhin, J. (1989). *Peasants and Nationalism in Eritrea: A Critique of Ethiopian Studies*. Trenton, NJ: Red Sea Press.

Gebreselassie, S. (2014). *The Ethiopian People's Revolutionary Party: Between a Rock and a Hard Place, 1975–2008*. Trenton, NJ: Red Sea Press.

George, A., & Bennett, A. (2005). *Case Studies and Theory Development in the Social Sciences*. Cambridge: Cambridge University Press.

Gerring, J. (2001). *Social Science Methodology: A Unified Framework*. Cambridge: Cambridge University Press.

Gersick, C. (1991). Revolutionary Change Theories: A Multilevel Exploration of the Punctuated Equilibrium Paradigm. *Academy of Management Review*, 16(1), 10–36.

Gilkes, P. (1989). Somalia: Conflicts Within and Against the Military Regime. *Review of African Political Economy*, 16(44), 55–58.

Gilkes, P. (2003). National Identity and Historical Mythology in Eritrea and Somaliland. *Northeast African Studies*, 10(3), 163–187.

Gill, P. (2010). *Famine and Foreigners: Ethiopia since Live Aid*. Oxford: Oxford University Press.

Gleditsch, N. P., Wallensteen, P., Eriksson, M., Sollenberg, M., & Strand, H. (2002). Armed Conflict 1946–2001: A New Dataset. *Journal of Peace Research*, 39(5), 615–637.

Goldthorpe, J. (1991). The Uses of History in Sociology: Reflections on Some Recent Tendencies. *The British Journal of Sociology*, 42(2), 211–230.

Goodwin, J. (2001). *No Other Way Out: States and Revolutionary Movements, 1945–1991*. Cambridge: Cambridge University Press.

Gott, R. (1996). Che Guevara and the Congo. *New Left Review*, I/220, 3–35.

Guevara, C. (1961). *Guerrilla Warfare*. New York, NY: Monthly Review Press.

Habteselassie, B. (1980). *Conflict and Intervention in the Horn of Africa*. New York, NY: Monthly Review Press.

Habteselassie, B. (1989). *Eritrea and the United Nations and Other Essays*. Trenton, NJ: Red Sea Press.

Hagmann, T. (2005). Beyond Clannishness and Colonialism: Understanding Political Disorder in Ethiopia's Somali Region, 1991–2004. *Journal of Modern African Studies*, 43(4), 509–536.

Hagmann, T. (2014). *Talking Peace in the Ogaden: The Search for an End to Conflict in the Somali Regional State of Ethiopia*. London: Rift Valley Institute.

Hansen, S. (2013). *Al-Shabaab in Somalia: The History and Ideology of a Militant Islamist Group*. Oxford: Oxford University Press.

Harbom, L., Melander, E., & Wallensteen, P. (2008). Dyadic Dimensions of Armed Conflict: 1946–2007. *Journal of Peace Research*, 45(5), 697–710.

Harrison, M., & John, M. (1978). Dynamics of Dissenting Movements within Established Organizations: Two Cases and a Theoretical Interpretation. *Journal for the Scientific Study of Religion*, 17(3), 207–224.

Hassen, M. (1990). *The Oromo of Ethiopia: A History, 1570–1860*. Cambridge: Cambridge University Press.

Hepner, T. R. (2011). *Soldiers, Martyrs, Traitors, and Exiles: Political Conflict in Eritrea and the Diaspora*. Philadelphia, PA: University of Pennsylvania Press.

Herbst, J. (2000). *States and Power in Africa: Comparative Lessons in Authority and Control*. Princeton, NJ: Princeton University Press.

Hess. R. (1964). The 'Mad Mullah' and Northern Somalia. *Journal of African History*, 5(3), 415–433.
Hirschman, A. (1970). *Exit, Voice, and Loyalty: Responses to Decline in Firms, Organizations, and States*. Cambridge: Harvard University Press.
Hobbes, T. (1981). *Leviathan*. London: Penguin Classics.
Horowitz, D. (1987). *Ethnic Groups in Conflict*. Berkeley, CA: University of California Press.
Huang, J. (2006). *Factionalism in Chinese Communist Politics*. Cambridge: Cambridge University Press.
Huang, R. (2016). *The Wartime Origins of Democratization: Civil War, Rebel Governance, and Political Regimes*. Cambridge: Cambridge University Press.
Humphrey, M., & Weinstein, J. (2006). Handling and Manhandling Civilians in Civil War. *American Political Science Review*, 100(3), 429–447.
Iyob, R. (1995). *The Eritrean Struggle for Independence: Domination, Resistance, Nationalism 1941–1993*. Cambridge: Cambridge University Press.
Jalata, A. (2005). *Oromia and Ethiopia: State Formation and Ethnonational Conflict*. Trenton, NJ: Red Sea Press.
Jardine, D. (1923). *The Mad Mullah of Somaliland*. London: Herbert Jenkins.
Jervis, R. (1976). *Perception and Misperception in International Politics*. Princeton, NJ: Princeton University Press.
Jervis, R. (2004). The Implications of Prospect Theory for Human Nature and Values. *Political Psychology*, 25(2), 163–176.
Johnson, D. (2003). *The Root Causes of Sudan's Civil Wars*. Oxford: James Currey.
Johnston, P. (2008). The Geography of Insurgent Organization and Its Consequences for Civil Wars: Evidence from Liberia and Sierra Leone. *Security Studies*, 17(1), 107–137.
Johnston, P. (2012). Does Decapitation Work?: Assessing the Effectiveness of Leadership Targeting in Counterinsurgency Campaigns. *International Security*, 36(4), 47–79.
Jonas, Raymond. (2011). *Adwa: African Victory in the Age of Empire*. Cambridge, MA: Belknap Press.
Jones, C. (2013). *Giving Up the Gun: Rebel to Ruler Transformations in Africa's Great Lakes*. Gainesville, FL: PhD thesis, University of Florida.
Jordan, J. (2009). When Heads Roll: Assessing the Effectiveness of Leadership Decapitation. *Security Studies*, 18(4), 719–755
Jordan, J. (2014). Attacking the Leader, Missing the Mark: Why Terrorist Groups Survive Decapitation Strikes. *International Security*, 38(4), 7–38.
Kahneman, D., & Tversky, A. (1979). Prospect Theory: An Analysis of Decision under Risk. *Econometrica*, 47(2), 263–292.
Kaldor, M. (1999). *New and Old Wars: Organized Violence in a Global Era*. Stanford, CA: Stanford University Press.
Kalyvas, S. (2001). New and Old Civil Wars: A Valid Distinction? *World Politics*, 54(1), 99–118.
Kalyvas, S. (2003). The Ontology of "Political Violence": Action and Identity in Civil Wars. *Perspectives on Politics*, 1(3), 475–494.
Kalyvas, S. (2004). The Urban Bias in Research on Civil Wars. *Security Studies*, 13(3), 1–31.

Kalyvas, S. (2006). *The Logic of Violence in Civil War*. New York, NY: Cambridge University Press.

Kalyvas, S. (2008a). Ethnic Defection in Civil War. *Comparative Political Studies*, 41(8), 1043–1068.

Kalyvas, S. (2008b). Promises and Pitfalls of an Emerging Research Program: The Microdynamics of Civil War. In S. Kalyvas, I. Shapiro, & T. Masoud, *Order, Conflict Violence* (pp. 1–14). Cambridge: Cambridge University Press.

Kalyvas, S., & Balcells, L. (2010). International System and Technologies of Rebellion: How the End of the Cold War Shaped Internal Conflict. *American Political Science Review*, 104(3), 415–429.

Kapteijns, L. (2012). *Clan Cleansing in Somalia: The Ruinous Legacy of 1991*. Philadelphia, PA: University of Pennsylvania Press.

Keller, E. (1981). Ethiopia: Revolution, Class, and the National Question. *African Affairs*, 80(321), 519–549.

Keller, E. (1991). *Revolutionary Ethiopia: From Empire to People's Republic*. Bloomington, IN: Indiana University Press.

Kibreab, G. (1985). *Refugees and Development: A Study of Organized Land Settlements for Eritrean Refugees in Eastern Sudan, 1967–1983*. Uppsala: PhD thesis, Uppsala University.

Kibreab, G. (1987). *Refugees and Development in Africa: The Case of Eritrea*. Trenton, NJ: Red Sea Press.

Kibreab, G. (2008). *Critical Reflections on the Eritrean War of Independence*. Trenton, NJ: Red Sea Press.

Kibreab, G. (2009). Forced Labour in Eritrea. *Journal of Modern African Studies*, 47(1), 41–72.

Kibreab, G. (2017). *The Eritrean National Service: Servitude for the Common Good & Youth Exodus*. Oxford: James Currey.

Kilcullen, D. (2009). *The Accidental Guerrilla: Fighting Small Wars in the Midst of a Big One*. Oxford: Oxford University Press.

Kilcullen, D. (2010). *Counterinsurgency*. Oxford: Oxford University Press.

King, G., Keohane, R., & Verba, S. (1994). *Designing Social Inquiry*. Princeton, NJ: Princeton University Press.

Koehler, K., Ohl, D., & Albrecht, H. (2016). From Disaffection to Desertion: How Networks Facilitate Military Insubordination in Civil Conflict. *Comparative Politics*, 48(8), 439–457.

Krause, P. (2014). The Structure of Success: How the Internal Distribution of Power Drives Armed Group Behavior and National Movement Effectiveness. *International Security*, 38(3), 72–116.

Krause, P. (2017). *Rebel Power: Why National Movements Compete, Fight, and Win*. Ithaca, NY: Cornell University Press.

Krause, P. (2018). Coercion by Movement: How Power Drove the Success of the Eritrean Insurgency, 1960–1993. In K. Greenhill & P. Krause, *The Power to Hurt in International Politics* (pp. 138–159). Oxford: Oxford University Press.

Kydd, A., & Walter, B. (2006). The Strategies of Terrorism. *International Security*, 31(1), 49–80.

References

Laitin, D., & Samatar, A. (1987). *Somalia: Nation in Search of a State*. Boulder, CO: Westview Press.
Lawrence, A. (2010). Triggering Nationalist Violence: Competition and Conflict in Uprisings against Colonial Rule. *International Security*, 35(2), 88–122.
Lawrence, A. (2013). *Imperial Rule and the Politics of Nationalism: Anti-Colonial Protest in the French Empire*. Cambridge: Cambridge University Press.
Lefebvre, J. (1991). *Arms for the Horn: US Security Policy in Ethiopia and Somalia 1953–1991*. Pittsburgh, PA: University of Pittsburgh Press.
Lefebvre, J. (1996). Middle East Conflicts and Middle-Level Power Intervention in the Horn of Africa. *Middle East Journal*, XIX(2), 387–404.
Levine, D. (2000). *Greater Ethiopia: The Evolution of a Multiethnic Society*. Chicago, IL: University of Chicago Press.
Lewis, I. M. (1994). *Blood and Bone: The Call of Kinship in Somali Society*. Trenton, NJ: Red Sea Press.
Lewis, I. M. (2003). *A Modern History of the Somali: Nation and State in the Horn of Africa*. Athens, OH: Ohio University Press.
Lewis, J. (2012). *How Rebellion Begins: Insurgent Group Formation and Viability in Uganda*. Cambridge, MA: PhD thesis, Harvard University.
Lewis, J. (2016). How Does Ethnic Rebellion Start? *Comparative Political Studies*, 50(10), 1420–1450.
Leys, C., & Saul, J. (1994). Liberation without Democracy? The Swapo Crisis of 1976. *Journal of Southern African Studies*, 20(1), 123–147.
Lidow, N. (2016). *Violent Order: Rebel Organization and Liberia's Civil War*. Cambridge: Cambridge University Press.
Lounsbery, M. O. (2016). Foreign Military Intervention, Power Dynamics, and Rebel Group Cohesion. *Journal of Global Security Studies*, 1(2), 127–141.
Lustick, I. (1996). History, Historiography, and Political Science: Multiple Historical Sources and the Problem of Selection Bias. *American Political Science Review*, 90(3), 605–118.
Lyons, T. (2016a). The Importance of Winning Victorious Insurgent Groups and Authoritarian Politics. *Comparative Politics*, 48(2), 167–184.
Lyons, T. (2016b). Victorious Rebels and Postwar Politics. *Civil Wars*, 18(2), 160–174.
Lyons, T. (2016c). From Victorious Rebels to Strong Authoritarian Parties: Prospects for Post-War Democratization. *Democratization*, 23(6), 1026–1041.
Mampilly, Z. (2011). *Rebel Rulers: Insurgent Governance and Civilian Life during War*. Ithaca, NY: Cornell University Press.
Manning, C. (2007). Party Building on the Heels of War: El Salvador, Bosnia, Kosovo, and Mozambique. *Democratization*, 14(2), 253–272.
Manning, C. (2008). *The Making of Democrats: Elections and Party Development in Bosnia, El Salvador, and Mozambique*. New York, NY: Palgrave Macmillan.
Marchal, R. (2011). *The Rise of a Jihadi Movement in a Country at War: Harakat Al-Shabaab Al Mujaheddin*. Paris: Sciences Po.
Markakis, J. (1987). *National and Class Conflict in the Horn of Africa*. Cambridge: Cambridge University Press.

Martin, L. (2000). *Democratic Commitments*. Princeton, NJ: Princeton University Press.
McDermott, R. (2004). Prospect Theory in Political Science: Gains and Losses from the First Decade. *Political Psychology*, 25(2), 289–312.
McLauchlin, T. (2010). Loyalty Strategies and Military Defection in Rebellion. *Comparative Politics*, 42(3), 333–350.
McLauchlin, T. (2014). Desertion and Collective Action in Civil Wars. *International Studies Quarterly*, 59(4), 669–679.
McLauchlin, T. (2014). Desertion, Terrain, and Control of the Home Front in Civil Wars. *Journal of Conflict Resolution*, 58(8), 1419–1444.
Mearsheimer, J. (2001). *The Tragedy of Great Power Politics*. New York, NY: W. W. Norton.
Medhanie, T. (1986). *Eritrea: Dynamics of a National Question*. Amsterdam: B. R. Grüner.
Melbaa, G. (1999). *Oromia: An Introduction to the History of the Oromo People*. Minneapolis, MN: Kirk House Publishers.
Mesquita, E. B. de (2008). Terrorist Factions. *Quarterly Journal of Political Science*, 3, 399–418.
Michels, R. (1968). *Political Parties: A Sociological Study of the Oligarchical Tendencies of Modern Democracies*. New York, NY: The Free Press.
Milkias, P. (2003). Ethiopia, the TPLF, and the Roots of the 2001 Political Tremor. *Northeast African Studies*, 10(2), 13–66.
Mohamed, I. A. (2015). Somali Women and the Socialist State. *Journal of Georgetown University – Qatar Middle Eastern Studies Student Association*, 1–10.
Negash, T. (1987). *Italian Colonialism In Eritrea: Policies, Praxis, and Impact 1882–1941*. London: Coronet Books.
Negash, T. (1997). *Eritrea and Ethiopia: The Federal Experience*. New York, NY: Transactions Publishers.
Negash, T., & Tronvoll, K. (2001). *Brothers at War: Making Sense of the Eritrean*. Athens, OH: Ohio University Press.
Nemeth, S. (2014). The Effect of Competition on Terrorist Group Operations. *Journal of Conflict Resolution*, 58(2), 336–362.
Olson, M. (1965). *The Logic of Collective Action: Public Goods and the Theory of Groups*. Boston, MA: Harvard University Press.
Olson, M. (1982). *The Rise and Fall of Nations: Economic Growth, Stagflation, and Social Rigidities*. New Haven, CT: Yale University Press.
Pakenham, T. (1992). *The Scramble for Africa*. London: Abacus.
Pateman, R. (1990a). *Eritrea: Even the Stones Are Burning*. Trenton, NJ: Red Sea Press.
Pateman, R. (1990b). Liberté, Egalité, Fraternité: Aspects of the Eritrean Revolution. *Journal of Modern African Studies*, 28(3), 457–472.
Patman, R. (1990). *The Soviet Union in the Horn of Africa: The Diplomacy of Intervention and Disengagement*. Cambridge: Cambridge University Press.
Pearlman, W. (2009). Spoiling Inside Out: Internal Political Contestation and the Middle East Peace Process. *International Security*, 33(3), 79–109.

Pearlman, W. (2011). *Violence, Nonviolence, and the Palestinian National Movement*. Cambridge: Cambridge University Press.

Pischedda, C. (2015). *Wars Within Wars: Understanding Inter-rebel Fighting*. New York, NY: PhD thesis, Columbia University.

Plaut, M. (2006). Ethiopia's Oromo Liberation Front. *Review of African Political Economy*, 33(109), 587–593.

Pool, D. (2001). *From Guerrillas to Government: The Eritrean People's Liberation Front*. Athens, OH: Ohio University Press.

Reeve, A. (2003). Equilibrium. In I. M. McMillan, *Oxford Concise Dictionary of Politics* (pp. 174–175). New York, NY: Oxford University Press.

Reid, R. (2003). Old Problems in New Conflicts: Some Observations on Eritrea and its Relations with Tigray, from Liberation Struggle to Interstate War. *Africa: Journal of the International African Institute*, 73(3), 369–401.

Reid, R. (2011). *Frontiers of Violence in North-East Africa: Genealogies of Conflict since c.1800*. Oxford: Oxford University Press.

Renders, M. (2012). *Consider Somaliland: State-building with Traditional Leaders and Institutions*. Leiden: Brill.

Reno, W. (2007). Patronage Politics and the Behavior of Armed Groups. *Civil Wars*, 9(4), 324–342.

Reno, W. (2011). *Warfare in Independent Africa*. Cambridge: Cambridge University Press.

Reyntjens, F. (2004). Rwanda, Ten Years On: From Genocide to Dictatorship. *African Affairs*, 103(411), 177–210.

Reyntjens, F. (2006). Post-1994 Politics in Rwanda: Problematising 'Liberation' and 'Democratisation.' *Third World Quarterly*, 27(6), 1103–1117.

Riker, W. (1962). *The Theory of Political Coalitions*. New Haven, CT: Yale University Press.

Rotberg, R., ed. (2003). *When States Fail: Causes and Consequences*. Princeton, NJ: Princeton University Press.

Sabbe, O. S. (1974). *The History of Eritrea*. Beirut: Dar Al-Masirah.

Sadri, H. (1997). *Revolutionary States, Leaders, and Foreign Relations: A Comparative Study of China, Cuba, and Iran*. Westport, CT: Praeger.

Schmidt, S., Scott, J., Landi, C., & Guast, L. (1977). *Friends, Factions, and Followers: A Reader in Political Clientelism*. Berkeley, CA: University of California Press.

Scott, J. (1976). *The Moral Economy of the Peasant: Rebellion and Subsistence in Southeast Asia*. New Haven, CT: Yale University Press.

Seymour, L. (2014). Why Factions Switch Sides in Civil Wars: Rivalry, Patronage, and Realignment in Sudan. *International Security*, 39(2), 92–131.

Shapiro, J. (2008). *The Terrorist's Challenge: Security, Efficiency, Control*. Palo Alto, CA: PhD thesis, Stanford University.

Shapiro, J. (2013). *The Terrorist's Dilemma: Managing Violent Covert Organizations*. Princeton, NJ: Princeton University Press.

Shay, S. (2008). *Somalia between Jihad and Restoration*. New Brunswick, NJ: Transaction Publishers.

Shay, S. (2014). *Somalia in Transition Since 2006*. London: Routledge.

Shepsle, K. (1991). Discretion, Institutions and the Problem of Government Commitment. In P. Bourdieu & J. Coleman, *Social Theory for a Changing Society* (pp. 245–265). Boulder, CO: Westview Press.

Sherman, R. (1980). *Eritrea: The Unfinished Revolution*. New York, NY: Praeger.

Shih, V. (2007). *Factions and Finance in China: Elite Conflict and Inflation*. Cambridge: Cambridge University Press.

Shuyun, S. (2006). *The Long March: The True History of Communist China's Founding Myth*. New York, NY: Doubleday.

Smith, L. (2013). *Making Citizens in Africa: Ethnicity, Gender and National Identity in Ethiopia*. Cambridge: Cambridge University Press.

Sorenson, J. (1993). *Imagining Ethiopia: Struggles for History and Identity in the Horn of Africa*. New Brunswick, NJ: Rutgers University Press.

Southall, R. (2013). *Liberation Movements in Power: Party and State in Southern Africa*. Pietermaritzburg: James Currey.

Staniland, P. (2012a). Between a Rock and a Hard Place: Insurgent Fratricide, Ethnic Defection, and the Rise of Pro-State Paramilitaries. *Journal of Conflict Resolution*, 56(1), 16–40.

Staniland, P. (2012b). Organizing Insurgency: Networks, Resources, and Rebellion in South Asia. *International Security*, 37(1), 142–177.

Staniland, P. (2014). *Networks of Rebellion: Explaining Insurgent Cohesion and Collapse*. Ithaca, NY: Cornell University Press.

Stedman, S. (1997). Spoiler Problems in Peace Processes. *International Security*, 22(2), 5–53.

Stein, A. (1990). *Why Nations Cooperate: Circumstance and Choice in International Politics*. Ithaca, NY: Cornell University Press.

Stewart, M. (2017). Civil War as State-Making. *International Organization*, 1–22. Online First Edition.

Tadesse, K. (1998). *The Generation, Part II: Ethiopia, Transformation, and Conflict: The History of the Ethiopian People's Revolutionary Party*. Washington, DC: University Press of America.

Tadesse, M., & Young, J. (2003). TPLF: Reform or Decline. *Review of African Political Economy*, 30(97), 389–403.

Tamimi, A. (2008). *Hamas: A History from Within*. Northampton, MA: Olive Branch Press.

Tamm, H. (2016). Rebel Leaders, Internal Rivals, and External Resources: How State Sponsors Affect Insurgent Cohesion. *International Studies Quarterly*, 60(4), 599–610.

Tanner, V., & Tubiana, J. (2007). Divided They Fall: The Fragmentation of Darfur's Rebel Groups. Small Arms Survey, HSBA Working Paper, 1–80.

Tareke, G. (1991). *Ethiopia: Power and Protest: Peasant Revolts in the 20th Century*. Cambridge: Cambridge University Press.

Tareke, G. (2009). *The Ethiopian Revolution: War in the Horn of Africa*. New Haven, CT: Yale University Press.

Tarrow, S. (1998). *Power in Movement: Social Movements and Contentious Politics*. Cambridge: Cambridge University Press.

Teiwes, F. C. (1990). *Politics at Mao's Court: Gao Gang and Party Factionalism in the Early 1950s*. Armonk, NY: M. E. Sharpe.

References

Thaler, K. (2017). Mixed Methods Research in the Study of Political and Social Violence in Conflict. *Journal of Mixed Methods Research*, 11(1), 59–76.

The Eritrean Revolution: 16 Years of Armed Struggle. (1977). Beirut: ELF Foreign Information Centre.

Tilly, C. (2003). *The Politics of Collective Violence.* Cambridge: Cambridge University Press.

Toft, M. D. (2003). *The Geography of Ethnic Violence: Identity, Interests, and the Indivisibility of Territory.* Princeton, NJ: Princeton University Press.

Trivelli, R. (1998). Divided Histories, Opportunistic Alliances: Background Notes on the Eritrean-Ethiopian War. *Africa Spectrum*, 44(1), 257–289.

Trotsky, L. (2008). *A History of the Russian Revolution.* Chicago, IL: Haymarket Books.

Tse-Tung, M. (2000). *On Guerrilla Warfare.* Champaign, IL: University of Illinois Press.

Tse-Tung, M. (2010). *Collected Writings of Chairman Mao, Vol. 3: On Policy, Practice and Contradiction.* El Paso, TX: El Paso Norte Press.

Tseggai, A. (1991). Triumphant Eritrea: Ten Reasons Why the EPLF Won the War. *The Journal of Eritrean Studies*, 5(1), 1–7.

Turner, R., & Killian, L. (1972). *Collective Behavior.* Englewood Cliffs, NJ: Prentice-Hall.

US Army and Marine Corps. (2007). *US Army and Marine Corps Counterinsurgency Field Manual.* Chicago, IL: University of Chicago Press.

Venosa, J. (2011). *Paths toward the Nation: Islamic Identity, the Eritrean Muslim League and Nationalist Mobilization, 1941–61.* Athens, OH: PhD thesis, Ohio University.

Venosa, J. (2012). "Because God Has Given Us the Power of Reasoning": Intellectuals, the Eritrean Muslim League, and Nationalist Activism, 1946–1950. *Northeast African Studies*, 12(2), 29–62.

Venosa, J. (2014). *Paths toward the Nation: Islam, Community, and Early Nationalist Mobilization in Eritrea, 1941–1961.* Athens, OH: Ohio University Press.

Vines, A. (1991). *Renamo: Terrorism in Mozambique.* London: James Currey.

Walt, S. (1987). *The Origins of Alliances.* Ithaca, NY: Cornell University Press.

Walter, B. (2001). *Committing to Peace: The Successful Settlement of Civil Wars.* Princeton, NJ: Princeton University Press.

Waltz, K. (1979). *Theory of International Politics.* New York, NY: McGraw-Hill.

Weinstein, J. (2005a). Resources and the Information Problem in Rebel Recruitment. *The Journal of Conflict Resolution*, 49(4), 598–624.

Weinstein, J. (2005b). Autonomous Recovery and International Intervention in Comparative Perspective. *Center for Global Development Working Paper*, 1–35.

Weinstein, J. (2007). *Inside Rebellion: The Politics of Insurgent Violence.* Cambridge: Cambridge University Press.

Weldemichael, A. (2009). The Eritrean Long March: The Strategic Withdrawal of the Eritrean People's Liberation Front (EPLF), 1978–79. *The Journal of Military History*, 73(4), 1231–1271.

Weldemichael, A. (2013). *Third World Colonialism and Strategies of Liberation.* Cambridge: Cambridge University Press.

Weldemichael, A. (2014). Formative Alliances of Northeast African Insurgents: The Eritrean Liberation Movement and the Ethiopian Armed Opposition between the 1970s and 1990s. *Northeast African Studies*, 14(1), 83–122.

Westad, O. A. (2007). *The Global Cold War: Third World Interventions and the Making of Our Times*. Cambridge: Cambridge University Press.

Woldegiorgis, D. (1989). *Red Tears: War, Famine, and Revolution in Ethiopia*. Trenton, NJ: Red Sea Press.

Woldemariam, M. (2011). *Why Rebels Collide: Factionalism and Fragmentation in African Insurgencies*. Princeton, NJ: PhD thesis, Princeton University.

Woldemariam, M. (2014). Battlefield Outcomes and Rebel Cohesion: Lessons from the Eritrean Independence War. *Terrorism and Political Violence*, 1–21. Online First Edition.

Woldemariam, M. (2015). Partition Problems: Relative Power, Historical Memory, and the Origins of the Eritrean-Ethiopian War. *Nationalism and Ethnic Politics*, 166–190. Online First Edition.

Woldemariam, M., & Young, A. (2016). After the Split: Partition, Successor States, and the Dynamics of War in the Horn of Africa. *Journal of Strategic Studies*, 1–37. Online First Edition.

Wood, E. J. (2006). The Ethical Challenges of Field Research in Conflict Zones. *Qualitative Sociology*, 29(3), 373–386.

Woodroofe, L. (2013). *Buried in the Sands of the Ogaden: The United States, the Horn of Africa, and the Demise of Détente*. Kent, OH: Kent State University Press.

Wrong, M. (2005). *I Didn't Do It for You: How the World Betrayed a Small African Nation*. New York, NY: Harper Perennial.

Yasin, Y. M. (2008). Political History of the Afar in Ethiopia and Eritrea. *Afrika Spectrum*, 43(1), 39–65.

Yasin, Y. M. (2010). *Regional Dynamics of Inter-ethnic Conflicts in the Horn of Africa: Analysis of the Afar-Somali Conflict in Ethiopia and Djibouti*. Hamburg: PhD thesis, University of Hamburg.

Yordanov, R. (2016). *The Soviet Union and the Horn of Africa during the Cold War: Between Ideology and Pragmatism*. Lanham, MD: Lexington Books.

Young, J. (1996). The Tigray and Eritrean People's Liberation Fronts: A History of Tensions and Pragmatism. *The Journal of Modern African Studies*, 34(1), 105–120.

Young, J. (1997). *Peasant Revolution in Ethiopia: The Tigray People's Liberation Front*. Cambridge: Cambridge University Press.

Zartman, I. W. (1989). *Ripe for Resolution: Conflict and Intervention in Africa*. Oxford: Oxford University Press.

Index

Page numbers in bold refer to tables or figures and 'n' attached to a page number denotes a footnote.

Abay Tsehaye, 189
Abd al-Qadir Kosar, 221, 224
Abdallah Abbakar Bashar, 3
Abdel Karim Ahmed, 138–9
Abdel Wahid-Nur, 3
Abdi Nassir Sheikh Aden, 203
Abdiqasim Salad Hassan, 236, 240
Abdirahman Tuur, 226–30
Abdiwali Hussein Gaas, 206
Abdulkadir Yahya Ali, 262
Abdulla Idris, 84n40, 110, 119, 120–1, 148–9, 153
Abdullah Sudi Arale, 260
Abdullahi Hassan Mohammed, 200
Abdullahi Maalim Mukhtar, 263
Abdullahi Sheikh Ahmed, 278–9
Abdullahi Yusuf, 240–1, 248, 264
Abidrizak Tibba, 204
Abraham Tewolde, 99, 137, 142–3
Abu Rijeila, 86
Abu Tiyara, 86, 90, 99, 144–5, 160, 179
Abu Ubaidah, 263
Abukar Omar Adane, 239–40, 244–5, 264
accidental guerrillas, 11–12
Adam Saleh, 146
Adem. *See* Idris Mohammed Adem
Adem Gendifel, 86
Aden Hashi Ayro, 259, 260, 262–3, 265
Afar clan, 112
Afar Revolutionary Democratic Unity Front (ARDUF), 206–8
Afeworki. *See* Issais Afeworki
Afghanistan, 232, 260, 284, 285
agents provocateurs, 8
Ahmed Abdi Godane
　Al-Ittihad schooling, 260
　Al-Shabaab leader, 265–6
　and *Amniyat* security branch, 275, 280
　conflict with Robow, 268, 274–5
　criticism from moderates, 274
　death, 280
　Emir, 263, 265
　failure of Ramadan offensive, 274–5
　ICU executive member, 263
　victory in extended power struggle, 277–80
Ahmed Adam Omer, 146
Ahmed Jimaale, 219
Ahmed Madobe, 263, 265, 269, 270–1, 276
Ahmed Mahmoud Silanyo, 222, 223–4, 227
Ahmed Mohammed Ibrahim, 139
Ahmed Mohammed Islam, Sheikh, 243
Ahmed Nasser, 108, 110, 112, 119, 120–1
Ahmed Sheikh Feres, 85n44
Al Urwa al Wutqa, 85
Al-Ittihad al-Islamiya
　aim, 232
　and Al-Shabaab network, 260
　Battle of Mogadishu, 233
　early military setbacks, 232–3
　Ethiopia campaign, 233–4
　split, 234
　and War on Terror, 237
Al-Qaeda
　Al-Shabaab alliance, 278
　in Kenya and Afghanistan, 235
　in Somalia, 234–5, 238
　and War on Terror, 237, 278
Al-Shabaab
　Al-Ittihad network members, 260
　Al-Qaeda alliance, 278
　Amniyat security branch, 275, 280
　break with ICU, 265
　clan politics, 261, 262, 268
　coalition within a coalition, 260–1
　continuing potency, 280

307

308   Index

Al-Shabaab (*cont.*)
  cooperation in face of external threats, 275
  counterterrorism targets, 262
  and Ethiopia's withdrawal, 267
  factionalism, 268, 274–5, 277–80
  famine tensions, 277–8
  foreign fighters, 261, 266, 279
  Godane–Robow rivalry, 268
  Hizbul Islam merger, 273–4
  Hotel Shamo attack, 257
  ICU militia, 252, 254, 257, 259, 260
  ICU radical wing, 263
  institutional structure, 265–6
  Italian cemetery training ground, 262–3
  Kenya–Ethiopia offensive, 276–7
  Kismayo capture, 268–71
  Madobe split, 269–72
  Mogadishu stalemate, 272–3
  pan-Somali Islamist group, 213
  political structure, 263
  Ramadan offensive (2010), 274–5
  Ras Kamboni merger, 273
  territorial expansion, 266–7, 272
  territorial losses (2011), 276–7
  violent attacks and assassinations, 262, 264–5, 266
  withdrawal from Mogadishu (2011), 276, 277
Ala group, 143, 147, 149, 150, 157–60, 161–3
Alemayehu Gesessew (Dirar), 189
Algiers Agreement (2000), 197–8
Ali Berhatu, 146
Ali Dheere, Sheikh, 235
Ali Isaq, 112
Ali Mahdi, 226, 235
Ali Mohammed Ossobleh, 223–4
Ali Mohamud Rage, 274
Ali Said Abdella, 100n73
Alliance for the Reliberation of Somalia (ARS), 259
Amhara elites, 55
Amharic language, 186
al-Amin Mohammed Said, 144–5
AMISOM, 249, 267, 272–3, 274–5, 276
Anglo-Ethiopian treaty (1897), 215
Arab-Israeli War (1967), 95, 100, 129
Aregawi Berhe, 188–9, 191
armed force, rebel organization criteria, 24
Asmerom Gerezghier, 157
Asrate Kassa, 94
Assuarta tribe, 85
Aweys. *See* Hassan Dahir Aweys
Azien Yassin, 148

Bahr Negash offensive (1985), 174, 176
Barre Hirale, 248, 269
Barut Hamse, 195–6
Bashar Abdi Hussein, 204
Bashir Rage, 239–40, 244–5
Battle of Adwa (1896), 76, 215
Battle of Afabet (1988), 175
Battle of Gereger (1973), 153–5
Battle of Salina (1977), 170
battlefield control. *See* territorial control
Beni Amer tribe, 83–4, 87
Bobassa Mohammed, 196
Bobe Yusuf, 221
Bolivia, 10, 28
Britain
  in Eritrea, 77–8
  Ogaden territory, 199
  Somali diaspora, 218–19
  and Somali territories, 215–16
  in Somaliland, 76n12
  in Sudan, 86, 87
Burma, Karen rebels, 28

Cabral, Amilcar, 10–11
case study selection, 60–5, **61**, 211–13
Castro, Fidel, 28
China
  cadres political training, 92, 138, 167–8
  and Jebha, 129
  Red Army, 9–10, 28, 30–1
  and Shaebia, 179
Christia, Fotini, 36–7
civil wars
  constraints on field research, 31–2
  duration affected by rebel fragmentation, 13–14
  ethnic defections, 35–6
  marginalized scholarship, 26–32
  new vs old civil wars, 20–1
  partisan bias in historiography, 29
Clapham, Christopher, 15
cohesive stalemate
  Al-Shabaab, 273
  ICU, 244
  Jebha, 101–3
  Shaebia, 174–5
  theories, 7, 38, 44–5, 46–7, 58, 283
  TPLF, 192–3
Commandis 101, 94
commitment problems, 43–4, 96–8, 118–19, 136, 191
Connell, Dan, 151, 171
counterinsurgency strategies, 11–12, 284–5, 286

Index

counterterrorism, 237–8, 245–6
coups, alternative to fragmentation, 48–50
credible commitments, 43–4, 96–8, 118–19, 136, 191
Cuba, 28
cycles of contention, 50, 51, 98, 109–10, 172–3, 224, 271–2

Darfur, armed rebellion, 3–5
Darood clans, 217, 240–1, 264
Dawit Woldegiorgis, 105
Dawud Ibsa, 197, 198
Debebe Hailemariam, 100
defection, 35, 48
demagogues, 8
democratic states, 64
Derg
  collapse, 193, 203
  in Eritrea, 192
  Marxism, 56
  military takeover, 103–4
  Operation Lash against WSLF, 202
  peace negotiations, 125–6
  and Soviet Union, 114, 123–4
diaspora
  EFLNA, 171–3
  Eritreans in Cairo, 80–3
  Eritreans overseas, 73
  OLF-Transitional Authority, 197
  ONLF leadership, 204
  Shaebia support, 178
  Somalia's Islamists, 231
Dima Nego, 194–5, 198–9

EFLNA (Eritreans for the Liberation of North America), 171–3, 178
Egypt, Jebha support, 128
Elemo Qiltu, 194
elite leaders, 38–9
Eritrea
  Algiers Agreement (2000), 197–8
  Ascari soldiers, 76–7
  British Military Administration, 77–8
  Ethiopian province, 78–9
  federation with Ethiopia, 77–9
  independence, 75
  Italian colony, 75–7
  maps, **62**, **72**
  Muslim–Christian divide, 75, 79–80
  racialized colonialism, 77
  social conditions, 167
  state-consolidating insurgency, 15
Eritrean Assembly, 79, 81
Eritrean Democratic Movement (EDM), 109

Eritrean Liberation Front. *See* Jebha (Eritrean Liberation Front/ELF)
Eritrean Liberation Front–People's Liberation Forces, 56–7
Eritrean Muslim League, 82
Eritrean People's Liberation Front (EPLF). *See* Shaebia (Eritrean People's Liberation Front/EPLF)
Eritrean People's Revolutionary Party (EPRP), 180
Eritrean refugees, 73, 95
Eritrean Relief Association, 178
Eritreans for the Liberation of North America (EFLNA), 171–3, 178
Ethiopia
  agriculture, 74
  and Al-Shabaab, 276
  Algiers Agreement (2000), 197–8
  Anglo-Ethiopian treaty (1897), 215
  backing for Somalia's TFG, 241–2, 248–9
  defeats ICU in Somalia, 250–2
  famine, 73
  maps, **62**, **72**
  pro-Christian bias, 79–80
  Red Terror, 113
  Somali invasion (1977), 114, 195, 216
  Somali withdrawal (2009), 267
  state-consolidating insurgency, 15
  TPLF victorious historiography, 28–9
  transitional government, 196, 203–4
Ethiopia civil war
  deaths, 73
  economic costs, 74
  ethnonational agendas, 55, 64–5
  ideological forces, 55–6
  slow government response, 91
  territorial ambitions, 54–6
Ethiopia military
  1st offensive (1978), 170–1
  army atrocities, 104
  Bahr Negash (8th) offensive, 174, 176
  Battle of Adwa (1896), 76, 215
  defections to OLF, 198
  expenditure, 123
  Red Star (6th) offensive, 173, 176, 193
  Soviet assistance, 74, 113–15, 123–4, 175
  technology, 123–4, 175
  troop numbers, 122–3
  US assistance, 114, 123–4
Ethiopia rebel organizations
  case selection criteria, 60–5, **61**, **62**, 65
  fragmentation, 57–9, **59**, **63**
  longevity and number, 57, **58**

Ethiopia Somali Democratic League (ESDL), 204
Ethiopian Democratic Union (EDU), 187–8, 190–1, 192
Ethiopian National Liberation Front (ENLF), 194
Ethiopian People's Revolutionary Democratic Front (EPRDF), 56, 64
Ethiopian People's Revolutionary Party (EPRP), 113, 187–8, 190–1, 192
Ethiopian Revolution (1974), 103–4, 187
external support
  Jebha, 92, 100, 127–30
  and rebel factionalism, 35, 52
  Shaebia, 176–9

factionalism
  alternative behaviors, 47–50
  definition, 5–6n2
Fallul uprising, 109–11
famine, 186, 277–8
Fazul Mohammed, 279
fragmentation. *See* rebel fragmentation
Fuad Shongole, 259, 268, 274, 275
Fur tribe, 3

Gaddafi, Muammar, 129, 150, 176–7
Galassa Dilbo, 197
Galula, David, 11
Gates, Scott, 34
Gebremichael Lilo, 173
Gemechu Ayana, 198
Gesessew Ayele (Sihul), 187, 188, 189, 190
Gettleman, Jeffrey, 253–4, 255
Ghebrehiwet, Yosief, 30
Giap, Vo Nguyen, 10
Gidey Zerastion, 189
Gilkes, Patrick, 30
Godane. *See* Ahmed Abdi Godane
Goitom Berhe, 162, 163, 168
Guardians of the Revolution, 180
guerrilla warfare, 8–9, 10, 11, 52
Guevara, Che, 10, 28

Habar Yunis clan, 222, 227–8
Hagos "Kisha" Gebrehiwet, 173
Haile Atsbaha, 192
Haile Gonfa, 198
Haile Selassie, Emperor
  and Adem, 81, 82
  and Eritrea, 78–9, 185–6
  and Ethiopian territory, 56
  ouster, 103
  Woyane rebellion, 186

Haile Woldense, 95, 151
Hailu Ragassa, 194
Hamid Saleh, 139
Harakat, 80–1, 86, 92
Hassan Dahir Aweys
  on Al-Qaeda link, 278
  frayed relationship with Al-Shabaab protégés, 259
  Hizbul Islam, 269
  Hizbul Islam–Al-Shabaab merger, 273–4
  ICU leader, 248–9, 252, 258, 259
  opposition to Djibouti agreement, 259
  surrender and house arrest, 280
  on US terrorist list, 237, 278
Hassan Isse Jama, 222, 226, 227
Hassan Turki
  Al-Ittihad leader, 237
  ICU hardliner, 252
  Kismayo ruling council, 269–70
  Ogaden clan displeasure, 269–70
  Ras Kamboni leader, 269
  on US terrorist list, 237
Hawiye clans, 217, 223–4, 232–3, 238, 240–1, 242
Hawiye Islamic courts, 235–6, 238
Hepner, T.R., 171
Herui Tedla Bairu, 107–9, 112–13, 148
Hirschman, A., 49
Hizbul Islam, 259, 269, 273–4
Hussein, Saddam, 178

Ibrahim Abdalla, Sheikh, 204
Ibrahim al-Afghani, 260, 279, 280
Ibrahim Dagaweyn, 228–9
Ibrahim Hassan Adow, 252, 256–7
Ibrahim Idris, 148
Ibrahim Shukri, Sheikh, 269–70, 271
Ibrahim Sultan, 81–2, 83
Ibrahim Totil, 120–1
Ibrahim Yarrow, 268
Idris Glawedos, 90, 93, 130, 139–41
Idris Hamid Awate, 83–5, 88, 90
Idris Mohammed Adem
  challenges to, 139–41
  factional disputes, 98, 99, 108
  flees Eritrea, 81
  and Ibrahim Sultan, 83
  Jebha leadership, 81–3, 90, 130
  Jebha recruitments, 83–4
  regains chairmanship, 148
  rehabilitation, 100
  Supreme Council tensions, 93
IGAD, Peace Support Mission in Somalia, 249

Index

insubordination, 48–50, 98
interorganizational alliances, 36–8
Iraq
  Jebha factionalism, 144n15
  Jebha support, 92, 95, 128, 149–50
  Shaebia support, 178
Isaaq clan
  grievances, 217–18, 219–20
  Guurti council, 225, 229
  refugees, 225
  See also Somali National Movement (SNM)
Islamic Courts Union (ICU)
  Al-Shabaab on executive council, 263
  business community interests, 239–41
  cohesive stalemate with warlords and TFG, 243–4
  criticism of leadership performance and absenteeism, 258–9
  defeat by Ethiopia, 250–2
  defeat in Kismayo, 254–6
  defeat in Mogadishu, 251, 252–4
  fragmentation, 249–50, 252–6
  hardline versus moderate factions, 252
  internal consolidation, 243
  Islamic ideology/edicts, 244, 249–50
  leadership conflicts, 256–9
  minimalist political program, 236
  motives of founding coalition, 236–43
  origins of founding coalition, 231–6
  pan-Somali Islamist group, 213
  qaat prohibition, 249–50
  territorial expansion, 246–9
  warlord confrontations, 239–40, 243
Islamic Federation for the Liberation of Oromia (IFLO), 196
Ismail Arale, 263, 265
Issais Afeworki
  Ala commander, 142–3
  Ala factionalism, 161–2
  background, 137–8
  leadership fissures, 174
  political training in China, 138
  Shaebia leadership, 180–1
Italy
  Battle of Adwa (1896), 76, 215
  Eritrea colonialism, 75–7, 185, 186
  Mogadishu cemetery incident, 262–3

Jaraa Abugaada, Sheikh, 194–6
Jebha (Eritrean Liberation Front/ELF)
  arms and ammunition, 84, 87, 89–90, 128–9
  background to rebellion, 137–42
  breakdown of military discipline, 116
  commitment to Eritrean self-determination, 91
  decline, 116–18
  diverse coalition, 87–8, 92–3
  early history, 83–8
  early leadership changes, 90–1
  early operational challenges, 88–90
  expanded tactics, 100, 129
  external offices, 86, 128–9
  external support, 92, 127–30
  factionalism. *See below*
  Kaida al-Amma council, 141, 144, 146
  loss of popular support, 95
  Marxist political education, 107
  numbers, 132–3
  organizational structure, 90–1, 100, 130–2
  origins, 80–3
  peace negotiations, 125–7
  recruitment, 91–2
  Sudanese military defectors, 86–7, 92
  Supreme Council, 90
  territorial gains, 105, **106**
  territorial losses, 96, **97**, 116, **117**
  withdrawal to Sahel, 114–15
  zonal commands, 92–3, 131
Jebha (Eritrean Liberation Front/ELF) factionalism
  Adhoba meeting (1969), 140–1
  Ala group, 143
  Aradib meeting (1968), 139
  breakdown in credible commitments, 118–19
  challenge to Supreme Council, 98–9
  Christian marginalization, 119
  Christian recruitment following Asmara raids, 104–5, 108
  Christians, tolerance for, 138
  Christians' executions, 96–8, 99, 142
  Eslah reform movement, 137
  Fallul uprising, 109–11
  and final demise, 118–21
  National Congress (1971), 147–9
  National Congress (1975), 107–8, 130
  potential unity agreement rejected by Shaebia, 164–5
  prepares to attack Shaebia, 148–51
  Sagem, 121
  and Shaebia, 74–5, 104
  Shaebia cooperation, 115
  Shaebia tensions, 115–16
  splinter groups, 101, 142–6
  Supreme Council tensions, 93, 143–4
  and territorial gains, 107, 113
  and territorial losses, 96–9

Jebha (Eritrean Liberation Front/ELF) factionalism (*cont.*)
  territorial stalemate and cohesion, 101–3
  Tripartite Unity Force, 139–40, 141, 144–5
  Yemen dissidents, 111–12
Juba Valley Alliance (JVA), 248
Justice and Equality Movement (Sudan), 4, 5

Kaida al-Amma council, 141, 143–4, 146
Kalyvas, S., 21, 33, 35–6
Kemal Gelchu, 198–9
Kenya
  and Al-Qaeda, 235
  and Al-Shabaab, 276, 277
  Somali conflict, 216
  Somali peace talks, 256–7
Khalif Adale, 262–3
Kibreab, Gaim, 121, 147
kidnappings, 100
Kilcullen, David, 11–12
Kismayo, 254–6, 268–71
Krause, Peter, 13
Kunama tribe, 94n64

Leencho Latta, 198–9
Lenin, Vladimir, 8–9
Liberia, 15, 35, 37
Libya, 129, 150, 176–7
Lidow, Nicholai, 35

Maalim Burhan, 280
Mahad Karate, 264–5
Mahber Showate, 80–1
Mahmouda Ahmed Gaas, 206, 207
Mao Tse-Tung, 9–10, 28, 30–1
maps
  Ethiopia/Eritrea, **62**, **72**
  Somali regions, **212**
Margarsa Bari, 195
Markakis, J., 152, 153, 154, 201
Martini, Fernando, 76
Marxism/Leninism, 33, 56, 107, 158, 167, 168
Mehari Debassai, 144–5
Mehari Tekle (Mussie), 187, 190
Melake Tekle, 110, 120
Meles Gebremariam, 158
Meles Zenawi, 193, 248
Menelik, Emperor, 55, 76, 185–6, 193, 215
Mengesha Seyoum, 190
Mengisteab Isaak, 172, 173
Mengistu Hailemariam, 74, 113

Menkhaus, Ken, 253
Mesfin Hagos, 144–5
Mesquita, E.B., 34
Minni Minawi, 3–5
Mogadishu
  Adane–Bashir Rage dispute, 244–5
  Al-Shabaab withdrawal (2011), 276, 277
  Al-Shabaab–AMISOM stalemate, 272–3
  Battle of Mogadishu (1993), 233
  business community, 239–40
  El Maan port incident, 239–40
  Ethiopia attack (2007), 264
  Hawiye business interests, 240–1
  Hawiye influence, 240
  Hawiye Islamic courts, 235–6, 238
  Hawiye–Darood rivalries, 240–1
  Hotel Shamo attack, 257
  ICU defeat by Ethiopia, 251, 252–4
  Italian cemetery, 262–3
  Ramadan offensive (2010), 274–5
  Second Battle of Mogadishu (2006), 245–6
  Shadow Wars (counterterrorism), 237–8, 262
Mogadishu warlords
  ARPCT (Alliance for the Restoration of Peace and Counter-Terrorism), 245–6
  and ICU, 239–40, 243
  in Mogadishu Shadow War, 237–8
  Second Battle of Mogadishu (2006), 245–6
  Western counterterrorism allies, 237, 238
Mohammed Abdi Yasin, 205
Mohammed Abdullah Hassan, Sheikh, 230
Mohammed Ahmed Abdu, 141, 145–6
Mohammed Ahmed Idris, 146
Mohammed Ali Omaro, 138, 144–5
Mohammed Dinai, 91
Mohammed Diriye Urdoh, 201, 203
Mohammed Farah Aideed, 226, 229, 232–3
Mohammed Ibrahim Egal, 216, 229
Mohammed Ibrahim Hapsade, 268
Mohammed Idris Haj, 86, 91
Mohammed Kahin, 227
Mohammed Omar Osman, 205–6
Mohammed Omar Yahya, 148
Mohammed Said Nawud, 112
Mohammed Siad Barre, 178
Mohammed Sirad Dolal, 205
Mohammed Suleiman Aden Gaal, 227
Mozambique, FRELIMO, 37

Index

Mukhtar Robow
  Al-Ittihad schooling, 260
  conflict with Godane, 268, 274–5
  flees Barawe, 280
  ICU executive member, 263
  infighting, 274
  and jihad, 236n37
  territorial gains, 266–7
Mussie Tesfamichael, 100n73, 159, 162
Mussolini, Benito, 77

Namibia, SWAPO, 28–9
natural resources, 63–4, 211
Negash, Tekeste, 76, 77
North Yemen, 129

Obel group, 146, 147, 150, 152, 160
Ogaden
  British protectorate, 199
  home of Ethiopia's Somalis, 199
  refugees, 217–18
  Somali invasion (1977), 114, 195, 216
  See also West Somali Liberation Front (WSLF)
Ogaden National Liberation Front (ONLF), 203–6
OLF-Change, 198–9
OLF-Transitional Authority, 197
Olson, M., 34, 132
Omar Damer, 144–5
Omar Dheere, 263
Omar Hammami, 255–6, 258, 260–1, 279, 280
Omar Izaz, 86
Omar Nur, 202
Omar, Sheikh, 263
Oromo Liberation Front (OLF)
  defections from Ethiopian military, 198
  expansion of operations, 198
  factional infighting, 195–6, 198–9
  historical background, 193–4
  origins, 193–4
  and Somali–Ethiopian war, 195
  in Somalia, 196–7
  in transitional government, 196
Osman Ajib, 146
Osman Hishal, 96–8, 99
Osman Saleh Sabbe
  Al Urwa al Wutqa, 85–6
  challenges to, 139–41
  departs Jebha, 129
  Eritrean nationalist spokesman, 85
  exile, 85
  external Jebha representative, 86
  General Secretariat (Jordan), 98–9, 143–4, 147
  History of Eritrea, 168
  Jebha leadership, 90–1, 130
  Jebha recruitment, 92
  and Popular Liberation Forces (PLF), 145
  pro-Arabism, 167
  and Shaebia, 150, 151, 154
  source of arms for Shaebia, 176–7
  split with Shaebia, 164–9
  Supreme Council tensions, 93
  vulnerability to Jebha, 149–50
  Yemin faction, 111–12

Pakistan, 85–6
peace agreements
  Algiers Agreement (2000), 197–8
  Djibouti Accords (2008), 259, 267
  Ethiopia/Somalia (1988), 225
peace negotiations
  brokered by Eastern Bloc, 175–6
  Darfur, 3–4
  Eritrea, 116
  government unwillingness to engage, 176
  ICU–TFG, 256–7
  Jebha, 125–7
  negative effect of rebel fragmentation, 13–14
  Shaebia/Derg, 172
  Somalia, 240
  spoilers, 34–5, 51
  strategies for success, 285–6
Plaut, Martin, 198
PLO, 129
political goals, rebel organization criteria, 24
Pool, D., 150
Popular Liberation Forces (PLF), 145–6, 147, 150
preference divergence, 42–3, 112, 136
prospect theory, 46–7, 287

Ramadan Mohammed Nur, 138, 144–5, 162, 180–1
Ras Kamboni militia, 263, 269–71, 273
realism, 41–2
rebel fragmentation
  alternative behaviors, 47–50
  and battlefield gains and losses, 35–8
  counterinsurgency, 11–12
  definition, 6, 24–6
  deleterious impacts, 12–13

rebel fragmentation (cont.)
  Ethiopian rebel organizations, 57–9, **59**, **63**
  formal exit, 25
  marginalized civil war scholarship, 26–32
  and military shocks, 40
  and military victory, 7, 27–9
  obstacle to peace, 285
  and organizational size and complexity, 52, 132–3, 181–2
  potential for increased violence, 13
  precipitated by internal factional struggles, 49–50, 142–6
  and state repression, 33–4
  sub-Sahara statistics, 16–20, **20**, 21
  theoretical analysis, 32–5
  theorist-practitioners, 7–12
  See also territorial control; territorial gains and fragmentation; territorial losses and fragmentation
rebel organizations
  benefits of hegemonic structure, 13
  definition, 17, 23–4
  effect of victory, 7, 27–9
  incentive to feign unity, 27
  material resources, 33
  and natural resources, 63–4, 211
  now in government regimes, 15–16
  and state behavior, 14–15, 51
  structure, 52, 90–1, 100, 130–2, 179–81
  survival as cohesive factor, 41–2
  See also Ethiopia rebel organizations
Red Star offensive (1983), 173, 176
refugees, 73, 95, 217–18
research
  archive sources and interviews, 65–6
  case study selection, 60–5, **61**, 211–13
  fieldwork, 31–2, 65, 66
  further avenues, 286–8
Robow. *See* Mukhtar Robow
Rodriguez, Carlos Rafael, 126
Rubattino Shipping Company, 75–6
Russian Revolution, 8–9
Rwanda, 15, 28–9

Sabbe. *See* Osman Saleh Sabbe
Sahel, 152–5
Saho tribe, 83
Saho/Assuarta tribe, 85
Said Hussein, 83, 90, 111–12
Salahudin Maow, 206
Saleh Ali Saleh Nabhan, 262
Saleh Eyay, 147–8
Saleh Hayouti, 146
Saudi Arabia, 85, 129–30, 218–19

Scott, James, 41
Sebhat Nega, 192
Seymour, Lee, 35, 51
Seyoum Ogbemichael, 110
Shaebia (Eritrean People's Liberation Front/EPLF)
  arms and ammunition, 178–9
  Congress (1977), 169, 180–1
  diversity, 152, 181–2
  early vulnerability to Jebha, 148–51, 152–5
  emergence, 98–9, 137, 147–52
  external support, 176–9
  factionalism. *See below*
  Fallul defectors, 110
  finances, 178
  Gehteb executive, 153, 179–80
  growth in numbers, 164
  Guardians of the Revolution (security unit), 180
  and Jebha, 74–5
  Jebha cooperation, 115
  Jebha tensions, 115–16
  Menka dispute, 159–60, 161–3, 169–70
  organizational size and complexity, 181–2
  organizational structure, 153, 179–81
  recruitment problems, 181
  Sahel stalemate, 173–5
  strategic withdrawal, 170–1
  territorial gains, 163–4
  territorial gains and growth, 116
  unity agreement, 151
  victorious historiography, 28–30
  victory, 75, 175
Shaebia (Eritrean People's Liberation Front/EPLF) factionalism
  EFLNA split (1978), 171–3, 179
  factional disputes and territorial gains, 155–63, 164–5, 168–9
  factional disputes and territorial losses, 170–3
  Obel opposition to full merger, 160
  rejection of Jebha unity agreement, 164–5
Shapiro, J., 33–4, 122
Sharif Sheikh Ahmed, 236, 252, 256–7, 259, 267
Sherman, Richard, 142
Siad Barre
  attempted coup (1978), 217
  Fourth Brigade opposition, 219–21
  Hargeisa Group arrests, 218
  Ogaden invasion (1977), 216
  ouster, 226

Index

scientific socialism, 231
and WSLF, 199–200, 201–3
Sihul. *See* Gesessew Ayele (Sihul)
SLA–Minni Minawi, 4–5
Smith, Gayle, 74
social networks, 33
Solomon Abraha, 137
Solomon Woldemariam, 157–8, 161, 169–70, 180
Somali Abo Liberation Front (SALF), 195, 200
Somali civil war, 213
Somali National Movement (SNM)
  ambiguous political program, 220–1
  amicable leadership changes, 221–2
  Berbera port, 228–9
  clan factionalism, 227–30
  clan lines reorganization, 225–6
  Ethiopian base, 219, 220
  Ethiopian help, 202
  growth in numbers, 225
  Hawiye split and further infighting, 223–4
  implosion, 229–30
  interim Somaliland administration, 226–7
  Isaaq *Guurti* council, 225, 229
  Isaaq refugees, 225
  origins, 217–19
  Saudi and London founding diaspora, 218–19
  Sheep Wars, 228
  split over military police force, 227
  stalemate and feuding, 222–3
  urban raids (1986), 223, 224
Somali Salvation Democratic Front (SSDF), 202, 217
Somalia
  attempted coup (1978), 217
  British rule, 76n12, 215–16
  colonial era, 213–14, 215
  colonial partition, 215
  Dervish rebellion, 230
  Eritrean-Ethiopian Friendship Society, 86
  Family Law (1975), 231
  famine, 277–8
  Fourth Brigade opposition to Siad Barre, 219–21
  Hargeisa Group arrests, 218, 219
  Isaaq discontent, 217–18, 219–20
  and Kenya, 216
  Ogaden invasion (1977), 114, 195, 216
  Ogaden refugees, 217–18
  political Islam, 230–1
  precolonial era, 214
  regional map, **212**
  Siad Barre socialism (*Hantiwadaag*), 231
  state collapse, 226
  state failure, 15
  state violence, 218, 224, 225, 231
  See also Transitional Federal Government (TFG); Transitional National Government (TNG); West Somali Liberation Front (WSLF)
Somalia Reconciliation and Restoration Council (SRRC), 240
Somaliland, 226
South Yemen, 128, 177
Southall, Robert, 29
Soviet Union, assistance to Ethiopian military, 74, 113–15, 123–4, 170–1
Staniland, Paul, 33, 283
state failure, 15
state repression, 33–4, 36, 51, 124–5, 175–6
Stedman, Stephen, 34–5
Sudan
  civil wars, 35, 72
  Eritrean refugees, 73, 95
  Gereger Battle (1973), 155
  and Jebha, 101, 128–9
  Jebha disarmament, 119–20
  military defectors to Jebha, 86–7
  and Shaebia, 178, 179
  support for EDU, 190
Sudanese Liberation Army (SLA), 3–4
Syria, Jebha support, 92, 95, 128, 149–50

Tadesse Birru, 194
Tahir Salem, 86, 91
Tareke, Gebru, 73, 200
Tarrow, Sidney, 50
Teranafit/Ethiopian Democratic Union (EDU), 187–8
territorial control
  and counterinsurgency, 286
  Ethiopian civil war ambitions, 54–6
  gains, losses, and absolute values, 45–7, **47**
  Jebha absolute position and fragmentation, 133
  Jebha ambition, 88–9
  Jebha gains, losses and fragmentation, 133–4, **134**, 135
  men and material inputs, 53–4
  Shaebia absolute position and fragmentation, 182

territorial control (*cont.*)
  Shaebia gains, losses, and fragmentation, 182–3, **183**, 184
  statistical measurement, 52–5
territorial gains and fragmentation
  Al-Shabaab, 267–8, 272
  counterinsurgency strategy, 284–5
  ICU, 249–50
  Jebha, 107, 113
  OLF, 198–9
  ONLF, 205–6
  Shaebia, 155–63, 164–5, 168–9
  theories, 36–8, 42–3
  TPLF, 188–9
  WSLF, 201–2
territorial losses and fragmentation
  Al-Ittihad, 234
  ICU, 252
  Jebha, 96–9
  OLF, 195–6
  ONLF, 204
  Shaebia, 170–3
  theories, 36, 43–4
  TPLF, 190–1
territorial stalemate and cohesion
  Al-Shabaab, 273
  ICU, 244
  Jebha, 101–3
  Shaebia, 174–5
  theories, 7, 38, 44–5, 46–7, 58, 283
  TPLF, 192–3
terrorism
  ARPCT (Alliance for the Restoration of Peace and Counter-Terrorism), 245–6
  War on Terror, 11–12, 237–8
Teshome Ergetu, 100
Tewdros Gebrezghier, 153, 154, 177
Tewolde Eyob, 157, 162–3
threats, as unifying force, 37–8, 91, 187–8, 207, 275
Tigray Nationalist Organization (TNO), 187
Tigray People's Democratic Movement (TPDM), 192
Tigray People's Liberation Front (TPLF)
  early rebellions, 186
  emergence, 186–7
  expansion, 189–90
  external threats underpin cooperation, 187–8
  factional infighting, 191–2
  historical background, 185–6
  organization, 188
  peasant faction discontent, 188–9
  and Shaebia, 187, 189, 192–3
  support for Shaebia against Jebha, 118
  in transitional government, 196, 203–4
  war with EDU, 187–8, 190–1, 192
  war with EPRP, 187–8, 190–1, 192
  war with OLF, 196
  war with ONLF, 203–4
Tigrayan United Student Association (TUSA), 187
Tigre/Beni Amer tribe, 83–4
Toft, M. Duffy, 55
Transitional Federal Government (TFG)
  Baidoa base, 241
  business concerns, 240–1
  concerns over ICU, 248–9
  Djibouti peace agreement (2008), 259
  establishment, 240
  Ethiopian backing, 241–2, 248–9
  ICU agreement, 247–8
  ICU defections, 249–50
  and Juba Valley Alliance (JVA), 248
  and warlords' anti-ICU campaign, 246
Transitional National Government (TNG), 236, 240
Trotsky, Leon, 9
Tsegai Keshi, 159
Tsegay Tesfay, 189

UCDP Actor Dataset, 56, 57
UCDP/PRIO Armed Conflict Dataset, 17–18, 23–4, 56
Uganda, 15, 28–9
United Somali Congress (USC), 224, 226
United States
  Al-Shabaab arrests and deaths, 265
  Battle of Mogadishu, 233
  counterinsurgency strategies, 284–5
  Ethiopian military assistance, 114, 123–4
  and Jebha, 129–30
  Somali peace talks, 256–7
  War on Terror, 11–12, 237–8

War on Terror, 11–12, 237–8
Weinstein, Jeremy, 15, 33, 283
West Somali Liberation Front (WSLF)
  clan divisions, 200
  divergent political objectives, 200, 201–3
  establishment, 199–200
  factional infighting and territorial gains, 201–2
  Isaaq fighters, 219
  military failure, 202
  stalemate and demise, 203
  territorial gains, 201

Index

Westad, O. A., 114
Woldai Kahsai, 98, 137
Woyane rebellion, 186
　See also Tigray People's Liberation Front (TPLF)

Yemin dissidents, 111–12
Yohannes Sebhatu, 100n73, 158, 162
Yohannes of Tigray, Emperor, 185

Yusuf Mohammed Siad Inda'adde, 247, 259
Yusuf Sheikh Madar, 221–2

Zaghawa tribe, 3–4
Zaire, state failure, 15
Zakariya Ahmed Ismail Hersi, 280
Zartman, I. William, 285–6
al-Zawahiri, Ayman, 279